D1599851

THE SERMONS OF
ST. MAXIMUS OF TURIN

Aɴᴄɪᴇɴᴛ   Cʜʀɪsᴛɪᴀɴ Wʀɪᴛᴇʀs

THE WORKS OF THE FATHERS IN TRANSLATION

EDITED BY

WALTER J. BURGHARDT

and

THOMAS COMERFORD LAWLER

No. 50

THE SERMONS OF ST. MAXIMUS OF TURIN

TRANSLATED AND ANNOTATED

BY

BONIFACE RAMSEY, O.P.

Sacred Heart Priory
Jersey City, New Jersey

NEWMAN PRESS
New York, N.Y./Mahwah, N.J.

Library of Congress Cataloging-in-Publication Data

Maximus, of Turin, Saint, 4th/5th cent.
    [Sermons. English]
    The sermons of St. Maximus of Turin / translated and annotated by
  Boniface Ramsey.
       p.   cm. . . — (Ancient Christian writers; no. 50)
    Translated from Latin.
    Includes bibliographies and indexes.
    ISBN 0-8091-0423-7: $22.95 (est.)
    1. Sermons, English—Translations from Latin.   2. Sermons, Latin—
Translation into English—Early works to 1800.   I. Ramsey,
Boniface.   II. Title.   III. Series.
  BR60.A35 no. 50
  [BR65.M3973]
  270 s—dc19
  [252'.014]

89-2970
CIP

Published by Paulist Press
997 Macarthur Boulevard
Mahwah, New Jersey 07430

PRINTED AND BOUND IN THE UNITED STATES OF AMERICA

CONTENTS

APPENDIX

NOTES

INDEXES

TO MY MOTHER

INTRODUCTION

THE LIFE OF MAXIMUS

The sole reference to Maximus of Turin from Christian antiquity appears in the late-fifth-century catalogue of Christian authors compiled by Gennadius of Marseilles and entitled *De viris inlustribus.* The 41st chapter, which treats of Maximus, reads as follows:

"Maximus, bishop of the church of Turin, a man fairly capable in the sacred Scriptures and able to teach the people as the occasion demanded, composed sermons in praise of the apostles and of John the Baptist and a general homily in praise of all the martyrs. But he also commented wisely and at some length on passages from the Gospels and from the Acts of the Apostles. In addition he produced two sermons on the life of Saint Eusebius, bishop of Vercelli and confessor, and on Saint Cyprian, and he published a special book on the grace of baptism. I have read his sermons on avarice, hospitality, on an eclipse of the moon, almsgiving, on the phrase in Isaiah which reads: *Your innkeepers mix water with their wine,* on the suffering of the Lord, on the general fast of the servants of God, on the special fast of Quadragesima and that there should be no frivolous behavior then, on the traitor Judas, the cross of the Lord, His sepulcher, His resurrection, on the Lord accused and judged in the presence of Pilate, and on the kalends of January; several homilies on the birth of the Lord, homilies also on the Epiphany, and on Easter and Pentecost; that fleshly enemies are not to be feared and that thanksgiving is to be made to God after eating, and on the repentance of the Ninevites, as well as many other homilies of his that he gave for different occasions, which I do not recall.

"He died during the reign of Honorius and the younger Theodosius."

I

A single other witness to Maximus' life, apart from the personal characteristics that his sermons reveal, is to be found at the beginning of the 33rd sermon. There he indicates that he was not a native of Turin. The text ("You yourselves know, brethren, that from the day I began to be with you I have not ceased to admonish you . . .") shows that he was not from Turin but that he was preaching as soon as he arrived there. It suggests, then, either that he was a bishop or priest already when he came to Turin or that he was ordained to the episcopacy or the priesthood very shortly after having gotten there. Although liturgical preaching was still primarily an episcopal function in Maximus' lifetime, i.e. at the end of the fourth and the beginning of the fifth century, priests are also known to have exercised this ministry in certain instances during this period,[1] and it may be that Maximus first preached as a priest and was then ordained to the episcopacy.

That Maximus would already have been a priest or a bishop before his time in Turin, however, seems at least somewhat unlikely. Although it was frequently observed in the breach, the 15th canon of Nicaea (325) forbade the transfer of a deacon, priest, or bishop from one diocese to another. Maximus, then, may either have been ordained and sent to Turin as its first bishop, since no previous bishop is recorded, or may have arrived there only to find himself, as was the case with Augustine,[2] suddenly and perhaps even unwillingly submitting to ordination by a bishop whose name is unknown to us.[3]

The province of Raetia, roughly corresponding to present-day Switzerland, has been proposed as Maximus' birthplace because of the apparent allusions in Sermon 105.1 to his having witnessed the martyrdom of Alexander, Martyrius, and Sisinius in the Val di Non in the Tyrol—an event that we know occurred in 397.[4] But Almut Mutzenbecher, the editor of the critical text of the sermons, gives convincing reasons why these allusions in fact prove nothing of the sort but are intended simply to make the martyrs spiritually present to the congregation in Turin.[5]

The upshot, then, is that we can say nothing certain about Maximus' birthplace except that it was not Turin itself.

Gennadius' reference to Maximus' having died during the reign of Honorius and the younger Theodosius seems to provide irrefragable evidence for the time of his death. The period of their joint reign was from 408 to 423, and that establishes—no further precision being possible—a space of 15 years within which his death must have taken place. Although this time is now accepted by most scholars without demur, another and later time for Maximus' death was proposed by the famous church historian Cardinal Baronius at the beginning of the 17th century. Baronius was convinced that a bishop of Turin named Maximus, who had signed the acts of the Council of Milan in 451 and those of the Council of Rome in 465, was the same Maximus to whom Gennadius referred in his catalogue. Baronius could not believe that two Maximuses living at different times could have governed the church at Turin in the fifth century, and he was sure that Gennadius' original text had been changed. He thought rather that Maximus had flourished (*claruisse*) during the reign of Honorius and Theodosius and that he had died at a great age sometime after the year 465. Indeed, because of his venerable age Maximus was given the privilege of signing the acts of the Roman council before any of the other prelates except the bishop of Rome himself. Only this could explain why the head of a relatively minor see like Turin would have been accorded such an honor.[6]

So influential was Baronius that his opinion dominated until the end of the 19th century. Yet it was not universally accepted, and when Bruno Bruni published his edition of Maximus' sermons at Rome in 1784 he raised the question as to whether there were not two Maximuses. Although he himself opted for Baronius' position, he acknowledged that it was a matter "disputed among scholars with considerable heat."[7]

Eventually, however, the view that there were two bishops with the same name in fifth-century Milan carried the day.[8] Mutzenbecher gives several arguments in favor of this more recent position in the preface to her critical edition of Maximus;[9] the most significant of these can be summarized here. In the first place, Gennadius has been shown to be generally a reliable chronicler.[10] The likelihood of his having made a mistake in placing Maximus' death sometime in the period from 408 to 423 is further reduced by the fact that the chapter on Maximus occurs between one on Orosius, who died after 417, and one on Petronius, who died before 450.[11] Another telling argument is that in the area of heterodoxy Maximus is exclusively concerned with Arianism.[12] Had he lived into the 460s, one would expect to find at least some traces in his sermons of a polemic against Pelagianism and Nestorianism as well, but of that there is nothing detectable.

Gennadius' accuracy appears vindicated, then, in this case. For the date when Maximus commenced his ministry, we may rely to a limited extent on the internal evidence of the sermons. Since nearly half of these recall ideas of Ambrose—mostly from his *Exposition on the Gospel of Luke*, which was composed in the 380s—we can date these sermons to the year 390 or after. The two sermons that treat of the martyrdom of Alexander, Martyrius, and Sisinius must, of course, date to 397 or after, while three other sermons that are evidently dependent to some degree on a letter of Jerome written in 400 date to that year or later.[13] A very precise date has been suggested for Sermon 18 because of its mention of a specific barbarian activity.[13a] But other references, whether to the eclipse of the moon spoken of in Sermons 30 and 31 or to barbarian incursions or to ecclesiastical events, are too vague to be of much help in dating.

A *terminus ante quem* cannot be established for the complete body of sermons, it is true, but only for about half. The earliest possible such *terminus* for these sermons would be about 390, when Ambrose would have published his *Exposition*. It seems convenient to use that year, if only for the sake of argument, as a general *terminus ante quem*. The conclusion is that we may date Maximus' ministry in Turin to the years between about 390 and 408/423.

THE PROBLEM OF THE TEXT[14]

When Bruni published his edition of Maximus' sermons at the request of Pius VI, he included 234 sermons and six *tractatus*. He had had no previous experience in editing and his criteria for authenticity were rather liberal. In earlier centuries, however, Maximus had frequently suffered from a lack rather than a surfeit. Many of his sermons were attributed to Ambrose or Augustine, even with the very titles that Gennadius had given for Maximus. On the other hand, sermons that were not his were occasionally attached to his name, and from these, to a great extent, Maximus gained the reputation that he enjoyed during the Middle Ages of being a great preacher.

In 1535 Joannes Gymnicus brought out the first independent edition of Maximus' sermons in Cologne. In this collection of 74 sermons, 35 were reassigned to Maximus for the first time after having been under Ambrose's name for centuries, but the other 39 have subsequently been judged as spurious. In the succeeding centuries, thanks in large part to the work of the Maurists, more sermons were added to Gymnicus' original 74 until, as we have seen, their number came to 240 in Bruni's edition, which was included in Migne's *Patrologia latina* as the 57th volume.

By the late 19th century Bruni's edition was being subjected to severe criticism, and in fact it was discovered that several sermons therein were 18th-century forgeries. No other text was published, however, until nearly two hundred years after Bruni's, when Almut Mutzenbecher brought out hers in 1962 in the 23rd volume of *Corpus christianorum, series latina*.

Mutzenbecher's edition is based on the information provided by Gennadius, who mentions 28 topics; on six manuscripts, which provide a total of 119 sermons; and on an investigation of the sermons published in Bruni's edition that were not already otherwise identified, which yielded two more sermons. Of these 119 sermons, 89 seem to have constituted a collection under Maximus' name by the end of the fifth century; yet seven of these 89 are judged spurious or doubtful by Mutzenbecher, including two listed by Gennadius himself (Sermons 7 and 8 on Saint Eusebius of Vercelli) and two that can be ascribed respectively to Jerome and to Basil as translated into Latin by Rufinus (Sermons 46 and 47). The remaining 30, which Mutzenbecher designates *sermones extravagantes*, or "sermons out of order," are for the most part authentic, although four are considered doubtful and two spurious. Thus, of a total of 119 sermons, all of which Mutzenbecher publishes in her text, 106 are authentic.[15]

MAXIMUS THE PREACHER

The sermons that are currently ascribed to Maximus can represent only a small part of the output of a preaching career that must have extended over at least 20 years. Given that a bishop in the ancient

Church would have preached every Sunday as well as on important feast days and frequently during Lent (there are examples in each category for Maximus), we probably possess barely a tenth of Maximus' homilies. The majority would have either lost their attribution to Maximus, in which event they still await discovery, or completely disappeared. This is the case, however, with most early Christian preachers.

Despite the great number of sermons that Maximus must have preached, though, not each of them was necessarily an entirely new production, as we know from the ones that have survived. Like preachers everywhere and at all times, Maximus was in the habit of repeating himself, and Mutzenbecher has listed nearly 30 places in which he repeats an idea or a phrase, some of them quite long, in her index of sources and imitations.[16]

Alexander Olivar, basing himself on Mutzenbecher's research, is of the opinion that Maximus' sermons were intended primarily to be heard rather than read: the proof of this is the relatively large number of expressions retained in the text that bespeak the presence of an audience.[17] In this regard Maximus is unlike Ambrose, for example, who was more a writer than a speaker, and whose sermons have survived for the most part under the form of treatises.[18] But, according to Olivar, Maximus must have written out his sermons beforehand, or at least provided himself with a sketch: the long citations from Ambrose, which occasionally occur, would ordinarily not have permitted extemporaneous preaching.[19] In relatively few cases, however, does Maximus actually cite Ambrose verbatim; usually he simply recalls the thoughts and images of his great contemporary, which is a process that would have been considerably less demanding on the memory.

Maximus' sermons can by no means be called great works of rhetoric; he is neither an Augustine nor a Leo, to mention two preachers of the first rank from about the same period. But his preaching is marked by the directness and sobriety that a mostly rural congregation, somewhat removed from the mainstream, would have appreciated. His sermons are models of a good popular homiletic style that must have been widespread, and therein lies much of their interest for us. In them we glimpse "a man fairly capable in the sacred Scriptures and able to teach the people as the occasion demanded," as Gennadius described him,[20] at work for his flock.

His Torinesi are a people still infected by pagan customs, particularly in the outlying farms, as numerous references make clear.[21] Three sermons speak explicitly of Arianism,[22] and several others of heresy in vaguer terms.[23] Phenomena such as these call forth words of reproof or warning, as does also his congregation's failure to turn out in full force on a Sunday or on a special feast day.[24] Once he indicates that he has not preached by way of punishment because so many had failed to come to church for the feast of Peter and Paul, and with a charming ingenuousness he tells them how much they missed.[25] In another sermon he threatens not to preach,[26] but ordinarily he realizes that he is obliged to speak rather than keep silent.[27] His rebukes are not only addressed to his congregation, for at the end of Sermon 79 he acknowledges in a revelatory passage that, although his congregation is at fault in a particular matter, the clerics of Turin are even more negligent than they; he himself, he says, is convicted by their unbecoming conduct. At other times, however, it is encouragement that is needed, as when, for example, barbarians appear in the vicinity.[28]

Familiar ascetic themes emerge, most notably those of fasting and almsgiving; there are numerous instances of each. The emphasis on fasting, however, and especially on keeping an unbroken fast throughout Lent—along with allusions to the fate that will overtake those whose observance of the fast has been less than perfect—strike one today as being somewhat out of order. Even Maximus' own contemporaries do not attach precisely the same importance to fasting that he seems to.[29]

Behind this preaching there lies a theory, which Maximus has left us in Sermon 42.2–3. This theory is based on Mk. 4.25: *To the one who has will be given, and from the one who does not have what he has will be taken away.* That is to say, as Maximus puts it, the virtuous are to be encouraged in virtue by a preacher who places before them the reward for their virtue, while the evil are to be told of the punishment that awaits them and of the deprivations that they will endure in hell. The former should be incited to act still more virtuously, but to speak of virtue to the latter would only earn their disdain, for, in the words of 1 Cor. 2.14, *the unspiritual person does not accept the things of the Spirit, for it is foolishness to him.* Whether Maximus was successful in the application of his insight we can only guess, but the notion of adapting the sermon to the audience is classic in its simplicity. Still relatively rare at this period (although there is a similar brief passage in Augustine's treatise *On Catechizing the Uninstructed*[30]), this reflection on how to preach looks forward to Gregory the Great's extremely influential *Book of Pastoral Care,* the bulk of which is devoted to the subject of fitting the preacher's words to his congregation.

In so many sermons from the patristic era we can even now catch a sense of dialogue between the preacher and his hearers, and this is certainly true in the case of Maximus. At least ten times he anticipates his listeners' difficulty in grasping a particular point by using the well-worn device or its equivalent: *Sed dicat aliquis fortasse*—"But perhaps someone might say. . . ."[31] He imagines out loud what the conversation of members of his congregation might be, or rather should be, about his preaching when they return home.[32] When one realizes that the bishop of a relatively small diocese in the early centuries of the Church would have been somewhat similar to the pastor of a large city parish today and that the congregations of both would have been about the same size, one can see how Maximus would have had more contact with his flock than perhaps most modern bishops do. The closeness of this contact is well reflected in the sermon *On the Eclipse of the Moon,* where we are given the impression that Maximus has been arguing with some of his flock in the streets of Turin over their adherence to pagan superstitions.[33] A passage from a Lenten sermon is still more striking in this regard. There he reproaches those in his congregation who are not observing the fast and says that they ought to be afraid lest he smell food on their breath when they exchange the kiss of peace with him during the liturgy.[34]

Maximus' extensive use of imagery is particularly noteworthy. This is perhaps the area in which his peculiar genius is most evident. Much of his imagery is, of course, borrowed from the common Christian fund and especially from Ambrose, but sometimes he develops a familiar image in a more or less original way, as in Sermon 37, where Ulysses is made a figure of Christ,[35] or as in Sermons 57 and 58, where Susanna has become a type of the Lord.[36] Sometimes, too, he creates what would appear to be an entirely new image. An instance of this is in Sermon 44.3, where we read that the Father receives the ascended Christ, still mysteriously suffering from the wounds of His passion, into His bosom and there provides Him with refreshment and healing. This picture anticipates an aspect of late medieval piety in a remarkable way.[37] Occasionally there is an unusual outpouring of eloquence around an image: this is the case at the beginning of Sermon 53 *On the Pasch*, which Adalbert Hamman has described as a vision of "cosmic fusion and incandescence."[38]

But Maximus does not want for some bizarre turns either. In Sermon 39.2 he interprets Ps. 5.9, *Their throat is an open sepulcher*, in a way that the sacred text could never have intended. For him the open sepulcher, far from being the place of horror and opprobrium that it was in the mind of the Psalmist, has become the throat of the Evangelists and is ultimately to be identified with the Scriptures, for the Lord now rests in them as once He did in the tomb. The Scriptures, like the Lord's sepulcher itself, reveal both "the sacrament of His suffering" and "the glory of His resurrection."[39] An interpretation such as this (and there are others in Maximus) serves to illustrate with special clarity a phenomenon that H.-I. Marrou observed with respect to Augustine and that is common to most of the Fathers: the tendency to break the Scriptures into isolated fragments, each of which was then examined separately and minutely. This was in turn the result of the strongly-held view that each detail of the Scriptures was of equal inspiration and hence of equal importance, so that any passage could be removed from its context without doing damage to it.[40]

If we are to speak of "theology" in the rather narrow sense that this word has acquired in recent times, we will find relatively little in the present collection of sermons. Sermons are, in any event, not always reliable sources for a systematic presentation of theology, since a certain allowance has to be made for the demands of rhetoric. But the sermon is the place par excellence for the use of images. Augustine recognized this when he wrote in his great work *On Christian Doctrine* that, although the meaning of a straightforward expression may be identical with that of an expression using elaborate images, the latter somehow pleases the hearer more; why, Augustine does not exactly know.[41] In itself Maximus' theology is unexceptional, and unexceptional as well. He speaks intelligently of most of the mysteries of Christ's life,[41a] for example, but Arianism, which denied the divinity of Christ or at least relegated Him to a secondary position in the Godhead, hardly tempts him to anything else than rebuke. For Maximus it seems enough to compare a heretic to a fox,[42] but much more than that perhaps his congregation did not require.

In his love of imagery Maximus is a product of his age. He is also a product of his age when he employs his command of imagery for less than admirable ends. In this respect the polemic against the Jews and a demeaning attitude toward women should be mentioned. Regarding the former, there are the regrettable references to, for example, "the faithless and ungrateful Jewish people,"[43] which we have unfortunately learned to expect from the Fathers. Ordinarily the Jews or the Synagogue appear simply in a generic sort of way as the group that is archetypally opposed to or contrasted with the Church. Thus the two women grinding grain in Mt. 24.41, one of whom is taken and one left behind, stand for the Church and the Synagogue, one of whom will be caught up into eternal rest while the other will be abandoned.[44] In Sermon 63.3, however, there is a passage on the Jews that has less a flavor of the generic and that seems to bespeak some acquaintance on Maximus' part with Jews. "We ought to avoid, though, the companionship not only of the pagans but also of the Jews, with whom even a conversation is a great contamination. For with their artfulness they ingratiate themselves with people, get into homes, enter into the palaces of governors, and disturb the ears of judges and of the common folk, and the more shameless they are the more influential they are." Such a passage must ultimately have been based on some experience that Maximus actually had with Jews in Turin or elsewhere and that he perhaps interpreted according to the preconceptions that he manifests in other sermons.

As is the case with most references to the Jews, women too are treated less as real persons than as archetypes. For Maximus, woman is the snare setter, symbolically depicted by Eve, of course, and by the portress who questions Peter about whether he is one of Christ's disciples.[45] But this understanding of the female sex is common among the Fathers.

In sum, we can say that Maximus is a preacher who is gifted, but not so gifted that he either overcomes the prejudices of his age (which, to be sure, he shares with such luminaries as Augustine and Chrysostom) or leads his flock into some of the deeper waters of theological speculation. His sermons, though short, are not necessarily characterized by cohesiveness, and with rare exception they lack the brilliant phrase and the play of words. Yet they do contain passages of great beauty; moreover, they are direct and easy to understand, and in them Maximus manifests his engagement with his congregation. In them, too, we are able to see a rural church, at once superstitious and devout, which must have loved its bishop while it often frustrated him. For in its hands, at least to a certain extent, lay the preservation of the preaching that he addressed to it.

THE PRESENT TRANSLATION

A collection of sermons from patristic times can never be considered closed; there is always the possibility of adding something else, if not perhaps of subtracting something. To that degree, then, Mutzenbecher's painstakingly researched and excellent edition must remain tentative. It is the edition from which the present translation has been made. In the very few cases in which I have deviated from Mutzenbecher's text, I have alerted the reader in the notes. The sermons that Mutzenbecher has designated *extravagantes* are listed as such in the notes. An appendix contains the 13 sermons that she found to be doubtful or spurious; these too are of historical value, and in some cases, as has been noted, they were already associated with Maximus' name by the end of the fifth century. I have not felt it necessary to mention Bruni's number for each sermon that appears in his text.

Translations of a few of Maximus' sermons, mostly in fragmentary form, are to be found here and there, notably in the Liturgy of the Hours used by the Roman Catholic Church. The only significantly large anthology of which I am aware is in Italian, translated by Filippo Gallesio and published in 1975; it contains parts of 69 sermons.[46]

The scriptural citations that Maximus makes are translated directly from the Latin, although whenever possible I have used the Revised Standard Version of the Bible as a kind of "guide" for the English. Occasional inconsistencies in the English rendering of certain passages correspond to inconsistencies in Maximus' Latin and indicate that at least sometimes he quoted the Bible from memory.

Inasmuch as Maximus is significant for his imagery, I have tried to give an account in the notes of as many of the images as possible, whether by citing the first use of the image in patristic literature or by giving a parallel, preferably from one of Maximus' contemporaries. I have also tried to indicate further literature, and in this respect I have often simply drawn the reader's attention to the relevant article in the extraordinarily helpful (but, alas, still far from complete) *Reallexikon für Antike und Christentum* or another such encyclopedic work. A dissertation has in fact been written by M. C. Conroy on Maximus' imagery, but it is almost exclusively devoted to merely cataloguing it rather than tracing it to its sources.[47]

It remains to say that the titles of the present sermons were not necessarily given by Maximus himself but are probably the products of later compilers. Consequently several of the sermons entitled "sequels" are perhaps not such, and I have mentioned this in the notes.

*   *   *

I want to thank Bede Shipps, O.P., in a very special way for having proofread the entire translation with a view to an accurate rendering of the Latin into English. I am also grateful to David Thomas Warner for having reviewed the English text for the sake of style. Needless to say, however, if there are any flaws in either translation or style, I bear the responsibility. Thanks, too, to the editors of Ancient Christian Writers for their encouragement and co-operation. Finally, I want to record my appreciation of my Dominican brothers and sisters at the Dominican House of Studies in Washington who expressed an interest in this project when I was pursuing it there.

THE SERMONS OF
ST. MAXIMUS OF TURIN

SERMON 1

On the Anniversary of Saints Peter and Paul[1]

1. Although all the blessed apostles are recipients of an equal share of grace from the Lord of holiness, nonetheless in some way Peter and Paul seem to stand out from the others and to excel by reason of a certain special virtue of faith in the Savior. Indeed, we are able to prove this by referring to the judgment of the Lord Himself. For to Peter, as to a good steward, He gave the key of the heavenly kingdom, and upon Paul, as one skilled in instruction, He enjoined the teaching office in the school of the Church.[1a] Thus those whom the one would educate to salvation the other would receive into peace, and while Paul would enlighten their hearts with the teaching of his words Peter would open to their souls the kingdom of heaven. Hence Paul also received, so to speak, a key from Christ, that of knowledge.[2] For whatever opens up the hard places of hearts to faith, lays bare the secrets of minds, and brings what is kept closed within out into the open by an intelligible presentation ought to be called a key. A key, I say, both opens the conscience to the confession of sin and inserts grace for the eternal saving mystery. Each, then, received a key from the Lord: the one of knowledge, and the other of power. The one dispenses the riches of immortality, the other distributes the treasures of knowledge. For there are in fact treasures of knowledge, as it is written: *in whom all the treasures of wisdom and knowledge are hidden.*[3]

2. Consequently blessed Peter and Paul stand out among all the apostles and excel by a certain special prerogative. But between these two it is uncertain who is to be placed first.[4] For I think that those who have suffered equally are equal in merits,[5] and that those who we see have attained the glory of martyrdom at the same time have pursued a life of like intensity of faith. Let us not imagine that they bore the savagery of one tyrant on one day in one place for no reason. They suffered on one day so that together they would attain to Christ, in one place so that Rome would lack neither, and under one perse-

cutor so that each would endure an equal cruelty. Thus the day was fixed with merit in mind, the place for glory, and the persecutor for virtue.

But where did they suffer martyrdom? In the city of Rome, which holds the leadership and the chief place among the nations, so that where the head of superstition had been, there the head of holiness might rest, and where the princes of the peoples used to live, there the princes of the churches might remain.

From this we are able to grasp how meritorious blessed Peter and Paul are: as the Lord illumined the region of the East with His own suffering, so He deigned to illumine the region of the West—lest it be inferior[6]—by the blood of the apostles who were acting in His place. And although His suffering is sufficient for salvation, nonetheless He has offered us these martyrs' as an example.[7]

3. On this day, then, the blessed apostles poured out their blood. But let us see why they suffered precisely these things. Note that, among other marvels, by their prayers they cast down the magician Simon from the airy void by a headlong fall.[8] For when this same Simon called himself Christ and claimed that he could ascend like the Son to His Father by flying, and when suddenly in his pride he began to fly by his magic arts, then Peter beseeched the Lord on his knees and conquered the magic flight by his holy prayer. The prayer ascended to the Lord before the flier did, the righteous petition before the wicked presumption. Peter, I say, from his place on the earth obtained what he sought before Simon attained to the heavenly places where he was going. Peter cast him down from the airy height as if he were bound, and striking a rock in his onrush he broke his legs. This occurred as a rebuke for what he had done: the one who a little before had tried to fly was suddenly unable to walk, and he who had assumed wings was deprived of his feet.

Yet lest perhaps it seem marvelous that this magician flew about in the air for a while in the apostle's presence, Peter accomplished the same thing by his suffering.[9] For God permitted Simon to ascend higher so that his fall would be greater. He wished him to be lifted up on high in the sight of all so that the eyes of all would see him when he fell. This, then, is the lifting up of wickedness, that a person should set himself up on high and raise himself upwards. But holy prayer puts down all pride and casts down all vanity.

Sermon 2

On the Anniversary of the Same[1]

1. As we observe today the anniversary of blessed Peter and Paul, we ought to enjoy different dishes and celebrate such a festival with great happiness. For, on the feast of men like these, who would not make elaborate preparations so that he might prove his love for the apostles by the amount that he spent? Yet there is no need to spend what is ours for our own refreshment; on his anniversary Saint Peter himself gives us to eat, for there is that vessel of his filled with every kind of good thing, which was brought from heaven to him when he was hungry.[2] Therefore the one who hungers as Peter did is himself refreshed along with Peter. Why should we ready our own meal, then, when we ought to be fed with apostolic food? Why should we seek after this-worldly dishes when we have a heavenly abundance? For Saint Luke says in the Acts of the Apostles that after prayer at about the sixth hour heaven was opened and a splendid vessel like a linen cloth was brought down to Peter, who was hungry. In it were all the four-footed beasts and crawling creatures of the earth and the birds of heaven, and the Lord said to him: *Peter, arise, kill and eat!*[3] Look at Peter! Elsewhere he says: *Gold and silver I have none,*[4] but now he has a banqueting plate more splendid than silver, and he who on account of Christ had resisted the beauty of silver is enriched by Christ with the brightness of silver. Peter, as he is about to dine, has neither the preparations of cooks nor the services of attendants. But, what is better, he does not want for divine ministrations, and, by an advantageous exchange, what the holy man lacks on earth abounds in heaven. For, so that Peter might eat, it is not a storeroom that is carefully unlocked but rather heaven itself that is instantly opened. We read in the sacred Scriptures that Elijah was fed in the desert by ministering ravens.[5] How much better Peter, who was not given a small amount of food by a loathsome bird[6] but was offered a whole banquet by an angelic multitude!

2. After his prayer, then, Peter eats. It is remarkable that hunger overtakes the holy man after praying, since hunger is usually driven away by prayer and the hungry soul is fed exclusively by its supplica-

tions. But I am of the opinion that, after having prayed, Peter hungered not for food but for the salvation of humankind, and that he was not oppressed by bodily fasting but afflicted by the lack of believers.[7] For when the faithless and ungrateful Jewish people did not believe him when he was preaching Christ, Peter experienced a certain kind of hunger in his ministry. For one who does not obtain the fruit of his own labor suffers hunger. Therefore he went quickly to the upper room to pray. Well does it say that Peter went to the upper room to pray, since whenever someone who is holy prays, leaving behind lower or earthly affairs, he is raised aloft in his mind, rapt on high in his senses, and drawn near to heaven in holy thought.[8] And there, for the salvation of the Jewish people, a vessel filled with animals of different sorts is offered to that hungry man, that is, to that man who is reflecting in the higher part of his heart, while God, as it were, tells him: "Your hunger is for the Jews only. Behold, I am assuaging the hunger of your faith with the diversity of all nations." For indeed the different animals collected in a single vessel are a type of the gathering of different nations collected in a single Church.[9] This Church, having neither spot nor wrinkle[10] anywhere on its splendid vessel, shines with the brightness of linen.[11] In it the first animal to be sacrificed to God from the nations is the centurion Cornelius.[12]

3. From this vessel of his, then, Peter feeds us. For when we see the throngs of the nations hasten to the Christian faith, we rejoice together with the apostles. For those whose anniversary we celebrate today are not dead but reborn. It is clear that they are alive because they have become partakers in Christ,[13] who is life.[14] Although their bodies have been slain in suffering, nonetheless the process of life has not been interrupted.[15] For they still give thanks to God and offer praises to the Savior, and in fact they adhere more closely to Christ inasmuch as their members are no longer bound together, as the apostle Paul says: *To be dissolved and to be with Christ is better by far.*[16] Thus that should not be called death which, when it occurs, separates us from our persecutors and joins us to Christ. It is clear that that should not be called death which associates the one who has died with Christ and brings gain to the dying, as the blessed Apostle says: *For me to live is Christ and to die is gain.*[17] But that is real death which binds by the death of sinners even the living person who, although he appears to be alive, seems nonetheless already given over to death on

account of his crimes. In this respect the Apostle says of that voluptuous widow: *While living she has already died.*[18]

SERMON 3

On the Gospel Pearl[1]

1. Beloved brethren, I think that it is a sufficient reproof to you that on the previous Sunday, when I was about to depart, I dispensed no spiritual gifts to you from the sacred Scriptures but upbraided and accused you because of your sin, dismissing you without any consoling preaching. For I wished you to understand this particular point: how gravely you have sinned when you have not deserved to hear the divine words. It is a strong and far-reaching punishment at the disposal of the priests[2] not to entrust to whoever is unworthy the sacraments[3] of the heavenly Scriptures nor, as the Lord says, to give what is holy to dogs or to cast pearls before the feet of swine so that they are trampled upon.[4] For whoever tries to set the grace of the heavenly pearl upon a vile sinner squanders it. A jewel, as you yourselves know, demands a setting of gold, and a pearl should only be placed in precious necklaces. Be, then, the finest sort of gold! Be a precious necklace, so that the spiritual pearl can be set in you! For Christ the Lord is the pearl which that rich merchant in the Gospel hastened to buy after having sold all his property; he chose to get rid of all the worldly jewels that he had just so that he might buy the one pearl of Christ.[5]

2. Hence, brethren, on account of the enormity of the transgression that you have committed, I have been unwilling to open to you the words of Gospel refreshment. Instead I indignantly press upon you your wrongdoing, first correcting you with spiritual blows and then enriching you with gifts of the pearl. I have chosen, I say, to lay blame on your sin with bitter accusation rather than to foster it with kindly dissimulation. For whoever does not reprove his brother when he sins is encouraging him, in a certain way, to sin. But I do not wish you to think that in striking you frequently I have no love for you; for the son who is worthy of chastisement is loved the more, as Scripture

says: *Whom the Lord loves He corrects; He chastizes every son whom He accepts.*[6] Tell me if this sin should not be lamented—that you were then so unmindful of your salvation that you did not honor the blessed apostles Peter and Paul, although you knew that they were the teachers of the nations, the first of the martyrs, and the princes of the priests; that you did not wish to celebrate their most solemn anniversary with us and partake of that heavenly banquet in which, for the sake of His martyrs' pleasure, the Lord Himself ministered to us the substance of life. Do you wish to know how many good things you were deprived of? Ask the brethren who were there at that time together with me how refreshed they were when they departed from the Lord's table and what sort of spiritual riches they brought back home with them. One thing I know—that if on that day someone noble and wealthy had invited you to a dinner for his son's birthday as far as ten miles away, you would certainly have gone because of the elaborate dishes and the large portions.

3. Therefore, brethren, whenever the memory of the martyrs is celebrated we ought to leave aside all worldly affairs and gather without delay to give honor to those who brought us salvation by the outpouring of their blood, who have offered themselves like sacred victims to the Lord on our behalf,[7] especially since Almighty God says to His saints: *Whoever honors you honors me, and whoever rejects you rejects me.*[8] Whoever honors the martyrs, then, honors Christ as well, and whoever rejects His holy ones rejects God too.

SERMON 4

On the Anniversary of Saint Laurence[1]

1. I believe that you are aware of the suffering of the most blessed Laurence, whose anniversary we celebrate today, and I have no doubt that your love[2] knows what sort of things he underwent in his persecution. So great is the glory of his martyrdom that he illuminated the whole world. Clearly Laurence illuminated the world by that torch with which he himself was set on fire, and the flames that he himself bore have warmed the hearts of all Christians. For, given this exam-

ple, who does not wish to burn for Christ with Laurence so that he might be crowned by Christ with Laurence? Who does not wish to put up with Laurence's fire for a while so that he will not have to suffer the eternal fire of Gehenna? By the example of blessed Laurence, therefore, we are incited to martyrdom, we are inflamed for the faith, and we glow with devotion. Even if the persecutor's flame is lacking to us, still the flame of faith is not. Indeed, we do not burn in body for Christ, but we burn in desire; the persecutor does not apply fire to me, but desire for the Savior sets me ablaze. In the Gospel we read that the Savior's fire exists when the same Lord says: *Do you not know that I have come to bring fire to the earth, and what do I wish but that it were blazing?*[3] Inflamed by this fire, Ammaus and Cleopas[4] said: *Was not our heart burning within us on the road, when the Lord Jesus opened the Scriptures to us?*[5] So Laurence, burning with this fire too, did not feel the blaze of the flames, and while he burned with desire for Christ he was not set ablaze by the persecutor's punishment. For to the extent that the ardor of faith glowed in him the torturing flame grew cold. Blessed Laurence endured a bodily burning, but Christ's divine fire extinguished the tyrant's material fire.[6] At one and the same time he is ablaze with the love of Christ and tormented by the persecutor's flame. For although his limbs are changed into glowing embers, yet the strength of his faith is not changed; he sustains the loss of his body, but he gains salvation.

2. For, brethren, blessed Laurence was not slain by speedy or simple suffering. Whoever is struck by the sword dies at once, and whoever is plunged into a fiery furnace is freed instantly, but he was tortured by a lengthy and involved punishment, so that death might color his sufferings but not end them.[7] For it is said that this punishment was devised for him by the cruel persecutor: stretched upon an iron grate over an exposed heap of burning coals, he was to be consumed by a slow flame that would not kill a person quickly by setting him ablaze but instead would torture him by burning him slowly, and whenever his persecutor noticed that one of his sides was burned he would expose the other to be burned by the flames.

We read that the most blessed youths Ananiah, Azariah, and Mishael, having been enclosed by the king in a fiery furnace, walked about in the flames that were intended to punish them and crushed the fiery coals beneath their feet.[8] Hence blessed Laurence is not to be honored with less glory. Although they walked about in the flames of their own punishment, he reclined in the very fire of his torture. They trampled upon the flames with their feet, but with his devotion he extinguished those burning his sides. They, I say, standing in the midst of their punishment, adored the Lord with elevated hands, while he, prostrate in his punishment, prayed earnestly to the Lord with his whole body.

3. Blessed Laurence, therefore, lying on his back, was turned from one scorched side to the other and his reins were burned with fire, so that the prophecy of the psalm which spoke about Laurence might be fulfilled: *Test me, Lord, and try me; burn my reins and my heart.*[9] *Burn,* it says, *my reins and my heart.* He asks, indeed, to be burned with a double fire. For if he had been speaking of the one fire which is merely of the world, it would have sufficed to have offered his reins alone to be consumed by the flames.[10] But the heart does not burn except by the flame of Christ. As Ammaus and Cleopas said: *Was not our heart burning?* And therefore he asks for a double fire for himself in order to prove his devotion, so that in his struggle he may manifest that in him the love of Christ avails more than a tyrant's vengeance. Therefore, brethren, let us honor blessed Laurence who, in conquering the flames of the persecutor with his faith, has shown us how to overcome the fires of Gehenna by the fire of faith, and by the love of Christ not to fear the day of judgment.

SERMON 5

On the Birthday of Saint John the Baptist[1]

1. In praise of the holy and most blessed John the Baptist, whose birthday we celebrate today, I do not know what is the most important thing that we should preach—that he was wonderfully born or more wonderfully slain. For he was born as a prophecy and murdered for truth; by his birth he announced the coming of the Savior and by his death he condemned the incest of Herod.[2] For this holy and righteous man, who was born in an uncommon way as the result of a promise,[3] merited from God that he should depart this world by an

uncommon death, that he should lay aside his body, which he had received as a gift from the Lord, by confessing the Lord. 2. Therefore John did everything by the will of God, since he was born and died for the sake of God's work.

Let us briefly go over the events relating to his birth. When his father Zechariah and his mother Elizabeth were worn out by their advanced age and were not enjoying the fruit of sons, and the best time for begetting children for themselves had gone by, so that the very desire to raise up offspring was lacking to them, suddenly they are given a promise by an angel, and holy Gabriel announces that John is to be born, saying: *Do not be afraid, Zechariah, for behold, your prayer has been heard, and your wife Elizabeth shall conceive and bear a son.*[4] *Your prayer has been heard,* he says. From this we understand that Zechariah's righteousness begot John by prayer rather than Elizabeth's old age did by the act of procreation. From this, I say, we understand that supplication and not pleasure brought forth John. For when the maternal womb had grown cold as a result of old age and the enfeebled members of the body had already lost the power of fecundity, contrary to the body's incapability and contrary to the sterility of the womb, by Zechariah's prayers Elizabeth's belly swelled and she conceived John not by nature but by grace. It was necessary for that holy child to be born in this way—he who was begotten not so much by embraces as by prayers.

3. Yet, brethren, we ought not to be so astonished that John merited such grace in his birth. For the precursor and forerunner of Christ ought to have had something similar to the birth of the Lord, the Savior. And indeed the Lord was begotten of a virgin and John of a sterile woman, the one of an unstained girl and the other of an already exhausted old woman. John's birth, then, also has something of the glorious and the wondrous. For although a matron's bringing forth would seem to be less noble than a virgin's, yet as we look up to Mary for having brought forth as a virgin we also wonder at Elizabeth for having done so as an old woman. Indeed, I think that this fact contains a certain mystery—that John, who was a figure of the Old Testament, should have been born of the already cold blood of an old woman, while the Lord, who would preach the gospel of the kingdom of heaven, came forth from a woman in the flower of glowing youth. For Mary, conscious of her virginity, marvels at the fruit hidden in

her belly, while Elizabeth, conscious of her old age, blushes that her womb is heavy with what she has conceived; thus the Evangelist says: *She hid herself for five months.*[5] How wonderful it is, though, that the same archangel Gabriel performs an office with respect to each birth![6] He comforts the unbelieving Zechariah and encourages the believing Mary. He lost his voice because he doubted,[7] but she, because she believed immediately, conceived the saving Word.

4. This too seems unworthy to pass over in silence in praise of John—that, not yet born, already he prophesies and, while still in the enclosure of his mother's womb, confesses the coming of Christ with movements of joy since he could not do so with his voice. For Elizabeth says to holy Mary: *As soon as you greeted me, the child in my womb exulted for joy.*[8] John exults, then, before he is born, and before his eyes can see what the world looks like he can recognize the Lord of the world with his spirit. In this regard I think that the prophetic phrase is apropos which says: *Before I formed you in the womb I knew you, and before you came forth from the womb I sanctified you.*[9] Thus we ought not to marvel that, after he was put in prison by Herod,[10] from his confinement he continued to announce Christ to his disciples,[11] when even confined in the womb he preached the same Lord by his movements.

SERMON 6

Another Sermon on the Birthday of the Same Saint John[1]

1. As we are about to celebrate the birthday of Saint John the Baptist today, I would like to be quiet and with silence set bounds to my labor and to my inexperience, but the power itself of his name does not permit me to be still. For the very sounding of his name draws out the secrets of our heart and unlooses what is hidden in our silence, and what is brushed over in concealment is pressed into the open in wonderment. For if even his father Zechariah received back his voice when he named him,[2] how much more are we promised abundant speech when we praise him! And if his father's mouth

opened when he was born in the world, how much more is our mouth fruitful when it is opened for Christ! For when Zechariah his father was punished with silence by the angel Gabriel because of his disbelief in his birth[3] and for a long time mutely veiled the secrets of his mind with his wordlessness, when John his son was born and among his neighbors there was concern about what name he should be given, writing tablets were offered to his father so that he himself could put down the name that he had decided upon, so that he might express in writing what he could not in speech. Then, in a wonderful manner, when he had taken the tablets in order to begin writing, his tongue was loosened, the written word gave way to speech, and he did not write "John" but spoke it.[4] Consider, then, the merit of the holy Baptist: he gave his father back his voice, he restored the faculty of speech to the priest. Consider, I say, his merit: John unloosed the mouth that the angel had bound. What Gabriel had closed the little child unlocked, although he himself was also an angel, as it is written of him: *Behold, I send my angel before your face.*[4] Think of John and of how great the power of his name is, so that the mentioning of it restored the voice to his mute father and the devout priest to his people! For when his tongue was silent he had neither son nor ministry, but when John is born the father suddenly becomes a prophet or priest, speech attains its use, love receives an offspring, the office recognizes the priest. Since such is the power of his name, then, we who are about to speak of it cannot be silent even if we want to be. John himself, in fact, is called *the voice of one crying.*[5] How could anyone praise his voice and be silent? How could anyone admire his outcry and be still? For he himself says of himself: *I am the voice of one crying in the desert.*[6] Notice what he says, for he does not simply say: *I am the voice,* but rather: *the voice of one crying.* It is for the sake of promoting faith that his voice penetrates ears and his outcry shakes hearts, that his voice foretells the kingdom and his outcry threatens judgment.

2. Great, therefore, is John, to whose greatness even the Savior bears witness when he says: *Among those born of women there is none greater than John the Baptist.*[7] He excels all, he outranks everyone, he comes before the prophets, he surpasses the patriarchs, and whoever is born of woman is inferior to John. But we ought to inquire care-

fully why the Lord said: *among those born of women,* rather than: "among the sons of men there is none greater" and so forth, since as a matter of fact women are not able to have children without men. He said this, though, because the offspring of women are more numerous than those of men, for there is a son of a woman who is not the son of a man. Holy Mary begot a son who did not have a man for a father. The Lord is the son of a woman and not the son of a man, as the Apostle says: *begotten of a woman, begotten under the law,*[8] so that He who has a mother on earth might have a Father in heaven. Therefore in praise of John his procreation by the more fruitful sex is mentioned so that no one's birth might be distinguished from his. But someone might say: "If John is greater than anyone born of woman, is he even greater than the Savior?" Perish the thought! For John was born of a woman, but Christ of a virgin; the one was brought forth from a corruptible womb, the other was begotten from the flower of an unsullied womb. When the generation of the Lord is considered along with the birth of John, then, let the Lord not falsely seem to share the human condition.[9]

SERMON 9

On the Anniversary of Saints Peter and Paul[1]

1. All of you know, brethren, and the whole world knows well indeed that today is the anniversary of the most blessed Peter and Paul. Such devotion can be hidden in no part of the world inasmuch as the prophet David is speaking of them: *Their sound has gone out through the whole earth, and their words to the ends of the world.*[2] The power of Peter's miracles has gone out through the whole earth, and the words of Paul's epistles have penetrated to the ends of the world. For who has not heard that the first thing that Peter did was to restore strength to the man sitting at the Beautiful Gate of the Temple, who was crippled and had been suffering from a weakness of the feet even from his mother's womb, apostolic grace thus repairing what nature had been unable to bestow?[3] For when the same cripple asked for a

little donation of money and thought that the apostles were about to give him some, Peter said to him: *Silver and gold I do not have, but what I have I give to you: in the name of the Lord Jesus Christ arise and walk!*[4] Blessed indeed is this largesse which, to be sure, did not bestow silver on the beggar but did bestow health! Blessed is this largesse which did not produce gold from its coffers but did produce medicine! And blessed is that cripple who, seeking an alms of money, received the riches of good health! For what he had been unable to purchase for want of money from the physicians he merited to be given by the apostles. The first wonder of his miracles, then, Peter performed by restoring a crippled man's feet.

We have frequently said that Peter was called a rock by the Lord. Thus: *You are Peter, and upon this rock I will build my Church.*[5] If, then, Peter is the rock upon which the Church is built, rightly does he first heal feet, so that as he maintains the foundations of the Church's faith he also strengthens the foundations of a person's limbs. Rightly, I say, does he first heal a Christian's feet so that he can walk upon the rock of the Church not as one who is fearful and weak but as one who is robust and strong.

And where are the words of Paul the apostle not read? Where are they not written down, kept in the heart, and preserved in speech? This Paul was called a vessel of election by the Lord.[6] A good vessel, in which the precious precepts of Christ's commandments are treasured! A good vessel, from whose fulness the substance of life is always poured forth for the peoples, and still it is full![7]

Rock and vessel—most appropriate names for the apostles, and necessary instruments for the house of the Savior! For a strong house is built of rock and rendered useful by vessels. A rock provides the peoples with something firm lest they waver, while a vessel shelters Christians lest they be tempted.

2. But there is no one who is not aware of how blessed their departure was from this world. And this is their first blessing, that the two of them are known to have suffered on one day, so that one day would crown with martyrdom those whom one faith had united in its service.[8] And on account of holiness this suffering, though different in each, nonetheless presupposed equal grace. For Peter, like the Savior, endured the death of the cross, and even in his death he was

not separated from a likeness of the Lord's oblation,[9] so that the one whom he imitated by faith he would also imitate in his suffering.[10] And it is said that when the executioner struck Paul's neck with his sword a stream of milk rather than blood poured forth, and wondrously at his very slaying the holy apostle stood out as resplendent with baptismal grace rather than covered with gore.[11] For why is it marvelous that the one who nourishes the Church should abound in milk? He himself says to the Corinthians: *I gave you milk to drink, not food.*[12] This is clearly that promised land which God promised to our fathers when He said: *I will give you a land flowing with milk and honey.*[13] For the land of which He is speaking is not the one which, as the waters well up, envelops the mire and mingles it with mud, but that land of Paul and those like Paul which constantly drips with what is pure and sweet. For which of Paul's epistles is not sweeter than honey and whiter[14] than milk? These epistles are like the breasts of the churches, nourishing the peoples unto salvation.[15]

From the neck of the Apostle, then, milk flowed instead of blood. We read in his own words: *For flesh and blood shall not possess the kingdom of God.*[16] Consequently Paul already possesses the kingdom, for the blood that is said to prevent one from reigning is lacking to him. Until this day, then, Paul has lain in the earth, but already he is transformed into the substance of the heavenly kingdom.

SERMON 10

On the Anniversary of Saint Cyprian[1]

1. Today, as everyone knows, we are celebrating the feast of Saint Cyprian, and with the birth[2] (as it is called) of the grape harvest, which is already imminent, we compare the birth of his martyrdom. So it is that our thoughts and those of the world meet: the world rejoices in the abundance of grapes, while we are gladdened by the suffering of the saints. Indeed, this suffering should be compared with the grape harvest, for as wine pours out when grapes are squeezed, so also when the saints are martyred blood is poured forth instead of wine, although the vine produces temporal fruits and suf-

fering everlasting ones.[3] Rightly, then, is martyrdom compared to the grape harvest, for it has both its own inebriation and its own cup, about which the prophet David says: *And your inebriating cup, how excellent it is!*[4] And the Lord Himself says in the course of His final suffering: *Father, if it be possible, let this cup pass from me.*[5] And again the prophet says: *I shall take the cup of salvation and call upon the name of the Lord.*[6] Rightly, I say, is the cup likened to martyrdom, for just as when a cup is drunk every noxious humor is burnt off by the heat of the wine, so when the cup of martyrdom is drained all the dregs of sin are diluted by the glory of suffering.

2. The salvation of martyrdom, then, is a kind of wine that rejoices the heart, warms the faith, and purifies the soul; this is clearly the spiritual wine from that grape which hung upon the tree for the salvation of all.[7] For as a cluster of grapes that will produce wine first hangs on the vine by the design of nature, so likewise Christ, when He is about to produce the spiritual wine of martyrdom, is fitted to the cross by divine providence. Plainly He is the grape cluster that those two spies, Joshua the son of Nun and Caleb the son of Jephunneh, carried back on a pole on their shoulders to the sons of Israel.[8] Indeed, even then this prefigured the coming of the Lord, the Savior. For the grape cluster hanging on the pole is an image of Christ hanging on the cross, and in the two bearers of the cluster on the pole two peoples are manifested, the Christian and the Jewish. Since the custom is with bearers that one precedes and the other follows, so the Jewish people is shown to be first and the Christian second. And as the one who comes first does not see what he is carrying and, always having it behind him, scorns it, as it were, by turning his back on it, while the one who follows always sees it with his eyes, always guards it with his glances, and is always in possession of it because of the nearness of his body, so it is with the Jewish and Christian peoples. For the Jew is first, bearing Christ in the law but not knowing it, and scorning Him, so to speak, by turning his back, since He is behind him, as the prophet says: *Let their eyes be darkened, so that they cannot see, and bend their back always.*[9] But the Christian people that follows always looks at Christ with their eyes, always guards Him with their glances, and always takes Him in possession by the nearness of their steps. And as much as the one people leaves Him behind after them-

selves on their wicked way, so much does the other people hasten to come to Him on a straight way.

SERMON II

A Sequel[1]

1. A few days ago, when we were celebrating the anniversary[2] of the most blessed martyr Cyprian, we rejoiced with great delight in his feast, for, as he suffered at the time of the grape harvest, so we also collected different sweet-tasting fruits from his suffering as from a grape harvest. He filled and refreshed us with the new wine of his martyrdom. For it is new wine that refreshes and inebriates the Christian, but that inebriation is sobering.[3] For whoever is inebriated with heavenly grace puts off the burden of sins.[4] The holy apostles, who were filled with this new wine, as Scripture says, spoke the wondrous deeds of God in foreign tongues and appeared, as they did so, both drunk and sober at the same time.[5] For they were thought to be drunk because another tongue sounded in them in a preternatural way, but they were sober because they praised the Lord with spiritual devotion in an ordinary way. Indeed, it did not happen through some kind of ecstasy or shameless behavior that the holy men spoke a foreign language,[6] but it was accomplished by divine providence so that the devotion of the mind would be released through many languages, since one tongue is insufficient to glorify God.

2. Therefore we are joyful because we have taken the fruit of refreshment from the vineyard of the Lord Sabbaoth. *But the vineyard of the Lord Sabbaoth*, as the prophet says, *is the house of Israel*,[7] and we are that house. For according to the faith we are Israelites, whence the Apostle says: *Because those who are of the faith are children of Abraham.*[8] Consequently we are Israel, we are the vineyard of the Lord. Let us be careful lest we produce from the vine sprout of our works not the grape of sweetness but the vinegary one, lest what was said to the Jews by the prophet be said to us: *I maintained it that it might bear grapes, but it brought forth thorns.*[9] How unfortunate it is that the landlord's possession, which ought to produce sweet fruits for him, should pierce him by the sharpness of its thorns! Thus the Jews, when they ought to receive

the Savior in the full devotion of faith, crown Him with the suffering of thorns. And this crown, as far as the Jews are concerned, was the abuse of injuries, but as far as the Lord is concerned it was the crown of virtues.[10] The Jews pierce the Lord, then, when they crown Him; they pierce Him when they crucify Him. For this reason holy Scripture says: *They shall look upon him whom they have pierced.*[11]

3. Therefore, brethren, beware lest it also be told us: *I maintained it that it might bear grapes, but it brought forth thorns.* That is to say, beware lest those thorns which the Jews pressed down on the Lord with bloody hands we also impose on Him with the wickedness of our minds, piercing Him not with thorny sharpness but with base deeds. These are the thorns of the heart, which they sewed together to wound even the Word of God. The Savior calls these to mind in the Gospel when He speaks of the sower's seed that fell among thorns, which grew up and choked what was sown.[12] What these thorns are He Himself says a little later: they are worldly cares which, when they grow up in the human heart, choke in it the commandments of the Savior.[13] For who has ever been able to be concerned about Christ if he is concerned about the world? Who has been able to look after the necessities of the Church if he has been looking to the gain of his own house? Thus the Apostle says: *The man who is without a wife is concerned about the affairs of the Lord, how to please God. But the man who has a wife is concerned about the affairs of the world, how to please his wife.*[14]

4. And so, brethren, be on guard lest your vineyard bring forth not grapes but thorns, lest your harvest produce not wine but vinegar. For whoever gathers in the harvest and does not give to the poor collects not wine but vinegar. Whoever reaps the harvest and does not minister to the needy has not stored up fruits for sustenance but has collected thistles of avarice. On account of this Scripture says of our earth: *Thorns and thistles it shall bring forth to you.*[15]

SERMON 12

On the Suffering or Anniversary of Saints Octavus, Adventus, and Solutor of Turin[1]

1. We ought to celebrate very devoutly the anniversary of all the holy martyrs, brethren, but the solemnity of those who have poured out their own blood in the places where we live is to be observed in

particular by us with total veneration. Now, although all the saints are everywhere and are useful to everyone, nonetheless those who have put up with suffering for our sake intercede specially for us. For when a martyr suffers he suffers not for himself alone but also for his cocitizens: he suffers for himself for the reward, for his cocitizens for an example; he suffers for himself for peace, for his cocitizens for salvation. For by their example we have learned to believe in Christ, to seek eternal life in reproaches, and not to fear death. See what we owe the martyrs, then: one has been tortured so that another might be saved, one has endured the executioner so that another might acknowledge Christ, one has been given over to death so that another might obtain eternal life, and, finally, the saint has been slain so that the sinner might escape. Blessed are the martyrs, then, who have neither lived for themselves nor died for themselves! They have left us an example of how to live by living well and of how to suffer by enduring courageously.[2] Consequently the Lord willed that martyrs should suffer throughout the whole world in different places so that, like apt witnesses, they might urge us on by a kind of presence through the example of their own confession. Thus human frailty, which hardly believed either in the Lord's preaching after having heard it for such a long time or in the testimony that can be seen with eyes, might give credence to the martyrdom of the saints.

2. All the martyrs, therefore, are to be very devoutly honored, but the ones whose relics we possess are to be especially venerated by us. For they all help us by their prayers, but these help us also by their suffering. Among them there is a certain familiarity with us: they are always with us, they tarry with us. While we are still living in our bodies they protect us lest the horror of hell overcome us. It was provided for by our ancestors that we should join our bodies to the bones of the saints,[3] for inasmuch as the underworld feared them punishment would not touch us, and while Christ shed His light on them[4] shadowy gloom would flee from us. Sleeping with the holy martyrs, we have escaped the shadows of hell—not by our own merits but nonetheless as sharers in holiness. The Lord says to Peter: *You are Peter, and upon this rock I will build my Church, and the gates of hell shall not prevail against it.*[5] If the gates of hell shall not prevail against the apostle and martyr Peter, then whoever is joined to a martyr will

not be held by the gate of the underworld. For the gate of hell does
not hold the martyrs because the kingdom of paradise receives them.
And we see that they already reign even here, for we notice that
frequently those obsessed by unclean demons are set free,[6] so that by a
celestial remedy the captive soul is snatched from the devil's snares,
and the devil himself, bound in fiery chains, is led forth captive in his
own captivity,[7] he who shortly before had preyed upon others now
falling prey himself. Everyone knows that these and other more powerful wonders are done by the saints. And therefore, brethren, let us
venerate in this world those whom we ought to have as defenders in
the one to come, and as we are joined to the bones of those who have
preceded us, so let us be joined to them by a like faith. For we shall
not be able to be separated from them if we are joined to them as
much in devotion as in body.

SERMON 13A

On Holy Epiphany[1]

1. We can see what thanks we owe to the Lord Christ because He
heaps good things upon good things and multiplies our joys by more
joys. Until now, see, we have been exulting in the newborn Savior,
and now we rejoice in Him as one reborn.[2] The festival of His birth is
not yet at an end and already the solemnity of His baptism is to be
celebrated. He has hardly been born to us and already He is reborn in
the sacraments.[3] For today—although many years have passed—He
was consecrated in the Jordan. The Lord has disposed of affairs in
such a way, then, as to join good things to good things, so that at one
and the same time He would be brought forth by a virgin and be born
by a mystery, and the feasts of the births of the flesh and of baptism
would be joined, so that just as we marveled then at His conception
from an unsullied virgin, now we might raise our thoughts to Him
who has gone down into the pure waters. Thus we shall glory in each
deed—that a mother begot a son (and she is chaste) and that water
cleansed Christ (and it is holy). Just as after childbirth Mary's chastity
was glorified, so after this baptism the cleansing of the water was

verified, except that the water was endowed with something greater than Mary was. For she merited chastity for herself alone, while it also conferred holiness on us; she merited not to sin, while it merited to purge away sins; she cast from herself her own sins, while it remits the sins of others in itself; upon her virginity was conferred, while upon it fruitfulness was bestowed; she gave birth to one (and she is pure), while it brings forth many (and it is a virgin); apart from Christ she knows no son, while with Christ it is the mother of nations.

2. Today, then, is another kind of birth of the Savior. We see Him born with the same sort of signs, the same sort of wonders, but with greater mystery. And the Holy Spirit, who was present to Him then in the womb,[4] now pours out upon Him in the torrent. He who then purified Mary for Him now sanctifies the running waters for Him. The Father who then overshadowed in power[5] now cries out with His voice. And He who then, as if choosing the more prudent course, manifested Himself as a cloud at the nativity now bears witness to the truth; for God says: *This is my beloved Son, in whom I am well pleased; hear Him.*[6] Clearly the second birth is more excellent than the first. For the one brought forth Christ in silence and without a witness, but the other baptized the Lord gloriously with a profession of divinity; from the one Joseph, thought to be the father, absents himself,[7] but at the other God the Father, not believed in, manifests Himself; in the one the mother labors under suspicion because in her condition she lacked a father, but in the other she is honored because God attests to His Son.

More noble, I say, is the second than the first birth, since in the one the father is discovered to be the God of majesty, while in the other he is perceived to be Joseph the workman.[8] And although the Lord was both born and baptized through the Holy Spirit, yet what cries from the heavens is more noble than what labors on the earth. Joseph the workman, then, is thought to be the father of the Lord, but God, the true Father of the Savior, is not excluded from this; for He is Himself a workman.[9] As a skilled workman He Himself contrived the plan of this world, and like a wise architect He hung heaven from the heights, founded the earth on a base, and bound the seas by His will. He Himself is the workman who, according to a certain measure, casts down the heights of pride and raises up the depths of humility.[10] He Himself is the workman who removes whatever is useless in what we accomplish and preserves whatever is useful. He Himself is the workman whose axe, John the Baptist warns, is laid to our root, so that the tree which goes beyond the proper length of time will be delivered over to the fire when it has been cut out by the roots,[11] while whatever keeps to the measure of faith will be pruned for the heavenly workshop.

3. Today, then, He is baptized in the Jordan. What sort of baptism is this, when the one who is dipped is purer than the font, and where the water that soaks the one whom it has received is not dirtied but honored with blessings? What sort of baptism is this of the Savior, I ask, in which the streams are made pure more than they purify? For by a new kind of consecration the water does not so much wash Christ as submit to being washed. Since the Savior plunged into the waters, He sanctified the outpouring of every flood and the course of every stream by the mystery of His baptism, so that when someone wishes to be baptized in the name of the Lord it is not so much the waters of this world that cover him but the waters of Christ that purify him. Yet the Savior willed to be baptized for this reason—not that He might cleanse Himself but that He might cleanse the waters for our sake.[12]

SERMON 13B

A Sequel[1]

1. Your holiness[2] remembers, brethren, that on the day of the most blessed Epiphany we said that the Lord was baptized in the Jordan, and we further said that He wished to be consecrated by this mystery more for our sake than for His own. It is clear that He accomplished all these things on our account. Why would a consecration have been necessary for His benefit, He who is Himself a sacrament?[3] What would the solemnizing of a mystery have profited Him in whom is the fulness of mystery? For fulness is in Him, as the Apostle says: *For in Him the whole fulness of divinity dwells bodily.*[4] And again the Evangelist says: *From His fulness we have all received.*[5] Thus He in whom the fulness of divinity existed did not lack for anything so as to require

completion by the mysteries of the sacraments, but He willed to go through the mystery not that He Himself might attain perfection but that the fulness of the mystery might profit us. For this reason, when John the Baptist resists Him and says: *I ought to be baptized by you, and do you come to me?* the Lord tells him: *Let it be so for now, for thus it behooves us to fulfil all righteousness.*[6] *To fulfil*, he says, *all righteousness*. When the Lord is baptized, then, righteousness does not justify Christ, but righteousness is itself made holy by Christ, and unfulfilled virtue is fulfilled by Him in whom is the fulness of virtues. Therefore John says: *I ought to be baptized by you*. He bears witness to the Lord's not having been baptized for His own sake because John demands that he be baptized before the Lord is baptized by him. In saying this he shows that there is a greater grace in the mystery of the Lord than there is in the master of the mystery. For how would he have been able to bestow consecration on Him from whom he himself desired to receive sanctification? The master of the mystery was inferior in his merits to the disciple in His holiness. For in comparison to Christ the master is inexpert, righteousness unfulfilled, and the water sullied. But when the Lord is baptized, by His blessing the master is perfected, righteousness is fulfilled, and the water is purged.

2. Although it had been harsh and cold, the water is purged and endowed with the warmth of the Lord's blessing, so that what had removed material stains a little before now cleanses the spiritual stains of souls.[7] Nor should we be surprised that we speak of water, which is something of bodily substance, as cleansing the soul. There is no doubt that it comes and penetrates into all that is secret in the conscience. For although it is already subtle and fine, yet, having become even more subtle by Christ's blessing, it passes through the hidden tissues of life to the recesses of the soul like a spiritual dew. For the current of blessings is more subtle than the flow of waters. Hence we have also said that in the baptism of the Savior the blessing which flowed down like a spiritual stream touched the outpouring of every flood and the course of every stream. When Christ stood in the Jordan the flood of waters moved wondrously, but the flood of blessings also flowed. In the one the river's stream was borne more violently, while in the other the most pure font of the Savior diffused itself. And in a certain wonderful way the consecration of that baptism went back to the source of the Jordan, and the flow of blessings

was carried in the opposite direction to the flow of the waters, which is the reason, I think, that David said: *The Jordan turned back.*[8] For in the baptism of Christ it was not the waters of the Jordan that turned back but the grace of the sacrament,[9] and it returned to the source of its own being in blessing rather than in substance, and inasmuch as the grace of consecration was dispersed to every stream, it may be seen that its own onrush was called back to the beginning of its flow.[10]

SERMON 13

On the Grace of Baptism[1]

1. Beloved brethren—I speak to you catechumens—because it is clear (as we showed a few days ago) that Jesus Christ was not baptized for His own sake but for ours, we ought to take up the grace of His baptism in all haste and draw the blessing of consecration from the river Jordan, which He blessed, so that our sins might be drowned in the water in which His holiness was submerged. Thus the same water that swirled about the Lord might also cleanse His servants, the holy stream profiting us from Christ's venerable washing to the extent that it can, and through the same contact and mystery by which it borrowed a blessing from the Savior might purify us with a more divine warmth, giving back to Christians the grace that it received from Christ.

2. Therefore, brethren, we must be dipped in the same stream as Christ was so as to be able to be what Christ was. Let me say this without detriment to the faith: although both baptisms are the Lord's, nonetheless I think that the baptism by which we are washed is more grace-filled than the baptism by which the Savior was baptized. For the former is celebrated by Christ, while the latter was celebrated by John; in the one the master asks to be excused, while in the other the Savior extends an invitation to us; in the one righteousness is incomplete, while in the other the Trinity is complete; to the one the holy one comes and departs holy, while to the other a sinner comes and leaves holy; in the one a blessing is conferred through the mysteries, while in the other sins are absolved by a mystery. We must therefore,

brethren, be baptized by the same stream as the Savior was. But in order to be dipped in the same water, we do not require the regions of the East nor the river in Jewish lands, for now Christ is everywhere and the Jordan is everywhere. The same consecration that blessed the rivers of the East sanctifies the waters of the West. Thus even if perchance a river should have some other name in this world, there is in it nonetheless the mystery of the Jordan.[2]

3. What was accomplished then is accomplished now by the same sacraments,[3] except that there is a greater grace. For then we saw the Trinity with bodily eyes, but now we contemplate the same Trinity with the eyes of faith; then the human face scarcely gazed upon Christ, but now the human mind embraces Him; then the Holy Spirit in the form of a dove poured over a man, but now by the same power of divinity He is poured within a man; then the Father came to us on account of His Son by a distant voice, but now He and His Son both come down upon us. That grace is fuller, therefore, wherein God does not descend to human beings under an assumed form but deigns to descend to His children in His own substance. For in the former He wishes, as it were, to draw unbelievers to faith by visible signs, while in the latter He desires to bestow grace on believers by a spiritual power. It is a greater grace, then, to see God as God than to see Him in such a way that you still seek Him. The one is the perfect Trinity, the other the still inscrutable Divinity. It is a greater grace, then, to know God by truth itself than to look upon Him in an assumed form.

4. Let us, therefore, do for ourselves what we see that the Lord has done for us. Let us do for ourselves what John desired might be done for him. If he who was a prophet, teacher, and saint yearned for the Savior's baptism, how much more ought we sinners, poor and ignorant, to pray for this grace! See the Savior's mercy: what the prophet begs for but does not merit to receive is freely offered to us! We should see why it was that John did not receive the baptism from Christ that he had asked for. For when he asks, the Lord says to him: *Let it be so for now, for thus it behooves us to fulfil all righteousness.*[4] Now we know that John the Baptist was a type of the law. Therefore it was proper that he should baptize the Lord, so that as the Savior was born from the Jews according to the flesh[5] the Gospel might also be born from the law according to the Spirit, and thus it might receive its

consecration whence it derived its origin. Therefore this is what he
said: *For thus it behooves us to fulfil all righteousness.*[6] And so it was
proper that He who had ordained the commandments of the law
should Himself fulfil them, as He says elsewhere: *I have not come to
destroy the law but to fulfil it.*[7]

SERMON 15

On the Anniversary of Saints Cantus, Cantianus, and Cantianilla[1]

1. Today is the anniversary of the most blessed Cantus, Cantianus,
and Cantianilla. How good and pleasant it is[2] that three martyrs are
named in what is nearly the same word! Nor is it to be wondered at if
those who are alike in suffering are alike in name, or if those who
have one calling before God have one name before humans. Together
they were called by the Lord, nor did they suffer at different times;
the same blow made martyrs of all of them together. Because of their
kinship it was granted them by Christ that as they agreed in name they
should share in dignity, that those who were blood kin should become
related by holiness, and that a confession of the same faith should
crown the souls of those whose limbs had been quickened by the
substance of a single body.[3]

2. But the story is told of these blessed ones that at the time of
their suffering, when their pursuer was looking for them, they sought
to escape in a high mule-drawn carriage. When they had gone not far
from the city walls, one of the animals that was under yoke collapsed,
and thus they were seized, bound by their pursuers, and led to the
place of punishment. We should understand how glorious this is, and
how well ordained by God. For God always leads those whom He has
chosen into the halls of the heavenly kingdom as if they were victors
in a lofty carriage.[4] For as Elijah went up to heaven in a kind of drawn
chariot,[5] so also they came to the place of martyrdom in a moving
vehicle. And as a horse-drawn chariot carried him up to his rest, so it
carried them to their glory. And although the one was fiery, still the
other should not be considered inferior because the former bore a
prophet while the latter carried three martyrs. If someone says: "The

fiery chariot was a more glorious vehicle than the earthly one," still this was no disadvantage as far as the holy men were concerned, for a fiery faith carried the martyrs just as a fiery chariot bore Elijah. Christ, I say, bore them—He who is light[6] and fire, and of whom it is written: *Our God is a consuming fire.*[7]

3. Therefore, when the pursuer pressed upon the blessed ones about whom we are speaking, they mounted a carriage. For what reason? So as to flee? Perish the thought! Not so as to flee but so as to come more quickly to their martyrdom, not so as to hide but so as to show themselves more manifestly as Christians to every passer-by. They had, after all, been able to conceal themselves quite safely among the many people in the city, to protect their flight in a safe manner through various stratagems on the part of each. But when someone leaves by a public road, with a crowd assembled, carriages prepared, and everything gotten ready, that should be called a progress rather than a flight. For when they had done this, the holy men, as if they were in a triumphal chariot, gave witness, crying: "O pursuer, look! we are setting out, we are going before you! Why do you hold back? Why do you delay? Follow our tracks! We do not want to appear unwilling in going to our punishment, we who profess that we are going on to glory."

SERMON 16

On the Anniversary of the Saints[1]

1. If the weakness of my body should continue for as long as I have to speak and you ought to listen, we would all in fact be excused—I from teaching the commandment and you from keeping it. But because we are smitten with sickness, so that we are unable to say what we ought, let the devotion of the mind excuse us whom the demand of preaching does not. That is to say, even if we cease from the praises of the Lord with our tongue, still let us bless His wonders with works of faith; if we do not speak His glory in words, let us pursue His grace in deeds, since deeds are prior to words.[2] For the Lord says in the Gospel: *Whoever does thus and teaches thus will be called great in the*

kingdom of heaven.[3] You see, then, that the deed precedes and teaching follows, because to act well is the first way of teaching. For, when words fail, a work of great goodness itself teaches a person as long as it is visible, so that even if it does not excite the ears by a sound it still pricks hearts with its power. For who, on seeing a good action, does not rejoice, admire and imitate it, does not use it as an example and learn from it as if from a silent teacher? Deeds precede words, then, and in fact without deeds words profit nothing. And this is how the Lord wished that teaching should be done, lest without good work there be just the useless and superstitious throwing about of words.

2. We are taught better by deeds, therefore, than by words. And even if the holy martyrs are silent, they teach us by the power of what they have done; even if they do not speak, they persuade by the suffering of their martyrdom. Thus, although a skilful speaker may teach me in an eloquent manner, nonetheless I learn what is useful for me more by the example of the saints than by the mouthing of words.[4] My eyes persuade me rapidly because they see—more so than my ears, which cannot absorb what passes them by. For what is heard falls quickly into oblivion, but what occurs before the eyes is always present in contemplation.[5] For who does not see at every hour and moment how the blessed martyrs underwent different tortures for the sake of Christ's name and triumphed somehow over the punishments themselves? The more they suffered, the more utterly victorious they believed they were. For a persecutor's sentence is a martyr's victory, as it is written: *And you will conquer when you are judged.*[6] For when a martyr is judged and condemned, then he conquers and overthrows. By such a judgment he is not doomed to death but set free for rest, and it is most evident from this that to have conquered is not to have perished.

3. It is clear, then, that the holy martyrs teach more by their suffering than by their voice, although suffering itself is not without a voice. For we read that their souls cry out from under the altar of God and say: *When, holy and faithful one, will you take vengeance on our blood?*[7] And God says to Cain with reference to Abel's blood: *The voice of your brother's blood cries out.*[8] Innocent blood that has been shed is said to cry out not by words but by its very existence.[9] And thus it is that the souls of the holy martyrs cry out, as they commend

their own faithfulness and innocence to our thoughts by their
suffering.

SERMON 17

On What Is Written in the Acts of the Apostles:
All Things Were in Common among Them,
and On Cain and Ananias[1]

1. We read in the book known as the Acts of the Apostles that
under those memorable men there was great devotion among the
people. Thus the beginnings of the Christian congregation flourished
to such an extent that, when the faith had been received, no one
claimed his home as his own and no one laid a claim to anything, but
all things were common to them by the law of brotherhood. Hence
those who were joined by religion would also share life together, so
that where there was one faith, there would also be one means of
subsistence, and where Christ was common to all, property would be
common as well.[2] For those religious men considered it shocking for
someone who shared in grace not to be accepted as a sharer in property, and so, in the brotherhood of charity, they possessed all things in
common, since brotherhood in Christ is something greater than
blood brotherhood. For blood brotherhood refers only to a likeness
of body, while brotherhood in Christ manifests a oneness of heart and
soul, as it is written: *But among the believers there was one heart and
one soul.*[3] He is truly a believer, therefore, who is related not so much
by body as by spiritual concord. He is a true brother, I say, who has
the same spirit and desire as his brother. And so, as I have remarked,
brotherhood in Christ is better than blood brotherhood. Blood
brothers are sometimes each other's enemies, while brothers in
Christ are always at peace; the ones divide things common to themselves by rivalry, the others share even what is their own in joy; the
ones often despise their brothers in what they possess together, the
others frequently receive strangers. As I have said, the devotion of the
Christian people at that time was so great that no one called his home
his own and no one claimed anything as his own, as Saint Luke says:

And no one called anything that he possessed his own, but all things were in common among them.[4] *For no one,* he says, *was in need among them.*[5] Blessed, therefore, that people which, while it had many who were rich in Christ, had no one who was in need in the world, and which, while it looked forward to eternal wealth, banished temporal poverty from among the brethren! *For,* as Scripture says, *they sold their lands and houses and laid the proceeds from what they had sold at the feet of the apostles, so that each could be given to according to his need.*[6] See the faith of these holy men, how for Christ's sake they despoiled themselves of their entire patrimony and left nothing for themselves! For, fearing lest anyone else be hungry, they were not afraid to be hungry themselves.

2. Such was the devotion among the people in the time of the apostles. What have we found like it today? Certainly the same Christ is in us. The same Christ is indeed in us, but the same spirit is not in us; the same faith is in the people, but that generosity is not in the people. Thus one person does not consider another's need, and thus what the Apostle speaks of occurs: *One is hungry, while another is drunk.*[7] Very many Christians not only do not distribute their own goods, but they even seize those of others.[8] Not only, I say, do they not lay the money that they have collected at the feet of the apostles, but they even drag their own brethren, who are seeking asylum, away from the feet of the bishops.[9] Now is that time which the blessed Apostle describes when he says: *In the last days the iniquity of many abounds and charity grows cold.*[10] For now the iniquity of avarice abounds, which was not a problem when there used to be the virtue of generosity, and fraternal charity grows cold, which used to burn with the love of Christ. In the time of the apostles brotherly love was such that poverty did not make an appearance in the congregation, but now the hypocrisy of Christianity is such that you hardly find anyone who is rich in our community. I say that a person is hardly to be found who is rich in works, however, not in property. For the Apostle says: *They should be rich in good works.*[11] He wished the person who is rich to be understood in the Church as the one who is rich in Christ.[12] And when it says there that no one was poor in the time of the apostles, it shows clearly that they were endowed with such grace of faith that they all abounded with the bountifulness of heavenly riches.

3. These days it is rare, then, that we find someone who is rich

among the Christian people. Even if very many are rich in gold in their homes, yet in the Church they are poor in righteousness. For since they do not even do what they are able on behalf of the poor, neither is what they offer agreeable nor what they hold back satisfactory. The Lord said to Cain, when he made offerings: *If you offer rightly but do not divide rightly, you have sinned; be still.*[13] You also, O Christian, do not divide rightly—you who, from so much gold, hold back the greater part for mammon rather than giving it to the Lord. Thus Ananias in the Acts of the Apostles, thinking that he rightly offered, but not rightly dividing, let perish the money that he offered and lost what he held back for his own house.[14] He lost, I say, both his money and his salvation. For since he kept back part of what he had promised, he was condemned both for sacrilege and for fraud—sacrilege in that he went back on his word to God, and fraud in that he thought that a certain portion of his offering could be subtracted from the whole. And thus the apostle Peter said: *You have not lied to human beings but to God.*[15] If Ananias is condemned then, brethren, because he did not give what he himself had promised from what was his, what do we think about the person who does not wish to give what another person has promised?[16] Look, then, brethren, at what you promised God when you first received the grace of faith! See how many strangers and foreigners there are in our city![17] Do what you promised, lest it be told you what was told Ananias: *You have not lied to human beings but to God.*

SERMON 18

A Sequel on Avarice and on Ananias[1]

1. Your love[2] remembers, brethren, when we were preaching a few days ago about the unanimity and generosity of the people in the time of the most blessed apostles, that we got as far as the avarice of Ananias, who was the only person like a sickly sheep then in the exemplary life of that whole flock. He was so infected by the disease of avarice that Saint Peter wished to condemn him rather than correct him; for he had read: *Expel the pestilent one from the assembly and all strife will depart with him.*[3] He was the only one who was unhealthy, then, in the holy con-

gregation—he who, while all were eager to gain life and disdained money, sought for gain in mere money rather than in salvation and, hoping for a profitable recompense, worked to his soul's disadvantage. Ananias, therefore, was found by the apostles to be avaricious. Thus our miserableness is excused. For it is hardly astonishing that these vices should flourish among us in view of the fact that they began to sprout in the time of the apostles. And if their authority was unable to correct them in Ananias, how can we be blamed if we cannot correct the same vices in so many of our brethren? For, had Peter been able to correct Ananias' avarice, he would not have punished him, but in punishing him he corrects others.[4] For he wished to punish the one but to instil fear in the many. Ananias, consequently, is set forth as an example to all the avaricious, that whoever is guilty of this crime will suffer the same punishment on the day of judgment.

2. Avarice is a great evil, then; indeed, it is the source of all evils, as the Apostle says: *The love of money is the root of all evils, and some who have that craving have wandered from the faith.*[5] You see, therefore, that whoever craves money loses the faith, whoever collects money squanders grace. For avarice is blindness and produces error in religion. Avarice is blind, I say, but it has eyes in the form of different kinds of deceit: it does not see what is divine but it contemplates what it lusts after. For although it is rich it is always thinking of how to derive gain from evil; it conceives of its whole life as a business;[6] it conceals all its profits in proportion as it sets interest on what it lends; it is embarrassed at the name of usury but not at usurious profit.[7] The person who is avaricious, therefore, always takes advantage of someone else; he feasts himself on others' downfall. Others' poverty is his gain, others' tears his delight, as we have seen has lately been the case. However many may lament what has been lost to them, as many rejoice in what has been seized. See how an old father mourns over his captive son, and you already boast of him as your slave. An innocent rustic groans over his lost bullock, and you get ready to cultivate your fields with it, thinking that you can make a profit from others' groans.[8] See how a devout widow weeps over her home, despoiled of all its furnishings, and you rejoice that your home has been outfitted with the same furnishings. Tell me, O Christian, are you not struck with guilt, are you not brought up short when you see the tears of others in your own neighborhood?[9]

3. Holy Scripture says to the children of Israel: *Do not touch something that has been savaged by a wild animal.*[10] For whatever has touched wild animals that are constantly thirsting for blood is polluted and contaminated, and thus whoever takes what a wild animal has left behind is more foul than the animal. Tell me then, O Christian, why have you taken up the pillage that has been left behind by the pillagers? Why have you brought into your house as gain something that is broken and dirty, as you yourself consider it? Why have you devoured, more savagely than a beast, what a wild beast has abandoned? People say that wolves are accustomed to follow in the tracks of lions and not to wander far from where they hunt so that they may sate their own appetite from others' plunder. What remains when the lions have eaten their fill is greedily devoured by the wolves. The wolves of avarice have likewise followed in the footsteps of predators so that whatever was left behind from the rapacity of the ones might fall to the ferocity of the others. But perhaps you say that you have purchased it and that consequently you are free of the crime of avarice. Not thus is buying and selling usually defined. It is good to buy—but what is sold in peace and willingly, not what has been seized in pillage. Regard carefully the source, the owner of what is being sold, and the price, and you will see that you are a partner in rapine and not a purchaser of something up for sale. How did bejeweled gold necklaces fall into the hands of a barbarian? How did someone who wears skins[11] get hold of silken garments? Whence, I ask, come these Roman properties? We know that they belong to the people of our province and to our cocitizens. A Christian and a citizen acts in such a way that he buys something in order to return it to its proper owner.

SERMON 19

Exhortation to the People, and On What Is Written in the Gospel:
Like a Flash of Lightning from Heaven,
So Also Will Be the Coming of the Son of Man,
and On the Two Men in One Bed[1]

1. Detained by business and called away by the needs of another church, I seem to have been absent from your assembly for a few days and not to have given you my accustomed attention. But although I

was not present to you in body, yet in love I was not absent from you; and although I journeyed away from you by the movement of my limbs, yet I was not removed from the concord of your spirit, and I even held you to myself by a greater desire, so that love made present to me those whose faces were absent, and I embraced in my heart those upon whom I could not gaze. For I was anxious each day whether you were in good health and whether you were hastening daily to church;[2] and, although I was certain of your devotion, still I was concerned because I did not see what I knew was in you. It is the characteristic of fatherly feeling that it does not so much rejoice in certain hope over absent children as despair over them with troubled thoughts, and that it loves them more the moment it ceases to see them. Hence we see that love between those who are present is agreeable, while between those who are absent from one another it is burdensome. Therefore I was anxious, troubled, and fearful about you, lest during my absence someone fall through neglect or be deceived by the snares of the devil, for I remembered that the fury of the wolves grows stronger in the absence of the shepherds. But thanks to the Lord that He guarded you unhurt and brought back my littleness unharmed!

2. Consequently, since after a lapse we should refresh ourselves with spiritual dishes, let us see what the Gospel reading is about. The Lord, as we have just seen, is speaking of the time of His coming: *Like lightning flashing from heaven, so also will be the coming of the Son of Man.*[3] And He adds a little later: *On that night there will be two men in one bed, and one will be taken and the other left; and two women grinding grain at one mill, and one will be taken and the other left.*[4] Perhaps you are interested, brethren, why the Lord, when speaking of His coming, says that He will come at nighttime, since indeed His coming ought to be received by everyone in all the brightness of day and with great splendor and fear. We have frequently heard it proclaimed in the sacred writings that before the Lord Christ comes the Antichrist will reign,[5] who will pour out the darkness of his wickedness on the human race so that hardly anyone will see the light of truth, and as this obscurity overwhelms human minds it will produce a kind of blindness in spiritual eyes. It is not to be wondered at if the devil sends out the darkness of iniquity, since he himself is the night of all sinners. And so Christ will come like a flash of lightning to drive away his

hideous darkness, and as night is overturned by the dawning day the Antichrist will flee before the brilliant Savior, and when the light of truth bursts forth he will no longer be able to spread about the darkness of his wickedness.[6]

3. But it says: *On that night there will be two men in one bed, and one will be taken and the other left.* Here merit with regard to the resurrection is already indicated, as well as how the grace of rising again is related to the kind of life that a person leads. And so great is the difference between each of these resurrections that even for two men sleeping and resting in like manner in one place there cannot be an equal taking up. For although they are understood to share the same bed, nonetheless on account of their merits one of them is snatched up to heaven and the other is left on earth. For this great mass of earth is, so to speak, our common bed in which our bodies lie down to rest in a most safe place. But in this bed whoever conducts himself more severely in life sleeps more softly. For we can call our bodies themselves our beds, in which our souls linger very comfortably as if in a bed.[7] I think that this is what the holy prophet means when he says: *You have turned his whole bed in his sickness.*[8] Blessed is the one whose bed the Lord turns in his sickness, so that the person who a little before was prone to anger, adulterous, wanton, and full of the infirmities of every crime becomes chaste, humble, and modest when the Lord turns his body that had been accustomed to evil. Concerning this bed the Lord speaks spiritually to the paralytic: *Rise, take up your cot, and walk.*[9] There is not as much to wonder at in the fact that a paralytic would carry the wooden parts of a broken-down bed as there is in the fact that the paralytic himself would bear the members of his healed body, which had been broken by sickness, as a kind of indispensable bed for his soul, and that in the presence of the Jews standing about he who had been carried by others' hands would betake himself away by his own feet. In this, as I have said, the prophetic words are clearly fulfilled: *You have turned his bed in his sickness.* Thus the bed in which a little before he had been carried he in turn carried, and his soul, which was previously borne in the vehicle of his body, afterwards itself led his body around in a more suitable manner. And so what was said, *There will be two men in one bed, and one will be taken,* can be thus understood: it refers to the

Christian people and to the Jewish people, who keep to one bed, which is the one law of the commandments, and they glory in a similar kind of resurrection. At that time, then, the blessed Christian people will be taken into glory, but the accursed assembly of Jews will be abandoned in hell.[10]

SERMON 20

A Sequel[1]

1. Last Sunday, when we were discussing the Gospel lesson, we touched on a certain part of it; it remains for us to go through the remaining part. For we were talking about what the Lord said: *On that night there will be two men in one bed,*[2] and so forth. Now then, let us see what else there is. The same divine word says: *There will be two women grinding grain at one mill, and one will be taken and the other left.*[3] The first thing to be considered is what the task of grinding grain consists in, then who the two women are who are said to be grinding grain, and third, what the mill is and what the effect of grinding is.

2. Everyone knows that grinding cannot be done without two stones that are prepared and fitted to each other, so that one lays on the other's flat side, the stone which is set down first being heavy, slow, and, as I might say, nearly idle; and were an upper stone not provided for, the lower would perhaps seem unnecessary. Thus while the former works the latter also appears useful. But the former (that is, the upper stone) rotates with such velocity that it deceives the eyes with its speed, and one would believe that it is standing still and think it immobile even as it moves. The more violent the movement, the more perfectly the operation is carried out. Consequently the first stone stands still, does not move, and is hardly of any use, but the other receives everything that is brought to it and seizes everything that comes, and through certain small cavities each gets what it works on. But whoever grinds is seen to have this responsibility—that with constant attention to the grains that have been roughly cracked he make the finest flour and meal from their kernels and from their

hidden interiors. And when the light chaff has been scattered into the open he produces only what is clean, and in preparing the purest bread from this he imitates the grace of the Lord.

3. I think, then, that these two millstones are the two covenants —that is to say, the law of Moses and the gospel of the Lord, which are so constituted and disposed that each fits the other, as the Savior says: *I have not come to destroy the law but to fulfil it.*[4] And that the millstones are set one on top of the other indicates the law, which was first given to human beings and was then transformed into the perfect gospel.[5] The law, like the lower millstone, was so slow, heavy, and nearly idle that whatever it received to work on it lost completely, as the prophet says of the Jews: *All have turned aside, all alike have become useless; there is no one who does good, no, not even one.*[6] Unless the gospel had been placed on top, therefore, the law would still be reposing on Jewish ground, slow and heavy and confined to the narrow limits of one province. Unless the gospel had been given, I say, the law would not have been necessary at all. But the law did as much without the gospel as one stone could do. It was able to crush, not to help, as the blessed Apostle says: *The law brings about wrath,*[7] but it does not offer grace. The gospel was given, then, when the law was in force, and now that it is superimposed on the old covenant each is complemented. And it revolves with such velocity that it circles the whole world with its turning, which is to say that it visits the nether regions, penetrates the heavens, and illuminates every part of the earth. This gospel, like the upper millstone, receives all believers, accepts all who come, and takes them within through the small cavities of the commandments, as it were, so that on each side, by the saving commandments of the two covenants, only what is pure may be produced once the roughness of paganism has been ground down. I think that the prophet Ezekiel treats of this when he speaks of a wheel within a wheel.[8]

4. Through the operation of these millstones—the new and the old covenants—the holy Church, then, acts with unceasing care so as to draw out the fine flour of a clean heart from hidden thoughts, once the roughness of sins has been scattered, and to produce spiritual food from their kernels when they have been cleansed by the heavenly commandments. The apostle Paul says about this food: *I gave you milk to drink, not food,*[9] and again: *Solid food is for the perfect, who have their*

faculties trained by habit,[10] and so forth. Purifying our hearts from all that is human, it strives to offer God as it were the finest wheat, as holy David says: *A broken spirit is a sacrifice to God*.[11] The gospel revolves with such velocity, however, that only the wise know of its movement, about which the blessed Paul says with understanding: *May the word of God speed on and be made glorious in us*.[12] But in the eyes of the foolish the gospel seems to stand still, I say, because they neglect its commands, for they do not believe that what has been written will come to pass.

5. The Synagogue also grinds, but it grinds in vain; indeed, it attempts to work with one stone, the old covenant alone, and consequently it does not so much grind as scatter and destroy. For this reason its work is displeasing, and the prophet says to the Jews: *And if you bring the finest wheat it is in vain*.[13] And the Lord Himself, reproving what they do, says: *Be on guard against the yeast of the Pharisees*.[14] The Synagogue tries to grind, then, while it sustains error. And indeed, since Moses received the two stone tablets of the covenant,[15] it thinks that it functions by means of two indispensable things, not knowing that that joining of tablets was prefiguring to it the coming of two linked covenants. And therefore the holy Church, which grinds a food of holiness for the Lord, will be taken up into eternal glory, but the polluted Synagogue will be left behind at the mill, where it will always tread along the course of its own faithlessness.[16]

SERMON 21

On Hospitality[1]

1. We have read in the book of Genesis that Abraham hastened to meet three men who were approaching him, fell on his face, and begged them to turn aside to his tent so that, for his hospitality to the saints, he would receive the reward of a blessing.[2] For he knew that this was the command of the Lord who said: *Whoever welcomes a prophet in the name of a prophet will receive a prophet's reward, and whoever welcomes a righteous person in the name of a righteous person*

will receive a righteous person's reward,[3] and so forth. For this reason, then, Abraham hastened to welcome the holy men so that by joining himself to them in hospitality he would merit to be joined to them in holiness, and while performing a service of kindness he might receive a share of justification. For this is the law of hospitality—that the person who is welcomed makes the one who welcomes him like himself. This is what John the Evangelist indicated most clearly with respect to those who welcomed the Son of God when he said: *But however many welcomed Him, to them He gave the power to become sons of God.*[4] You see, then, how great the grace of hospitality is, that it even makes a son of God out of one who welcomes the Son of God in the guest house of his heart.[5] If, therefore, whoever welcomes the Son of God becomes a son of God, how much more will the one who welcomes a righteous person merit the grace of a righteous person! For this is, as I have said, the good characteristic of hospitality—that when a holy man comes, by the association that results from a friendly welcome he makes his host to be what he himself is. Under such a condition who would not wish to welcome a holy person hospitably into his home, so that, by sharing a dwelling place with him, he might share his holiness? And even if he had been a sinner up until that moment, who would not wish to be righteous himself by welcoming a righteous person, as the prophet David says: *With the holy you will be holy, and with the innocent you will be innocent?*[6]

2. Therefore, brethren, if Abraham our father, knowing what the grace of hospitality was, hastened to meet the three men approaching him, who were the one Lord, fell on his face and begged them to come under the roof of his tent, how much more ought we to go out to meet the holy bishops[7] who come to us and with every friendly greeting to welcome them into our dwellings so that, as David says, we may be holy with our holy guests! Let no one be apprehensive because he knows that he has sinned, let no one despair of mercy: whoever gives hospitality to a bishop[8] has already been justified. Although a little before you had been committing crimes, although you had been evil, when you welcome an innocent man you are reformed by the merits of innocence, as the prophet says: *With the innocent you will be innocent.* Therefore, brethren, since we are children of Abraham let us do the works of Abraham.[9] He came out to meet three holy men; let us also run to meet the many bishops.[10]

Although he was righteous he gave hospitality to the blessed in order to become more righteous; let us, because we are sinners, welcome the bishops[11] in order that our sins might be washed away and we might be righteous. Let us welcome the saints, I say, so that our sins against nature might be forgiven us. For on account of his hospitality the righteous Abraham, because he had no sin, was given[12] a son, Isaac, contrary to nature. He was given, as I have said, so contrary to nature that frigid old age despaired that he could be born and his mother Sarah laughed.[13] Sarah laughed, I say, because she begot a son not through nature but through grace. Blessed the offspring, then, whose birth has been preceded by mirth and not by tears! She should surely have laughed who conceived with the help of God. Such, then, is the hospitality of the blessed that it always bestows joy on the hosts. Sarah laughs because she is no longer sterile, I laugh because I put down my sins; she is freed from a bodily defect, I am washed clean of the sins of my soul; she rejoices because by her hospitality she has begotten a son, Isaac, and I am glad because I have acquired mercy with righteousness. But perhaps someone might say: "In those three men who came to Abraham the Lord also came." This in fact is true, for so Scripture tells us. But I say that even now Christ comes to us in his bishops.[14] Let us, then, brethren, imitate our father Abraham. But why do I say Abraham? Let us imitate God our Father! For if God wished people of different races to dwell in the one hospice of heaven, why do not we, who are brothers, stay with one another in one hospice? And if He desired our diversity to be contained within the one home of this world, why is not our concord maintained by the holy dwelling of His tabernacles?

SERMON 22

On Almsgiving, and On When the Lord Jesus Sat by the Well of Samaria[1]

1. Sacred Scripture says: *As water extinguishes a fire, so almsgiving extinguishes sin.*[2] It is clearly a great judgment and one to be sought after by all which promises those who are nearly dead and withered away by the ulcers of their sins that, with almsgiving, water as it were

will be poured out upon the faint, as moisture and refreshment to what is dried up. That is to say, miserable people who had been languishing in death because of their sins will come back to life through almsgiving. Mercy will be a fountain of salvation for those to whom avarice had been a fiery death so that the flames which they had enkindled for themselves by sinning they may quench by freely giving. And by a more profitable business transaction a person who had once spent money in order to commit adultery now expends money in order to cease being an adulterer, and the person who used to purchase sin for himself now, so to speak, purchases innocence for himself.[3] For the Lord tells His disciples: *Give alms, and behold! all things are clean for you.*[4] Although you are unclean, then, although you are hedged in by numerous crimes, if you give alms you have begun to be innocent. For almsgiving purifies what avarice polluted, and the stain which you had contracted by seizing other people's property you remove by giving away your own. See, then, what the grace of mercy is—a virtue which by itself alone is the redemption of all sins![5]

2. Now let us consider the meaning of that sacred phrase so that we may understand to what almsgiving is compared. For it says: *As water extinguishes a fire, so almsgiving extinguishes sin.* Thus water is compared to mercy. But since I realize that water comes forth from a source, I have to look for the source of mercy too. And I discover the source of mercy: He Himself is the source of mercy, He of whom the prophet says: *For with you is the source of life, and in your light we shall see light.*[6] He Himself, I say, is the source who, in the Gospel that we have recently heard read, asks for water from the Samaritan woman but pardons her sins; He rejects the water from the well but bestows the water of eternal life.[7] For He says: *Anyone who drinks of this water will thirst again, but whoever drinks of the water that I shall give him will not thirst forever.*[8] The Savior asks for water from the woman, then, and feigns thirst so that He might give eternal grace to the thirsty. For the source was not able to be thirsty,[9] nor was He in whom there is living water able to draw water full of earthly sediment. Did Christ thirst, then? He thirsted, to be sure, but for salvation and not for human drink; He was thirsty not for the water of this world but for the redemption of the human race.[10] In a wonderful way, therefore, the source sitting by the well produces streams of mercy in that very place, and with coursing, living water He purifies

the woman who is fornicating with a sixth man, not her husband but an adulterer. And in a new kind of miracle the woman who had come to the well of Samaria as a prostitute returned chaste from the source of Christ, and she who had come to look for water brought back chastity. As soon as the Lord points her sins out to her she acknowledges them, confesses Christ, and announces the Savior, and abandoning her pitcher she brings not water but grace back to the city. She seems, indeed, to return without a burden, but she returns full of holiness. She returns full, I say, because she who had come as a sinner goes back as a preacher, and she who had left her pitcher behind brought back the fulness of Christ, without the slightest loss to her city, for even if she did not bring water in to the townspeople, still she brought in the source of salvation. Sanctified, then, by faith in Christ, the woman goes back home.

3. I think that the prophet said about this woman: *Such is the way of a prostitute: when she has washed herself she says that she has done nothing wrong.*[11] Clearly this is said of her who, after having washed herself at the source, does not remember the vices of her sins, assumes the virtue of preaching, and, wiping away her stains with living water, has no more awareness of her sin but is urged on by the ardor of faith. For in a certain way she says that she has done nothing wicked now that she has become a messenger of the truth, and by forgetfulness she renounces her impurity now that she preaches chastity in her devotion. For this is the power of Christ the Lord, that even a sinner who washes himself in his water returns afresh to virginity and forgets what he had done before. And in his new birth he manifests the innocence of infancy, he does not know the sins of youth, and although he had been an adulterer because of the corruption of sin, he becomes a virgin because of faith in Christ.

SERMON 22A

On Almsgiving[1]

1. Your love[2] remembers that a few days ago, when we were giving you a sermon on alms, we wanted first to look for the origin of mercies and, when we had found the source of those virtues, we showed that the water of Christ washed away the stains of the Sa-

maritan woman better than the water of Samaria did[3] and that mercy wipes away sins more effectively than well water. It is obvious that mercy destroys stains more effectively than well water because well water only cleanses the skin of the body, while the bounty of mercy purifies the interior regions of the soul. We also showed that this woman of the Gospel was to be compared with that prophetic prostitute who, after she washes herself with living water, forgets her wickedness and exults in the splendor of purity.[4] The prophet does not say this about a prostitute from this world, whose uncleanness water does not wash away and who even makes unclean what she so much as touches, as the Apostle remarks: *Whoever joins himself to a prostitute forms one body.*[5] If by a touch a person forms one body and joins one who clings to him into members of ignominy, how can she who makes unclean herself be purified?

2. Let us inquire carefully, then, who this prostitute is—this Samaritan woman whose adulterous stains the water of Christ washed away. I think that this woman is the Church gathered from the Gentiles which had completed five thousand years and had submitted in the six thousandth to fornication with idols,[6] but which cleansed away every uncleanness when the font who is Christ came, through faith in Christ removed the stains that it had contracted by adulterous sacrileges, and, abandoning as useless the first water, the worship of its fathers, announced to the whole world the coming of the Lord. This, I say, is that prostitute who, after she has washed, says that she has done nothing wicked. For when the Church has been purged by the brightness of baptism[7] it does not recall its diabolical impiety but exults in the true religion and, having been transformed from a prostitute into a virgin, does not remember its former crimes but glories in the fulness of the virtues.[8]

3. The prophet says, therefore: *As water extinguishes fire,*[9] and so forth. Frequently indeed we see that water poured out extinguishes a fire. But sometimes we see the opposite—that huge balls of fire consume streams of water and that the flames grow more vehement, drawing strength from the water as if from food, so that the water does not seem to put out the burning but to aggravate it. What, then, is that water which consumes flames but is not itself consumed? It is, I think, that which, flowing in the bath from the fountain of Christ, is

not consumed by sins but consumes the fires of Gehenna, and which, once poured out on people in baptism, itself both lives in them and puts out the fire of hell. It is clear that it lives in people from what the Lord says: *But the water that I will give him will become in him a source of water leaping up,*[10] and so forth. But in a wonderful way the water of Christ both vivifies and extinguishes by one and the same operation. For it vivifies souls and extinguishes sins; the ones it renews by the refreshment of its bath, the others it consumes by its surging stream. And as far as the higher grace of baptism is concerned, in the heavens a mystery is celebrated and in hell Gehenna is extinguished; in the one the waters flow, in the other the fire grows cold; in the one we are submerged in the bath, in the other we are set free from the underworld. Yet there is nothing astonishing if hell is opened by the sacrament of baptism[11] since heaven is also unlocked. For these places are opened so that freedom and grace might come together in the bath of Christ—grace from heaven and freedom from hell. Freedom is given to those who will rise, grace to those who will reign; the ones are snatched from punishment, the others received into glory; the ones who used to be slaves of sin become children of righteousness, the others who used to be held by the troubles of the world gaze upon the delights of paradise. In the baptism of Christ, then, both heaven and the underworld are opened—the former so that the Holy Spirit might come, the latter so that the mercy of the Savior might penetrate. Life is brought down from heaven, death is destroyed in the underworld. Thus it is that almsgiving extinguishes sin as the water of baptism extinguishes the fire of Gehenna.

4. Therefore almsgiving is another kind of washing of souls, so that if perchance after baptism a person should commit a fault through human frailty he has but to be cleansed again by almsgiving, as the Lord says: *Give alms, and behold! all things are clean for you.*[12] With all due respect to the faith, I would say that almsgiving is more indulgent than baptism, for baptism is given once and offers pardon once, but as many times as you give alms you win pardon. These, then, are the two sources of mercy, which both give life and forgive sins. Whoever keeps to each will be enriched with the honor of the heavenly kingdom, but whoever betakes himself to the streams of mercy, if he has sullied the living fountain, will himself attain mercy.[13]

SERMON 23

Opening Words and a Rebuke to the Congregation[1]

It is obvious that we preach willingly and do the work of God joyfully. But when we see many of the brethren coming to church sluggishly and particularly on Sundays not taking part in the heavenly mysteries, we preach reluctantly—not because we dislike speaking but because our preaching oppresses the negligent rather than changes them. Therefore we preach reluctantly and cannot be silent. For our preaching brings either the kingdom or punishment to our congregation—the kingdom to believers but punishment to the faithless. For when a brother does not participate in the sacraments[2] of the Lord, he is, before God, necessarily a deserter from the divine camp. And how can one excuse himself who, on the day of the sacraments,[3] scorns the heavenly meal while preparing a meal at home for himself and, in seeing to his stomach's needs, neglects his soul's medicine?

SERMON 24

On the Mustard Seed, and On the Martyr Saint Laurence[1]

1. The Lord says in the holy Gospel, as the lesson that was read testifies: *What is the kingdom of God like, and to what shall I compare it? It is like a mustard seed that someone took and cast into his garden, and it grew and became a tree, and the birds of heaven roosted in its branches.*[2] Perhaps you wonder why the kingdom of God, so splendid and magnificent, is compared to a tiny mustard seed, and why the great consolation of our hope is said to be like such an insignificant thing, particularly when the same Lord tells His disciples elsewhere: *If you had faith like a mustard seed you would say to this mountain: Be uprooted and hurled into the sea.*[3] If it is a remarkable faith, then, that can uproot mountains from their very foundations, the mustard seed to which we are urged to liken our faith is consequently a great thing. Yet I would say that it is a great thing not in its appearance but in its power, and it

should be compared to faith not in regard to its being a plant but because of the strength of its sharpness. And if we consider the matter carefully we discover that this image was rightly used by the Lord. For a mustard seed, when one sees it at first, is small, mean, and contemptible, not having any taste nor giving off any odor nor suggesting any attractiveness. Yet, as soon as it is rubbed it immediately gives off its odor, manifests its sharpness, breathes out a fiery taste, and is ablaze with such burning heat that it is a cause for wonder that so great a fire should be locked up in these paltry seeds. People collect the food of this seed particularly in winter time on account of its great usefulness in warding off the cold, drawing out the humors, and warming the internal organs. And frequently they apply a medicine made from this to the head, so that whatever is ailing and unwell may be cured by the mustard's fire.

2. So also the Christian faith at first sight seems small, mean, and trifling, not showing its power nor giving evidence of a lofty spirit nor proffering grace. Yet, when it begins to be rubbed by different temptations, all at once its vigor appears, it manifests its sharpness, breathes forth the warmth of the Lord's faith, and is diffused by such heat of the divine fire that it burns itself and compels whatever partakes of it to burn as well. So Ammaus and Cleopas[4] said when the Lord was speaking with them after His passion: *Was not our heart burning within us on the road, when the Lord Jesus opened the Scriptures to us?*[5] Thus the mustard seed warms the bowels, but the strength of faith burns up the sins of hearts; the one removes the harsh chill of the cold, but the other expels the diabolical chill of sins. Mustard, I say, burns away the humors of the body, but faith consumes the floods of the passions. Medicine for the head is gotten from the former, but our spiritual head, which is Christ the Lord,[6] is more frequently restored by faith. And we also enjoy the holy odor of faith that is similar to mustard, as the blessed Apostle says: *For we are the good odor of Christ to God.*[7]

3. And so we are able to compare the holy martyr Laurence to a mustard seed—he who, by the different sufferings that rubbed him, merited grace to glow with his own martyrdom throughout the world; who before, when his body was sound, was humble, unknown, and insignificant; who afterwards was abused, struck, and burned up; and who has poured out the odor of his nobility on all the churches

throughout the world. Justifiably, therefore, is this comparison made, since the mustard seed is enkindled when it is rubbed, and Laurence is set ablaze when he suffers; the one gives up its heat by being rubbed, the other breathes forth fire because of much suffering. Mustard, I say, is steam-cooked in a hot vessel, Laurence is roasted by fire on a flaming griddle.[8] Thus the blessed martyr was ablaze without because of the tyrant's cruel fire, but the flame of Christ's love within tortured him still more. And although the wicked king put down logs and laid bigger fires, still Saint Laurence, burning with faith, does not feel these flames, and as he meditates on Christ's commands all that he undergoes is cold to him.[9] For he who possessed the refreshments of paradise in his mind is unable to feel the fiery torments in his bowels. Although his burnt flesh, his lifeless corpse, lies at the feet of the tyrant, nonetheless he whose soul abides in the heavens suffers no loss on earth. He is stretched out over the fiery balls of flame, then, and often tormented on his side, but the more pains he suffers the more greatly he fears Christ the Lord. And—new wonder!—one torments him while others carry out the tortures of the fiend, but as the punishments grow crueler they make Laurence more faithful to his Savior.

SERMON 25

A Sequel on the Mustard Seed[1]

1. Last Sunday we were discussing one of the Lord's parables, in which He says: *What is the kingdom of God like, and to what shall I compare it? It is like a mustard seed,*[2] and so forth. We said a great deal in order to show that the kingdom of God is not inappropriately compared to a mustard seed, and that the difference exists only so far as words and not virtues are concerned, since the Christian faith, which is the kingdom of God,[3] possesses the same strength as the nature of mustard has at its disposal. For, when we eat the juice of mustard, our face takes on a pained expression, our forehead wrinkles, we are moved to tears, and we promote the health of our body with, as it were, bitter weeping (for on the one hand the bitterness

vexes us and the sharpness penetrates us, while on the other the heat of the fiery taste burns us, and once our whole body has been discomfitted we become more healthy the more we suffer). Likewise, when we understand the commandments of the Christian faith our soul is saddened, our body is afflicted, we are moved to tears, and we obtain our salvation, as it were, with weeping and bitterness (for on the one hand fasting wears us out, while on the other the knowledge of our sins distresses us, and, too, the loss of our inheritance disturbs us, and once all our behavior manifests contrition we draw nearer to salvation the more we weep, as the Lord says: *You will weep and lament, but the world will rejoice*[4]). But just as, when our head must sometimes be treated with mustard, we are bidden to shave our hair and get rid of all that covers the skin in order that the medicine may have a more far-reaching effect on the bare member, so also, when the soul is to be looked after by faith, we are asked to dispose of what we have accumulated in this world and put away impediments of gold and silver in order that the spiritual medicine may have a more powerful effect on the soul, naked and alone.[5] For the medicine of faith will not profit whoever is wrapped up in earthly concerns and the riches of this world. What mustard juice does in the body, then, the Christian faith does in the soul.

2. But since in these same words of the Lord there stands written: *That someone took and cast into his garden, and it grew and became a tree, and the birds of heaven roosted in its branches,*[6] let us look more closely to find out to whom all these things pertain. We said before that the nature of mustard can resemble the holy martyrs because they are rubbed by different sufferings. But inasmuch as Scripture says: *And it grew and became a tree, and the birds of heaven roosted in its branches,* I think that this is more properly compared to the Lord Christ Himself, who in being born a man was humbled like a seed and in ascending to heaven was exalted like a tree.[7] It is clear that Christ is a seed when He suffers and a tree when He rises. He is a seed, I say, when He endures hunger and a tree when He satisfies five thousand men with five loaves.[8] In the one He endures barrenness in His human condition, in the other He bestows repletion by His divinity. I would say that the Lord is a seed when He is beaten, scorned, and inveighed against, but a tree when He enlightens the blind, raises the dead, and forgives sins. That He is a seed He Himself says in the

Gospel: *Unless the grain of wheat, falling upon the earth, dies.*[9] The Jews, then, not enduring the mustard-like harshness and bitterness of this seed, that is of the Lord the Savior, disdained to accept the juice of heavenly discipline, saying to that blind man who had been enlightened: *You are his disciple, but we are disciples of Moses.*[10] Yet they were also completely ignorant of the commands of Moses himself, who ordered them specially to eat this bitterness when he established the paschal sacraments for them to observe and said: *You will eat it with bitterness, for it is the Pasch of the Lord.*[11] For he did not order, as they think, the consuming of the very bitter juices of insignificant herbs with the roasted flesh of a lamb, but he commanded the fruitful devouring of the bitter words of Christ's precepts with the sacrament of the Lord's passion. For do not the words of the Lord seem to be bitter when He says: *If you wish to be perfect, leave all that you have and come, follow me?*[12] And when He says that one is not to possess two tunics nor a wallet nor sandals,[13] that bitterness of words is a medicine for souls.

3. But when the Gospel says: *That someone took and cast into his garden,* who do we think that this person is who took a seed like a mustard seed and sowed it in his little garden? I think that he is the person to whom the Evangelist refers: *But behold! Joseph, who was a decurion from Arimathea, approached Pilate and asked to bury the body of the Lord that had been taken down; and he took it and brought it to the place of burial, which had been made ready in a garden.*[14] Therefore Scripture says: *That someone took and cast into his garden.* Joseph's garden, then, was full of the fragrance of different flowers, but no such bud as this had ever been planted there. Indeed, the spiritual garden of his soul was ablaze with the manifold sweetness of the virtues, but he had never put Christ with His spices in the recesses of his heart. Thus, when he buried the Savior in the tomb of his little garden he laid Him, rather, in the innermost parts of his soul.[15]

But let us consider the branches of this tree. You will see that Peter is a branch, Paul is a branch, all the apostles and martyrs of the Savior are branches.[16] If anyone wishes to cling to them he must not drown beneath the waters of the world but rather, hiding in their shade, escape Gehenna's heat, secure both from the storm of the diabolical tempest and from the fire of the burning judgment.

SERMON 26

On What Is Written: Give the Things That Are God's to God,
and On Soldiers[1]

1. Some of the brethren who are in military service[2] or who occupy public office are accustomed to excuse their sins, when they sin
gravely, by saying without further ado that they are soldiers. And if
sometimes they do not act rightly they complain that they are involved in an evil occupation—as if it were the army and not the will
that was at fault! Thus they ascribe what they themselves do to the
positions that they hold. For it is not a sin to be in military service, but
it is a sin to soldier for the sake of plunder; nor is it a crime to hold
public office, but to act toward the common weal in such a way that
you increase your private property[3] is understood to be condemned.
On this account a certain foresight has provided payments for soldiers lest plunder be taken in a search for recompense.[4] But it happens
that when a misdeed has occurred and some are accused by their
seniors and one of them is confronted as to why he got drunk or why
he broke into another's property or why he committed a violent act of
murder immediately he responds: "What was I, a man of the world or
a soldier, supposed to do? Did I profess the monastic life or the
clerical state?" As if everyone not a cleric or a monk were permitted
to do what is impermissible! Consequently sacred Scripture provides
a rule of life for all stations, and each sex, every age and rank is
challenged to behave well.[5] Therefore let no one excuse himself for
his public actions, let no one complain of his soldier's status. Among
all Christians the first soldiery must be of honorable conduct.

2. Now, in order to prove what we are saying by Gospel authority,
let us look at the reading that was read a short while ago. The Gospel
says: *But tax collectors also came to John in order to be baptized by him,
and they said to him: Master, what shall we do? And he said: You should
exact no more than has been determined for you.*[6] Clearly the tax collectors' question is an honest one, and the holy prophet's response is
just. They ask him carefully, lest either in ignorance they commit sin
by exacting too much or, ceasing altogether, they fail to perform their

public duty. And with moderation he commands them both to give no place to evil and to collect the tax that has been decreed. For he did not say: "Exact nothing," but: *You should exact no more.* . . . Hence we see that with God it is not tax collecting that is condemned so much as wicked tax collecting. For the Lord Himself says: *Give the things that are God's to God and the things that are Caesar's to Caesar.*[7] Consequently what Caesar orders is to be borne and what the emperor decrees is to be endured; but it becomes unendurable when it is heaped up as the plunder of exaction. But what sort of thing is this—that those who carry out such obligations pile sins upon sins, that they call their frauds and pillage proper, although by plunder itself something improper is done? This they add to their crimes— that those who they see are defenseless they trouble the more, and they think that they have deceived the public interest unless they have seized[8] the homes of orphans, so that the children whose father was a friend, colleague, or brother two days ago are, now that he has died, considered unknown, mean, and insignificant. If there is a widow, either she is harassed by intimidating acts so that she marries or, if she wishes to devote herself to chastity, is hardly able to keep her property because of the gifts that she gives.[9] When they have fattened their wallets by means of these deceits, then, you see them hastening to church, satisfied and punctilious, to thank God, as if this money had been given them by Him! So they sin also in this—that they wish God to be a partner in their crimes.

3. But the holy Gospel says: *The soldiers also questioned him: And what shall we do? John said to them: Do not intimidate anyone or injure anyone, but be content with your pay.*[10] Everyone in military service ought to see that he is being addressed here. For Scripture does not speak only of soldiers who are on the front lines; whoever is in military service is considered to be a soldier. Consequently these words, for example, are spoken to bodyguards and to everyone of rank.[11] Whoever receives money that has been publicly set aside for him is condemned, in John's words, as a cheat and an extortionist if he looks for more. Up until now, however, this evil has grown so that it is almost a matter of course that laws are sold, rights corrupted, and even a judicial sentence is venal, and there are an infinite number of judicial actions.[12]

4. But this divine word, which is spoken to soldiers, can also be

turned back on clerics who, although they do not seem to be in military service in the world, are nonetheless soldiers for God and the Lord, as the Apostle says: *No one soldiering for God involves himself in secular affairs.*[13] We seem, I say, not to be soldiers in our loose and flowing tunics, but we have our military belt, by which we are bound to an interior purity.[14] About this belt the Lord says to His apostles: *Let your loins be girt and your lamps burning in your hands.*[15] We, then, are soldiers of Christ[16] and we receive our pay and our reward from Him, as the blessed Apostle says: *who has given us the Spirit as a pledge.*[17] That is to say that He has enriched us with the recompense of the Holy Spirit. But if any Christian is perhaps not satisfied with this gift and seeks something more, he begins to lack the very thing of which he was worthy. This has particular reference to the Arian heretics. For while they seek I know not what more, in discovering the spirit of error they have lost the grace of the Holy Spirit.[18] A Catholic cleric should take warning from this, for if he is not satisfied with the pay that he receives from the altar, as the Lord has ordered, but practices a trade, sells his prayers, and wilfully seizes the property of widows, he can be considered more a businessman than a cleric. Nor are we able to say: "No one accuses us of taking property forcibly, no one accuses us of violence," as if greedy flattering words could not entice forth more booty than tortures do.[19] It does not matter to God whether a person usurps someone else's property by force or by deceit, so long as he holds on to that property in some way.

SERMON 27

A Sequel[1]

1. A few days ago we rebuked clerics who conduct business, and we reproved them by a basically just verdict. But if we look at the matter correctly, our office is truly a business, and the exercise of the priestly ministry[2] is a kind of exercise of spiritual transaction. For we expend earthly things in order to gain heavenly things; we give out the money of this world in order to acquire eternal riches; we feed

others by our hunger, not so that our own sustenance may perish but that it may increase.[3] For what does our feeding the poor, our covering the naked, our visiting the imprisoned[4] have as its aim if not that money given out on their behalf not be lost but be increased, and that this business, so to speak, gain interest for the giver? For a poor and hungry person is, as it were, a rich person's treasure chest: he does not consume the alms given him but guards it. Even if someone's flesh be dissolved and he return to dust, still the holy work lives and abides in him, and on the day of judgment you will have as a sympathetic witness one who has been unable to feed himself, so that he will be believed with respect to your works even if he is not believed with respect to his own actions. See, then, if almsgiving is not a business! What you give to a friend perishes to you, what you leave your children perishes to you; the only thing that does not perish to you is what you give to a beggar. For on the day of judgment the poor will be of service to you, while your friends and children will be of no service at all; the former will take up your cause, but the latter will be unable to defend their own.[5]

2. To be a Christian is a kind of business, then, and the priestly function is a very lucrative business. For we receive the money of the Lord—the words of the Savior, which are to be distributed to the people. About these words the Lord says in the Gospel to that greedy and unskilled businessman of the priesthood: *Wicked servant, you ought to have given my money to the bankers, and on returning I would have demanded it back with interest.*[6] He is reprimanded because by his silence he held back the divine commandments that had been entrusted to him, which by his preaching he should have multiplied.[7] He is reprimanded, I say, because he has not sown seed by giving, which he would be able to gather in at the harvest, as the Apostle says: *What a person sows he also harvests.*[8] Therefore the Lord says: *On returning I would have demanded it back with interest.* Understand, then, that this business is transacted when interest is demanded as if for a loan—not that interest, however, by which the minds of the avaricious are fed by the lucrative receiving back of money and in which what is owed the creditor is constantly repaid and never cleared. The interest that is demanded is not a reckoning up of denarii but a conversion of manners; it is not a question of capital bearing interest but of the fundamental principle of salvation.[9] For we are debtors, and we re-

main bound in debt not by a written record but by the record of our sins. Hence the Apostle, speaking of the Lord, says: *destroying the record that was unfavorable to us.*[10] We are ordered, then, to pay the interest on this debt. The Lord refers to a debtor in the Gospel when He says that he is to be handed over to the tax gatherer, thrown into prison, and not released until he pays the last penny.[11] We also owe the interest on those words, brethren. For "usury" comes from "use,"[12] and we have to account for how we use these words.[13] For the Gospel does not preach in vain, the Apostle does not cry out for nothing, the priests do not speak without reason, and those whose ears hear the holy words sound will either be blessed because of their attentiveness or condemned by their own attestation.[14]

SERMON 28

On What the Prophet Says to the Children of Israel: Your Innkeepers Mix Water with Their Wine[1]

1. Not inappropriately a few days ago we discussed the priestly[2] function as a kind of business to be conducted, and we said that the clerical office is of no little gain. It is clearly no little gain when it is not the profit of money which is acquired but that of souls. This is a great business, where the buying back[3] of humankind consists not in the giving of a price but in the proclamation of the commandment. For the commandment of Christ is, as it were, a precious talent by which salvation is acquired and life bought back. And this is a great buying back, when a price is given but no money is seen. The talent, therefore, is the great commandment of the Savior, which can be lucrative to the capable in place of wages, while among the negligent it cannot be lost. To some it is restored with grace multiplied over, while from others it is required with the interest of penalties. For Christ, who is the creditor, must needs demand back the talent which He bestows and give grace to the one who is freed of his debt rather than subject him to punishments. It is clearly the way of the world to subject a person to punishments. Thus a debtor who is unable to make satisfaction by returning property pays his debt by bodily punish-

ment. Therefore, brethren, we give this talent to your hearts by our preaching in order to turn over to the Lord the profit of your salvation. We shall have to render an account about how both our preaching is profitable and your obedience bears fruit.[4] For not without reason is the Gospel proclaimed, does the Apostle cry out, and do the priests[5] speak, and he whose ears hear the holy words sound will either be blessed because of his attentiveness or condemned by his own attestation.[6] For we speak blessedness to believers, but we bring judgment to the wicked.

2. Thus the priestly ministry[7] is a trade. Hence the prophet says to the children of Israel: *Your innkeepers mix water with their wine.* For holy Isaiah is not speaking about the innkeepers who, in the course of their publican ministrations, deceptively mix pure wine with a measure of water; it could not be a matter of concern to the blessed man, as if he were a civil judge, that people would dilute tavern vessels to make a less inebriating drink. He is speaking rather about the innkeepers who preside not over taverns but churches, who offer thirsty people a goblet not of wanton desire but of virtue, who do not minister the cup of drunkenness but the Savior's cup. Those innkeepers he censures and rebukes, and he complains that they mix water with wine. This he blames in them—that although they are set over divine functions, they have become followers after human things, as the prophet himself says: *Each of you follows his own house.*[8] For if any priest[9] has abandoned the priestly office[10] and delights in worldly pleasures, he mixes water with wine; that is to say, he mingles vile and cold things with holy and warm things.

3. So we can also believe that the Jewish priests likewise mixed water with wine when they did not accept the saving Lord as God but judged Him to be a man, and when they wished to introduce something filthy and base into His true and pure divinity, saying to Him: *because, although you are a man, you make yourself God,*[11] and: *We were not born from prostitution.*[12] For while they excuse themselves from the impurity of prostitution, they try to make Him impure in the divinity of His birth. But let us look still more closely at what is said here: *They mix water with wine.* We read that wine is particularly abundant in the Church, for it is said in the Gospel that new wine is to be kept in new skins,[13] which means that the grace of the Holy Spirit is to be bestowed on new persons, on neophytes. If, then, the

precious and spiritual grace of wine abounds in the Church, where is the vile and brackish water to be sought if not in the Synagogue?[14] For brackish is this water of the Synagogue which does not wash away sins by its baptism but begets them, which does not purify a person by its washing but makes him dirty. And as the Church is honored in its skins of wine, so also with its skin of water the Synagogue is cast out. Hagar, who was an image of the Synagogue[15] and about whom Abraham is told: *Drive out the slave*,[16] betakes herself from the tents, when indeed she is driven out, with a skin not of wine but of water. Certainly the house of Abraham was rich and abundantly wealthy, but even so she did not take wine, oil, or bread, which are the most essential foods of life. And the Synagogue does not rightly take the food of life because it does not know the life who is Christ † but only the waters by which † [17] a person's sickness is prolonged and his weakness drawn out. It was appropriate, then, that she not take the nourishment of the living nor accept the consolation of the dying. Therefore the priests of the Jews are censured because they wished to mix the water of the Synagogue, which was already worthless and rejected, with the Church's precious wine. For it is not a custom in the Church for water to be mixed with anything[18] but to be transformed, which happened at the wedding feast, when the Lord did not mix the jars full of water with wine but transformed them into wine;[19] he preferred to change the nature rather than pollute the substance, lest anything of Jewish baseness remain at the holy feast.

SERMON 29

On Psalm 21, and On the Passion of the Lord[1]

1. We should first consider carefully the successive parts of the psalm which is about to be gone over and which has just been read and see what is contained in the title. Thus when its beginning has been understood we might more easily grasp its meaning, and in the clarification of the first words we shall see better how the other parts are arranged.

It is inscribed in this way: *Unto the end, for the rising of the dawn. A psalm of David himself.*[2] Unless I am mistaken, the rising of the dawn always precedes the rising of the sun, and before the sun's clear brightness casts its light upon the earth dawn puts an end to the darkness of the night, and gradually, when the shadowy gloom has been driven away, a certain form and light is bestowed on all things. And although the world had lain in confusion, as if under one cover of darkness, with the arrival of the dawn different things take shape in the variety of their forms; that is to say that although all things had been blind, now the eyes of all are restored. For night, so to speak, removes the world's eyes and dawn restores them; and we so enjoy the dawn's rising beforehand that afterwards we may possess more gloriously the sun's brightness.

But since, as the Apostle says, there is a spiritual law[3] and spiritual things are to be compared with spiritual things,[4] I think that this is to be called the sun of justice[5]—that is, Christ the Lord. He pours out the light of His heavenly teaching upon us who are sunk in the darkness of ignorance and the blindness of sins, and the eyes of the heart, which we did not have, He gives to us. And He sent out His apostles as, so to speak, rays of light who would set us free from the most shameful night of wrongdoing, and gradually, when the darkness of sins had dissolved in us, they would accustom us by the dawn's rising to be able to bear more easily the warmth of the sun as perfect persons. That is to say, they would first instruct us by simpler precepts, with the result that we would be rendered more capable of the heavenly mysteries. All the darkness of our sins is destroyed by the dawn of this sun of justice, as the prophet himself says, speaking in the person of the Lord: *In the morning I slew all the sinners of the earth.*[6] In other words, when the sun of justice rises in us, who are the dwelling place of the Lord,[7] every evil thought is cast down. Blessed Solomon also recalls this sun in the person of sinners who are reflecting within themselves and saying: *The sun has not risen upon us and the light of justice has not illuminated us.*[8] In the holy Gospel we are also able to ascribe this rising of the dawn to Mary Magdalene who at the right moment, early in the morning, was in her watchfulness the first to receive the resurrection of the Lord, the Savior, at the tomb.[9] As the world's sun was growing bright she alone, before anyone else, recognized the rising of the sun of justice, and with the coming of the dawn she rejoiced in the return of day, but still more she rejoiced in Christ risen from the dead. And in this the prophecy was fulfilled: *At evening weeping will be prolonged, but in the morning there is joy.*[10]

2. But this whole psalm is arranged with respect to the person of the Lord, the Savior, even though of course more things are said about Him in the New Testament. Thus it says: *God, my God, look upon me,*[11] and so forth. Why does it plead the cause of the man who was assumed[12] and seem, as it were, to ask: "God of all things, who are my God, why have you abandoned me? For I am aware of no guilt on my part"? For, according to the prophet, He did not know sin, nor was there deceit in His mouth.[13] He says these things in order to show that He was abandoned on account of us whose sins He bore,[14] and that we might see and learn how to die for Him who is holy and just,[15] since He died because of sin.[16]

Then in His suffering He used these words, as we read in the Gospel: *Heli, heli, lama zapthani.*[17] *That is, God, my God, why have you forsaken me?*[18] He used these words, I say, so that what the prophecy had foretold would be proven by the outcome.

3. And since the things that follow are hardly clear at all, let us examine the verse in which it is said: *But I am a worm and not a man.*[19] Why the Lord of every creature should wish to be compared to a worm is something that we can ascribe first of all to humility, which is the saints' greatest virtue. This is why holy Moses acknowledges before God that he is an irrational animal[20] and David often characterizes himself as a flea.[21] But I think that what the Lord says ought to be taken more literally, since a worm is procreated with no admixture of a foreign substance but from the virgin earth alone. Consequently a worm is comparable to the Lord, since the Savior Himself is begotten from the virgin Mary alone.[22] We also read in the books of Moses that worms were bred from manna.[23] The comparison is clearly a worthy and good one—the worm produced from manna and the Lord Christ begotten of a virgin. Why should I not rather say that Mary herself is manna?[24] For she is subtle, splendid, sweet, and virginal; coming in a heavenly way she gave forth a food sweeter than honey to all the peoples of the churches, and whoever fails to eat and feed upon it will be unable to have life in him. The Lord Himself says: *Unless a person eat my flesh and drink my blood he will not have life in him,*[25] but instead that very food will be turned

into a judgment, as the Apostle says: *Whoever eats and drinks unworthily. . . .*[26] This was prophesied in a veiled manner to the children of Israel in the Old Testament. For to those acting against the divine precepts worms were produced from the manna—that is, revengers and judges of stubbornness.[27] This similitude points to Christ the Lord, whom the one who has neglected to consume the delightful food and sweet drink will have as his judge, as He Himself says: *For the Father does not judge anyone, but He has given all judgment to the Son.*[28] And that worm and judge are one and the same is shown by the prophet when he speaks of sinners: *Their worm shall not die and their fire shall not be quenched until the present day.*[29]

4. As to its being said that *they divided my garments among themselves, and over my garment they cast lots,*[30] we have seen that this was done in the Gospel and that the four soldiers who crucified the Savior divided His garments in four parts among themselves. But for the garment of His that was not sewn but woven from top to bottom they played dice.[31] Let us look closely, then, at these garments, at the soldiers, and at the other garment. I think that these garments are the prophecies and the lessons of the heavenly Scriptures by which the sacrament of Christ the Lord[32] was announced. The adversaries of the Savior (that is, the wicked heretics who daily lay impious hands on Him as the soldiers did[33]), who proclaim one thing and announce it everywhere, by so doing wilfully divide these prophecies among themselves and scatter the garments of the one body in different places, and as they strip the Lord they clothe Him in their own false teachings. We can show that the unsewn garment of His, however, is His heavenly wisdom, since it[34] says[35] that it was woven from top to bottom.[36] For our wisdom, which is human, is sewn: it is sewn together when we give our children to studies, hand them over to grammarians, and have them taught by philosophers so that they might acquire the wisdom that they do not possess.[37] But the Lord's wisdom is not sewn or acquired. He did not study with a teacher, as the Jews themselves remark: *How does this man have learning when He has not studied?*[38] And He Himself answers: *My teaching is not of this world but from Him who sent me.*[39] This is what He says of the garment woven from top to bottom. In this garment and in all these garments the Catholic Church has always been clothed, as the prophet says: *The queen stood at your right hand in golden raiment.*[40]

SERMON 30

On the Eclipse of the Moon[1]

1. You yourselves see, brethren, that my humility does not cease to labor among you solicitously in order to convert you speedily to good works, yet the more I labor among you the more I am confounded by you. For when I see that, despite so many warnings of mine, you have made no progress, my labor gives me reason not to rejoice but to blush. The blessed Apostle says: *Who has planted a vine and does not eat its fruit? Who pastures a flock and does not get the flock's milk?*[2] See, I pasture Christ's flock and am unable to obtain the fruit of the flock; I pasture the Lord's flock and receive no nourishment of the milk of devotion from it. It has no sweetness of faith to rejoice me, but whatever flows forth from it is harsh and bitter. For the shepherd of the Christian flock is refreshed by milk when he rejoices in the splendor[3] of its good works.

2. For who, brethren, would not take it to heart (yet I do not speak of everyone, for there are those among you whom you ought to take as examples of religious practice)—who, I say, would not consider it a serious matter that you are so unmindful of your salvation that you even sin with heaven as witness? When I reproached a large number of you a few days ago because of your avariciousness,[4] that very day toward evening such an outcry was raised by the people that its impiousness penetrated to the heavens. When I asked about the reason for the shouting, they told me that your outcry was helping the moon in its labor and that the shouting was aiding its eclipse.[5] I laughed and marveled at this vanity, that seemingly devout Christians were helping God. For you cried out lest on account of your silence He lose the heavenly body—as if He were feeble and weak and unable to protect the heavenly lights that He had created unless He were helped by your voices! Well do you do this, you who show concern for the Divinity, so that with your help He might rule heaven! But if you want to do more than this, you ought to keep vigil each and every night. For while you are sleeping how often do you think that the moon has suffered violence and still has not disappeared from heaven? Does it not always undergo an eclipse toward evening, and is

it not sometimes in labor toward dawn? But with you it is only accustomed to labor in the evening hours, when your stomach is filled with an abundant supper and your head is nodding from heavy drinking. Then it is that, with you, the moon labors, when the wine also labors; then, I say, among you the lunar sphere is moved by songs, when your eyes also are moved by wine cups. How, then, when you are drunk, are you able to see what is happening to the moon in the heavens when you are unable to see what is happening to yourself on earth?

3. This is clearly what holy Solomon says: *The fool is changed like the moon.*[6] For you are changed like the moon when, foolish and stupid, you who had been a Christian begin to be sacrilegious in response to its movement. For a sacrilege is committed against the Creator when some defect is imputed to the creature. You are changed like the moon, then, so that you who shortly before were shining with a devout faith are afterwards eclipsed by the weakness of unfaith. You are changed like the moon when your mind is emptied of wisdom as the lunar sphere is deprived of light; and just a small covering of clouds passes over it, but you the vilest darkness of the mind invades. And if only, O fool, you were changed like the moon! For it quickly returns to its fulness, but not even over a long time are you converted to wisdom; it speedily gathers up the light that it had lost, but not even slowly do you get back the faith that you denied. Your change, consequently, is more serious than the moon's is: the moon undergoes an eclipse of light, but you do of salvation. How well, then, it is written: *The fool is changed like the moon,* since it is written of the wise: *He will endure with the sun!*[7] The one who is wise endures with the sun as long as the constancy of his faith endures with the Savior. But suppose someone says: "Does the moon, then, not labor?" That it labors we are unable to deny, but it labors along with the other creatures, as the Apostle says: *For all creation groans and brings forth until now,*[8] and before that: *because creation itself will be freed from slavery,*[9] and so forth. It will be freed, it says, from slavery. You see, then, that the moon does not labor with songs but with obedience; it does not labor in dangers but in duties; it does not labor in order to disappear but in order to serve. *For creation has been subjected to vanity not of its own will,*[10] and so forth. It has been subjected, it says, not of its own will. The state of the moon, there-

fore, is changed not of its own will, but of your own will you are changed in your mind; it is led by its condition into a diminution of itself, but you are drawn by your will to the detriment of yourself. I do not wish, then, brother, that you be like the moon in its eclipse, but be like it when it is full and perfect. For it is written of the just: *like the perfect moon for ever, and a faithful witness in the heavens.*[11]

SERMON 31

A Sequel[1]

1. A few days ago, brethren, we spoke against those who think that the moon can be escorted from the heavens with magicians' incantations, and we inveighed against the foolishness of those who undergo no less a diminution of soul than it undergoes a diminution of light. We also exhorted them to leave behind their pagan error and to return as quickly to wisdom as it is changed back to its fulness; and as it speedily gathers back the light that it had lost, so should they quickly retrieve the faith that they have denied. Moreover, let them put aside the cloud of stupidity and begin to consider the moon no longer with a bodily but with a spiritual eye, and let them understand that its rise and eclipse is from design rather than from some weakness. For would the Creator have subjected all things to such change unless this were His design for them?[2] See how the element of the sea ebbs when the moon wanes and the tide is high when it waxes, so that at its movement either the waters return into themselves or the floods do not contain themselves; thus as frequently as the moon's light is changed the sea's waters are changed. The very swimming creatures of the sea are said to be fuller of flesh when the moon is full, but thinner and smaller when it wanes. Great, then, is the moon's design and great is its excellence, which by its own strength thus diminishes the elements in order to magnify them again, and increases them in order that they may be diminished again, so that the alternating changes are agreeable because the restoration is complete. But how much increase the earth is given is known to everyone, for the nocturnal dew refreshes the pastures[3] that the warmth of the midday sun

had dried up, and in fair weather moisture is wondrously offered to those things that are thirsty because of the heat. For when the moon casts its light in a new way, fair weather renders the earth moist.

2. There is, then, a great design as far as the moon is concerned—indeed, a great mystery. It empties itself of its light in order to recreate all things with moisture. Thus also Christ the Lord emptied Himself of His divinity in order to fill us with immortality, for which reason the blessed Apostle says: *who, although He was in the form of God, did not consider it robbery to be equal to God, but emptied Himself, taking the form of a slave.*[4] Christ emptied himself in order to offer life to us, then, and the moon empties itself in order to be of service to the elements. But we read of the Savior that He Himself is the sun of justice.[5] How, then, do we compare the sun to the phases of the moon? There is clearly no great difference: these luminaries are like one another, since the moon by a certain fraternal relationship borrows light from the sun, and it receives the brightness of its own splendor from having been struck by rays of sunlight. Hence if Christ is legitimately compared to the sun, to what shall we compare the moon if not the Church?[6] For, like the moon, in order to shine among the nations it borrows light from the sun of justice, and when it has been struck by Christ's rays—that is, by the apostles' preaching—it receives from Him the brightness of immortality. For the Church is resplendent not with its own but with the Savior's light, and it glows not with its own brilliance but with its brother's, as it is said through the Apostle: *But it is no longer I who live, but Christ lives in me,*[7] and again: *that he might be the first-born among many brethren.*[8] Rightly is the Church compared to the moon, since it also gains increase and suffers loss. For often it wanes, and frequently it waxes: it is diminished under persecution and enlarged with preaching; it decreases when it loses its children and increases when it is crowned with martyrs; and the very thing that causes it to wane also causes it to wax. For frequently the very ones whom it mourns as persecutors it receives as confessors.[9]

3. How often do you think that magicians' incantations have tempted the Church,[10] as they have the moon? How often have evil arts tried to lead it from the heavenly kingdom? First the magicians Jamnes and Mambres tried to subvert the Church when they resisted Moses with wondrous signs, but the enchanters' incantation was

unable to do harm to the sacred words.[11] For enchanters can do nothing where the song of Christ is sung.[12] Then, when the magician Simon opposed the apostle Paul before the proconsul Sergius Paulus, he tried the vessel of the Church and sought to crush him with magical arts, but he was convicted by him with such force that he blinded him by depriving him not only of his art but also of his eyes, and at one and the same time both his incantation and his sight were removed from him.[13] For he who did not have spiritual eyes did not deserve to have bodily eyes. And what shall we say of the apostle Peter, who by the strength of his prayers cast down the other Simon, who was disturbing the foundations of the Church in the city of Rome? For when he had been raised up by his magic arts so that he even flew through the air, he so struck him down by the power of his faith that the higher he had flown the deeper he fell. For truly Peter, like a solid rock,[14] broke him into pieces by his fall, so that he who promised him a heavenly kingdom would perish by the hardness of a death on the earth.[15]

SERMON 32

On What Is Written in the Gospel, When the Lord Says:
It Is Easier for a Camel to Pass through the Eye of a Needle
Than for One Who Is Rich to Enter the Kingdom of Heaven[1]

1. The Lord Jesus Christ says in the holy Gospel: *Amen, I say to you: It is easier for a camel to pass through the eye of a needle than for one who is rich to enter the kingdom of heaven.*[2] I fear that these words may not suit you—you who either have or seek after the riches of this world. For like the camel, which is twisted and deformed and whose very crookedness of body does not permit it to pass through the extremely narrow hole of a needle, their very deformity of life does not permit the rich, who are weighed down by avarice and defiled by desire, to enter through the strait way of the kingdom.[3] For the same Lord says: *Strait and narrow is the way that leads to life.*[4] In the camel it is the construction of its body that makes the passage difficult, but in the one who is rich the greatness of his sins causes the impediment.

For a hump is, as it were, to think or to do something base of soul, and it is a kind of twisted deformity of mind always to incline toward unclean things and to be withdrawn from the holy threshold of the church by worldly concerns. Hence it seems to me that the prophet, when he spoke spiritually of this bodily deformity, alluded instead to a moral hideousness when he said: *Let no one who is crooked boast as if he were upright.*[5] It is as if he were saying: "Let not the sinner boast who is distorted by the wickedness of his vices, as the righteous boasts who is made upright by the sincerity of a good conscience." For although, O sinner, you rejoice in your tall stature, although you are glad because of the straightness of your shoulders, nonetheless your soul is deformed by your evil way of life. Rightly, then, is a rich person compared to a camel, since bodily ungainliness prevents the one from passing through a needle, while concern for his property hinders the other from entering the church. And just as a small needle cannot receive the one, which is burdened by the grossness of its body, so also the sacred portal cannot take in the other, who is encumbered by the weight of his offenses. Each has his own burden: the one is weighed down by his physiognomy, the other by his sins. And just as the one cannot pass through the needle's tiny eye, so the other is unfit for the most blessed kingdom of God, except that the camel's body is disordered by nature, while the rich person's will makes him evil.

2. But I say these things, brethren, about those who are prevented by the shackles of their property from celebrating the high festival of holy Epiphany in church and who are bound by a kind of earthly fetter that prevents them from coming to the house of the Lord. It is not that someone hinders them but that they are so burdened by their own deeds that they have already lost the ability to live of their own power, and while they show concern for their property they do not ask within for medicine for their souls. Do you think that you convince me, O you who are rich, when you say that there is not enough time? Why do you offer a sudden obligation as an excuse? If you have a heart, understand that the obligation of salvation is greater than any other obligation, and that it is more urgent to see to life first and afterwards to make up for one's financial losses, lest while seeking an increase of property we discern a decrease in our soul. But perhaps you fear the judge, whom you have left in his council chamber.

Believe me, you have more reason to fear God the Judge, who will judge your very judge himself! You fear, then, one who will soon have a successor, but God, whom no one ever succeeds, you do not fear. Consider, therefore, the oncoming day of judgment and the unquenchable flames of Gehenna,[6] the horrible gnashing of teeth,[7] and the final torment of darkness, and see if, with the Church now left behind, you are able to carry on worldly affairs! For I fear lest, while you are on the watch for the riches of the world, you find instead the riches of sins and, with the treasures of the world in hand, lose heavenly treasures.

SERMON 33

On What Is Written: The Kingdom of God Is Like Leaven[1]

1. You yourselves know, brethren, that from the day I began to be with you[2] I have not ceased to admonish you with all the Lord's commandments,[3] and partly by encouraging and partly by rebuking to repeat the divine precepts to you, so that I have been an affectionate father to many but a hard master to some. Whoever has freely embraced my words has rejoiced in me as his father, but the one who has been pained by having his conscience struck by my preaching has experienced me as a hard master. Yet that is of no concern to me so long as, whether affectionately or reproachingly, Christ is announced to you[4]—although a reproach itself may be a token of affection that is used toward one's more negligent sons so that they may learn through fear what they had neglected because of love. Not that a father's love toward all his sons should be unequal but that fatherly gentleness might be capable of an affectionate feeling with respect to a variety of ways of behaving—that it would spur on the obedient son with encouragement but meet the stubborn one with harshness, yet that it would be sure of the correction of each, since it strikes the one with love and chastises the other with severity, as the blessed Apostle says: *Of course any punishment does not seem at the moment to be joyful but bitter; afterwards, however, it bears the peaceful fruit of righteousness for those who have been exercised by it.*[5]

2. Consequently, since I believe that you have made progress on account of my many sermons, I would like to discuss with you some things from the sacred Scriptures so that I may see with what liveliness of faith you seize upon what I say. The Lord says in the holy Gospel: *To what shall I compare the kingdom of God? It is like leaven that a woman took and concealed in flour until everything was leavened.*[6] Doubtless the power and characteristics of leaven are known to everyone. For although it is small in size, simple in appearance, and common in nature, it has such power within it that, when it has been concealed in flour, by its inherent energy it makes the whole mass to be what it itself is. And it so diffuses itself throughout the lump by the force of its spreading that it causes the whole mass of flour to become leaven, and thus the thing itself, by its own power, acquires for itself a mass that shares its own strength. Women do this so that they may diligently produce for their husbands a nourishing bread and a useful food.

3. But since there is a spiritual law[7] and the Gospel consists particularly in parables, let us see what the leaven, the woman, and the flour are. We read in the holy Gospel that Christ the Lord says of Himself: *Unless the grain of wheat falls in the earth and dies, it remains by itself, but if it dies it bears much fruit.*[8] Therefore if the Lord is wheat the Lord is also leaven, since leaven is made only from wheat. Rightly, then, is leaven compared to the Lord who, when He was a man in form, little in humility, and cast down in weakness, was interiorly so powerful because of His wisdom that the world itself barely grasped His teaching. And when He began to spread Himself about through the whole earth by the power of His divinity, He immediately drew the entire human race into His substance by His own strength. Thus, in pouring out the energy of His Spirit on all the saints, He made every Christian to be what Christ is.[9] For when the Lord Jesus was a man in the world, alone and by Himself like leaven hidden in a lump of dough, He made it possible for everyone to be what He Himself was. Whoever, therefore, sticks to the leaven of Christ becomes in turn leaven as useful to himself as he is helpful to everyone else and, certain of his own salvation, he is made sure of the redemption of others.

4. Leaven, then, when it is about to be sprinkled in a lump of dough, is broken up, crumbled, dispersed, and completely destroyed

in order to bring together that scattered grain by its strength and join it into a solid unit (that leaven which in its dissolving seemed inert like dust), and by this joining it makes a useful mass, since it seemed useless when it was scattered. Likewise the Lord Jesus Christ, when He was the leaven of the whole world, was broken, beaten, and destroyed by His various sufferings, and for our salvation He poured out His energy, which is His precious blood, in order, by adding Himself to it, to solidify the human race, which was formerly lying scattered in different parts. And thus we have been bound together as if we were leaven, we who seemed to be meal from the nations.[10] We, I say, who were lying interiorly scattered and diminished throughout the whole world were brought back by the power of Christ's passion to His own body, as the blessed Apostle says: *since we are the body of Christ and its members*.[11] We, then, of the nations, who were cast about like dust upon the face of the earth, have grown into a solid mass by the sprinkling of the Lord's blood.

5. But the woman who is said to conceal the leaven in the meal—who is she if not the holy Church, which daily seeks to conceal the teaching of Christ the Lord in our hearts? It itself, I say, is that woman who elsewhere is said also to grind grain, as the Lord says: *Two women will be grinding grain; one will be taken and one left behind*.[12] For the holy Church grinds by the law, by the apostles, and by the prophets when it makes catechumens and scatters and crumbles the harshness of the nations so that, when they are ground into flour, it may prepare them to be bound together by the leaven of the Lord's blood. For I would say that the leaven of faith is all the Lord's suffering. The leaven of our salvation is the very symbol that is handed on;[13] without this leaven or symbol no one is able to merit the substance of eternal life.

6. And since the Gospel describes two women grinding grain, and we have said that one is the Church grinding unto salvation, what must we consider the other one to be if not the Synagogue? For it also grinds by Moses and the prophets, but it grinds in vain, as the Apostle says of the Jews: *They have zeal for God, but not according to knowledge*.[14] In vain, I say, the Synagogue grinds, since the teaching of Christ is not mixed into its mass. And therefore the Lord warns that the leaven of the Synagogue is to be avoided when He says: *Be on guard against the leaven of the Pharisees*,[15] for it was mixed with the

bloody and cruel deeds of the Jews, who said of the Lord: *Let His blood be upon us and upon our children.*[16] Hence the Gospel says: *Two women will be grinding grain; one will be taken and one left behind.* For the holy Church, which has ground a food of holiness for the Lord, will be taken up into eternal rest, but the polluted Synagogue will be left behind at the mill, where it will always tread along the course of its own faithlessness.[17]

SERMON 34

On Hospitality in the Gospel[1]

1. Your holiness,[2] brethren, has attended to the Gospel reading and to how the Lord set down for His disciples, among the other virtues that they were to pursue, the laws of hospitality as well. For He says: *In whatever city you enter, ask in it who is worthy, and remain there until you leave,*[3] and so forth. Clearly these are holy and divine words, which both gave the disciples the privilege of choosing first and also completely did away with any lightmindedness. For in establishing a norm He saw to it that a holy man would neither be quick in making a judgment nor frivolous in changing his host. For just as He conceded to us the ability to make a decision, so He also wished us to remain constant. How reprehensible it is when a man who announces the Gospel and teaches others not to go astray himself begins to wander about in different places, to abandon the house that he had greeted with peace[4] and to sadden the host upon whom he had brought a blessing! For hospitality is a great grace and ought not to be easily violated: it is open to all, ready for all, and both gladly welcomes saints and patiently puts up with sinners.

2. But let us repeat the holy and divine phrase itself. For if it is pleasing from the literal point of view, perhaps in mystery it will be yet more pleasing. It says, then, that when we enter the city we should ask who in it would be a worthy host and what would be a fitting house, and where we should stay until the day of departure arrives. This phrase offers us a higher meaning. For it does not seem to me to have ordered us to inquire diligently about a host or a house in this

world so much as about Him who, as an unoffended and unhurt host, can safeguard us until the day of our departure.[5] Now we quickly hurt and quickly offend a host of this world, and sometimes we also displease him after three days.[6] It was ordered that a faithful house and worthy host be sought after. What house is more faithful than the Church, what host more worthy than the Savior?[7] He takes in strangers as sons, while she refreshes those who have been taken in as infants; He longs to wash the feet of His guests,[8] as we have experienced,[9] while she hastens to set the table. The ones the Savior refreshes with living water,[10] while the others the Church restores with heavenly foods. The Evangelist orders us, then, to seek out this host, and he commands us to live with Him until the day of our death, lest perhaps for some frivolous reason we leave in the middle of our stay for someplace else. This is so that we who have once believed in Christ will not return again, like transgressors, to idols. For it is written: *No one can serve two masters.*[11] For while he seeks to please the one, he notices that the other is angry. Therefore we must not desert Christ our host, as the apostle Peter did not abandon the Lord when his other contemporaries were deserting Him; but let us say what he said to the Savior: *Lord, to whom shall we go? You have the words of eternal life, and we believe.*[12] Behold the one who carries out the heavenly commandments and who, because he did not leave Christ's hospice, deserved to share the heavenly kingdom with Christ!

SERMON 35

On the Fast at the Beginning of Quadragesima[1]

1. The holy Apostle presents testimony from the prophets when he says: *At an acceptable time I heard you, and on the day of salvation I helped you.*[2] And this follows: *Behold, now is the acceptable time; behold, now is the day of salvation.*[3] Hence I also testify to you that these are the days of redemption, that this is the time, as it were, of heavenly medicine, when we shall be able to heal every stain of our vices and all the wounds of our sins if we faithfully implore the physician of our

souls and do not, as people scarcely worthy of the undertaking, despise His precepts. For a person wearied of his illness has found healing when he very carefully observes his doctor's orders; but if he does one thing when another is ordered, then the transgressor and not the physician is guilty if the sickness is aggravated. But the physician is the Lord Jesus Christ, who says: *I will kill and I will give life*.[4] For the Lord kills—in a certain manner—before He gives life. First, by baptism He kills in us murders, adulteries, crimes, and robberies, and with that, by the immortality of eternity, He gives life to us who are like new persons. For we die to our sins through the bath, but we are reborn to life through the Spirit, as the holy Apostle says: *For you have died to your sins, and your life is hidden with Christ*.[5] *For in baptism you have been buried with Him in death*.[6] Now we have been killed in a certain manner when we cease to be what we have been. By a new kind of piety both death and life are at work in one and the same person, for the lust of sins dies and the order of virtues comes to life. In one and the same person the impious and the adulterer are slain so that one who is merciful and chaste might be reborn; idolatry is destroyed so that religion might be generated; the fornicator and the drunkard are annihilated so that the continent and the sober might come to birth. Thus, therefore, the Lord kills in order to make alive, thus He slays in order to make good, thus He strikes in order to correct. This is, then, the extent of His severity toward His servants —that in them sins be punished, the soul preserved, detestable vices abstained from, and the best virtues nourished. Thus far we notice that, by the Lord's kind slaying, many have been converted inasmuch as they have made progress to what is better, going from very bad to very good, so that when you see them you would think that they were changed persons, although you would not see that they were changed in appearance. For, to the extent that what we were previously is destroyed, removed, and annihilated in us, let us believe that what we are since then has been born anew. Hence this second birth signifies that the former life has come to an end.

2. But He says: *I will strike and I will heal*.[7] Clearly the Lord strikes sinners by His precepts in order to heal them, He inflicts blows with His commandments in order to correct, He orders fasts, imposes continence, threatens judgment, and applies a healing remedy by instilling a dismal dread of Gehenna, so that while we fear future

things we may correct what is present. It was thus that, by striking the apostle Paul, He restored him to health. For, when he was an impious and blasphemous persecutor hastening to Damascus to destroy the churches, suddenly He struck him with the terror of a heavenly flash so that He might fill him with the light of gospel splendor. And He punished him with blindness in his fleshly eyes so that He might illuminate the sight of his spiritual eyes. He terrified him with weakness of body so that He might heal him with the zeal of faith. Rising from the ground, then, Paul to be sure saw neither people nor sky with his external eyes, but by the eyes of his soul he saw Christ and heaven.[8] Having been struck by the Lord in that way was of such profit to him that from a Jew he became a Christian, from a blasphemer an apostle, and from Saul Paul; and so much did he change the old man with his habits that he even changed his name as well.[9]

3. Since we have a physician of this sort, then, who heals by striking and gives life by causing death, let us be subject to Him in all patience for the sake of our health, so that whatever He sees in us that is shameful, whatever is filthy because of our sins, whatever is evil-smelling because of our ulcers He might remove, lop off, and cut away, so that when all the wounds of the devil have been cut away He might cause to remain in us only what is of God. But this precept of His is first, that during these 40 days we give our attention to fasts, prayers, and vigils. For by fasts the wantonness of the body is subdued, by prayers the devout soul is nourished, and by vigils the snares of the devil are repelled. When this time has been filled up with the keeping of these commandments, then the soul, purged and wearied by so many observances, is, upon coming to baptism, refreshed with an outpouring of the Holy Spirit. Whatever in it that the heat of different maladies had dried up is moistened with the dew of heavenly grace so that, as the corruption of the old man is removed, it may acquire the character of a new youth. And in marvelous fashion holiness follows upon sinfulness, righteousness upon wickedness, and infancy upon old age in one and the same person; and by a new kind of birth someone else is reborn from the very one who sinned.

4. Thus Elijah, with a fast that was drawn out for 40 days and nights,[10] merited to allay the prolonged and extreme drought of the whole world[11] with a shower and to moisten the arid dryness of the earth with the bounty of a heavenly rain.[12] We know in fact that this

occurred as a figure of ourselves[13] so that we also who are fasting during the course of these 40 days might merit the spiritual rain of baptism, that a heavenly shower from above might pour down upon the arid ground of the whole world for our brethren, and that the inundation of the saving bath might wet the prolonged drought of the Gentiles.[14] For whoever suffers drought and heat in his soul does not experience the moisture of baptismal grace.[15] Fasting these 40 days and nights holy Moses too merited to speak with God, to stand and stay with Him, and to receive the precepts of the law from His hand.[16] For although this human condition prevented him from seeing God, yet the grace of his fasting drew him into close contact with the Divinity. For to fast frequently is a portion of God's virtues in ourselves, since God Himself always fasts.[17] He is more familiar, intimate, and friendly with the person in whom He sees more of His works, as Scripture says: *And Moses spoke with God face to face like one speaking with his friend.*[18] Hence the Lord Jesus Christ also, when He was about to receive the glory of the resurrection, consecrated His virtues by a fast of 40 days and nights in order to show that bread was not the life of human beings but that the commandments were.[19] And so[20] with these fasts of 40 days God is appeased, the heavens are opened, and hell is shut. Therefore we too, beloved brethren, ought to fast continually and devotedly in this space of time so that the Lord might be propitiated by us, the heavens opened to us, and hell not prevail.[21]

SERMON 36

A Sequel:
That There Should Be No Wantonness during the Time of the Fast[1]

1. Last Sunday we said that this was the first work of our faith—to fast most devoutly during the course of these 40 days—and that it was the cause of our salvation if at this time we would devote our attention to abstinence. Therefore, beloved brethren, we ought to consider what kind of fasting this is so as to be aware of how useful it is.

For sometimes there exists a useless and empty fast which, although it empties the stomach and all the inner organs of their fulness, is nonetheless unacceptable to God because it does not empty the mind and the inmost senses of the fetters of wickedness. For what use is it to fast in the stomach while acting wantonly at the hunt, to abstain from food while wandering in sin, to subdue the body by not eating while exercising the mind in wickedness, to refrain from strong wine while getting drunk with thoughts of evil, except that it is easier to excuse someone who is full or drunk than someone who is both wicked and fasting? The former occasionally ceases from sinning since, being drunk, he sometimes falls asleep, but the latter does not cease from his error since, practiced in evil deeds and hungry, he is ever watchful. Hence such a fast is empty and useless: this abstention from food weakens the body and does not free the soul from perdition. About this fast the holy prophet, speaking in the person of the Lord, says: *Why do you fast for me? I have not chosen such a fast, says the Lord.*[2]

2. Do you think that a person fasts, brethren, who is not keeping watch in church at the first light of dawn, who does not seek out the holy places of the blessed martyrs[3] but, upon arising, gathers his slaves together, gets his nets in order, leads out his dogs, and goes all through the woodlands and forests? The slaves, I say, who were perhaps hastening to church he drags out, adding others' sins to his own pleasures and not knowing that he will be guilty both of his own crime and of his slaves' damnation. He whiles away the whole day, then, at the hunt—at one time raising an unseemly clamor and at another stealthily demanding silence, happy if he should catch anything but angry if he has lost what he did not have. And he acts with great zeal, as if hunting were the publicly appointed fast. Among these excesses, then, brethren, tell me what worship there is of God, what devotion of spirit there can be in one who fasts not so as to have leisure for God and prayer but so as to spend the whole day, idle and unoccupied, in the exercise of his own pleasures. Although you who behave like that, brother, return home in the evening and eat while the sun is setting,[4] you may seem to have eaten at a rather late hour, yet you have not fasted for the Lord, nor may it be thought that, while exercising your own will, you have done the will of the Lord. For this is the Lord's will, that we fast both from food and from sins, that we

impose abstinence on the body in order that we may be able to make the soul abstain more from its vices, for a worn-out body is a kind of brake on the wanton soul. For whoever fasts and sins may seem to have made a profit with respect to food but he has not with respect to salvation. By acting sparingly he may seem to have stuffed his pantry with supplies but he has not filled his mind with virtues.

3. Some people, however, who are heedless of the divine precepts, exercise such an absolute power over their slaves and those subject to them that they do not hesitate these days to cut them to pieces with scourges, to fasten them with fetters, and, if perchance the waiter is a little bit late when mealtime has come, to lacerate him at once with blows and to satiate themselves with the slave's blood before doing so with the pleasures of the table. Such is the fast of these people that they fast not in order to call forth the divine mercy but to pour out the cry of their groaning household. But whoever wishes to deserve mercy from God must first himself be merciful, for it is written: *By the same measure that you have meted out it will be meted out to you.*[5]

And, what is still more tragic, these days a Christian master does not spare his Christian slave and does not consider that, even though he is a slave by condition, nonetheless he is a brother by grace, for he has also put on Christ,[6] participates in the sacraments and, just as you do, has God for his Father. Why would he not have you as his brother? For there are many who, on returning from the hunt, pay more attention to their hounds than to their slaves. Not caring if their slaves die of hunger, they have their hounds recline or sleep next to them while they themselves feed them a daily portion. And, what is worse, if the food has not been well prepared for them, a slave is slain for the sake of a dog. In some homes you may see sleek and fat dogs running around, but human beings going about wan and faltering. Will such persons ever take pity on the poor when they are without mercy for their own households?[7]

4. We ought to know, then, brethren, that this is the fast acceptable to God, not only that we chastise our bodies with abstinence but also that we clothe our souls with humility. Let us be gentle to our slaves, amenable to those not of our household, and merciful to the poor. Rising at the first light of dawn, let us hasten to church, offer thanks to God, and beg pardon for our sins, asking for indulgence concerning past crimes and for vigilance concerning future ones. Let

us spend the whole day in constant prayer and reading.[8] If someone does not know how to read, let him look for a holy man and be nourished by his conversation. Let no worldly deeds hinder sacred deeds, let no gaming tables distract the mind, no pleasure in hounds lead the senses astray, no success in business pervert the soul with avarice. For whatever you do other than God's commandment, although you may abstain you do not fast. This is the saving fast, that just as the body abstains from feasting, so the soul should refrain from wickedness. This also, brethren, should not go unsaid with respect to the perfection of fasting: we who abstain and do not eat during this time should give our meals to the poor.[9] For this is true justice, that while you go hungry someone else is satisfied with your food, and that you who are fasting should beseech the Lord because of your sins and the one who has been filled should pray on your behalf.[10] Both profit you—your hunger and the beggars' fulness. But the person who fasts in such a way that he gives nothing of his food to the poor seems to have turned his fast to his own advantage and, by scrimping, to have acted in a businesslike way. For he has abstained to this end—not to please God but so that he not have to spend much. And therefore almsgiving is good with fasting, so that it not be a kind of business whereby one may live sparingly or like that abstinence which monks and clerics flaunt: they do this for no other reason than for gain, whereas we do it for our salvation; they weaken their souls in order to make money, but we chastise our bodies for our souls' profit.[11]

SERMON 37

On the Day of the Holy Pasch, and On the Cross of the Lord[1]

1. Age-old is the story of the famous Ulysses who, cast about on the sea's uncertain paths for ten years, was unable to return to his homeland when the course of his sailing brought him to a certain place where the lovely song of the Sirens resounded with cruel sweetness and caressed those who were approaching with its alluring melody in such a way that they would not enjoy the pleasurable

spectacle but rather cause the shipwreck of their well-being.[2] For their singing was so delightful that whoever heard its sound would be taken captive, as it were, by a certain charm and would no longer head toward the port that he sought but would proceed on to a death that he was not seeking.[3] Consequently, when Ulysses unexpectedly fell upon this sweet trap[4] and wanted to resist its dangerous delightfulness, he is said to have bound himself to the ship's mast after having put wax in his companions' ears. There he was immune from the baleful charms of the singing, and this also prevented him from endangering the ship's course.

2. If, then, the story says of Ulysses that having been bound to the mast saved him from danger, how much more ought there to be preached what really happened—namely, that today the tree of the cross[5] has snatched the whole human race from the danger of death![6] For, because Christ the Lord has been bound to the cross, we pass through the world's charming hazards as if our ears were stopped; we are neither detained by the world's destructive sound nor deflected from the course of a better life onto the rocks of wantonness. For the tree of the cross not only hastens the person who is bound to it back to his homeland but also protects those gathered about it by the shadow of its power. That the cross causes us to return to our homeland after many wanderings the Lord says when He speaks to the thief on the cross: *Today you will be with me in paradise.*[7] Indeed, this thief, a wanderer and a shipwrecked man in another way, would have been unable to return to the homeland of paradise that the first man had left had he not been bound to the tree. For a ship's mast is like the cross of the Church which alone, in the midst of the charming and destructive traps[8] of the whole world, is safe to cling to. On this ship, then, whoever binds himself to the tree of the cross or stops his ears with the divine Scriptures will not fear the sweet tempest of wantonness. For the alluring manner of the Sirens is a kind of enervating desire for pleasures, which weakens the steadfastness of the captive mind with its evil blandishments.

3. Therefore the Lord Christ hung on the cross so that the whole human race would be freed from the shipwreck of the world. But let us pass over the story of Ulysses, which is fiction and not fact, and see if we can find something similar by way of example in the divine

Scriptures, which the Lord, who was later to fulfill everything in Himself, might have intimated beforehand through His prophets.

We read in the Old Testament, when holy Moses led the children of Israel out from the captivity of Egypt and the same people were struggling in the desert because of a devastating attack of serpents and were unable to defend themselves against them by force of arms, that holy Moses, filled with the divine Spirit, then erected a bronze serpent attached to a pole in the midst of the crowds of the dying. He ordered the people to place their hope for health in that sign, and from that object there came forth such relief from the serpents' bite that whatever wounded person either looked at the cross with the serpent or hoped in it immediately received back his health.[9] The Lord Himself recalls this fact in the Gospel when He says: *Just as Moses lifted up the serpent in the desert, so the Son of Man must be lifted up.*[10] Thus, if the serpent fixed to the wood brought health to the children of Israel, how much more does the Lord, crucified on the gibbet, offer salvation to the nations! And if the sign was of such advantage, of how much greater profit do we believe the reality is!

4. The serpent, then, is crucified first; rightly was it the first to be slain by the sentence of the cross because the devil had been the first to sin before God. It is crucified on wood; mystically was this done so that man, who had been deceived in paradise through the tree of desire, would now be saved through a tree of wood, and the same material that had been the cause of death would be the restoration of health.[11] Finally, after the serpent, man is himself crucified in the Savior[12] so that the instrument of crime would be punished after its perpetrator. For by the first cross he was avenged against the serpent and by the second against the serpent's poisons; that is, first the perpetrator itself is punished and then its wickedness is condemned. The venom that it had poured into the man by its persuasive speech is now rejected and healed. For when a person is addicted to lust he is not handed over to death but the deadly crime in him is corrected. The Lord did this by the man whom He took up,[13] so that while He suffered in innocence the disobedience of that diabolical transgression in man would be corrected and from then on he would be free from guilt and free from death.

5. Since we possess the Lord Jesus, then, who has freed us by His

suffering, let us always gaze upon Him and hope for medicine for our wounds from this sign of His. That is to say, if perhaps the poison of avarice spreads in us we should look to Him and He will heal us; if the wanton desire of the scorpion stings us we should beseech Him and He will cure us; if bites of worldly thoughts tear us we should entreat Him and we shall live. For these are the spiritual serpents of our souls. In order to crush them the Lord was crucified, and concerning them He Himself says: *You will tread upon serpents and scorpions and they will do no harm to you.*[14]

SERMON 38

A Sequel on the Cross and on the Lord's Resurrection[1]

1. Yesterday we said that the cross of the Lord has brought salvation to the human race, and it is true; for His suffering is our redemption and His death is our life. He bore all these evils so that we might know every good thing; He wished cruelty to be wreaked upon Himself so that mercy might be ours; He so desired our good that He was severe with Himself. He removed the wounds of the human race by His cross and destroyed them all in His suffering so that nothing more would ever hurt us.

2. Great, therefore, is the sacrament of the cross.[2] And if we understand aright, by this sign the world itself is also saved. For, when sailors cleave the sea, the first thing they do is erect the mast and unfurl the sail, and the waters are broken by the cross of the Lord that has been made; and, safe because of this sign of the Lord, they seek the port of salvation and escape the danger of death. For the sail hanging on the mast is a kind of figure of the sacrament—as if it were Christ lifted up on the cross.[3] Confident in the coming mystery, then, people disregard the stormy winds and fix their minds on voyaging. But the Church is unable to stand without the cross, just as a ship is imperiled without a mast. For at once the devil disturbs the one and winds bring the other into danger. But where the sign of the cross is erected the wickedness of the devil is immediately repelled and the stormy wind is calmed.[4]

3. But the good farmer also, when he prepares to turn the soil in order to plant life-sustaining foods, undertakes to do this by nothing other than the sign of the cross. For when he sets the share beam on the plough, attaches the earthboard, and puts on the plowhandle, he imitates the form of the cross, for its very construction is a kind of likeness of the Lord's suffering.[5] Heaven, too, is itself arranged in the form of this sign, for since it is divided into four parts—namely, east, west, south, and north—it consists in four quarters like the cross.[6] Even a person's bearing, when he raises his hands, describes a cross; therefore we are ordered to pray with uplifted hands[7] so that by the very stance of our body we might confess the Lord's suffering.[8] Then our prayer is heard more quickly, when Christ, whom the mind speaks, is also imitated by the body. Holy Moses is an example of this as well: when he was waging war against Amalek he overcame him neither by arms nor by the sword but by his hands uplifted to God. For thus you see it written: *When Moses lifted his hands Israel conquered, but when he lowered his hands Amalek regained his strength.*[9] By this sign of the Lord, then, the sea is cleaved, the earth is cultivated, heaven is ruled, and human beings are preserved unhurt. By this sign of the Lord, I say, hell is unlocked. For by it the man, the Lord Jesus, who was carrying that cross and who was buried in the earth, caused to spring up all the dead whom it held—when the earth was broken by it, so to speak, and ploughed up.

4. But let us see what happens to the Lord's body itself after it is taken down from the cross. Joseph of Arimathea, a righteous man, as the Evangelist says, took it and buried it in his new tomb, in which no one had ever been laid.[10] Blessed, therefore, is the body of the Lord Christ, which in birth comes forth from a virgin's womb and in death is placed in the grave of a righteous man! Clearly blessed is this body, which virginity brought forth and righteousness held! Joseph's grave held it incorrupt, just as Mary's womb preserved Him unharmed. In the one He is not touched by a man's impurity, in the other He is not hurt by death's corruption; in every aspect holiness is conferred upon that blessed body, and in every aspect virginity. A new womb conceived Him and a new grave enclosed Him. The Lord's is the womb, then, and it is virginal, and virginal is the sepulcher. Or should I not rather say that the sepulcher itself is a womb? There is in fact no small similarity. For just as the Lord came forth alive from His mother's

womb, so also He rose alive from Joseph's sepulcher; and just as then He was born from the womb in order to preach, so also now He has been reborn from the sepulcher in order to evangelize. But the latter birth is more glorious than the former. For the former begot a mortal body, whereas the latter brought forth an immortal one; after the former birth He descends to hell, whereas after the latter He returns to the heavens. The latter birth is clearly more religious than the former. For the former kept the Lord of the whole world locked in the womb for nine months, whereas the latter held Him in the bowels of the grave for only three days; the former offered hope to all more slowly, whereas the latter raised up salvation for all more speedily.[11]

SERMON 39

A Sequel on the Sepulcher of the Lord, the Savior[1]

1. Perhaps someone might say of last Sunday's sermon, in which we preached that there was no less glory in Joseph's grave receiving the Lord than in holy Mary's womb begetting Him: "What comparison can there be between the womb and the grave, since the one brought forth a son from its innermost bowels while the other only gave Him a place of burial?" But I say that Joseph's love was no less than Mary's since she conceived the Lord in her womb and he did so in his heart.[2] She offered the secret place of her inmost members to the Savior; he did not deny Him the secret place for his own body. She wrapped the Lord in swaddling clothes when He was born; he wrapped Him in linen cloths when He died. She anointed His blessed body with oil; he honored it with spices.[3] Each one's service is similar and each one's love is similar; hence each one's reward must also be similar. But there is this difference: an angel called Mary to her service, but righteousness alone persuaded Joseph.[4]

2. And so Joseph placed the Lord in his own sepulcher. We read in the prophet: *Their throat is an open sepulcher.*[5] If, then, the human throat is an open sepulcher, let us see whether perhaps, according to this figure of speech, Joseph placed the Lord not so much in an earthly tomb as in the sepulcher of his heart and received Him for

safekeeping not so much by the frail memorial of stones as by the holy memorial of virtues. For this is the faithful memorial of virtues which, containing Christ within it, does not permit Him to be injured by the corruption of heretics. The Lord says about this memorial in the sacraments:[6] *As often as you do this you do it in memory of me, until I come.*[7] For as often as we speak of Christ we safeguard Him by the memorial of a holy tongue. Therefore the human throat is an open sepulcher. Rightly does the prophet say this, for Christ's open sepulcher is the Evangelists' blessed throat, by which they have fashioned it[8] as an eternal repository of writings. It is called an open sepulcher because whoever wishes to come to the mystery of Christ does not enter into it except by the secret way of the Gospel writing. For the Lord has been placed, so to speak, in a new repository of sacred writings. Whoever desires to see Him, then, both finds the sacrament of His suffering and recognizes the glory of His resurrection there. Consequently the throat of the saints is open, which is why the Apostle says to the Corinthians: *Our mouth is open to you, O Corinthians.*[9] He is inviting them, through the ever-open portal of his preaching, to enter into the secret mysteries of Christ. In this memorial of the heart, then, the Lord is placed by Joseph so that there He may rest in a place of righteousness and so that the Son of Man may have a place to lay His head.[10]

3. Let us see, then, why the Savior is placed in someone else's grave and has none of His own. He is placed in another's grave because He died for the salvation of others. For that death was not inflicted upon Him but was borne for us; that death did not befall Him but profited us. Why should He, who did not have His own death in Himself, have His own grave? Why should He, whose dwelling remained in heaven, have a burial place on earth? Why should He have had a grave who for a space of only three days did not so much lie as one dead in a sepulcher as rest as one sleeping in a bed? Indeed, the brief period of time itself bespeaks sleep rather than death. But a sepulcher is the dwelling place of death. Therefore Christ, who is life,[11] had no need of a dwelling place of death, nor did He who is always living require an inhabitation of the deceased. Rightly, however, have we laid up this life[12] in our own sepulcher so that, as He gives life to our death, we may rise up with Him from the dead.

4. Hence also Mary Magdalene, who looked for the Lord among the other dead in the sepulcher, is reproached and told: *Why do you seek the living with the dead?*[13] That is to say, why do you seek in hell Him who, it is evident, has already returned to the heights? Still not understanding or recognizing Him, she responds to Him: *Sir, if you have carried Him away, tell me where you have laid Him, and I will take Him away.*[14] For she considered Him, as Scripture says, to be the gardener. This holy and simple woman, then, looked for Christ from Christ, and with interior devotion she prophesies without realizing it. She says to the Lord of Himself: *If you have carried Him away, tell me.* Rightly does she ask *if you have carried Him away,* for He Himself who raised up His own body carried it away; He Himself who brought it forth from the sepulcher carried His body away; He Himself who by His own inbreathing revived His body as it lay asleep carried it away; He Himself who brought it to heaven, bearing it by virtue of His divinity, carried His body away. And therefore the woman wisely asks and questions: *If you have carried Him away, tell me where you have laid Him.* That is to say, if you have taken it from the sepulcher, have you carried it away to paradise? (For she had heard him speaking to the thief: *Today you will be with me in paradise.*[15]) Or have you perhaps taken it from hell to the Father's right hand? As the Apostle says: *Seek the things that are above, where Christ is at the right hand of God.*[16] Blessed the one, then, who so seeks Christ the Lord that he believes Him to be dwelling in paradise and gathered up in the heavens! But to the one who looks for Him in hell or in the graves it is said: *Why do you seek the living with the dead?*

SERMON 39A

On Mary Magdalene[1]

1. You still retain in your memories, brethren, what we preached a very few days ago—that Mary Magdalene was sternly reproved because she was seeking the Lord in the sepulcher after His resurrection. Not remembering His words to the effect that He would return from the underworld on the third day, she thought that He was being

held under the laws of hell. Not lightly is she chided because she does not recall the promise of the resurrection and searches for an indication of death. For humble and inexperienced faith seeks what it does not know[2] and forgets what it has been taught. It hastens, indeed, to pay its duties to the dead, but it is not perfect in believing; it is anxious about a hurt done to the Lord's flesh, but it is uncertain about the glory of the resurrection; it weeps out of love for Christ, to be sure, but it laments in despair over His body not found; it thinks that He has perished who, it was evident, is already reigning, for it searches in the grave for one whom it ought rather to call down from heaven.

2. Holy Mary is reproached, then, as one who is slow to believe; and, although she recognized the Lord in the evening, the Savior tells her: *Do not touch me, for I have not yet ascended to the Father.*[3] *Do not touch me* is a reproach; that is to say, do not touch me with your hands because you do not touch me with a perfect faith. You cannot hold me with bodily embraces because in your forgetfulness you do not hold on to my resurrection. She whose memory[4] has slipped is forbidden to touch.[5]

Do not, he says, *touch me, for I have not yet ascended to the Father.* Let us see how Christ has not yet ascended to the Father, since He Himself says: *For the Father is in me and I am in the Father.*[6] He is never separated from Him on account of the undivided substance of the Divinity. For, inasmuch as one abides in the other, this means that the Father and the Son are always together.[7] Or does the Son say that He is ascending to that place where He is dwelling before He ascends? For the same Lord said: *Who has descended from the heavens except the Son of Man who is in heaven?*[8] If therefore the Savior is in heaven when He descends, all the more is He in heaven before He ascends. But let us see if perhaps, at Mary's reproach, those words pertain that are said a little before to the one seeking the Lord among the sepulchers: *Why do you seek the living with the dead?*[9] To this is now added: *Do not touch me, for I have not yet ascended to the Father.* That is to say, why do you wish to touch me, you who, while seeking me among the graves, do not believe that I have just ascended to the Father; you who, while searching for me among the lower regions, hesitate to believe that I have returned to the heavenly places; you who, while seeking me among the dead, do not hope that I am living with God the Father? *I have not yet,* He says, *ascended to the Father.* That is to say, as far as you are concerned I have not yet ascended to the Father; with respect to your faith I am still being held in the sepulcher.[10] For from your point of view I am still tarrying in the earth, I am still clinging to this world, because your faith has not yet lifted me up to heaven. Why, then, do you hasten to touch me as if I were the Son of God when you do not follow Him with a devout spirit as He returns to the Father?

3. Whoever, therefore, wishes to touch the Savior must first, by his faith, set Him at the right hand of the Divinity and, by believing in his heart, place Him in the heavens rather than search for Him among the dead. To that person, who believes that He is always in the Father, the Lord ascends to the Father. To the blessed apostles He ascends to the Father, saying to them: *The one who sees me sees the Father too.*[11] He ascends to John the Evangelist, who sought Him and found Him with the Father, so that he says: *And the Word was with God, and the Word was God.*[12] He ascends also to blessed Paul, who, not content just with knowing what he knew, also taught us how we should seek for the Savior in the heavenly places, saying: *Seek the things that are above, where Christ is seated at the right hand of God.*[13] And, so that he might remove us interiorly from this earthly and terrestrial seeking of Mary, he adds: *Have a taste for the things that are above, not for those that are on earth.*[14] Therefore we ought no longer to look for the Savior on the earth or in the earth or according to the flesh if we want to find Him and touch Him, but according to the glory of divine majesty, so that we might say with the apostle Paul: *But now we have not known Christ according to the flesh.*[15] Consequently blessed Stephen, by his faith, did not seek the Lord upon the earth but recognized Him standing at God's right hand; he found Him where he sought Him with devotion of mind. But Stephen not only sees the Lord in heaven; he touches Him by his martyrdom. For he touches the Lord when, praying for his enemies and holding Him as it were by his faith, he says: *Lord, do not count this sin against them.*[16] Understand, then, the glory of devotion that is here: Mary, who stands near the Lord, is not worthy to touch Him, but Stephen, on earth, touches Christ in heaven; she does not see the Savior present among the angels, but Stephen discerns the Lord absent among the Jews.

Sermon 40

On Pentecost, and On the Psalm: The Lord Said to My Lord[1]

1. I believe that you know, brethren, why we celebrate this vener-able day of Pentecost with no less joy than we accorded the holy Pasch, and why we observe this solemnity with the same devotion that we gave to that feast. For then, as we have done now, we fasted on the Sabbath, kept vigils, and prayed earnestly through the night.[2] It is necessary, therefore, that a like joy follow a like observance. The joy is plainly similar, for then we received the Savior rising up from hell, while now we await the Holy Spirit from the heavens; then, anxious and concerned, we were praying for the coming of Christ, while now, fearful and fasting, we desire the coming of the Paraclete. In all things God has provided for human salvation; for then the Savior opened the underworld for us so that we might rise, while now the Paraclete has unlocked the heavens for us so that we might reign; and by ever-advancing steps, as it were, we learned then to return from death to life, while now we reflect upon the ascent from earth to heaven.

2. All these things are brought about in us by Christ the Lord who, before He returned to heaven, made this promise to His disciples: *But when I ascend I shall ask my Father and He will send you another Paraclete, who will be with you for ever, the Spirit of truth.*[3] Thus it must be believed that Christ has ascended to the Father when we see that the Paraclete has descended upon the apostles. It must be believed, I tell you, that He sits at the right hand of God, as David says of the Savior, because we see the Holy Spirit, as the Lord promised, exult-ing in the disciples. Consequently the prophetic psalm says: *The Lord said to my Lord: Sit at my right hand.*[4] According to our custom the right of sitting is offered to one who, like a victor returning from having accomplished a great deed, deserves to be seated for the sake of honor. And so the man Jesus Christ, who overcame the devil by His suffering and unlocked the underworld by His resurrection, re-turning to heaven like a victor after having accomplished a great deed, hears from God the Father: *Sit at my right hand.* And it is not to be wondered at that sitting on the same seat is offered to the Son by the

Father, since by nature He is of one substance with the Father. But perhaps someone is puzzled that the Son is said to be on the right. For although there are no degrees of dignity where the fulness of divinity is concerned, nonetheless the Son sits on the right not because He is preferred to the Father but so that He not be believed to be inferior.[5] And the Son is on the right because, according to the Gospel, the sheep will be gathered on the right but the goats on the left.[6] It is necessary, therefore, that the first lamb occupy the place of the sheep and that the unsullied leader come before the unsullied flock that will follow Him, as John says in the Apocalypse: *These are the ones who follow the Lamb of God wherever He goes, who have not defiled themselves with women.*[7] Therefore the prophet David says: *The Lord said to my Lord: Sit at my right hand.* That is to say, the Lord who is Father offers the lofty seat of His throne to the Lord God Christ, who is His Son, and for the sake of honor He places Him at His right on an eternal seat.

3. We read in the Acts of the Apostles that blessed Stephen, when he is stoned by the Jews, says: *Behold, I see the heavens opened and the Lord Jesus standing at the right hand of God.*[8] Let us see, then, why the same Lord is prophesied by David as sitting, but is preached by Stephen as standing. First, how can the God of all things, who is incorporeal and invisible (for He is a spirit, as the Lord says: *God is spirit*[9]), either sit or stand? And then, on what kind of seat would God sit—He who is infinite and immeasurable and who contains everything created within Himself? I think that these things are said about the Lord by holy men for this reason—not to contradict each other but to describe His power at one time and His mercy at another time. Now, indeed, sitting is spoken of with reference to a king's power, while standing calls to mind an intercessor's benevolence. For the blessed Apostle says: *For we have an advocate with the Father, Jesus the Lord.*[10] Christ is a judge, therefore, when He sits and an advocate when He rises. It is clear that He is a judge to the Jews and an advocate for Christians. On the one hand, standing before the Father of the Christians, even though they are sinners, He pleads their cause, while on the other He sits with the Father of the Pharisees, who are persecutors, condemning their sins. Angry with the ones, He wreaks harsh vengeance on them, while He gently has mercy on the others, interceding on their behalf. On the one hand He stands in order to

receive the spirit of the martyr Stephen, while on the other He sits in order to condemn the guilty deed of the betrayer Judas.

SERMON 41

On What the Lord Says in the Gospel:
The Foxes Have Holes, *and So Forth*[1]

1. If your love[2] paid close attention to the section of the Gospel that was read, that section would have moved your feelings deeply. For the Lord, as Scripture says, upon having been told by someone that he would follow Him wherever He went for the sake of religious service, says instead to another person: *Follow me.*[3] And, having spurned and disdained the one, He chooses the other in his place—a person who expected nothing and was silent, although a voluntary offering is usually more acceptable, and service is more pleasing when it is spontaneously rendered and not commanded. Why is the one[4] rejected, then? Why is he refused as if he were unworthy? For the Lord says to him: *The foxes have holes and the birds of heaven have nests, but the Son of Man has nowhere to lay His head.*[5] This is the first thing that we must consider, therefore—that the Lord is not an accepter of persons,[6] for He is a just and evenhanded judge, but that He gives love in repayment of virtuous deeds and does not choose the one who is quick with words and slow in devotion but the one whose tongue is silent and whose mind is devout. About such a one the prophet says: *If you practice silence you will appear to be wise,*[7] but with regard to the one who speaks at every occasion Scripture has it: *not everyone who says to me: Lord, Lord, but the one who does my will.*[8] From this we learn, then, that the Lord ought not to be cried out to so much from the mouth as from the heart. Therefore, when our Savior, who sees human thoughts and feelings, hears a voice offering service but recognizes a crafty mind, He compares him to that animal whose voice says one thing but whose actions perform another. For the fox barks like a dog but is a deceitful robber.

2. Therefore He takes the one who is silent and who expects nothing. His tongue was silent, to be sure, but he spoke in spirit. For

we understand how devoted he was who, as he himself maintained, left his dead father so as to lay hold of the Lord of life. For he says: *First permit me to go and bury my father.*[9] The one whom he had left behind as dead he begs that he might return and bury. Sorrow did not hold him nor death detain him, because he was hastening to life. He had not yet closed the eyes of the dead man, not yet buried the stiff limbs, but as soon as he learned that the Lord had come he forgot the feeling of paternal piety, believing that there was a greater piety in loving Christ more than one's parents. Perhaps he had read the prophetic passage that says: *Forget your people and your father's house.*[10] So he forgot his father and remembered his Savior. Perhaps he had also heard the Lord's Gospel words: *The one who loves his father or mother more is not worthy of me.*[11] Thus, as Tobit is justified because he abandons his meal for the sake of a burial,[12] this man is approved because he abandons the burial of his father for the sake of Christ. For the one is not afraid to pass over his meal because some earthly work intervenes, while the other fears lest some delay cause him to omit the eating of heavenly bread. Hence, although in consideration of Christ we owe burial to everyone, this man forsook his father's burial out of love for Christ.[13]

3. Let us discuss first the words of the one man and the reply of the Lord, the Savior: *He said: I will follow you wherever you go.*[14] This declaration is prompt indeed, but proud. The Lord, about to go to His suffering, was to descend to hell and ascend to heaven. Is human frailty able to follow Him in everything? This is foolish presumption rather than a religious confession, since in fact the Lord says to the apostle Peter, when he thought that he would follow the Savior in every circumstance: *Where I am going you are not able to follow me now.*[15] And, when he obstinately insisted and said that death would not separate him from Him, he heard that he would deny the Lord three times;[16] in this he was condemned, as it were, for his pride. Thus the one who promised, while confessing Christ, that he would not be separated from Him by death is cut off from fellowship with Him by a little maidservant's[17] question.[18] And, unless the Lord had set a kind of limit, so to speak, by saying that he would deny Him three times, perhaps he would have denied Him more had he been questioned more.[19]

4. How, then, does He reply to that forward man? *The foxes have*

holes and the birds of heaven have nests where they may rest, and the Son of Man has nowhere to lay His head. See to what he is subtly compared![20] For this kind of animal is deceitful, always intent upon tricks and practicing thievery, leaving nothing safe, free, or secure, seeking its prey even among human habitations. I think that this comparison is written not only with respect to that man but even with respect to many Christians who confess the Lord by their mouth but who tarry in the deceitfulness of foxes by their deeds. For every Christian who wishes to hide his sins is spiritually a fox. For just as a fox lives in hidden places because of its deceitful deeds, so also the sinner conceals himself in dens, guarding silence because of his knowledge of his sins. And just as the one does not dare to manifest the deceitfulness of its deeds in the midst of humans, so also the other is ashamed to confess the wickedness of his life in the midst of the Church. I would call any Christian a fox who sets up a snare for his neighbor, who daily strives to nibble away at others' property, steal their fruits and devour their animals and, what is common in our day, like wolves seize swine and not simply chickens, as foxes do. Although he is able to live by his own labor, he takes pillage with the madness of wild beasts.

5. I think that all the heretics, as well, are to be compared to foxes.[21] Since they are unable to dwell in the house of the Lord, they set up conventicles for themselves, so to speak, like dark holes. There, tenaciously concealing themselves, they lie in wait for the Church so that, if perchance an innocent soul should appear, they might swallow him up like a chick. The foxes, I say, lie in wait for the Church. That is to say, the heretics lie in wait for that Gospel hen about which the Lord says: *How often I have wished to gather your children as a hen gathers its chicks under its wings!*[22] Let us avoid, then, brethren, let us avoid the pestilential deceits of the insidious foxes. Let us avoid the deadly frauds of wicked persons lest, like the foxes which that famous strong man Samson once sent into the Philistines' fields, bearing torches on their tails that burned up everything with their flames,[23] the foxes of perverse teachings in like manner either get hold of the fruits of our fields by deceitful traps or consume them by burning flames. Let us, therefore, as we read, be simple and clever —that is to say, simple as doves and clever as serpents,[24] so that the cleverness of the serpents might protect the simplicity of the doves.

And let us not know how to do evil so that we might be able to avoid it, through our Lord Jesus Christ, to whom be honor and glory.

SERMON 42

A Rebuke to the People, and On What Is Written in the Gospel:
To the One Who Has Will Be Given,
and: We Sang for You and You Did Not Dance[1]

1. I have often thought to myself, brethren, that I should deprive you of the Sunday sermon and not dispense so frequently the sacraments of the heavenly words;[2] for it is of no profit to offer food to someone who refuses it and to proffer a drink to someone who is not thirsty, since what you offer will not be drunk willingly but be given back with aversion as if it were turbid. And so it happens both that the purity of the cup is sullied and that the fastidious drinker discovers causes for offense. In the same way it is perhaps superfluous to present the preaching of the Lord's cup[3] to your charity,[4] since your soul, with bowels sealed, does not thirstily drain it but deceptively pours it out. For the one who does not hearken to it and whose heart does not embrace it pours out the Lord's commandment. The one who receives it, so to speak, on the outer part of his body and does not make it present within forgets what he has heard and spills out the words that have been preached, and so the person who had left church full returns home empty.

For, tell me, which one of you says when he returns home: "Today we heard the bishop[5] talking about almsgiving. He preached something beneficial, and we ought to show kindness to the poor. He also spoke about the disgusting worship of idols. Let us look lest unbeknownst to us there be an idol in our possession. He admonished us, too, that we ought to hasten the catechumen to the grace of faith. Let us tell our household that any unbelievers ought to accept the faith lest perhaps we be called to a reckoning with regard to their salvation, for their life depends on our decision." No one thinks of the things of God, no one speaks of the day of judgment, as if we were either going to conquer completely or die completely![6] Believe me, in this world we live in such a way that we shall die bodily, and we die in such a way that we must live to render an account. For, although a person may die for a while, yet his acts are still liable to judgment. But while the case is pending it means that the person connected with the case is still living, as the prophet says: "Behold the man and his works."[7]

2. I had wanted, then, to deprive you of the Sunday sermon—not angrily but so that I might observe the Gospel words. For the Lord says: *To the one who has will be given, and from the one who does not have what he has will be taken away.*[8] He ordered, then, that the one who has be given to, and not only that the one who does not have not be given to but even that what he has be taken away. These words might seem superfluous to you, but I am saying rightly and wisely what the Lord commanded. It is ordered, then, that the one who has be given to. Clearly he deserves to receive who has so labored that he has acquired spiritual riches by his concern for his soul. For example, someone who, with a strong resolution of continence, has begun to hold to the virtue of chastity deserves to hear what the future reward of chastity is, so that by adding the glory of the reward to the observance of the virtue he might more easily be able to pursue the struggle that he has begun. Another person who is disposed to mercy ought to hear that the Lord will be merciful to him. And it is necessary that one who has weighed the stuff of this earth against heavenly riches should, on hearing of the exchange of heavenly rewards, pursue the Lord's work more readily and willingly and add the increase of liberality to the good of mercy that he has.[9] Consequently the Lord says: *To the one who has will be given.* That is to say, whoever is rich in good works[10] will be more enriched by Gospel preaching.

3. On the other hand, if you preach to a fornicator and tell him that he should remain a virgin[11] or to an avaricious person and tell him that he should part with all his goods and give them away, to such it is foolishness. He considers this preaching to be ridiculous, as the Apostle says: *But the unspiritual person does not accept the things of the Spirit, for it is foolishness to him.*[12] For to preach what is perfect to these persons is like wanting to clothe a ragged beggar with silk or to delight a hungry rustic with pastry. Of course this offering would be refused by both, for silk displeases the one, who wants clothing more suitable to the cold, and pastry is bitter to the other, since he requires a more filling food. From these persons, then, the things that are their

own are to be taken away, as the Gospel says: *Even what he has will be taken away from him.* That is to say, the fornicator will be forced to cast off the rags of his corruption and the avaricious person will be compelled to cast out the bread of his desire.

4. But I fear, brethren, that there may apply to many of you the Gospel reading which says: *We sang for you and you did not dance; we wailed and you did not weep.*[13] For we announce to you the joy of the heavenly kingdom and your hearts are not moved by eagerness. We preach the dour judgment and your feelings do not bring forth tears of repentance. It is a kind of lack of faith in divine things neither to rejoice in prosperous affairs nor to weep over difficult ones. Therefore the Lord demands dancing of us—not, to be sure, the light movement of a flexible body but the holiness of faith lifting itself up. For just as a person who dances bodily is at one moment suspended in the air, at another jumps into the heights, and at still another springs brilliantly with successive leaps from place to place, so also the person who dances spiritually with the help of faith is at one moment lifted up into the air, at another raised to the height of the stars, and at still another springs brilliantly with various leaps of thought to paradise and to heaven. And just as the person who dances bodily and exercises himself by the movement of his limbs does so in the form of a round, so also the person who dances spiritually and moves himself about by the swiftness of faith has the whole round world for himself.

5. But, as the custom is with vows, particularly at marriages, people are in the habit of dancing or singing, and thus we have marriages to which a vow is attached and at which we are expected to dance or sing. For our vows are celebrated when the Church is united to Christ, as John says: *The one who has the bride is the bridegroom.*[14] Because of this marriage, therefore, it behooves us to dance, for David, at once king and prophet, is also said to have danced before the ark of the covenant with much singing.[15] In high rejoicing he broke into dancing, for in the Spirit he foresaw Mary, born of his own line, brought into Christ's chamber,[16] and so he says: *And He, like a bridegroom, will come forth from His chamber.*[17] Thus he sang more than the other prophetic authors because, gladder than the rest of them, by these joys he united those coming after him in marriage. And, by inviting us to his own vows in a more charming way than usual,

having danced with such joy in front of the ark before his marriage, he taught us what we ought to do at those other vows. The prophet David danced, then.[18] But what would we say that the ark was if not holy Mary, since the ark carried within it the tables of the covenant, while Mary bore the master of the same covenant? The one bore the law within itself and the other the gospel, but the ark gleamed within and without with the radiance of gold, while holy Mary shone within and without with the splendor of virginity; the one was adorned with earthly gold, the other with heavenly.[19]

SERMON 43

Where the Lord Healed a Withered Hand on the Sabbath[1]

1. I believe, brethren, that you paid close attention to the Gospel lesson that was just read, where the Lord Jesus Christ went into a synagogue on the Sabbath and with spiritual medicine healed the withered hand of a man who was there, restoring health to the body not by applying herbal potions or concocting medicinal ointments but by oral command and angry admonishment. In anger, I say, he restores the well-being of his hand, as the Evangelist tells us.[2] From this we understand how health-giving the Lord's mildness is when such is the healing property of His indignation, and how profitable His gentleness is if He is so merciful when He is angry. By a word, then, He commands the veins to pour their strength into the withered hand. It is not to be marveled at that He who formed the whole body from dry dust[3] should heal a dried-up hand, nor that He should restore by oral command what He established in the beginning by the labor of creation. For, recognizing its Creator, so to speak, the created thing obeys, even in a small part of its being, Him to whom it owes the totality of that being.

2. But let us see whether this hand that is in the Synagogue and that is of no profit to its body has not dried up because of its works. We want to know also when it first began to be withered. For it is not one person's concern only that is taken up by the Savior, nor is it one

person's sickness that is attended to, but it is the illness of the whole human race that is cured.

Everyone knows that the hand—which is, as it were, a rather noble part of the whole body—performs the office of providing food for the body every day and, by a certain foresight, feeds and nourishes the other members so that life may be sustained.[4] I would say, then, that with respect to the Jewish people this hand is the scribes and doctors who, set up by the Lord as a rather noble part in the body of the Pharisees, neglected to feed their other members with the oracles of the prophets. That is to say, they did not want to give Christ to their body—the one who, according to the oracles of the prophets, is, as it were, the food of eternal life. And consequently their teaching withered up like an unhealthy hand because it did not seek after the source of perennial wisdom. Thus it happened that this hand, as if it had been closed tight, was unable to hold the key of knowledge, as the Lord says: *Woe to you, scribes and Pharisees, who have hidden the key of knowledge,*[5] and so forth. But this key is Christ the Lord, by whom the hidden places of our hearts are unlocked to believing faith. This key was lost by the Pharisees and found by the apostles, as the Lord says to Peter: *I shall give you the keys of the kingdom of heaven.*[6] Therefore the hand of the Synagogue, abandoning Christ, withered up among the leaders of the Jews. Therefore the hand of the Synagogue grew unhealthy, for whoever deserts the source, who is Christ, immediately gets sick and, indeed, is found to be more sick than all the other members.

3. But I know that this hand was once better than all the other members. For holy Moses, the leader of the Jewish people, was like the glorious hand of his body when he merited to receive the law that was to be given him by God.[7] Holy Moses was, I say, a hand—he who, like a provident hand, fed the children of Israel with heavenly manna.[8] This was clearly a hand that overcame the magicians Jamnes and Mambres with the splendor of snowy brightness.[9] For thus you see it written: *When Moses withdrew his hand from his breast it shone with a brilliant white light.*[10] And so the magicians' darkness was destroyed, for the shining hand of Moses gleamed with merit.

4. But let us see when this hand first began to be withered or dead. I am certain that it first began to wither in Adam. For when, against

the prohibition of the Lord, it plucked the fruits of the forbidden tree it lost the vigor of immortality.[11] And then it dried up to a certain degree when by his sin he dissolved the human person, formed in the image of God,[12] into dust. If only the wicked hand alone were held by sin! What is worse, the entire body was sentenced to death when the first hand sinned. Nor should you wonder if the member that is the hand did not remain whole in Adam, for the vigor of eternity dried up in it. Just as the hand of Moses, who was keeping the commandments of the Lord, shone with snowy splendor, so also the hand of Adam, who acted against the precepts of God, was clenched tight with a deadly pallor. It is this hand of Adam's that the Savior heals in the synagogue. That is to say, He is eager to cure the sickness of the whole human race, and so this medicine is universal. For He says to him: *Stretch out your hand!*[13]—he who clenched it by sacrificing to idols. He says to him: *Stretch out your hand!*—whose hand dried up by accepting usury. He says to him: *Stretch out your hand!*—he who used it to seize the goods of orphans and widows. But you who think that you have a healthy hand, beware lest avarice close it tight. Rather, stretch it out frequently to the poor for mercy's sake, more frequently to the traveler for hospitality, and always to the Lord because of sin. Be merciful, be generous, and observe what the prophet says: *Let not your hand be extended when it is time to receive and clenched when it is time to give.*[14] For thus your hand will be able to be healthy if it is held back from evil deeds but stretched out for good works.[15]

SERMON 44

On Pentecost[1]

1. Your holiness[2] should know, brethren, why we celebrate this holy day of Pentecost and why for 50 days we have a continual and uninterrupted festival, such that during this entire time we neither proclaim a fast to be held[3] nor prostrate ourselves to implore God but, as we are wont to do on Sunday, celebrate the resurrection of the Lord while standing erect and in festal mood.[4] For to us Sunday is

venerable and solemn because on it the Savior, like the rising sun, broke forth with the light of resurrection and scattered the darkness of the nether regions, and consequently this day is called the day of the sun by people of the world because, since Christ the sun of justice[5] has arisen, He illuminates it.[6] The whole course of 50 days is celebrated on the model of Sunday, then, and all these days are counted as Sundays, since the resurrection is a Sunday.[7] For the Savior, rising on a Sunday, came back to men, and after the resurrection He remained the whole 50 days with them.[8] It is necessary, then, that there be an equal celebration of those things whose holiness is equal.[9] For the Lord arranged it that, just as we mourned over His suffering with the fasts of a 40-day period, so we would rejoice over His resurrection during the festivals of a 50-day period.

2. And so we do not fast for 50 days because the Lord abides with us during these days. We do not fast, I say, when the Lord is present because He Himself says: *Can the friends of the bridegroom fast as long as the bridegroom is with them?*[10] For why should the body abstain from food when the soul is filled with the presence of the Lord? The one who is refreshed by the Savior's grace cannot be a faster, for the companionship of Christ is a kind of food for the Christian. We are refreshed, then, in this 50-day period when the Lord is with us. But when He ascends to heaven after these days we fast again, as the Savior says: *But the days will come when the bridegroom will be taken from them, and then they will fast in those days.*[11] For when Christ ascends to heaven and is removed from our sight we suffer hunger not of body but of love, and we are burdened not so much by want of food as by desire. For our eyes suffer a kind of desire when they do not see the one whom they seek, as the prophet says: *My eyes have grown dim while I hope in my God.*[12] The eyes of the prophet grew dim because he did not yet see the one whom he hoped that he would see. In the same way the eyes of the apostles also grew dim when they were unable to see the Lord going to heaven, as Luke says: *And in their sight he was lifted up, and a cloud took him from their eyes.*[13] The blessed apostles stood, their bodies completely tense, and followed the Lord ascending to heaven with their eyes since they could not with their feet, and although human vision failed to catch the Savior, nonetheless faith's devotion did not fail. For their eyes follow Christ up to the cloud, but up to the heavens they are united with Christ by the eagerness of

faith. Hence the Apostle says, knowing that our faith is in heaven with the Lord: *But our way of life is in heaven.*[14]

3. The cloud, then, removed the Savior from the eyes of the apostles. Let us see, therefore, what this cloud is, so splendid and so brilliant, that deserves to receive Christ, the light of the world. It could not have been night-like or bleak or darksome, since it is written: *And the darkness did not grasp it.*[15] For the darkness was unable to bear the light. But this is the cloud that caught up Christ in His ascent, which also bore testimony to Christ on the mountain; about it the Evangelist says: *A voice from the cloud was heard saying: This is my beloved Son, hear Him.*[16] It was not a cloud that received Christ, then, but God the Father who received His Son, and by a kind of loving embrace He grasped the ascending one to His tender bosom.[17] The Father, therefore, is said to receive the Son in the shady place of the cloud so that by this refreshment, so to speak, He might be shown to care for the wounds of His suffering. For after the cross, after the violence, after the nether world there is no greater refreshment for Christ than to be overshadowed by the power of the Divinity, as is said to Mary at His conception: *And the power of the Most High will overshadow you.*[18] The most high Father, then, who at Christ's conception overshadowed Mary in His power, received Him in a cloud when He was ascending. For God always leads to rest those who have suffered violence and protects them under the shadow of His cloud, as He protected the children of Israel, freed from Egypt, by the pillar of cloud.[19] And that He might lead them into the land of promise after much toil He cares for them in a shady place of refreshment, as the prophet says: *He spread a cloud to cover them.*[20] He spread a cloud lest they grow weary from the sun's heat in the dryness of the desert.

4. Let us be glad, then, on this holy day, just as we were glad at Easter. For on each day there is one and the same solemnity. At Easter all the pagans are usually baptized, while at Pentecost the apostles were baptized,[21] as the Lord said to His disciples when He was about to ascend to heaven: *John baptized with water, but you will be baptized with the Holy Spirit, whom you will receive after a few days.*[22] And therefore Luke says: *But when the days of Pentecost were completed, suddenly there was a sound from heaven as of the powerful coming of the Spirit, and He rested upon each one of them.*[23]

SERMON 48

On What Is Written:
Who Is the Greatest in the Kingdom of Heaven?[1]

1. If you listened carefully to the Gospel reading you are able to understand what reverence is due the ministers and priests[2] of God and how it behooves the clerics themselves to surpass one another in humility. For as the disciples were arguing over which of them would be the greatest in the kingdom of heaven, the Lord, showing them all a little child, said: *Whoever humbles himself like this child will be the greatest in the kingdom of heaven.*[3] From this we understand that the kingdom is attained by humility and that by simplicity heaven is penetrated. Whoever, then, desires to grasp the summit of divinity must pursue the depth of humility. Whoever wishes to surpass his brother in reigning must first surpass him in serving, as the Apostle says: *surpassing one another in showing honor.*[4] Let him overcome him in kindly behavior in order to overcome him in holiness. For if your brother has not harmed you he deserves kindness so that you may love him, but if perchance he has harmed you he deserves kindness all the more so that you may overcome him. For this is the principal point of our Christianity, that we should requite those who love us with love in return and those who harm us with patience.

2. The one who is more patient in the face of hurt, then, will be established as more powerful in the kingdom. For the reign of heaven is not attained by pride, wealth, or the administration of a province but by humility, poverty, and mildness. *But strait and narrow is the way that leads to the kingdom.*[5] Whoever, therefore, is puffed up by honors and enlarged by treasures of gold is, like a burdened and heavily-laden animal, unable to pass along the strait road of the kingdom. And just as he thinks that he has arrived he is obliged to turn around, forced back from the threshold because the small gate cannot receive his baggage. For the heavenly gate is as strait to the one who is rich as the eye of a needle is small to a camel; this is why the Lord says: *It is easier for a camel to pass through the eye of a needle than for one who is rich to enter the kingdom of heaven.*[6] For as the narrow eye of

a needle does not permit the camel, a twisted and deformed animal, to pass through it, neither does the strait door of heaven permit one who is rich, avaricious, and a liar to enter it.[7]

3. Now then, we are born naked in the world, naked we come to be washed,[8] and naked also and unencumbered[9] let us hasten to the gate of heaven. But how incongruous and absurd it is that one whom his mother begot naked[10] and naked was received by the Church should wish to enter heaven rich! Consequently the Savior said to the young man in the Gospel who saw himself as righteous and holy and as one who had fulfilled all the commandments of the law: *If you wish to be perfect, sell all that you have and give to the poor.*[11] To such an extent is bare virtue[12] fitting for heaven that, no matter how righteous or holy someone possessing gold or riches is, he is unable to be perfect.[13] For the Lord wanted that young man to return to paradise in the same state that Adam had been when he was cast down from paradise's height, for Adam was nude when he was a dweller in paradise. But after the sin, seeing his own nudity, he covered his shameful parts with a leaf;[14] before he had sinned, however, he was clothed in the condition of virtue. And thus it was not nature that created nudity as something vicious but criminal sin that revealed it to be so. Are the holy angels who are splendidly adorned clothed in tunics and mantles?[14a] Yet, although they are bereft of anything material by reason of their origin, they appear to be clothed because they are holy. So therefore Adam, maintaining the dignity of angelic virtue, was indeed unclothed as far as earthly apparel was concerned, but he was covered with the splendor of immortality. His eyes looked upon nothing evil, nor did his heart consider anything base; to virtuous minds nudity was itself clothed. For, as among wicked persons a vile thought is not kept from wanton desire by garments, so among holy men virtuous simplicity is not drawn to wanton desire by nudity; but as all things have been laid bare for the sake of corruption as far as the wicked are concerned, so all things have been covered over for the sake of chastity as far as the devout are concerned.

4. But what does the Gospel reading say? *Whoever offends one of these least ones who believe in me, it would be better for him if a millstone were hung on his neck and he were drowned in the depths of the sea.*[15] It calls "least ones" not those who are children in age but those who are

babes with respect to evil, as the Apostle says: *Be babes in evil so that you may be perfect in your thinking.*[16] Who are these if not worthy clerics, devout monks, and laypersons? Whoever, then, is disrespectful or abusive to these is struck with this brutal punishment: to be hurled into the sea with a hideous rock tied to his neck. But let us see why this punishment is decreed for those who offend Christians and what the judgment itself means, for I think that a mystery is contained therein. As if some kind of small stone were not enough for drowning a person in the sea, so that a huge millstone, such as would be turned by an ass, has to be attached to his neck, and a necessary and useful thing is lost along with the person who is about to perish!

Now in the Scriptures the race of the Gentiles is given the symbol of the ass which with eyes closed is drawn in the circle of its own error round about the millstone of ignorance, toiling unwillingly in another's employ while aimlessly going over its own tracks again and again.[17] Does the race of the Gentiles not seem to you to turn a millstone so long as it is turned about in the toil of its own ignorance? It is held in the bonds of nature so that it may grind the Word of God and seek the Lord of heaven, but so filled with the blindness of a closed mind is it that it cannot lift up the face of its soul to God or raise the eyes of its heart to heaven. But since it is true that this stone is a millstone, let us see if it is also the millstone of the pagans. Without a doubt it is, for the millstone of the pagans is the stony Jupiter and Hercules, around whom they revolve with blind eyes and in constant error. I would say, indeed, that the eyes of those are blind who think that they see what they do not see. For, looking at a rock, they are sure that they see God. But whoever uses a millstone is sure that sometime he will finish his task, and he hopes to lay aside the work that had to be done. Yet the one on whose neck a millstone is hung carries a stone that has refused to bear the yoke of the Lord. The ass, therefore, at the millstone, the blind person at the stone, the pagan at the rock is the one who adores Him whom he neither sees nor knows.[18] For God does not dwell in things made by hands,[19] nor is He known in metal or stone. The Gentile people, then, when they persecute the Christian, are struck with this punishment so that they, along with their sacrilegious millstone, are drowned in the waters that bring judgment to the world.[20]

SERMON 49

On the Two Boats in the Gospel[1]

1. How many miracles the Lord Jesus Christ performs we can see from this Gospel reading, which describes so many benefits that He has conferred upon the people that the excited crowds rush forward to hear Him rather than request to do so. They do not hope for the medicine of salvation through the grace of humility but through rude behavior, such that desert waste does not keep the onrushing crowds from the Lord Jesus, as the Gospel says, neither does the Synagogue repel them nor reverence for the Divinity hold them in check. For it is the custom of the sick that, in their eagerness to cure their ailments, neither place nor time nor embarrassment restrains them from their importunate demand. But the more the healer offers a remedy, the more the sufferer is importunate. Hence when the Lord Jesus, unable to keep away from the pushing crowds on land, sees two boats in the sea, He gets quickly into Peter's boat so that the water might keep Him from being harmed by the press, which reverence for the teacher did not prevent, and from Peter's boat He begins to pour forth the words of His teaching upon the people. See the mercy of the Savior! He is separated from the people in body, to be sure, yet He is joined to them by the benefit of His teaching. Everywhere He shows pity, everywhere He is available: on land He heals bodily afflictions by a touch, on the sea He cures the soul's wounds by his teaching.

2. But let us see what Simon Peter's boat is, which the Lord judged the more fitting of the two to teach from and which keeps the Savior safe from harm and brings the words of faith to the people. For we have discovered that the Lord previously set sail in another boat and was provoked by serious wrongs. For He sailed with Moses in the Red Sea when he led the people of Israel through the waters,[2] but He was hurt by serious wrongs, as He himself says to the Jews in the Gospel: *If you believe Moses you would also believe me.*[3] The wrong inflicted upon the Savior is the Synagogue's disbelief. Therefore He chooses Peter's boat and forsakes Moses'; that is to say, He spurns the faithless Synagogue and takes the faithful Church.[4] For the two were

appointed by God as boats, so to speak, which would fish for the salvation of humankind in this world as in a sea, as the Lord says to the apostles: *Come, I will make you fishers of men.*[5]

Of these two boats, then, one is left useless and empty on the shore, while the other is led out heavily laden and full to the deep. It is the Synagogue that is left empty at the shore because it has rejected Christ as well as the oracles of the prophets, but it is the Church that is taken heavily laden out to the deep because it has received Christ with the teaching of the apostles. The Synagogue, I say, stays close to land as if clinging to earthly deeds. The Church, however, is called out into the deep, delving, as it were, into the profound mysteries of the heavens, into that depth concerning which the Apostle says: *O the depth of the riches of wisdom and knowledge of God!*[6] For this reason it is said to Peter: *Put out into the deep*[7]—that is to say, into the depths of reflection upon the divine generation. For what is so profound as what Peter said to the Lord: *You are the Christ, the Son of the living God?*[8] What is so trivial[9] as what the Jews said about the Lord: *Is this not the son of Joseph the carpenter?*[10] For the one, by a higher counsel, assented in divine fashion to the birth of Christ, while the others, with a viper's mind,[11] considered His heavenly generation in fleshly wise. Hence the Savior says to Peter: *because flesh and blood has not revealed this to you but my Father who is in heaven.*[12] But to the Pharisees he says: *How are you able to speak good things when you are evil?*[13]

3. The Lord, then, gets only into this boat of the Church, in which Peter has been proclaimed pilot by the Lord's words: *Upon this rock I will build my Church.*[14] This boat so sails upon the deeps of this world that, when the earth is destroyed, it will preserve unharmed all whom it has taken in. Its foreshadowing we see already in the Old Testament. For as Noah's ark preserved alive everyone whom it had taken in when the world was going under,[15] so also Peter's Church will bring back unhurt everyone whom it embraces when the world goes up in flames.[16] And as a dove brought the sign of peace to Noah's ark when the flood was over,[17] so also Christ will bring the joy of peace to Peter's Church when the judgment is over, since He Himself is dove and peace, as He promised when He said: *I shall see you again and your heart will rejoice.*[18]

4. But since we read in Matthew that this same boat of Peter, from

which the Lord is now drawing forth the sacraments of His heavenly teaching,[19] was so shaken about by violent winds as the Lord was sleeping in it that all the apostles feared for their lives,[20] let us see why in one and the same boat at one time He teaches the people in tranquillity and at another He inflicts the fear of death upon the disciples in stormy weather, especially inasmuch as Simon Peter was there with the other apostles. This was the reason for the danger: Simon Peter was there, but the betrayer Judas was also there. For although the faith of the one was the foundation of the boat, still the faithlessness of the other shook it. Tranquillity exists when Peter alone pilots, stormy weather when Judas comes aboard. Although Peter was firm through his own merits, nonetheless he was shaken by the criminal deeds of the traitor. As the disciples were fearful, then, and Peter was distressed, the Lord slept. Perhaps it appears unfeeling that the Lord slept while Peter was anxious. He slept to Peter lest He also be awake to Judas.

The deserts of all are affected, then, by the crime of one; Christ sleeps; gusts of wind are stirred up. For whoever commits a sin immediately causes the Lord to sleep in his regard and raises up a storm of unclean spirits for himself. It must be, though, that a diabolic tempest arise when the Lord is peacefully at rest. Therefore, if all the apostles are endangered by the sin of the one Judas, we should, given this example, beware of a treacherous person, beware of a traitor, lest we, the many, drown on account of one. Would that we would cast such a person from our boat, so that the Lord would not sleep but be awake to us, and so that, as He keeps watch, no storm of spiritual evil may strike us! For where faith is whole, there the Savior teaches, keeps watch, and exults; there is calm, there tranquillity, there healing for all. But where faithlessness is mixed in with faith, there Christ slumbers, sleeps, and is sluggish; there is fear, there tempest, there danger for all. It is as a result of our own actions that the Lord either sleeps or wakes to us.

SERMON 50

On the Fasts, and On Holy Quadragesima[1]

1. Some Christians, brethren, thinking that they are keeping the divine precepts more devoutly by omitting the observance of Qua-

dragesima, the beginning of which we celebrate today, deceive themselves by observing Quinquagesima, since this is neither commanded by the sacred writings nor has it been handed down on the authority of the ancients.[2] They do this only out of an obstinate spirit, and while thinking that they are acting devoutly they are behaving superstitiously. The one who is hardly able to observe Quadragesima says that he is observing Quinquagesima! Of course it is good to fast at all times, but it is better to fast during Quadragesima with Christ, for the Lord consecrated these 40 days for us by His own fast. I said "by His fast" and not "by His fasts" because the Lord's fast was one: for 40 continuous days and nights He took no food at all.[3] Whatever Christian, then, does not observe these consecrated 40 days by fasting is held guilty of disregarding his duty and of arrogance, since by eating he annuls a law divinely given for his salvation. For you who do not hold to the Lord's example of fasting annul the law.

What kind of Christian are you, that you eat while the Lord is fasting? What kind of Christian are you, that you refresh yourself while Christ goes hungry?[4] He undergoes hunger for your salvation, but you fear to fast for your sins. Tell me (I speak to you who take food during Quadragesima), do you not have guilty consciences, since you alone eat, contrary to the Lord's commandment, while all the people abstain? Are you not ashamed to go out in public lest someone who is fasting meet you? Or, when you go to church, do you not think about how you will extend peace to the bishop,[5] lest perhaps on account of the very smell of your kiss he reprove[6] you? If you do not think about these things, perhaps you are in serious error. For you ought to know that when one who has eaten meets one who has fasted during the days of Quadragesima, the one who fasts does not judge the other benignly. I say this because I hear that many—and what is worse, they are the faithful—abstain in alternate weeks during Quadragesima and violate that consecrated number of days by gluttonous intemperance; that is to say, for the space of seven days they eat and for seven days they fast. I say this to them: even on those seven days when they fast they are deceiving themselves, because such a fast is of no use to them. For even though someone abstains on certain days, even though he does not eat more delicate foods, still the fast of Quadragesima is not credited to the person who does not fast for 40 days. I am ashamed to say that old men and old women observe Quadragesima, while the rich and the young do not.

Let us celebrate this most holy time with every care, then; let the day not pass us by without fasting; let not one week overtake us without vigils. For the one who observes Quadragesima by fasting and keeping vigil ascends to the Pasch. Just as fasting during the rest of the year is profitable, so not to fast during Quadragesima is sinful. For the one fast is voluntary, the other necessary; the one comes from free choice, the other from the law; to the one we are invited, to the other obliged.

2. But let us see where this most sacred number of 40 days had its beginning.[7] We read first in the Old Testament that in the time of Noah, when criminal wickedness had seized the whole human race, torrents of water poured forth from the opened floodgates of heaven for just as many days.[8] In a kind of mysterious image of Quadragesima, this inundation of the earth refers not so much to a flood as to baptism.[9] This was clearly a baptism in which the wickedness of sinners was removed and Noah's righteousness preserved. For this reason, then, the Lord has given us 40 days now as well in imitation of that time, so that for this number of days, while the heavens are opened, a celestial rain of mercy might pour upon us and, with the flood, the water of the saving washing might enlighten us[10] in baptism and—as was the case then—the wickedness of our sins might be quenched in us by the streams of water and the righteousness of our virtues preserved. For the very same thing is at issue with regard to Noah and in our own day: baptism is a flood to the sinner and a consecration to the faithful; by the Lord's washing, righteousness is preserved and unrighteousness is destroyed. We see this done in one and the same person in the apostle Paul, who, before he was washed in the spiritual commandments, was a blasphemer, a persecutor, and Saul. But when the rain of the celestial washing poured over him the blasphemer was destroyed, the persecutor destroyed, Saul destroyed, and the apostle was given life, the righteous man given life, Paul given life. To such an extent did it destroy the old man with his deeds that his name was changed along with his way of living.[11] In whoever keeps the Lord's commandments during this observance of Quadragesima, then, diabolical wickedness will be destroyed but apostolic

grace will be preserved. And as he observes it he dies to himself in a certain way in that part of himself which is sinful, but he is restored to life in that part which is righteous.

3. Let us also see if we are able to find Quadragesima's mystical number somewhere else in the Scriptures. We read that holy Moses fed the children of Israel with heavenly manna in the desert for the space of 40 years.[12] Good is the number, then, which always opens heaven. Good is the number, I say, by which Noah's righteousness is preserved and the children of Israel are fed. For this reason let us also observe this number so that the heavens might be opened to us in order that the rain of spiritual grace might fall upon us and the manna of the spiritual sacraments[13] refresh us. For, after the fashion of our fathers, by this observance of Quadragesima we are both made righteous and nourished: we are made righteous by the washing and nourished by the sacraments.

But someone says that when the children of Israel were in the desert they did not fast when they were filled with manna. I say, however, that they applied themselves then to nothing but abstinence and that consequently they deserved the grace of a heavenly sustenance. For, first of all, the desert is all emptiness,[14] and the fear engendered by solitude drives away the desire for food. And secondly, where in the desert can one find elaborate dishes, costly wines, or anything at all to last for a space of 40 years? We understand, then, that the children of Israel fasted inasmuch as we know that a supply of food was lacking to them, and that they had something to eat whenever it pleased the Lord, the giver. The one who refreshes himself with Christ's will fasts long enough. But to such a degree did the abstinence of the children of Israel in the desert please the Savior that even the intemperance of a few of them was noticed, so that when someone who was more greedy had collected a double portion of manna he suffered this—he discovered that he had not kept food but rather worms for himself.[15] That is to say that because he had desired more than a moderate amount of food he was oppressed, as it were, by worm-like pricks of conscience.[16] Therefore we also, brethren, keeping the daily and moderate fasts of Quadragesima and living, so to speak, in the desert, ought not to think of worldly delights, and no pleasure of bodily desires ought to occupy us. Let us be sober, let us be chaste. Although we live in cities, let us dwell in the desert in our minds. If we thus act abstinently we too shall be refreshed by the sustenance of heavenly manna and not be pricked by the stings of worms.

SERMON 50A

A Sequel on Quadragesima[1]

1. As your love[2] well remembers, brethren, on the previous Sunday we preached that the Lord himself consecrated holy Quadragesima by abstaining. By not taking any food during the course of that many days and nights, He established one continuous period of fasting, which it is a sacrilege not to observe in its entirety and a sin to violate in part. This He did for the sake of our salvation, that He might not only teach what was useful by words but also instil it by examples, so that on the very path that we hasten to faith we might take steps to abstinence. But let us see why the Savior appointed fasts and why He Himself, as the good physician of the human race,[3] first fasted. (For a good physician first tastes the potion that he is about to give to the sick person in order to demonstrate beforehand the skill of his art on himself, so that when the sick person takes what has been tried he may be certain about the potion and more certain about his health.) And then let us see why He established this time for fasting in the place that He did, for the Evangelist says that the Lord abstained 40 days and nights in the desert.[4]

2. I think that this is the reason for fasting—that since the first Adam, when he was in paradise, had forfeited the glory of immortality through his gluttonous intemperance,[4a] Christ, the second Adam,[5] might restore the same immortality through His abstinence. And now, because he had incurred the sin of death by going against the commands of God and tasting of the forbidden tree, the Lord in His fasting, in conformity with the commandment, might merit the righteousness of life.[6] The Savior did this so that He might purge our crimes by taking the same path on which they had been committed. That is to say, He repairs by abstaining what the man had perpetrated by eating, and by fasting He despises the same woman whom the man

had known by eating. For Adam would not have known Eve except that he was provoked by intemperance; but as long as they abided in undefiled abstemiousness they abided in unstained virginity as well, and as long as they fasted from forbidden food they fasted also from shameful sins.[7] For hunger is a friend of virginity and an enemy to lasciviousness, but satiety drives out chastity and feeds wantonness. The Lord did this, then, as I have said, so that by these decisions which had made humanity subject to sin it might be freed. For this reason He wished to be born according to the likeness of Adam in every respect, so that in the likeness of Adam He might destroy all the sins of humanity. For Adam was born of the virgin earth[8] and Christ was begotten of the virgin Mary; the maternal soil of the one had not yet been broken by hoes, while the hidden place of the other's maternity was never violated by desire. Adam is formed from mire[9] by the hands of God, while Christ is formed in the womb by the Spirit of God.[10] Each comes forth with God as father, then; each has a virgin for mother; each, as the Evangelist says, is a son of God,[11] but Adam is a creature and Christ is a son in substance.[12]

3. The Lord did this, then, as a second Adam, so that what the former man had lost by eating, the other might regain by fasting. And in the desert He kept the law of abstinence that had been given in paradise, for He knew that God's precept was not for one place but for the whole world. It makes no difference with respect to the divine command whether you keep it at home or in your field, since the one who gave the command is everywhere. In the desert, then, the Savior fulfils the command of God, so that He might save the wandering Adam in the very place where he had been dispossessed of paradise, for Adam, when he was cast out of paradise, endured the desert places of a harsh world. It is in the desert, then, that salvation is first restored to humankind—there where there are no rich foods, where there are no pleasures, where (what is the cause of every evil) there is also no woman. For Adam would have been able to remain unshaken among those pleasures of paradise had Eve not been in the same place with her diabolical snares. The desert, then, is fitting for salvation—there where there is no Eve to persuade, no woman to entice. Behold a remarkable thing: in paradise the devil contends with Adam, and in the desert the devil struggles with Christ; everywhere he lays a snare for

man, everywhere he accosts him, but where he has found a woman he conquers, and where he has not found a woman he retires conquered.[13]

4. In having done this, then, God gave us the form of fasting, in order that dwelling in the desert, so to speak, during the time of the fasts we might abstain from rich foods, from pleasure, and from womankind, so that Eve might not be united with us, lest by her charming persuasiveness she subvert us from our chaste observance. For a person who fasts and is chaste seems to dwell in the desert in a certain way at the time of Quadragesima. The very body of the Christian is in a sense a desert when it is not filled with food and cheered with drink but is neglected in the desolation of parched fasting. Our body, I say, is a desert when the flesh pines away with abstinence, paleness is induced by thirst, and the unadorned appearance of the whole person grows filthy through the contempt of material goods.[14] Then Christ the Lord inhabits the desert of our body— when He has found that our land is desolate because of hunger and parched because of thirst, according to what the prophet David says: *I have appeared to you in the holy place as in a land that is desolate, impenetrable, and waterless.*[15] For we are unable to appear to Him in the holy place unless the land of our body is desolate of worldly pleasures, impenetrable to diabolical lusts, and unmoistened by wanton desires. Then the Savior dwelling in this desert of our body overcomes there all the factions of the devil, and safe and secure from the thoughts of this world He takes it for His habitation, so that from then on we might see heaven and earth within ourselves as in a solitude; that is to say, we might think of nothing other than the Lord of the heavenly kingdom and the author of earthly resurrection.

SERMON 51

On the Lord's Fasting in the Desert, and That One Does Not Live on Bread Alone[1]

1. Your love[2] ought to remember what I preached on the previous Sunday: I gave a reason why the Lord fasted for 40 days and why He carried out those fasts in the desert. We said that He had observed all

these things not for the sake of His own justification, He who was a virgin in all things, but for our salvation, so that the generation that had sinned by intemperance might be healed by abstinence. Let us see, then, what took place at that time and in that solitude.

The Evangelist says that the devil was there and that the Savior was tempted by his cunning. For the sacred reading says that the Lord was hungry and that the devil told Him: *If you are the Son of God, tell this stone to become bread.*[3] See how skilful the Lord was, circumventing His adversary by deceit! After much fasting He makes believe that He is hungry so that by hungering He might again trick the devil, whom He had already conquered by fasting.[4] For He seemed to give him the hope of a struggle, so that in fighting against one who appeared to be weak he might be all the more gloriously overcome. This is the true victory, that the one who[5] had ruined the deathless, glorious, and feasting Adam is now conquered by a man subject to death, humble, and hungry. Seeing the Lord hungry, the devil thinks that He is a man and doubts that He is the Savior, and so he says: *If you are the Son of God, tell this stone to become bread.* O what a miserable and desperate encounter for Satan! In the desert the devil does not find his customary weapons of temptation: he lacks the pleasant trees of paradise, he lacks his counsellor Eve, he lacks the beautiful deception of the fruit. And since he finds no food to offer to the one who is hungry, he asks that stones be turned into food. Cut off on all sides, deceived on all sides, he betakes himself to stones. He shows quite clearly that the wasteland in its vastness has withstood him when he thinks that on account of the lack of materials even the elements can be changed. Therefore he asks that stones be changed into bread. Cunning and shrewd, he knows what he is asking for, he knows that what he is talking about has been done, for he remembers in the Old Testament that water flowed from a rock for those who were thirsty; he himself also wishes food to be produced from a rock for the one who is hungry. He recalls that the hardness of the rock was dissolved into springs of water; he himself also wants the roughness of the rock to be transformed into the sweetness of bread.[6] For he suspects that this man is the Christ, who should be accustomed to producing these things from the nature of stones. As the apostle Paul says: *They drank from the spiritual rock that followed them, but the rock was Christ.*[7] He suspected, I say, that He was the Christ when he asked Him to make bread from stone, but he thought that He was only a man when he saw Him hungry.

2. The Savior, however, condemns his cunning with a wonderful response. He does not do what the devil says lest He appear to make known His glorious power at the nod of His adversary, nor yet does He reply that He is unable to do it, since He could not deny what He had already frequently done. Therefore He neither accedes to the petitioner nor turns away from the one who is probing Him, and so He both reserves the power of His strength to His own free choice and confutes the cunning of His adversary with divine eloquence. He responds to him: *A person does not live on bread alone but on every word of God*[8]—that is to say, not on earthly bread and not on material food, with which you deceived Adam, the first man, but on the word of God, which contain the provisions of heavenly life. But the Word of God is Christ the Lord, as the Evangelist says: *In the beginning was the Word, and the Word was with God.*[9] Whoever feeds, then, on the word of Christ has no need of earthly nourishment, nor is one who is fed with the bread of the Savior able to desire the bread of the world. For the Lord has His own bread; indeed, the Savior Himself is bread, as He taught when He said: *I am the bread that has come down from heaven.*[10] About this bread the prophet says: *And bread strengthens the human heart.*[11]

3. What to me, then, is the bread that the devil offers when I have the bread that Christ bestows? What to me is the food on account of which, as I remember, the first-formed man was cast down; Esau, as I have seen, was cheated out of his status as first-born;[12] and Judas Iscariot was marked by the crime of betrayal? For Adam lost paradise because of food, Esau abandoned the honor of the first-born for a lentil, Judas laid down the lofty office of apostle for a morsel—for from the time when he took the morsel he began to be no longer an apostle but a traitor. Thus you have it written, as the Lord says: *The one to whom I give the bread that has been dipped, he will hand me over. And directly after the morsel Satan entered into him.*[13] Evil is the food after which the enemy finds access! Evil is the food after which Christ is rejected and the antichrist is devoured! Evil is the food that lacks a blessing but that is filled with cursing! That food is needful for

us, then, which offers life and nourishes the soul, upon which Christ
enters and the enemy is shut out. We must take that food which the
Savior and not the devil follows upon, which makes the one who
takes it a confessor and not a traitor. During His time of fasting, how
well it was that He said that the word of God was food, so as to show
that our fasts ought not to be taken up with worldly affairs but kept
busy with the sacred writings![14] For the one who is intent upon the
food of reading disregards bodily hunger, and the one who obtains the
nourishment of the heavenly word will be unable to worry about his
stomach. This is the repast that fills the soul, that fattens a person
within, when we take from the divine Scriptures the food of unfailing
eloquence. This is the food that gives eternal life and keeps the snares
of diabolical temptation away from us. And the Lord testifies that the
reading of the sacred Scriptures is life when He says: *The words that I
have spoken are spirit and life.*[15]

SERMON 52

A Sequel on the Fasts of Quadragesima[1]

1. Thanks to the divine graciousness, see, we have now almost
gotten through the prescribed fasts of Quadragesima and by our
devotion to abstinence fulfilled the commands of Christ the Lord.
What remains now is that, as His servants Moses and Elijah merited
grace by observing this most sacred number, we might also gain merit
by holding to this same length of time. As there is a like effort in
carrying out the fast, so may there be a like return in the receiving of
the reward. For Elijah, when heaven was closed on account of human
wickedness and no abundance of rain poured forth upon the things of
earth, when everything lay under the desolation of a prolonged
drought and a great famine beset the whole human race (for since
heaven gave no rain the earth produced no food)—then with his fasts
holy Elijah opened heaven and made the earth fruitful with his
prayers.[2] The drought of the one he turned to rain, the sterility of the
other he made productive. So much rain watered the earth because of
his prayers that what was dry came back to life again, what was dead

arose, and what was weakened was restored. A kind of stream coursed into all things such that, because of the purification effected by the rain, the crimes of every creature were washed away, and the renewed beauty of the whole earth was resurrected as a result of that inundation.

2. Hence we also, observing the same fasts as Elijah, with our attentive prayers open a closed heaven to those requesting baptism,[3] so that the rain of the saving washing may enlighten them.[4] For heaven is closed to them as long as the Holy Spirit has not yet come from heaven and enlivened their hearts. They suffer a drought, as it were, because they are not yet watered with the grace of baptism,[5] and they also labor under a severe famine because, like hungry people, they long for the heavenly sacraments.[6] We open heaven to them, then, so that when the spiritual rain has come from on high their land might be filled with water and, having put off the sterility of their sins, they might bring forth the fruits of the virtues. And indeed the heavenly shower destroys sinful blemishes, produces an increase of righteousness, gets rid of the dry dust of wantonness, rejoices the beneficial purity of chastity, buries the sordid filth of avarice, and nourishes the perennial generosity of mercy. For, just as when Elijah's rain came the land produced every food, so also when Christ's washing comes the soul brings forth all righteousness. And just as in the former the rain water moistened the earth so that the already dead seeds of vegetation might come to life, in the same way the water of baptism moistens the human race so as to bring to life the dead hearts of souls. This is the reward, then, of those who observe these fasts: by their prayers either the world is renewed or their brethren are reborn.

3. And so heaven must be opened to those requesting baptism[7] since it is still closed to them. For heaven is closed to them because they do not yet see the mystery of the Trinity. Inasmuch as heaven is closed to them they are unaware of what is taking place above heaven, nor can they know what the substance is of the Son and the Father unless they first transcend the elements of the world. Then a person will be able to look upon the divine mysteries of the Trinity, when he has opened the heavens by his own virtue, as the blessed martyr Stephen opened the heavens for himself by his martyrdom and saw the Savior standing at the right hand of the Father, as he himself said:

Behold, I see the heavens opened and Jesus standing at the right hand of God.[8] Therefore, when the heavens have been closed to a person they must be opened to him so that he may see Christ standing above the heavens, for as long as they are closed to someone he is unable to see Christ reigning.

But we ought to find out how the heavens that have been closed are to be opened. I believe that they cannot be opened unless we take the keys of the apostle Peter, which he took when the Lord gave them, as He Himself says: *I will give you the keys of the kingdom of heaven.*[9] Let us by all means ask Peter, as the good gatekeeper of the heavenly kingdom, to open it to us.

4. But let us consider carefully what this key might be. I would say that Peter's key is Peter's faith, by which he opened the heavens, penetrated the underworld, and securely and fearlessly trod the seas underfoot.[10] For such is the strength of the apostolic faith that all the elements are open to it; that is to say, the angelic portals are not closed to it, the gates of the underworld do not prevail against it,[11] and floods of waters do not overwhelm it. But this key, which we call faith—let us see in what it consists and how it is made. I am of the opinion that it is cast by the labor of 12 workers. For the holy faith has been summarized in the symbol of the 12 apostles, who, collaborating like skilled workmen, have cast a key according to their own design.[12] For I would say that the symbol itself is a kind of key by which the darkness of the devil is revealed and the light of Christ comes. The hidden sins of one's conscience are opened up so that the manifest work of righteousness might shine forth. Therefore this key must be shown to our brethren so that they also, like disciples of Peter, may be used to unlocking the nether regions and opening the heavens for themselves.

SERMON 53

On the Pasch[1]

1. Not without cause, brethren, is the psalm read today in which the prophet orders exultation and jubilation,[2] for holy David invites all creatures to the celebration of this day. On this day the underworld

is opened by Christ's resurrection, the earth is renewed by the Church's neophytes, and heaven is unlocked by the Holy Spirit: for the underworld, now that it is opened, returns its dead; the earth, having been renewed, brings forth the risen; and heaven, unlocked, receives those ascending. At last the thief ascends into paradise,[3] the bodies of the saints enter into the holy city,[4] the dead turn into the living, and all the elements, by a kind of progressive movement, betake themselves to the heights in the resurrection of Christ. Those whom the underworld holds it returns to the upper regions, those whom the earth encloses in burial it sends to heaven, and those whom heaven receives it presents to the Lord. By one and the same operation the Savior's suffering lifts up from the depths, raises up from the earth, and gathers in the heights. For Christ's resurrection is life to the dead, pardon to sinners, and glory to the saints. Therefore holy David invites every creature to the celebration of Christ's resurrection, for he says that there must be exultation and jubilation on this day that the Lord has made.[5]

2. But suppose someone says: "If this is to be a day of rejoicing, there ought to be rejoicing with respect to the things that the day itself encompasses, yet heaven and the underworld are set beyond the day of this world. How, then, can those elements which are not contained within the day's ambit be called to the celebration of this day?" But this day, which the Lord has made,[6] penetrates all things, contains all things, and encompasses heaven, earth, and the underworld. For the light of Christ is not obstructed by walls, not divided by the elements, and not obscured by darkness. The light of Christ, I say, is a day without night, a day without end; everywhere it shines, everywhere it radiates, nowhere does it fail. That this day is Christ the Apostle says: *The night has passed, but the day has drawn near.*[7] He says that the night has passed, not that it is about to follow, so that you may understand that with the coming of the light of Christ the darkness of the devil is taking flight and the obscurity of sin will not ensue; and by this constant shining the mists of the past are dispelled and sins that would steal in are prevented. Scripture bears witness that this day—Christ—illuminates heaven, earth, and the underworld. That it shines upon the earth John says: *He was the true light that enlightens everyone who comes into this world.*[8] That it shines in hell the

prophet says: *Light has risen upon those who sat in the region of the shadow of death.*[9] That this day abides in the heavens David mentions when he says: *I shall establish His seed forever and His throne as the day of heaven.*[10] But what is the day of heaven if not Christ the Lord, of whom the prophet says: *Day utters a word to day?*[11] For the Son Himself is the day, to whom the Father, the Day, utters the secret of His own divinity. He Himself, I say, is the day who says through Solomon: *I have established it that an unfailing light should arise in heaven.*[12] Just as night, then, does not at all follow the day of heaven, neither does the darkness of sin follow the righteousness of Christ. For the day of heaven is forever resplendent, luminous, and shining, and no obscurity can enfold it. In the same way the light of Christ is always brilliant, radiant, and gleaming, and no gloom of sinfulness can encompass it, which is why the Evangelist John says: *And the light shines in the darkness, and the darkness did not grasp it.*[13]

3. All the elements, then, glory in the resurrection of Christ. I think that the sun itself is unusually brighter on this day, for it must be that the sun should rejoice in the resurrection of the one at whose suffering it had lamented. As it responded to His death with a kind of doleful gloom, so it should receive back His life with the splendor of a more radiant light; and as a good servant who hid himself, so to speak, at the rites of burial, so now it should gleam at the rites of resurrection.[14] For at the suffering of Christ it enclosed itself in a night of mists, and with the world as witness it groaned over the Jews' wicked deed. That it should have abdicated its light-giving office is an indication of sorts of the sun's sorrow at such a crime, and as a kind of revenge it poured darkness into the eyes of the Jews so that blindness would fill the eyes of those whose minds had been laid hold of by blindness, nor would the world's light shine on those by whom the light of salvation had been put out. Condemnation is meted out to the Pharisees so that already in the upper regions they might suffer the darkness promised to sinners on the day of judgment.[15] Darkness lingers in the upper regions, then, since Christ has been crucified. Why should it be remarkable that darkness is in the upper regions, when the light has descended into the nether regions?

4. Therefore, brethren, we ought all to rejoice on this holy day. Let no one draw back from the common celebration because of his

awareness of sin. Let no one stand off from the public acts of worship because of his burden of crimes. Although one may be a sinner, on this day he ought not to despair of pardon. This is no small privilege. If even the thief merited paradise, why should not the Christian merit pardon? And if the Lord, when He is crucified, has mercy on the former, will He not all the more have mercy on the latter when He rises? And if the humiliation of His suffering has so much to offer to the one who confesses Him, how much will the glory of the resurrection bestow on the one who beseeches Him? For joyful victory, as you yourselves know, is accustomed to be more generous than fettered captivity.

SERMON 54

A Sequel on the Holy Pasch[1]

1. Brethren, God has given us a great and marvelous gift this saving paschal day, on which the risen Lord offers resurrection to all creatures. Ascending from the depths to the heights, in His own body He has lifted us as well from the nether regions to those that are above, for, according to the Apostle, all of us Christians are the body of Christ and its members.[2] In Christ's resurrection, then, all His members have necessarily risen with Him. For while He passes from the depths to the heights, He has made us pass from death to life.[3] For in Latin the Hebrew word *pasch* means "passage" or "progress," because by this mystery a passage is made from what is worse to what is better.[4] It is a good passage, then, to move from sins to righteousness, from vices to virtue, and from old age to infancy. But I would speak of infancy not with respect to age but with respect to simplicity, since merits and faults have their own ages. For by the old age of our sins we first lived in frailty, but by the risen Christ we have been renewed in the innocence of children. Christian simplicity also has its infancy: just as an infant does not know how to grow angry, cannot deceive, and does not dare to strike back, neither does the infancy of

Christianity get angry with those who cause injury, resist those who plunder, or fight back those who deal blows. And, as the Lord has ordered, it even prays for its enemies, leaves its cloak to one who takes its tunic, and offers its other to the person who strikes one cheek.⁵ In this, however, the infancy of Christ is better than that of nature: the one cannot sin, but the other disdains to; the one is harmless through weakness, the other is innocent through virtue. It is more praiseworthy not to wish to do evil than to be unable to do it.⁶

2. Therefore, as we have said, there are certain ages for merits and faults, and a moral old age is found in children, while the innocence of babes is met with in the old. That an old age of goodness, so to speak, may be in the young the prophet says: *Old age is not venerable on account of length of time, nor is it reckoned by number of years, for a person's understanding is his gray hair.*⁷ And to the apostles, who are already older in years, the Lord says: *Unless you change and become like this child you will not enter into the kingdom of heaven.*⁸ He calls them back to that from which they came and He insists that they return to their infancy, so that those who had grown old in their frail body might be reborn in good habits of innocence, as the Savior says: *Unless one is reborn of water and the Holy Spirit he will not enter the kingdom of God.*⁹ For this reason the apostles are told: *unless you change and become like this child.* He does not say "like these children" but *like this child.* He chooses one, he proposes one. Let us see, then, who He might be, who is proposed to the disciples to be imitated. I do not think that He is from the people, nor from the ordinary crowd, nor from the vast multitude—this one who was given, through the apostles, as an example of holiness to the entire world. I do not think, I say, that He is from the ordinary crowd but from heaven. For He is the child from heaven about whom the prophet Isaiah says: *A child is born to us, a son is given to us.*¹⁰ Clearly He is the child who, like an innocent, did not curse when He was cursed, did not strike back when He was struck,¹¹ but rather in His very suffering prayed for His enemies saying: *Father, forgive them, for they know not what they do.*¹² Thus simplicity, which nature has given to infants, the Lord augmented with the virtue of mercy. This is the child, then, who is proposed to little ones to be imitated and followed; for He Himself says: *Take up your cross and follow me.*¹³

SERMON 55

A Sequel[1]

1. Your holiness[2] recalls, brethren, how I preached very recently that the human person is reformed into a more youthful state through righteousness and, although worn out by age, is born again into childhood by innocent behavior so that, once the mystery[3] has taken place, we may see old people turned into babes. For it is a kind of renewal to cease what you were and to take up what you had once been. This renewal, I say, is why they are called neophytes, since in a kind of newness they cast off the stains of oldness and receive the grace of simplicity, as the Apostle says: *Laying aside the old man with his practices, put on the new, which has been created according to God.*[4] Hence also holy David says: *Your youth shall be renewed like an eagle's.*[5] It is understood that by the grace of baptism what is failing in our life can live again and what had broken down in us by reason of the old age of sin can be renewed by a certain youthfulness.[6] But in order for you to see that the prophet speaks of the grace of baptism, he compares this very renewal to an eagle, a bird that by a continual changing of its vesture is said to live to a great age.[7] Its old and already decayed plumage it makes youthful with a new set of feathers so that, once renewed, when it has laid down its old covering it clothes itself in fresh garments. From this we understand that it is not an eagle's body but its plumage that feels old age. Therefore it reclothes itself, and as her feathers sprout an old mother bird becomes an eaglet again. She is to be compared to a young bird when, with pinions outspread, she has to practice flying again and gain control over the once seasoned apparatus of her wings, just as if she were a newly-hatched bird lying sluggish in its nest. For although she is well accustomed to flying, nonetheless she lacks confidence because of the sparsity of her feathers. The holy Psalmist, therefore, prophesied this with the grace of baptism in mind. For, indeed, our newly-baptized neophytes have laid aside their old vesture like eagles and have put on the new clothing of holiness.[8] They have shed their former sins like light feathers and they are adorned with the new grace of immortality. Thus in them the feeble sins of old age grow old, but life does not

grow old, for as an eagle becomes an eaglet so they become babes. From their way of life they are familiar with the world, but thanks to their renewal they are secure in righteousness.

2. Let us look still more closely at what holy David says. For he does not say that "your youth shall be renewed like the eagles' " but *like an eagle's*. He declares, then, that the youth of one eagle is to be renewed in us. I would say that this one single eagle is Christ the Lord, whose youth was renewed when He rose from the dead.[9] For when He laid aside the vesture of bodily corruption He flourished anew by taking on new flesh, as He Himself says by the prophet: *And my flesh flourished anew, and willingly I shall confess to him.*[10] *My flesh,* He says, *flourished anew.* Notice how He expresses Himself: He does not say "flourished" but *flourished anew,* for something does not flourish anew unless it had flourished before. But the flesh of the Lord flourished when first it came forth from the Virgin Mary's unsullied womb, as the prophet Isaiah says: *A shoot shall come forth from the root of Jesse and a flower shall spring up from his root.*[11] It flourished anew, however, when, the flower of the body having been cut by the Jews, it sprouted from the sepulcher with the renewed glory of the resurrection, and like a flower it breathed forth upon everyone an odor as well as the splendor of immortality—spreading around the odor of good works with its sweetness, manifesting the incorruptibility of an eternal divinity with its splendor.[12]

SERMON 56

On Pentecost[1]

1. Several days ago, brethren, as you remember, we preached not inappropriately and described how the revivified flesh of the Lord sprouted from the grave with, as it were, the beauty of a flower. The Evangelist bore witness that the tomb was located in a garden,[2] which not unfittingly we pursued. For it was appropriate that a precious flower should spring up in a garden and that the seed of good fruit committed to the earth amidst sheltered domestic and pleasant plants should bud forth salvation for all, for the resurrection of Christ is the

redemption of all peoples. In the garden, then, the Savior takes on a renewed body, and among the flowering trees and white lilies He blossoms anew in a flesh already dead, and He sprouts from the grave in such a way as to reveal all sprouting and lovely things. For after the icy burial, so to speak, of a rigorous winter all the plants made haste to bud forth so that they themselves might rise with the rising Lord. Indeed, as the result of Christ's resurrection the air is healthier, the sun warmer, and the earth more fertile; as a result of it the young branch comes into leaf, the green stalks grow into fruit, and the vine ripens into vine sprouts.[3] If all things, then, are clothed in flowers when the flesh of Christ blossoms anew, then it must be the case that when it bears fruit everything else must bear fruit as well, as the Lord says: *Unless the grain of wheat falls in the earth and dies, it remains alone, but when it dies it bears much fruit.*[4] The Lord budded forth anew, then, when He rose from the tomb; He bears fruit when He ascends to heaven. He is a flower when He springs up from the lower parts of the earth, fruit when He is re-established on the most high throne. He is grain, as He Himself says, when alone He suffers the cross, and He is fruit when He is surrounded by the very great belief of the apostles. For, having conversed with these disciples for 40 days after His resurrection, He taught them with all the wisdom of maturity, and with all the fertility of knowledge He converted them into good fruits. Then He ascended to heaven, presenting the fruit of His body to the Father, leaving the seeds of righteousness in His disciples.[5]

2. The Lord ascended, then, to the Father. Your holiness[6] remembers that I compared the Savior to that eagle of the Book of Psalms whose youth, we read, was renewed.[7] This is, to be sure, no insignificant comparison. For just as an eagle leaves behind low places, seeks high places, and mounts into the reaches near the heavens, so also the Savior left behind the low places of the underworld, sought the higher places of paradise, and penetrated the heights of the heavens. And just as an eagle, when it has abandoned the mean things of the earth and is flying on high, enjoys the wholesomeness of purer air, so also the Lord, leaving behind the filth of earthly sins and ascending in His saints, rejoices in the simplicity of a purer life. In all respects, therefore, the comparison with an eagle is appropriate to the Savior.[8]

But how shall we handle the fact that an eagle frequently snatches prey and frequently seizes what belongs to others? Yet neither in this is the Savior dissimilar, for in a manner of speaking He made off with prey when He took the human being that had been held captive in the jaws of the underworld and carried him to heaven, leading the slave who had been rescued from the captivity of another's domination— that is, diabolical power—as a captive to the heights, as it is written in the prophet: *Ascending on high He led captivity captive, He gave gifts to men.*[9] This phrase is to be understood in this way—that the captivity of the human being, whom the devil had captured for himself, the Lord captured for Himself by rescuing him, and this very captive captivity, as it says, He took to the heights of the heavens. Both captivities are called by the same name, then, but both are not equal, for the devil's captivity subjects a person to slavery, whereas Christ's captivity restores a person to liberty.

3. *Ascending,* it says, *on high He led captivity captive.* How well the prophet describes the triumph of the Lord! The parade of captives was accustomed, so they say, to precede the chariots of the triumphant kings.[10] Look, as the Lord goes into the heavens a glorious captivity does not precede Him but accompanies Him; it is not led before the car but it itself bears the Savior. For, by a kind of mystery, as the Son of God takes the son of man to heaven captivity itself is carried and carries. And what it says—*He gave gifts to men*—is a sign of the victor, for after a triumph the victor always bestows gifts, and when he is seated in his own kingdom he gives gladness to his servants. Thus also Christ, the Lord and victor, seated at the Father's right hand[11] after His triumph over the devil, has today bestowed gifts on His disciples. These are not talents of gold or ingots of silver but the heavenly gifts of the Holy Spirit that make it possible, among other graces, for the apostles even to speak in different tongues. That is to say, they make it possible for a person of the Hebrew nation to sound forth the glory of Christ with the splendor of Roman eloquence, and for the ears of foreigners who are unable to grasp preaching in the language of Judea to know, in their own speech, of the redemption of the human race.[12] Every tongue is loosed for the preaching of Christ so that every language might tell His majesty, as holy David says: *There are no languages or words whose voices are not heard.*[13]

But do not be surprised that we have said that the Son sits at the Father's right hand. For He sits at His right hand not because He is greater than the Father but that He might not be thought less than the Father,[14] as the heretics are in the habit of saying blasphemously.[15] For as divinity knows no grade of honor, so sacred Scripture knows how to prevent blasphemies.

SERMON 57

On the Lord Accused before Pilate, and On Susanna[1]

1. It might seem remarkable to you, brethren, that the Lord should be accused by the chief priests before the procurator[2] Pilate and should be silent, and that He should not refute their wickedness by His response,[3] since indeed a defense which follows quickly is the only way to refute a persistent accusation. It might seem remarkable, I say, brethren, that the Savior should be accused and should remain silent. Silence is occasionally understood as avowal, for when a person does not wish to respond to what is asked of him he appears to confirm what is raised against him. Does the Lord, then, confirm His accusation by not speaking? Clearly he does not confirm His accusation by not speaking; rather He despises it by not refuting it. For one who needs no defense does well to keep silent, but let one who fears to be overcome defend himself and one who is afraid of being vanquished hasten to speak. When Christ is condemned, however, He also overcomes, and when He is judged He also vanquishes, as the prophet says: *that you should be justified in your words, and should vanquish when you are judged.*[4] Why was it necessary for Him, therefore, to speak before being judged, when for Him judgment was a complete victory? For Christ conquers when He is judged, because in this way He is proven innocent, and hence Pilate says: *I am innocent of the blood of this just man.*[5] It is a better case, then, which is not defended and still is proved; it is a fuller righteousness that is not added to with words but is still supported by the truth. It must be that the tongue should keep silent when justice itself is present to itself. Let the tongue keep silent in a good affair, inasmuch as it has also

been accustomed to speak out in favor of bad causes. I do not want righteousness to be defended in the same manner that wickedness is usually excused. It is not by reason of speech but because of virtue that Christ vanquishes, for the Savior, who is wisdom, knows how to vanquish by keeping silent and how to overcome by not responding, and therefore He prefers to establish the truth of His case rather than to speak about it. What, in fact, would compel Him to speak when silence is enough to conquer? But perhaps fear would compel Him, lest He lose His life.[6] Yet this was precisely the reason for His victory: He lost His own life in order to gain life[7] for all; He preferred to be conquered in Himself in order to be the victor in everyone.

2. But why should I speak of Christ? The woman Susanna was silent and vanquished her enemies.[8] For she did not defend herself before Daniel the judge with much talk, she was not protected by a word of pleading, but chastity spoke on behalf of the holy woman while her tongue was silent. Susanna's chastity was present at her trial, and it defended her in the garden; in the one it provided for her modesty, in the other for her salvation; in the one it did not permit her purity to be sullied, in the other her innocence to be condemned. Susanna's chastity, then, both refutes the lascivious priests in the garden and prevails against the false accusers at her trial, and twice the victor makes guilty of perjury those whom she had made guilty of adultery. But still, what kind of judge does chastity merit? The boy Daniel, not yet of the age of puberty. Purity, then, deserves well from God since it merits a virgin judge. For chastity is sure of victory when it is to be judged by virginity. No one but a pure man dared to hear the case of purity; chastity merits such a judge, in whose presence modesty is not jeopardized.

3. Once Daniel is made aware of Susanna's position, when the ignorant mob wants to condemn her on false accusations, he says: *I am innocent of the blood of this woman.*[9] Having said this he undoes the error of a sinful people. Daniel uses the expression with respect to Susanna that Pilate used with respect to the Lord. For Pilate said: *I am innocent of the blood of this just man.* Righteousness is also acquitted with the same sentence, then, by which purity is held guiltless. But Daniel is better than Pilate, for the one does not condemn but sets free pure blood, while the other confesses and hands over righteous

blood. What did it profit to have brought forth a testimony of innocence and to have judged someone guilty of wickedness, so to speak, when in fact it is a graver sin to pronounce innocent the very same person whom one hands over as a criminal? For he is a witness of his own iniquity who acquits with his mouth and condemns in his heart. Although Pilate washed his hands,[10] nonetheless he does not wash away his deeds, and although he thought that he had wiped the blood of a just man off his hands, still his spirit is contaminated by that very blood, for one who has given Christ over to be killed has killed Him himself. The firm and just judge, lest he be responsible for the blood of an innocent person, must not give in either to envy or to fear. Therefore Daniel is better than Pilate; the former undid the error of a sinful people, but the latter confirmed the sacrilege of the raging Synagogue.

SERMON 58

A Sequel[1]

1. A few days ago we described how the trial of holy Susanna was very similar to the trial of the Savior, and how the chastity of that renowned woman was subject to the same calumnies as was the integrity of Christ, for purity bore with persecutors in the case of Susanna just as righteousness did in the case of Christ. Although she convicts the priests for their adultery, she is herself detained as if she were an adulteress; although He reprimands the Pharisees for sacrilege, He is Himself accused as sacrilegious. What indeed is a sacrilege in the Pharisees can be called a greater adultery, for an adulteration of religion is more serious than one of the body, and there is more involved in offending against divine integrity than there is in violating human integrity. Susanna, then, is condemned, and the Lord is also condemned—she because she guarded bodily chastity, He because He defended the purity of religion.

The case to be judged in each regard was similar, then, although Susanna had a better judge than the Lord. The procurator[2] judges Him, but a prophet judges her; a man who was terrified by the quarrels of the Pharisees hears Him, but a boy who was filled with the Holy Spirit hears her; one pronounces faithfully what he knows, but the other does not stand by what he pronounces, for Susanna's judge absolves and frees her, while the one who recognizes the Lord absolves Him and hands Him over. In nearly all aspects, therefore, the trial of Susanna and that of the Lord were similar, nor was the accusation in either instance dissimilar: the elders indict Susanna, while Judas accuses the Lord; her own teachers charge her, His very disciple Him. Pseudo priests,[3] I say, assail Susanna, while a pseudo bishop[4] betrays the Savior, for Judas was a bishop,[5] as the prophet says in reference to him: *May his days be few, and may another accept his episcopate.*[6] But neither does the place seem, brethren, to be dissimilar in either instance: Susanna is set upon by her accusers in her husband's garden, while the Lord is beset by His betrayers in a small garden; she submits to those who lie in wait for her in the one place, He endures His betrayer in the other.

2. But let us see the outcome of both trials. The accusers of Susanna are subjected to the prophetic sentence as false witnesses, and those who longed to condemn innocent blood are punished as being guilty of the same crime. I see, however, that the Lord's betrayer was not condemned by the judge, for Pilate does not condemn him, neither do the people condemn him, but, what is worse, he condemns himself and, after the judge's sentence has been pronounced, he is judged by his own sentence.[7] For a person whom someone else judges can perhaps be excused, but one who is condemned by the judgment of his own conscience is inexcusably guilty. A person whom someone else judges can perhaps hope for a remission of punishment from his judge, but from whom will one who judges himself seek forgiveness? Judas, referring to the price of the Lord's blood, says to the Jews: *I have sinned because I have betrayed innocent blood.*[8] It is a great witness to the Lord's innocence, therefore, that His accuser both confesses his crime and is guilty of accepting money. For as the wretched man pours out the price of his sale, he thinks that he is able to destroy his criminal contract, but he is not absolved, and in fact the shameful behavior of the Jews is confuted; although he is guilty of perpetrating this sale, they are convicted by the fact that they entered sacrilegiously into the wicked contract. The traitor Judas, then, is con-

demned by his own judgment. But perhaps it appears strange to you that the people did not judge him nor the procurator sentence him. This is the usual judgment of a sacrilegious person—that he himself should ponder over and punish his own impiousness, and that in recognizing his crime he should also avenge it. So he exceeds the sentences of everyone else, for he is condemned by his own conscience and his own sentence.[9]

3. This, I say, is the usual judgment of a sacrilegious person—that, aware of his deed, he should damn himself, as the apostle Paul says about the heretic: *Avoid a heretical person after a first and a second correction, knowing that someone of this sort is ruined and, when he does wrong, stands condemned by his own judgment.*[10] For the heretic damns himself when he casts himself out of the Catholic Church and under no compulsion leaves the gathering of the saints. He who separates himself from everyone by his own judgment shows what is merited from everyone. The heretic himself, I say, damns himself because, although all the wicked are cast out from the Christian assembly by the sentence of the bishop, the heretic departs himself, by the judgment of his own will, before anyone's wishes are expressed. The heretic is condemned, then, to the same punishment as Judas, so that the same person might be both guilty of the crime and judge of the punishment. The heretic, I say, is condemned to the same punishment as Judas. Nor is this undeserved, for the Lord whom the one sold the other blasphemes, whom the one handed over to the persecutors the other persecutes daily, for the heretic persecutes the Lord when he strips divinity from Him and claims that He is a creature.[11]

SERMON 59

A Sequel[1]

1. Your love[2] recalls that last Sunday we preached that Judas Iscariot, condemned by his own judgment, returned the price of the Lord's blood to the Pharisees and, driven by remorse, poured out the cost of the sale,[3] but he did not absolve the crime as far as his

conscience was concerned. After having brought back the money he hanged himself with a noose, so that he who had been punished with respect to his money would also be punished with respect to his life. For, knowing what a great crime he committed, it was not enough for him to deprive himself of the price of his sacrilege unless he deprived himself of his life[4] as well. He judged himself worthy of death because he had betrayed Christ, the life of all. Judas is his own most severe judge, therefore, and in his punishment he confesses the one whom he had denied by betraying Him. He gives back the money to the Pharisees, then, but the Pharisees do not take it. They say that it is not lawful for them to have it in their treasury. See what power the Lord's money has, which Judas on the one hand rejects and the Pharisees on the other do not put in their coffers! For wickedness fears to possess the cost of righteous blood.

2. Yet the Pharisees devise a plan to establish a potter's field with it, in which the bodies of travelers may be buried. I think that this, in fact, was done providentially, so that the price of the Savior would not furnish provisions for sinners but provide rest for travelers, so that it would not be for the pleasure of the sacrilegious but be used as a tomb for the dead, that from there Christ might redeem the living with His own blood's suffering and receive the dead as His precious possession.

With the cost of the Lord's blood, then, a potter's field is established. We read in the Scriptures that the salvation of the whole human race was purchased by the blood of the Savior, as the apostle Peter says: *For you have not been purchased with corruptible gold or silver but with the precious blood of the pure and spotless lamb, Jesus Christ.*[5] Therefore, if the price of our life is the blood of the Lord, see that it is not an ephemeral earthly field that has been purchased but rather the eternal salvation of the whole world. As the Evangelist says: *For Christ did not come to judge the world but in order that the world might be saved through Him.*[6] See, I say, how it is not so much a small portion of field that has been furnished with that money as the vast property of the whole world, as the prophet David says: *Ask of me and I shall give you the nations as your inheritance and the ends of the earth as your possession.*[7] This field, then, is this entire world,[8] in which we who have been dispersed and scattered bear the fruit of good work unto the Lord.

3. Yet perhaps you would inquire of me, if the field is the world, who the potter might be who could have the ownership of the world. Unless I am mistaken, the potter is the one who made the vessels of our body from clay. Of Him Scripture says: *And God made man from the clay of the earth.*[9] The potter is the one who, with the warmth of His own breath, animated the slimy clay of our flesh and, with fiery heat, molded the fluid and earthy matter. The potter, I say, is the one who fashioned us unto life with His own hands and refashioned us unto glory through His Christ, as the Apostle says: *We are being refashioned to the same image from glory to glory.*[10] That is to say that we who from our previous condition have broken to pieces because of our own misdeeds are restored in a second birth through the loving-kindness of this potter. We who have been struck by death because of Adam's transgression rise anew through the grace of the Savior. Clearly this potter is the one of whom the blessed Apostle says: *Does what is molded say to the one who has molded it?* And again: *Does the potter not have power to make from the same lump of clay one vessel for honor and another vessel for abuse?*[11] For from the same clay of our body God preserves some persons for the kingdom on account of their individual merits and keeps others for punishment.

4. The field of this potter, then, was bought with Christ's blood for travelers. For travelers, I say, who were without home or country and were cast about as exiles throughout the earth, rest is provided by the blood of Christ, so that those who have no possession in the world might have a burial place in Christ. Who do we say that these travelers are if not very devout Christians who, renouncing the world and possessing nothing in the world, rest in the blood of Christ? For the Christian who does not possess the world possesses the Savior utterly. Christ's burial place, then, is promised to travelers so that the one who preserves himself from fleshly vices like a traveler and stranger may merit Christ's rest. For what is Christ's burial place if not the Christian's rest? We, therefore, are travelers in this world, and we sojourn in this life as passers-by, as the Apostle says: *While we are in this body we are away from the Lord.*[12] We are travelers, I say, and a burial place has been bought for us at the price of the Savior's

blood. *We have been buried with Him,* the Apostle says, *through baptism in His death.*[13] Baptism, therefore, is Christ's burial place for us, in which we die to sins, are buried to evil deeds, and are restored to a renewed infancy,[14] the conscience of the old man having been dissolved in us for the sake of another birth. Baptism, I say, is the Savior's burial place for us, because there we destroy our previous way of life and there we receive a new life. Great is the grace of this burial, then, in which a beneficial death is provided for us and a more beneficial life is bestowed on us! Great, I say, is the grace of this burial, which both cleanses the sinner and gives life to the dying!

SERMON 60

To Be Given before the Birthday of the Lord[1]

1. You well know what joy and what a gathering there is when the birthday of the emperor of this world is to be celebrated; how his generals and princes and soldiers, arrayed in silk garments and girt with precious belts worked with shining gold, seek to enter the king's presence in more brilliant fashion than usual. For they believe that the emperor's joy is greater if he sees his household engaging in a more elaborate preparation and that he will be happy to the extent that they throw themselves into his celebration. And so, inasmuch as the emperor, being human, does not look into hearts, he may see their love for him by looking at how they are dressed. Thus it happens that whoever loves the king more devotedly attires himself more splendidly. And, since they know that on his birthday he will bestow generous gifts on his servants and on those who are considered to be insignificant and mean in his house, they first hasten to fill his treasuries with a variety of rich things so that an abundant largesse might not be wanting for as long as he wishes to dispense it and so that the desire of the giver might not exceed the substance of the gift. They do these things carefully, then, because they hope for a greater recompense for themselves in return for their care.[2]

2. If, therefore, brethren, those of this world celebrate the birth-

day of an earthly king with such an outlay for the sake of the glory of present honor, with what solicitude ought we to celebrate the birthday of our eternal king Jesus Christ, who in return for our devotion will bestow on us not temporal but eternal glory! Nor will He give us the administration of an earthly honor, which comes to an end when someone else inherits it, but the dignity of a heavenly empire which has no end. The prophet says what kind of reward this will be: *Eye has not seen, nor ear heard, nor has it entered into the human heart what the Lord has prepared for those who love Him.*[3] With what garments does it behoove us to be fitted out! But I have said "us," which is to say our souls, since Christ our king does not demand splendid clothing so much as loving souls. He does not look at bodily ornaments but considers the hearts of the deserving, nor does he admire the workmanship of a fragile belt girding one's loins but rather that of a strong chastity restraining wantonness for the sake of modesty. Let us seek, then, to be found before him proven in faith, bedecked with mercy, and arrayed in virtues. And whoever loves Christ more devotedly is more shiningly intent upon the observance of His commands, so that He may really see that we believe in Him when we so shine on His feast day; and the purer He sees us the happier He is.

3. Before many more days, then, let us make our hearts pure, let us cleanse our consciences and purify our spirits, and, shining and without stain, let us celebrate the coming of the spotless Lord, so that the birthday of Him whose birth was known to be from a spotless virgin may be observed by spotless servants. For whoever is dirty or polluted on that day will not observe the birthday of Christ and fulfil his obligation. Although he is bodily present at the Lord's festivity, yet in mind he is separated by a great distance from the Savior. Nor can the impure and the holy, the avaricious and the merciful, the corrupt and the virgin keep company. Indeed, an unworthy person commits an offense when he intrudes himself and does not announce himself. For, although he wishes to be courteous, he appears insulting, like the one in the Gospel who, in the midst of the saints, was invited to the wedding and dared to come without his wedding garment.[4] And although some were bright with righteousness, others were brilliant with faith, and still others were resplendent with chastity, he alone, contaminated by his filthy conscience, was despised by

all the shining ones because of his unsightliness. And the more the holiness of the blessed ones reclining at table gleamed forth, so much the more was the depravity of his sins manifest—he who would perhaps have been less displeasing had he not forced himself upon the assembly of the righteous. He was expelled, then, and carried out by his hands and feet into the outer darkness not only because he was a sinner but because, despite the fact that he was a sinner, he claimed the reward of holiness for himself.

4. Therefore, brethren, let us who are about to celebrate the Lord's birthday cleanse ourselves from all the filth of our sins.[5] Let us fill his treasuries with gifts of different kinds so that on the holy day there might be the wherewithal to give to travelers, to refresh widows, and to clothe the poor. For what sort of thing would it be if in one and the same house, among the servants of a single master, one should vaunt himself in silk and another should be completely covered[6] in rags; if one should be warm with food and another should endure hunger and cold; if, out of indigestion, one should be belching what he had drunk yesterday and another should not have compensated for yesterday's dearth of food? And what will be the effect of our praying?[7] We ask to be freed from the enemy,[8] we who are not generous with our brethren. Let us be imitators of our Lord! For if He wished the poor to be sharers with us in heavenly grace, why should they not be sharers with us in earthly goods?[9] Nor should those who are brethren as far as the sacraments[10] are concerned be strangers as far as means of sustenance are concerned; indeed, we shall plead our case before God better through them, so that at our expense we ought to feed those who will give thanks to Him. However much a poor person blesses the Lord, it profits the one whose deed prompts the blessing. And as it is written of one: *Woe to that person through whom the name of the Lord is blasphemed,*[11] so it is written of another: *Peace to the person through whom the name of the Lord, the Savior, is blessed.*[12] But what is the recompense of the giver? That someone should act in the quiet of his own home and through many should beseech the Lord in the Church, and that while perhaps he would not dare to petition the Divinity, by reason of the prayers of many petitioners he might receive even what he was not hoping for.[13] Recalling this assistance of ours the blessed Apostle says: *that thanks*

might be given by many on our behalf;[14] and again: *that your offering might be acceptable, sanctified in the Holy Spirit.*[15]

SERMON 61

A Sequel on the Coming Birthday of the Lord[1]

1. Last Sunday I believe that I spoke sufficiently and at length about how we ought to celebrate the birthday of the Lord in brilliant and shining fashion and to reflect upon His coming feast with every desire to please—to reflect upon it, I say, so that even when the solemn day passes, still the happiness of His sanctification may remain with us. For this is the saving Lord's birthday grace—that it should pass into the future for the sake of the predestined and remain in the past for the sake of the devout. It behooves us, then, to be pure in holiness, clean in chastity, and shining in virtue, so that when we see the festal day approaching more closely we may enter into it more carefully. For if housewives who are about to celebrate some feasts are in the habit of washing the stains out of their clothes with water, why do not we who are about to observe the Lord's birthday all the more wash out the stains of our souls with tears? And if these insignificant things are very filthy, so that water alone cannot remove the stains, they add a soft oil soap and rub them harshly. And we too, if our sin is so serious that it cannot be washed away with tears alone, add the oil of mercy and the harshness of fasting. For no misdeed is so serious that it cannot be cleansed by abstinence and extinguished by almsgiving. And indeed the holy prophet says: *As water extinguishes a fire, so almsgiving extinguishes sin.*[2]

2. Great, therefore, is almsgiving, which cools the masses of burning offenses with the water of its kindness and by the moisture, as it were, of its generosity overcomes the flames of misdeeds so that, although God is displeased and provoked by the offenses, because of almsgiving He is compelled to free the one whom He had determined to punish because of his sins. Indeed, He is compelled by us to a certain extent inasmuch as He is obliged to change His judgment on account of our actions, and with respect to one and the same person

He is sometimes moved by a judge's severity, and sometimes He invites with a father's love. For God is a father to us when we act well, and He is our judge when we sin. On account of our works, then, the Lord is constrained to bestow His mercy on us, and therefore He Himself says in the holy Gospel: *From the days of John the Baptist the kingdom of heaven is taken by force.*[3]

Let us see what meaning this phrase has. The kingdom of heaven is nothing other than Christ the Lord, who reigns in the heavens.[3a] The word "forced"—that is, "condensed"[4]—is ordinarily used when something liquid is solidified by constant activity. Hence, therefore, John the Baptist announced the coming of the Savior, from which the kingdom of heaven proceeded, which first lay fluid and slack among the Jews and began to solidify by the activity of believing peoples; then all that liquidity of the kingdom started to take solid form as a result of frequent preaching. For so liquid was the kingdom among the Jews that it went over to the Gentiles, so fluid was it that it spread to the nations. Now, however, it is forced or condensed with such a density of believers that it remains fixed and solid forever, as Scripture says: *And of His kingdom there will be no end.*[5]

3. We force the kingdom of heaven, then, and exercise a certain violence, as the Gospel reading says: *And the violent seize it.*[6] We exercise violence on the Lord, I say, not by constraint but by weeping, not by provoking with insults but by beseeching with tears, not by blaspheming through pride but by becoming deserving through humility. O blessed violence that is not mottled with provocation but devoted to mercy! Blessed violence, I say, that elicits kindness from the one who suffers the violence and is beneficial to the one who inflicts it! An evil thing is perpetrated and religion is advanced. For whoever is more violent to Christ is considered more devout by Christ. We approach the Lord on the road, then, since indeed He Himself is the way,[7] and, as thieves do, we endeavor to despoil Him of what is His. We desire to snatch from Him His kingdom, His treasures, and His life, but He is so rich and generous that He does not refuse or resist and, although He gives everything away, still He keeps everything. We approach Him, I say, not with a sword or a club or a rock but with gentleness, good works, and chastity. These are the arms of our faith, with which we contend in the struggle. But, that we may be able to use these arms in inflicting violence, let us first

exercise a measure of violence on our own bodies and cast out the evil deeds of our members so that we may attain the rewards of virtue. For we ought first to exercise control over ourselves so that we may be able to seize the Savior's kingdom.[8]

4. For this reason the Gospel says: *And the violent seize it.* We are plunderers, therefore, but plunderers seize nothing except what belongs to others. I acknowledge this as true, for the Church snatched Christ from the Synagogue, and foreign nations, by exercising violence, possess the kingdom. The Savior—sent under the law, born in the law, and brought up according to the law[9]—is taken possession of by the Gentiles inasmuch as He is neglected by the Jews, and He is found by sinners inasmuch as He is lost by priests, as He Himself says: *Publicans and sinners precede you in the kingdom of heaven.*[10] We are plunderers, therefore. No wonder, since we descend from that sort of ancestor! For it is written of our forefather Benjamin that he was a rapacious wolf,[11] since he seized what was not his. So we also, as offspring of a rapacious wolf, snatch away the shepherd of others' sheep by means of our desire, as He Himself says: *I have not been sent except to the lost sheep of the house of Israel.*[12] Christ is seized, then, when He is deserted by the Jews and preached by foreigners. Christ is seized when He is slain by the Jews and buried by us. Christ is seized by His watchful disciples and lost by the sleeping Pharisees, as they themselves acknowledged in lying fashion when they placed guards at the sepulcher after the Lord's resurrection, saying *that His disciples came at night and stole Him while we were sleeping.*[13] Hence we understand spiritually that all those who sleep lose Christ and all those who stay awake find Him. And therefore the Apostle says: *Wake up, you who sleep, and arise from the dead, and Christ will shine upon you.*[14] You see, then, that one who sleeps thus is dead, so that he does not keep watch over the Savior; and consequently those Pharisees, like dead men, were unable to keep hold of a living man. Therefore, brethren, let us not sleep, but let us keep watch over the Lord our Savior, so that with guards constantly posted no one may remove him from the sepulcher of our heart, nor shall we ever say: "They came and stole him while we were sleeping." For we have enemies who make an effort to remove Christ from our hearts if we are sleeping. Hence let us keep Him with unremitting solicitude in the

sepulcher of our souls. There let Him rest, there sleep, there rise when He desires.

Sermon 61a

Given before the Birthday of the Lord[1]

1. Even if I should be silent, brethren, the season warns us that the birthday of the Lord Christ is very near, since the extreme conclusion of the cycle of days has anticipated my preaching. For by this very brevity the world tells us that something is about to happen by which it will be restored to a better state, and with increasing longing it wishes for the brilliance of the shining sun to cast light on its darkness. While it dreads to have its course come to an end because of the shortness of the hours, it shows by a kind of hope that its year is to be formed anew. This longing on the part of creation,[2] then, also persuades us to long that the new sun,[3] the risen Christ, may cast light upon the darkness of our sins, and that by the power of His birth the sun of justice[4] may scatter the protracted gloom of sin in us; and it persuades us not to let the course of our life come to a close with shocking abruptness but to let it be extended thanks to His power. Therefore, since we know the birthday of the Lord because the world points to it, let us also do what the world is accustomed to do; that is to say, just as on that day the world extends the period of its light, so let us also prolong our righteousness. And just as the brightness of that day is common to poor and rich, so let our generosity also be common to travelers and needy folk. And just as the world has then thrown off the gloom of its nights, so let us also cut off the darkness of our avarice. And, as is the case in the winter season, just as seeds are sustained in the ground when the frost is broken up by the sun's warmth, so let the sluggish seed of righteousness in our hearts grow strong when our hardness is broken up by the Savior's radiance.

2. Therefore, brethren, let us who are about to celebrate the Lord's birthday adorn ourselves in pure and shining garments. I speak, however, of the soul's garments and not of those for the flesh. For the garment intended for the flesh is a mean piece of clothing, but

the soul's vesture is a precious object; the one has been put together by human hands, the other has been formed by the hands of God. And therefore more care is required to preserve the work of God without stain than to keep human works unsullied. For if worldly clothing gets dirty a hired launderer can wash it out, but if the soul's garb once gets soiled it can hardly be cleaned except by special and unremitting works. The hand of a skilled worker is of no avail, neither is a launderer's toil, for water can wash the polluted parts of one's conscience but it cannot clean them. These are the soul's precious garments, which the Evangelist Mark praises in the Savior when he says: *And His clothes became shining, exceedingly white like snow, such as no launderer on earth could make them.*[5] Christ's raiment is praised, then, because it shone not on account of its texture but on account of grace. His raiment is praised not because it was put together with fine weaving but because it was conceived in bodily integrity. His garment is praised not because women's hands wove it but because Mary's virginity begot it. And therefore the grace of brilliance is magnified in Him, for it was not the care of a skilled worker that made it stainless. *Such as no launderer on earth*, he says, *could make them.* Obviously a launderer is unable to do such with Christ's clothing, for a launderer can produce brightness, cleanness, and purity, but he cannot produce virginity, righteousness, or goodness: the one is a question of skilled work, the other is in the realm of virtue. The holy Evangelist praises these garments of virtue in the Lord Christ, which blessed David also preached in a similar way when he said: *myrrh and aloes and cassia from your precious garments.*[6] By these odors of holy aromas the garments of virtue are signified.

3. Therefore, brethren, let us who are about to celebrate the Lord's birthday cleanse our conscience from all filth.[7] Let us array ourselves not in silken vesture but in precious works. For shining garments can cover limbs but they cannot adorn the conscience, and in fact it is all the more shameful to go about with handsome limbs while the senses within are foul. Let us first, therefore, adorn the disposition of the interior person so that the clothing of the exterior person may be adorned as well. Let us wash away spiritual stains so that our fleshly robes might shine on us. It is of no profit to wear shining robes and to be filthy with criminal deeds, for where the conscience is dark the whole body is in shadow. But we have the

means of washing away the stains of our conscience, for it is written: *Give alms and everything is clean for you.*[8] Good is the command to give alms, by which we act with our hands and are cleansed in our heart.

SERMON 62

On the Birthday of Our Lord Jesus Christ[1]

1. Well it is that people frequently call this day of the Lord's birth "the new sun" and assert it with such force that even the Jews and pagans agree to the name.[2] This should willingly be accepted by us, since with the rising of the Savior there is salvation not only for the human race, but even the brilliance of the sun itself is renewed, as the Apostle says: *that He should restore all things through Him, whether in the heavens or on the earth.*[3] For if the sun is darkened when Christ suffers,[4] it must necessarily shine more brightly than usual when He is born. And if it poured forth darkness upon the Jews who dealt Him death, why should it not show its brilliance to Mary who brought Him into life? And why should we not believe that when Christ was born a more resplendent sun should come to pay Him homage, since a brighter star went before the Magi as a sign?[5] And if a star performed a service out of season during the day, why should we not believe that the sun also subtracted a little from the night hours by a speedier appearance?

I think, then, that for these reasons the night waned while the hastening sun, out of homage due the Lord's birth, produced light for the world before the night had finished its accustomed course. Indeed, I do not even say that this was a night—wherein shepherds keep watch, angels rejoice,[6] and the stars attend—or that it had any element of darkness. Nor ought we to be surprised that at the birth of Christ all things were made new,[7] since the fact that a virgin bore a child was itself a new thing. But, if this birth was out of the ordinary, the homage that was offered was also out of the ordinary. At the birth of the Lord, then, shepherds keep watch, angels rejoice, the sun shows reverence, and a star is in attendance. And the angels and the shepherds speak their joy in their own tongues and in words, but the elements, since they have no voice, bear witness to these joys of theirs by their ministry. The sun, consequently, contrary to custom, shone early in the morning on this festival. Nor is this surprising, for if at the prayer of Joshua, the son of Nun, it stood fixed throughout the day,[8] why, at the birth of Jesus Christ, should it not advance hastily in the night?

2. The people, then, call this day "the new sun" and, although they say that it is new, yet they also show that it is old. This world's sun—which undergoes eclipse, is shut out by walls, and is hidden by clouds—I would call old. I would call old the sun that is subject to vanity, is fearful of corruption,[9] and dreads the judgment. For it is written: *The sun will be changed into darkness and the moon into blood.*[10] Old, indeed, would I call that which is implicated in human crimes, does not flee adulteries, does not turn aside from murder, and, although it does not wish to be in the midst of the human race when some offense is perpetrated, stands here alone amongst all the evil deeds.

Therefore, inasmuch as it has been shown to be old, we have discovered that nothing is new but Christ the Lord, of whom it is written: *The sun of justice will rise upon you,*[11] and of whom the prophet also says in the person of sinners: *The sun has not risen upon us, and the light of justice has not shone upon us.*[12] For, when the whole world was oppressed by the darkness of the devil and the gloom brought on by sin was laying hold of the world, at the last age—that is to say, when night had already fallen—this sun deigned to bring forth the rising of His birth. At first, before the light—that is, before the sun of justice shone—He sent the oracle of the prophets as a kind of dawning, as it is written: *I sent my prophets before the light.*[13] But afterwards He Himself burst forth with His rays—that is, with the brightness of His apostles—and shed upon the earth a light of truth such that no one would stumble into the devil's darkness.

This, then, is the new sun that penetrates the places that are shut, unlocks the nether regions, and enters hearts. This is the new sun that, by His Spirit, gives life to what is dead, restores what is decayed, and raises what has already died, and that, by His warmth, cleanses what is filthy, burns away what is weak, and melts away what is wicked. He is, I say, the one who gazes upon all our works in everything that we do and not so much condemns our misdeeds as corrects them. He is clearly the just and wise sun that, like the sun of this world, revolves without prejudice over good and bad alike[14] but, by a certain truthful judgment, casts light upon the holy and slays the sinner. And this is the difference between the two suns, that the one fears judgment and the other threatens judgment, that the one is a slave of corruption[15] and the other is Lord of eternity, that the one is a creature and the other the Creator.

3. Nonetheless, when day has not yet broken, it is customary, according to human usage arising from need, for a lamp to precede the earth's sun before it appears. Christ the sun also has His own lamp, which preceded His coming, as the prophet says: *I have prepared a lamp for my Christ.*[16] What this lamp is the Lord shows when He says of John the Baptist: *He was a burning lamp.*[17] But John himself, as the small light of the lamp that went ahead, says: *Behold, one is coming after me the strap of whose sandals I am not worthy to loose. He will baptize you in the Holy Spirit and in fire.*[18] Likewise, realizing that his light was going to be overwhelmed by the rays of the sun, he foretells: *He must increase, but I must decrease.*[19] For, as the brightness of a lamp is done away with by the coming of the sun, so also John's baptism of repentance[20] was rendered void when the grace of Christ overtook it.

4. Now let us see from what source this our new sun is born. Indeed, God is the progenitor from whom He arises. The Son, therefore, is divine—of a Divinity, I say, that is incorrupt, whole, and inviolate. I understand clearly that this is a mystery. For this reason his second birth was of the immaculate Mary—because she had been rendered inviolate beforehand by the Divinity,[20a] so that the second birth of Him whose first birth was glorious might not be demeaning —that is to say, that just as a virginal Divinity had brought Him forth,[21] so also the virgin Mary would conceive Him.

It is also written that among men He had a father, as we read in the Gospel when the Pharisees say: *Is not this the son of Joseph the workman, and is not his mother Mary?*[22] In this also I perceive a mystery. The Father of Christ is called a workman. Clearly God the Father is a workman—He who fashioned the structure of the whole world. Clearly He is a workman who, in the flood, built Noah's ark with the skill of a workman.[23] He is a workman, I say, who set up Moses' tent,[24] constructed the ark of the covenant,[25] and erected Solomon's temple.[26] I would call Him a workman who refines unyielding minds, cuts away proud thoughts, and raises humble deeds. This workman also applies the iron to trees, as we read in the Gospel when John says: *The axe has already been placed to the roots of the trees. Every tree that does not produce good fruit will be cut down and thrown into the fire.*[27] All this He does so that in the time to come He may bring together the useful trees of the heavenly workshop, but that the unfruitful ones, which have been pulled up by their roots, He may destroy in a blazing fire.[28]

SERMON 63

On the Kalends of January[1]

1. I have no small complaint against a great number of you, brethren. I speak of those who, while celebrating the Lord's birthday with us, have given themselves over to pagan feasts and, after the heavenly banquet,[2] have prepared a meal of superstition for themselves, so that those who beforehand had taken delight in holiness are afterwards besotted with foolishness. They do not realize that a person who wishes to reign with Christ cannot rejoice with the world, and that one who wishes to find righteousness must turn away from wantonness. The goal of eternal life and the hopelessness[3] of this-worldly licentiousness are two different things: one ascends to the former by virtue but descends to the latter in perdition. Therefore the person who wishes to be a participant in divine things may not enjoy the companionship of idols, for the idol's portion is to besot the mind with wine, to distend the stomach with food, to torture the limbs with dancing, and to be so busied with evil deeds that you cannot help but be unaware of the existence of God. Hence the holy Apostle, foreseeing these things, says: *What portion does righteousness have with*

wickedness? Or what fellowship is there of light with darkness? Or what partnership does a believer have with an unbeliever? What agreement is there between the temple of God and idols?[4] If, then, we are the temple of God,[5] why is the festival of idols observed in the temple of God? Why is gourmandizing, drunkenness, and licentiousness brought into the place where Christ dwells, who is abstinence, temperance, and chastity? The Savior says: *No one can serve two masters—that is, God and mammon.*[6]

2. How, then, are you able to celebrate the Lord's Epiphany religiously when, with your greatest devotion, you have celebrated the kalends of Janus? For Janus was a human being, the founder of a city that is called Janiculum,[7] in whose honor the kalends of January have been named by the pagans. Hence the person who celebrates the kalends of January commits sin because he offers divine homage to a dead man. This is why the Apostle says: *You observe days and months and seasons and years. I fear that I may have labored among you in vain.*[8] One who has observed a day or a month is one who has either not fasted on these days or not gone to church. Whoever observed a day yesterday went not to church but to a field.[9] Therefore, brethren, let us turn away with all our might from the festivity and the feasts of the pagans so that, when they banquet and enjoy themselves, we might be sober and fasting, thereby making them realize that their pleasure is condemned by our abstinence.

3. We ought to avoid, though, the companionship not only of the pagans but also of the Jews, with whom even a conversation is a great contamination. For with their artfulness they ingratiate themselves with people, get into homes, enter into the palaces of governors, and disturb the ears of judges and of the common folk, and the more shameless they are the more influential they are.[10] And this is not something new as far as they are concerned: it is an inveterate and ancient evil. For once already they persecuted the Lord and Savior within the governor's palace and condemned Him with the judge's approval. In the governor's palace, then, innocence is oppressed by the Jews, hidden things are revealed, and religion is condemned. For, when Christ is slain, all truth and righteousness is condemned in Him, since He Himself is innocence, holiness, and mystery. Amen.

SERMON 64

On Epiphany[1]

1. There are very many who, on this holy day of Epiphany, commemorate the marvelous deeds enacted by the Lord at the time when, upon having been importuned at a wedding feast, He changed the substance of water into the appearance of wine and, by His blessing, turned spring water to a better use.[2] The servants who had drawn water from the wells discovered wine in the jugs and, by a profitable loss, what they had filled them with disappeared and they found what had not been there. With this marvelous sign the power of His divinity was made manifest for the first time.

Some, however, refer on this holy day to His having been baptized by John in the Jordan.[3] In the grace of His washing, God the Father was present in voice, and the Holy Spirit came down. Nor is it remarkable if the mystery of the Trinity was not absent at the Lord's washing, since the sacrament of the Trinity[4] makes our washing complete. For the Lord had to demonstrate first in Himself what He would afterwards demand of the human race, since He accomplished everything not for His own sake but for our salvation. Or did He wish to be baptized on his own account even when He had no sin? As the prophet says: *He did no sin, nor was deceit found in His mouth.*[5] But [He was baptized][6] for our sake—we who, subject to punishment because of our many crimes and sins, needed to be cleansed in Christ's baptism. And therefore the Lord came to the washing not so that He Himself might be purified by the waters but so that the streams of waters might purify us, for He went down into the waters, thereby destroying the sins of all believers. But it was necessary that He who bore the sins of all should destroy the sins of all, as the Evangelist says: *This is the lamb of God, this is the one who takes away the sins of the world.*[7] In a wonderful way, then, one man goes down into the waters and the salvation of all is restored.

2. God the Father is present, then, when the Lord is baptized, and the Holy Spirit is present. See the kindness of the Savior because of which, in His suffering, He submitted Himself all alone to outrages:

alone in His washing He did not seek grace, alone He does not wish to partake of glory. He is present, therefore, as I have said; the Father is present and also the Holy Spirit. And inasmuch as God cannot be seen, the Spirit descended as a dove and the Father as a voice. And this manifestation of the Savior was only necessary to build up the faith of human beings, for our faith depends on nothing but hearing and seeing; consequently the Spirit submits Himself to our eyes as a dove and the Father gives Himself over to our ears in a voice.

Now it would not have been necessary for these things to happen except for the sake of our belief; the Father and the Spirit, as God unseen, could have come down upon the Word, the Son, by an unseen descent. For the sake of our faith, then, when heaven was opened, the Spirit came down to Christ, the Father to the Son, a voice to the Word. For Christ is the Word, of whom it is written: *In the beginning was the Word.*[8] Rightly, I say, is the Father called a voice and the Son the Word, because a word comes only from a voice. Voice and Word belong together, then, and in mysterious conjunction they provide for human salvation.

But let us see why the Holy Spirit came upon Christ in the form of a dove. Is there some similarity between the dove and the Lord, as there is between the voice and the Word? Clearly there is no small similarity, for I would also call the Lord Himself a dove, since He is quick, gentle, and simple. He is a dove because He commands His holy ones to be as doves when He says: *Be simple as doves.*[9] But the prophet speaks of what Christ the dove is when, in His person, he describes His return to heaven after His suffering: *Who will give me wings like a dove, and I shall fly away and be at rest?*[10] When Christ the Lord, therefore, initiated the sacraments of the Church a dove came down from heaven. I understand the mystery and I recognize the sacrament. For the very dove that once hastened to Noah's ark in the flood[11] now comes to Christ's Church in baptism. Then it announced safety to the one with an olive branch, now it bestows eternity on the other with a token of divinity; then it bore a sign of peace in its mouth, now it pours out peace itself—Christ, in His own substance.

3. In the Jordan, then, the Lord is baptized. The Scripture recounts that many marvelous deeds were frequently done in this river. It says, among other things: *And the Jordan turned back.*[12] But I think that what happened when the Lord Jesus Christ was there was more

marvelous. For in the past the waters turned back, but now sins are turned back; and just as the surging river left its bed then, so also now the surge of sins withdraws from a person in error. I think that this already happened in the time of the prophet Elijah. For just as Elijah made a division of waters in the Jordan,[13] so also Christ the Lord worked a separation of sins in the same Jordan: the one commanded the waters to stand still, the other sins. And just as under Elijah the waters sought the primordial sources from which they had come, so also under Christ the Lord human beings have turned back to their beginning, from which they had sprung in infancy.

SERMON 65

Given after Epiphany[1]

1. I believe that my preaching on the holy day of Epiphany reached all of you, brethren, especially you catechumens. In it we spoke to those who assert that water was changed into wine then[2] and also to the many who testify that the Lord was baptized in the Jordan on that day.[3] Although it is believed by different people that only one of these took place, nonetheless I hold that both took place and that one is a sign of the other, for both took place. For when the Lord was baptized He instituted the mystery of washing and also, by contact with the Divinity,[4] changed the human race—brackish water, as it were—into an eternal substance. Likewise, when He turned the jars full of spring water into wine He did both things: He presented something far better to the wedding feast and also showed that, by the washing, the bodies of human beings are to be filled with the substance of the Holy Spirit. The Lord declared this in clearer fashion elsewhere when He said that new wine was to be stored in new skins,[5] for in the newness of the skins the purity of the washing is signified, and in the wine the grace of the Holy Spirit.

2. Therefore it behooved you catechumens to have listened to this quite closely. There is greater need that your understanding, which is now as chilly as water because of ignorance of the Trinity, should become as warm as wine with a knowledge of the mystery, and that

the brackish and weak liquid of your souls may be decanted into a precious and strong grace. Thus, instead of wine we may taste what is good and be redolent of what is sweet, and hence we can say, in the words of the Apostle: *For we are the good odor of Christ to God.*[6] For a catechumen is like water, cold and pale, before he is baptized, but a believer is strong and red like wine. A catechumen, I say, is like water, having no taste or smell, valueless, useless, unpleasant to drink, and unable to keep.[7] For just as water spoils and smells when it is kept a long time and has deteriorated within itself, so also a catechumen becomes worthless and goes to ruin when he remains a catechumen a long time, for he deteriorates within himself.[8] As the Lord says: *Unless one is born again from water and the Holy Spirit he will not enter into the kingdom of heaven.*[9] The one who does not enter into the kingdom, however, necessarily remains in hell. But rightly is the faithful compared to wine, for just as every part of the whole creation goes to ruin as it gets older and only wine improves with age, so, while all are perishing of old age from throughout the human race, only the Christian improves with age. And just as wine acquires a pleasant savor and a sweet odor as its bitterness diminishes from one day to the next, so also the Christian takes upon himself the wisdom[10] of the Divinity and the agreeable aroma of the Trinity as the bitterness of his sins diminishes with the passing of time.

3. On this holy day, then, the Lord was baptized. See how well He ordained that He should be born on His birthday and reborn on the Epiphany, so that the vows[11] of human salvation might not be too distant from Him and that we might constantly give eternal thanks to the Savior. Then our vows were also solemnized, when the Church was united to Christ, as John says: *The one who has the bride is the bridegroom.*[12] Because of this marriage, therefore, it behooves us to dance, for David, at once king and prophet, is also said to have danced before the ark of the covenant with much singing.[13] In high rejoicing he broke into dancing, for in the Spirit he foresaw that through Mary, born of his own line, the Church was to be joined in Christ's chamber;[14] about this he says: *And He, like a bridegroom, came forth from His chamber.*[15] Thus he sang more than the other prophetic authors because, gladder than the rest of them, by these joys he united those coming after him in marriage. And to his own vows he invited, with more than customary charm, all the nations,

and he taught us what we ought to do at this wedding feast, inasmuch as, before the wedding feast, he rejoiced in utter joy.

SERMON 66

On Holy Quadragesima[1]

1. A few days ago, while preaching on the observance of holy Quadragesima, we produced examples from the sacred writings in order to prove that this number 40 was not of human origin but divinely consecrated, not initiated by earthly deliberation but commanded by the heavenly majesty. And therefore a person who fails to observe the established number by eating on one day is not accused of being the violator of one day but is charged with having transgressed the whole of Quadragesima. Hence it is good for a person to strive after the holiness of all of Quadragesima to an equal degree in order to fast without difficulty on a particular day. These are not so much the commands of priests,[2] however, as they are of God, and consequently the one who disdains them disdains not a priest but Christ,[3] who speaks in His priest.

2. Let us see, then, when the Lord enjoined this observance on us, whether He did not wish all the elements to make progress through this devotion.[4] For look, when Quadragesima is proclaimed the earth that had been held in bonds by the winter frost is set free, and when the ice has melted the flowing streams course again. Thus also, in this same season, the sins that have been occasioned by the crimes of our flesh are pardoned, and when the diabolic chill has been dispelled our renewed life returns to its original course. Once Quadragesima has been proclaimed the earth, I say, lays aside the harshness of winter, and once Quadragesima has been proclaimed I reject the harshness of my sins. The earth is cut by plows so that it might be suitable for heavenly seeds. For as one who works a field by frequently digging it up receives a more abundant return, so also one who works the field of his body by frequently fasting receives a greater grace. For look, during the time of abstinence the young crop of standing corn grows

again into harvest corn, the tree's young twig bursts into fruit, the vine branch buds forth, and all things raise themselves from the depths to the heights. Thus in this same season people's faint hope is made alive again, lost faith is restored to glory, temporal life advances into eternity, and the whole human race, raising itself from the depths to the heights, mounts together to the heavenly regions. Now the farmer, wielding his knife, prunes the vine twigs, as now also the bishop,[5] preaching the gospel, cuts off the sins of his people. And in this space of 40 days all creatures do this, so that they may lay aside what is superfluous and may proceed well prepared and adorned to Easter.

3. Now all things are in travail so that later they may be found fruitful. For then, contrary to nature, the thorn produces the rose, the reed shines with the lily, withered bushes give forth sweetness, and everything is so laden with flowers that creation itself seems to celebrate the festivity of the great day with its own resplendence. During this time of fasting, therefore, we also produce roses from our thorns—that is to say, righteousness from sins, gentleness from severity, and generosity from avarice. For these are the thorns of our body, which suffocate the soul, about which Scripture says: *The earth will bring forth thorns and thistles to you.*[6] My earth brings forth thorns to me if it pricks me with the tickling of bodily wantonness; it begets thistles to me when it torments me with the desire for worldly riches. The root of his avarice is a thorn to the Christian, and ambition for honor is a thorn to the good person; to all appearances they seem to be beautiful, but they are harmful. We are not able to be free of them, therefore, except by watchfulness and fasting, and indeed by abstinence the thorns themselves are turned into a rose. For by fasting wantonness produces purity, pride humility, and drunkenness sobriety. These are the flowers of our life, which sweetly give forth an aroma to Christ and which breathe forth a good odor to God, whence the Apostle says: *For we are the good odor of Christ to God.*[7]

4. The Lord, then, has given us these 40 days so that during this time we may conceive the seeds of the virtues after the fashion of the whole of creation, and thus on the day of Easter we shall produce the fruit of righteousness. For a space of 40 days the Lord Christ Himself was exercised, not in order that He Himself might grow but in order to show us the growth of salvation.[8] For in Him there was no thorn of

sin that would be changed into a flower: He was Himself a flower, born not of a thorn but of a shoot, as the prophet says: *A shoot shall come forth from the root of Jesse and a flower shall spring up from his root.*[9] The shoot was Mary, fertile, delicate, and virginal,[10] who brought forth Christ like a flower in the integrity of her body. During the course of 40 days and nights, then, the Lord observed this fast without hungering, but the Evangelist says that He was hungry afterwards.[11] Yet how could it be that one who did not feel hunger and thirst for so many days would be hungry afterwards? Clearly He was hungry, nor can we deny that He was hungry, for He hungered not for the food of human beings but for their salvation, and He wished not for banquets of worldly foods but desired the holiness of heavenly souls.[12] For Christ's food is the redemption of the peoples, Christ's food is the accomplishment of the Father's will, as He Himself says: *But my food is to do the will of the Father who sent me.*[13] Hence let us also hunger for the food that is not provided in earthly banquets but that is drawn from the reading of the divine Scriptures.[14] For the one nourishes the body in time, but the other refreshes the soul for eternity.

SERMON 67

A Sequel on Quadragesima[1]

1. Last year we frequently gave an account of holy Quadragesima, the beginning of which we are celebrating today, and we often explained why we fast for so many days. For we said that the Lord Jesus Christ consecrated this same number by His fast and that by not taking food for 40 successive days and nights He established one period of fasting.[2] That is to say that, although the course of day was broken by the coming of night, nonetheless the course of fasting was not broken. Hence with the Lord there were indeed many successive moments but one day of abstinence, showing us that we ought to fast this whole number through in such a way that, since we are unable to fulfil[3] Quadragesima by one uninterrupted fast, we nonetheless celebrate Quadragesima by an uninterrupted succession of daily fasts.

Thus if anyone omits a single day of abstinence he violates all of Quadragesima and loses the fruit of much labor for the sake of food eaten in a short time.[4]

2. But suppose someone says: "We have heard the reason for Quadragesima from time to time and we have frequently been told that it was consecrated by the Lord, but we want to know why this same Quadragesima has 42 days."[5] We read in the Old Testament that, when holy Moses rescued the children of Israel from the yoke of the bondage of Egypt in order to lead them into the promised land, he came to the aforementioned land in stages of 42 days.[6] And he took possession of what was promised through the same number of times as that by which we also rejoice in the enjoyment of the things that have been promised us by the Savior. By the same number of stages, I say, that Moses came to the place of rest we also hasten to heaven by fasts.[7] For fasts are our stages, so to speak, by which we proceed along through strength of soul as we make our spiritual journey, and by daily progress we come closer to the land promised us, in such a way that the one who fasts more devoutly arrives more quickly. The swift feet of the soul, so to speak, are faith and fasting, which quickly go up from the depths to the heights, quickly ascend from the earth to the heavens. About these feet the Apostle said: *How beautiful are the feet of those who announce peace, of those who announce good things!*[8] The Lord has commanded these feet to be washed, as the Apostle says with respect to the widow: *if she washes the feet of the saints.*[9] For worthy of honor are the feet of those who announce peace, which ascend—spiritual and resplendent in their teaching—through human hearts.

3. Over the space of 42 days the people of Israel came to the streams of the Jordan, and over the same period the Christian people comes to the streams of baptism. And as the prophet says: *The Jordan turned back.*[10] In the one case when the Israelite went into the deeps of the river the water avoided him, while in the other when the Christian goes down into the font the sins of his evil deeds are scattered. And in a marvelous way the river that has been turned back returns to its origins in the one case, while in the other a human being who has been called back is restored to his infant beginnings.[11] In the one case the water seeks the source from which it had sprung forth,

while in the other innocence recognizes the person from whom it had departed. In the one case the river bed is emptied of its streams, while in the other hearts are rid of their misdeeds, so that in the former the muddy water does not drench the servants of God, while in the latter a soiled conscience does not pollute the servants of Christ. For the Jordan is a kind of bath through which the person who is entering the promised land passes, leaving his filth behind. In this number 42, then, the people of Israel leave Egypt and pass over the waters of the Red Sea, and we also leave the Egypt of this world[12] and cross over the waters of burning Gehenna. The water does not touch them in the stream, nor does the flame burn us in the fire; for them the water is made solid and for us the flame is cooled. And, contrary to nature's custom, the sea is dried up by heat,[13] while Gehenna is tamed by the baptismal font.

4. In this mystical number, I say, the children of Israel, arriving at Marah and being unable to draw the water because of its bitterness (for the well had water but no sweetness, and it was pleasing to the eye but polluted to the taste), drank water that became sweet and mild as soon as wood was thrown into it by Moses:[14] the sacrament of the wood[15] removed the harshness that the noxious water bore. I believe that this happened as a sign,[16] for I think that the bitter water of Marah is the Old Testament law, which was harsh before it was tempered by the Lord's cross.[17] For it used to command *an eye for an eye and a tooth for a tooth*[18] and, austere as it was, it offered none of mercy's consolation. But, when it had been tempered by the wood of gospel suffering, at once it changed its bitterness into mildness and presented itself as a sweet drink to all, as the prophet says: *How sweet are your words to my taste, more than honey and the honeycomb to my mouth!*[19] For sweet are the words that command: *If anyone strikes you on your cheek, offer him the other as well; if anyone takes your tunic from you, leave him your cloak too.*[20] This, then, is the bitterness that has been changed into sweetness: the austerity of the law has been tempered by the grace of the gospel. For the letter of the law is bitter without the mystery of the cross; about this the Apostle says: *The letter kills.*[21] But when the sacraments of the passion are joined to it, all its bitterness is spiritually buried, and about that the Apostle says: *But the Spirit gives life.*[22]

SERMON 68

A Sequel[1]

1. You still remember, brethren, that last Sunday we preached that those 42 stages by which the people of Israel entered the promised land by a daily advance after they had left Egypt,[2] mounting as it were by saving steps from the yoke of slavery to the kingdom, contained an image of this our Quadragesima. There was in those stages, I say, an image of our fasts not only in number but also in the observance of the virtues. For the children of Israel did not so much walk with bodily steps on the desert road as make progress with deeds of religion in the way of the Lord. Clearly they walked in the way of the Lord, which both bore them along in streams and fed them from heaven. For to those hungering in the desert there was no lack of manna,[3] and from those endangered in the sea the land did not withdraw:[4] here the sea is stretched out like a path, there heaven is opened for food. For the sake of the servants of God the Jordan holds back its streams[5] and Marah changes its waters.[6] In the one case the water that used to be behind, having been turned back on itself, now takes the lead, and in the other case the well that used to distil bitterness, having been tempered into something better, is now sweetened, and in a wonderful way the river abandons its course and the spring of water its taste.

2. But having said that the children of Israel who came to Marah were oppressed by the bitterness of the water and were able to drink it only by throwing in wood, and that this was also an image of the Old Testament, let us see where this wayfaring people went from there. They arrived at a place called Elim, where there were 12 very pure springs of water and a multitude of 70 flourishing palm trees.[7] See the mystery of God—how, after the bitterness of the law, the richness of gospel piety abounds. There the one spring is harsh to drink, but here the many are all sweet to imbibe; there there is no refreshment after weariness, but here there is refreshment after labor. For springs are at the disposal of the thirsty, and palms are offered to victors. Palms are offered to victors, I say, because after the hardness of the law it is a victory to have arrived at the grace of the gospel. For part of the victor's reward is to moisten his mouth from a flowing

spring and to take the triumphal palm in his hand. With the spring the confessor's tongue is purified, and with the palm the martyr's hand is honored—the former because it has praised the glory of Christ, the latter because it has refused the altar of sacrilege. The martyr's palm is a prize: it furnishes sweet fruit to the confessing tongue and gives a glorious ornament to the victorious hand. Clearly for martyrs the palm means something delicious to eat, a shady place to rest, and a worthy triumph; it is always flourishing, always covered with leaves, always ready for the victor. And the palm does not wither for the same reason that the victory of the martyrs does not wither.[8]

3. These very palms are offered to the Lord by the people as He sits upon an ass and comes to the temple.[9] For, when the disciples spread out their garments and made safe Christ's path with their cloaks,[10] there was no greater prize than the palms that the people offered Him in their devotion. By the garments spread out on the road it is signified that His way in the world is unsullied, and by the palms that were offered that He is victor over the world. He, I say, is the victor about whom Scripture says: *The lion of the tribe of Judah has conquered.*[11] He is clearly the victor who destroyed diabolical death and illuminated eternal life. Palms, therefore, are raised at Christ's coming. It is written: *The righteous will flourish like the palm tree.*[12] Justifiably, then, are the banners of righteousness raised at the coming of the righteous one and the titles of His triumphs presented to their author. Before the palms are taken, however, the Lord's path up to the temple is covered over with the disciples' garments, and in order that the Savior's way may be clean it is protected with the apostles' cloaks. This, I think, was done in a mystery, for the way of Christ that leads to the temple is His faith and teaching. In order that we might walk without stumbling, the disciples stripped off the clothing of their own body by their martyrdom, spread out this road and, amidst the crowds of different nations, protected the path of righteousness with the blood of their own members, laying down the garments of their members and covering up the world's filthy disorder, thus showing forth the unsullied way of the Savior.

4. After Marah, then, the people of Israel come to the 12 springs. We read in the prophet: *Bless the Lord from the springs of Israel.*[13] This is the Lord Christ, who is not blessed except by the mouths of the apostles and the teaching of the disciples. The apostles are to be called

springs: like very pure springs they abound in the grace of preaching and, after the bitterness of the law, from the bountiful wisdom within themselves they distil the sweet cup of the sacrament.[14] Nor is it to be wondered at if the drink of the springs is sweet when, in their midst, the food of the palms is sweeter. The apostles, then, are springs that water the face of the whole earth with the streams of their teaching and set before the wearied peoples of the nations the drink of the divine mystery. But the 70 palms growing near the apostolic springs I would call those 70 disciples who, in the next grade after the apostles, are sent out by the Lord for the salvation of humankind, who the Evangelist Luke in his writing asserts were appointed in groups of two,[15] who, like palm trees, return with rejoicing after having cured people and boast to the Lord that even the demons are subject to them.[16] Rightly, then, are they compared to palm trees who have been rewarded with palms and who have shown themselves victorious over the devil.

SERMON 69

A Sequel[1]

1. I think that you have understood, brethren, why I compared these fasts of ours to those stages in which the people of Israel, equipped for battle, so to speak, overcame Pharaoh the king by daily toil and warded off their enemies at their post as if from armed camps (their stopping places), so that if any of that multitude did not hold to his post every day he was either seized by Pharaoh or lured away by the wasteland.[2] Thus we also ought to exert ourselves to keep to the 40-day journey that has been set before us and secure ourselves by the devotion of our fasts as if by armed camps. For our fasts are camps for us, which protect us from the diabolical onslaught. And they are called posts because, when we stand[3] and stay in them, we can parry the stratagems of our enemies. It is clear that fasts are armed camps for Christians, and if a person wanders away from them he is either set upon by the spiritual Pharaoh[4] or devoured by the wasteland of

sins: whoever forsakes the company of the saints endures the wasteland of sins.

2. Fasting is a kind of wall, then, for the Christian—impregnable
to the devil, inaccessible to the enemy. For what Christian has ever
fasted and been taken captive? Who has stayed sober and been overcome? The devil has entree with the drunken, the enemy lays seige to
the gluttonous. But when he sees a fast he flees, he is afraid and struck
by fear; he is terrified by its pallor, unnerved by its hunger, struck
down by its weakness. He is struck down by its weakness, I say,
because Christian weakness is strength; hence the Apostle says: *When
I am weak, then I am strong.*[5] But suppose someone asks how weakness may be strong. Weakness is strong when the flesh dwindles
away with fasting and the soul grows fat with purity, for to the extent
that the nourishment of food is withdrawn from the former the
power of righteousness is increased in the latter. It is then, indeed,
that a person is incapable of worldly works but able to do divine ones,
for it is then that he thinks more of God, then that he fears the
judgment more, and then that he conquers the enemy more defini-
tively. As the Savior says of the devil: *This kind is not cast out except by
fasting and prayers.*[6] He says that someone possessed by the devil
cannot be cleansed except by fasts. See, then, what the power of
fasting is: as much as it offers grace to the one who practices it, it
serves as a healing to someone else; while it renders holy the one who
observes it, it purifies another person. This is a wonderful thing: one
fasts and the benefit of fasting profits another.

3. Therefore, brethren, let us not lay down the arms of abstinence,
and let us observe the fasts of 40 days without intermission.[7] For this
is the perfect number for conquering. For the Lord vanquished the
devil after he fasted for 40 days[8]—not that He would have been
unable to conquer him before fasting, but that He might show us that
we can be victorious over the devil when, by fasting for 40 days, we
have been victorious over fleshly desires, while the one who has
violated this consecrated number by immoderate eating is, like someone frail and miserable, easily able to be overcome by the enemy. For
how is a person who does not conquer immoderate eating in himself
able to conquer the devil's depravity in someone else? First conquer
yourself, man, in order to conquer another! For within you are your
own enemies, who daily assault you. Look, avarice besets you with

the desire for riches, gluttony seizes you with enticing dishes, heresy leads you astray with false knowledge. Conquer your own enemies, then, so that you may be able to conquer others! For it is no light sin, brethren, for the faithful to violate the 40-day period that has been appointed by the Lord and to annul consecrated fasts because of a ravenous stomach. As it is written: *The one who says that he abides in Christ ought himself also to walk as He walked.*[9] If you wish to be a Christian, then, you ought to do what Christ did. He who had no sin fasted for 40 days. You, a sinner, do not wish to fast for 40 days? He, I say, had no sin, but He fasted for our sins. What sort of Christian does your conscience tell you that you are, when you eat while Christ fasts for you, when you refresh yourself while the Savior goes hungry for you?[10]

4. It is no light sin, as I have said, to violate the appointed fast. In order to demonstrate this briefly by examples, we read in the Book of Kings[11] that when Saul the king of Israel was waging war against the foreigners he proclaimed a fast for his entire army, and when all were abstaining he began to fight against the opposing forces. This is obviously a good king, who overcame his enemies not so much by arms as by devotion, and who fought more by piety than with spears. When, therefore, Saul had proclaimed a day's abstinence for all his men and his son Jonathan, unaware of the command, had tasted some honeycomb into which the tip of his staff had been dipped as the victorious army was proceeding into the midst of the enemy, suddenly such indignation was aroused that the victory was delayed and the Divinity offended. And neither was an end put to the war nor a prophetic response given to the king. From this we understand that Saul used to overcome his enemies not so much by the might of his soldiers as by the abstinence of his soldiers. And so by the sin of one person guilt is laid upon all, and by the crime of one person weakness is produced in all, for the army's strength failed when the observance of the fast failed. But since Saul recognized the sin from the fact that the Divinity had been offended, he immediately said that Jonathan should not be pardoned but that the sin which he admitted should be atoned for by the shedding of his blood. See how religious was the behavior of Saul the king, who desired to pacify the offended Lord even by the slaying of his kin! And see what guilt attaches to the broken fast, which is only punished by the shedding of blood! And if

the unwitting Jonathan is delivered over to death because he broke the fast proclaimed by his father, what would a person deserve who knowingly broke the fast proclaimed by Christ? Therefore, brethren, let us most carefully observe the fast that has been decreed for us so that we may overcome our spiritual and fleshly enemies. For we have, as you know, fleshly enemies as well. Let us fast, then, so that our army, like Saul's, might overcome and seize them, and let us not, having determined to abstain, turn away for a honeycomb. For a honeycomb is, so to speak, the pleasure and vices of the world, *which,* as it is written, *are sweet in the throat for a time, to be sure, but in the end are more bitter than gall.*[12]

SERMON 70

A Sequel[1]

1. We should not be so saddened, brethren, as to be subject to distressful temptation during these 40 days, since we see that our Savior was tempted during the same 40 days.[2] We slaves, therefore, ought to lament less inasmuch as we have the example of our master, for where there is a devotion like Christ's, there is temptation like Christ's. For the condition of fasting imposes upon us a condition of enduring. We believe, however, that as our Savior prevailed over the devil when He was tempted, so we also are able to conquer our enemies when we are in distress. For Christ's fasts may be liable to temptation but they cannot be overcome. There are trials, indeed, in the practice of them, but they bestow benefits for salvation.

2. Let us see, then, how skilfully the devil, among his other temptations, provoked the Lord. For when the Savior was standing upon the pinnacle of the temple the devil said: *If you are the Son of God, throw yourself down,*[3] and so forth. Truly does he argue with his customarily clever diabolical deceit. He is always attempting to hurl devout persons down from the heights to the depths,[4] and he strives to make them fall away from holy and noble deeds to earthly and filthy ones, so that the one who, in purity of mind, stands at the summit of the temple may, by contact with sin, cast himself down to

the depths of hell. Now, when he tries to hurl the Lord down from the pinnacle of the temple, he is attempting to take him away from the perfect practice of religion, for the pinnacle of the holy place is the perfection of the heavenly sacrament.[5] Rightly is the Lord said to stand on the pinnacle of the temple, since it is written of Him: *He who walks on the wings of the winds.*[6] For the Lord walks on the wings of the winds, so to speak, when He walks with joy upon the brisk[7] pathway of our virtues. For virtues are wings to us, which raise us up from the low places of the earth to the heights of heaven and, by a kind of flight of the mind, snatch us from the darkness of the nether world and lead us to the pleasures of paradise.[8] Desirous of having these wings of virtue, the prophet says: *Who will give me wings like a dove, and I shall fly away and be at rest?*[9] On this pinnacle of the temple, then, the Savior is said to stand—that is to say, to abide, as it were, in a kind of temple of our faith. For this reason the Apostle says: *You are the temple of God, and the Spirit of God dwells in you.*[10] Standing on this temple, then, and not drawing back, the Lord reproaches the devil, saying: *It is written: You shall not tempt the Lord your God.*[11] That is, you shall not tempt Him who you think ought to be driven as a human being into the nether regions, but rather you shall know that He is to be adored as God and Lord.

3. In these days of fasting, then, we are tempted in the likeness of the Savior, for in the same way our enemies also attempt to dislodge us from the pinnacle of the temple—that is to say, from the observance of Quadragesima. As they heap up terrors and prepare traps, they want to carry us away forcibly from the stronghold of religion. But to them it is said by the Lord: "You shall not tempt the holy ones and the servants of God, for those who you think are to be trodden underfoot as lowly, you will see are to be honored as powerful." For there are, as I have said, many brethren whom our enemies carry away forcibly from the perfection of religion, who, fearing the evil that is present to them, think that God is unmindful of our salvation, not realizing that God forgets no one and is unmindful of no one. But we make Him unmindful of us when we sin, for when we do evil deeds He turns away His face,[12] and when we say wicked things He covers His ear. Therefore God Himself does not so much withdraw His goodness from us as our sins reject Him. For, through the prophet,

the same Lord says to those who were in distress: *Is my hand not able to save you?*[13] and so forth.

You see, then, that sins cause a separation between God and humankind. Therefore, remove the sins from your midst and you have drawn God near to you. For how is God able to forget us, brethren —He who in the Gospel says that even the hairs of our head have been numbered?[14] If He remembers our hairs, much more does He remember our souls. For we take numbering to mean care and solicitude in our regard, since no one numbers something unless he wants to be particularly attentive to it; no one numbers unless he is concerned that he might be defrauded because of not taking a count. A shepherd frequently numbers his flock in order to keep it safe. When one sheep out of a hundred sheep had gone astray, the Lord, who is the good shepherd,[15] went over the number again and carried it back to the flock on His own shoulders.[16] One who is numbered, then, is in such safekeeping that when he goes astray he is brought back on His own shoulders[17] lest the number be diminished. Do not think, therefore, brethren, that God forgets even the least. He remembers everyone, recalls everyone, so much so that forgetfulness comes upon Him only if our sins get in the way.

SERMON 71

On Fasting and Almsgiving[1]

1. I do not doubt, brethren, that you are saddened as often as necessity causes me to be absent from you, for when you do not see the person whom you love you are afflicted, like good children, by the goads of affection. But I, although I am sometimes absent from you in body, nonetheless do not leave you in spirit. Wherever I go, your love follows me; wherever I am, there your brotherliness lingers with me. For it must be that whoever abides in Christ's commandments clings to Christ's bishop,[2] and, although He may seem far away, yet He becomes very close as long as the grace of one faith stands in His place. By all means let the one who is separated from Christ because

of evil deeds reckon himself separated from the bishops.[3] Therefore, brethren, you who keep the Savior's commandment, although you may have been absent from me in body, still you have not been wanting in love for me. So it is that the grace of Christ is accustomed to join together those whom earthly distance separates.

2. But there are a few of you, brethren, whose hearts we know are in the open country even if we should see their faces in church, and, to be sure, we gaze upon their presence in the congregation, but we are aware that their thoughts are on their lands. For they always think of the earth, talk about the earth, and are engaged with earthly things.[4] To them pertains the divine word: *You are earth, and to earth you will return.*[5] These people come to church from time to time, then, not because they are Christians but lest they not be considered Christians by others. When a fast is appointed for them they always excuse themselves on account of the inconvenience of the season. For in the summer months they say: "The day is long and the sun is so hot. We are unable to bear thirst; we have to refresh ourselves with a few drinks." But in wintertime they say: "There is a heavy cold spell and its rigors are very severe. We cannot endure the chill; we have to warm ourselves up with food." Thus people who are always thinking of eating look for reasons for their eating, and they blame the Creator's seasons as they excuse themselves from fasting. Tell me, O delicate Christian unable to bear fasting in the summer, is the heat that you are about to endure more burning than Gehenna? Is the winter more savage than the darkness into which you must be thrust? *For sinners will be cast into the outer darkness. There there will be weeping and chattering of teeth,*[6] as the Lord says. There will be chattering of teeth in that darkness, He says, such as occurs in wintertime. Therefore, just as people shiver when the winter cold penetrates the whole body, so also grave sinners' teeth are made to chatter when the chill consciousness of their crimes comes upon them. While here the miserable sinner fears the rigor of winter, there he incurs the cold of darkness; while here he escapes the heat of the sun, there he will endure the fire of Gehenna.

3. But when you tell these very people that they should give something to the poor, at once they object to you: "There are endless needs, the taxes are heavy, we are unable to keep our financial affairs in order." And so many things do they keep saying to you that they

act as if you were a criminal for wanting them to bear this in mind. They do not understand that the need of salvation must supersede every other need, and that to pay taxes profits someone else, while to give alms is of value to the giver himself. For the paying of taxes confers a benefit on the receiver, but the doing of almsdeeds bestows a benefit on the one who performs them. The paying of taxes, I say, brings a loss to the one who pays, but the giving of alms is gain for the giver, for the merciful person becomes richer after he begins to have less as a result of his generosity to the poor. Blessed, then, is almsgiving, which both renews the recipient and rejoices the giver, *for God loves a cheerful giver,*[7] and for this reason it is better to give to Him first. Joyful, therefore, and cheerful is the one who attends to the poor. Quite clearly is he joyful, because for a few small coins he acquires heavenly treasures for himself;[8] on the contrary, the person who pays taxes is always sad and dejected. Rightly is he sad who is not drawn to payment by love but forced by fear. Christ's debtor, then, is joyful, and Caesar's sad, because love urges the one to payment and punishment constrains the other; the one is invited by rewards, the other compelled by penalties.

The holy Apostle says: *Command the rich of this world not to be haughty*[9] and so forth. You see, then, O rich person, that your riches are uncertain.[10] Why, then, do you heap up gold, in which there is no real assurance? Let avarice cease and your gold will be earth; let your overweening desire be removed and your solidi[10a] will be filth. For your gold and silver are vile and worthless stuff. But where human concupiscence has grown, there ambition has also joined up with these objects. For nature did not cause gold and silver to be precious, but human willing made it so.[11]

SERMON 72

*That Spiritual Enemies Are More to Be Feared
Than Fleshly Ones, and That Thanksgiving Is to Be Made
to God after Eating*[1]

1. I have frequently warned you, brethren, that while there is still time you should give heed in every way to your salvation and in this

short life provide an eternal life for yourselves. For anyone who is wise knows that this human life has been given not for quiet rest but for toil—that is to say, so that the one who toils here may rest afterwards. But here there is no rest,[2] for this life is filled with such evils that in comparison to it death ought to be considered a relief and not a punishment.[3] God made life short, then, so that its troubles might be ended in a brief span of time, since they could not be ended by good fortune.

2. Holy Job says: *Human life is a pirates' den*,[4] which is to say either that in this life people experience every evil (for in Latin experience can be called a *piraterium*)[5] or—and this is certainly a pirates' den—that in this life the devil rages furiously, like a pirate, against human beings; for a *piraterium* is a pirates' den. We are in piratical circumstances, then, so long as in this flesh we lie prey to the temptations of spiritual beings. Although flesh-and-blood pirates, who are barbarians, are also not wanting to us in this life, yet I fear less those who are unable to remove righteousness even if they do remove property. If they take gold away, certainly they cannot take Christ away; if they seize silver, they cannot seize the Savior. Who, therefore, would not hasten to possess Christ for himself, whom neither the plunderer can seize nor the enemy bear away nor captivity separate from? For the one who has Christ fears no human enemy. What can happen to the wise person? Suppose someone takes his flocks. The plague does this as well. Suppose someone seizes his herd. This loss he has already gotten used to from putting up with cattle thieves. Perhaps someone even kills him. He does not bring burdens but removes them from him. This has been inflicted upon him because a fever would carry him away with greater pain, especially inasmuch as the Lord says: *Fear not those who kill the body but are unable to kill the soul.*[6]

More to be feared, then, are those spiritual pirates who are used to despoiling not only people's bodies but their souls as well, who strive to remove not so much the gold of the world as the gold of faith, who plunder not so much worldly property as Christ's wisdom. Now these spiritual enemies themselves dispatch these fleshly things against us, so that when we are in tribulation we might be made to prove how trusting we are in God and how[7] we should seek relief from Him alone. For there are some who, when they undergo tribulation, say that their enemies are overcoming them by evil arts and that therefore they have to be overcome by those same arts; so they beg for victory from demons while despairing of God. Unhappy people, they know not what they do or what they say, for in their anxiety about their property they have forgotten religion and faith. Perhaps, indeed, they will not lose their property, but, what is more important, they have lost their souls. Holy Job says: *If we have received good things from the hand of the Lord, why should we not endure evil things as well?*[8] That is to say, if we take delight in the good things that happen, why should we not be consoled also in adverse circumstances? For the endurance of adversity is an exercise in virtue for the one who is wise, but an occasion of transgression for the fool.

3. I have frequently said, then, that in this short life you should provide an eternal life for yourselves, which I regret that you disdain to do. For when we say that there must be fasting, no one fasts except for a few. When we say that almsdeeds are to be performed, avarice constrains you more. But I believe that most of you also do not know what praying and giving thanks to God is—those who get up early in the morning and think of nothing but eating and who go off to bed after they have eaten without ever thanking God, who gave them both food for refreshment and sleep for rest.[9] You, Christian, if you are to do the right thing, should remember whose bread you eat and give praise to Him. Tell me, if you give something of yours to someone, do you not expect him to thank you and to bless the house from which a kind act has been shown him? And if perhaps he does not thank you, how you call him an ingrate! So also the God who feeds us expects us to render Him thanks for the food given by Him and, when we are full, to praise Him for these gifts of His.[10] For this is the recompense of divine benefits—that when we have been refreshed we should acknowledge that we have received well. Otherwise, if we are silent and heedless when we receive the gifts of God, we shall be deprived of their bounty as ungrateful and unworthy, so that the God whom we did not recognize in His kind deeds we might beseech when evils fall upon us, and so that we who did not give thanks for the good things that we enjoyed might be incited to implore because of adversity. So now it happens that, since we have been slow to give praise in time of peace, we live anxiously now in tribulation, so that we may bemoan its trials.

SERMON 73

A Sequel[1]

1. Last Sunday I believe that I spoke at sufficient length for the correction of those who do not give thanks to the Creator for the divine gifts that they enjoy and who, while benefiting from heavenly kindnesses, like ungrateful and unworthy persons do not acknowledge the author of the kindnesses. They are ungrateful, I say, who neither fear God as slaves do their master nor honor Him as children do their father. God says through the prophet: *If I am a master, where is my fear? If I am a father, where is my love?*[2] That is to say, if you are a slave render the Master the service of fear, if you are a son show your Father a reverent love. But when you do not give thanks you neither love nor fear God; hence you are an insolent slave or a proud son. The good Christian, therefore, ought always to praise his Father and Master and to do all things with a view to His glory, as the blessed Apostle says: *Whether you eat or drink or do anything, do all for the glory of God.*[3]

See what sort of meal the Apostle wished there to be for the Christian: it is the faith of the Christian rather than bodily nourishment that is to be consumed, and the frequent invocation of the Lord's name rather than a variety of dishes and an abundant table that is to refresh him. Devotion fills the hungry better than food! *Do all,* he says, *for the glory of God.* He wishes, then, for all our actions to be accomplished with Christ as companion and witness for this reason, namely, so that we may do good things with Him as the author and avoid what is evil for the sake of His fellowship. For one who knows that Christ is his companion is ashamed to do evil. In good things, however, Christ is our helper, and in the face of evil things He is our defender.

2. Therefore, when we get up in the morning we should thank the Savior before we leave our room, performing an act of piety before any of our worldly actions, for He watched over us as we slept peacefully in our beds. For who but God watches over the one who sleeps and is so relaxed in slumber—unaware of his own human life

and abstracted from himself—that he does not know what he is or where he is and is certainly unable to be present to himself? Necessarily, then, God is present to those who sleep because sleepers cannot be present to themselves, and He protects the human race from snares by night because no one else keeps vigil then to guard it. Therefore I owe thanks to Him who keeps vigil so that I may sleep soundly. For God Himself receives us in the bosom of peace, so to speak, when we are about to go to bed, and He keeps us concealed in the treasure house of peace and, by the safeguard of darkness, as it were, protects us until the dawn, so that the wickedness of the enemies of humanity, which cannot be expelled in kindness, may be driven away by darkness. And let darkness offer that peace to the weary which human kindness did not. For when a person does not know where the enemy is that he is pursuing, the peace that he had not wished to extend willingly he extends unwillingly.[4]

3. When we arise, then, we ought to thank Christ and to perform all the day's work under the sign of the Savior. When you were still a pagan, were you not accustomed to search for propitious signs for things and to subject them to a thorough examination? Now I do not want you to fall completely into error. Know that under the one sign of Christ is the prosperity of all things. The one who has begun to sow under this sign will acquire the fruit of eternal life; the one who sets out on a journey under this sign will come even to heaven. In this name, therefore, all our actions are to be directed, and to it the movement of our whole life is to be referred, as the Apostle says: *In Him we live and move and have our being.*[5]

4. But also, when evening closes the day, we ought to praise Him with the Psalter and sing His glory in pleasant tones so that, when the struggle of our labors has come to an end, like victors we might merit rest, and the forgetfulness of slumber might be, as it were, the palm of our toil. We are not only taught by reason that we should do this, brethren, but we are also admonished by examples. For, when the dawn brings forth the breaking day, do we not see the smallest birds in the tiny bedchambers of their nests first proceed to sound forth with manifold loveliness and to do this assiduously, so that they may delight their Creator with sweetness, since they are unable to do so with language?[6] And do we not see how each one of them offers a

service in melody since it cannot in speech, so that it seems to itself to give more devout thanks the more sweetly it has sounded forth? And do we not see that it does the same thing when the day has drawn to an end? What, then, does this ordered singing at particular times and this constant effort mean if not a kind of unmeasurable confession of thanks? For the innocent bird charms its shepherd with sweetness since it cannot do so with words. For the birds also have their shepherd, as the Lord says: *Consider the birds of heaven, that they neither spin nor reap, and your Father, who is in heaven, feeds*[7] *them.*[8] But with what food are the birds fed? With the meanest and most earthly. The birds, therefore, give thanks for mean food, but you are fed with the costliest dishes and are ungrateful.

5. What human being, then, would not blush to end the day without praying the Psalms, when the birds themselves burst out with the sweetness of the Psalter in order to give pleasure, and who would not, with the loveliness of verses, sound forth the glory of Him whose praise the birds pronounce in delightful song? Imitate, then, the smallest birds, brother, by giving thanks to the Creator morning and evening. And if you are more devout, imitate the nightingale which, since the day alone does not suffice it for praise, runs through the night hours with wakeful song. And you, then, binding the day together with your praises, add the course of the night to your work and lighten the sleepless activity of the toil that you have taken up with a series of Psalms. And inasmuch as I have mentioned these birds that keep vigil through the night, I do not want you to imitate the night owl:[9] although it stays awake during the night it is nonetheless lazy and blind by day, and with its huge eyes it loves the gloom of darkness but shudders at the brightness of the sun. Marvelous to say, it is given sight in darkness and blinded by light. This creature is an image of the heretics and pagans. They embrace the darkness of the devil and shudder at the light of the Savior, and with the huge eyes of disputation they look at vain things but do not observe what is everlasting. Of these the Lord says: *They have eyes and do not see; they walk in darkness.*[10] For they are acute as far as superstitions are concerned but dull with respect to divine matters. While thinking that they are flying about with subtle words they are confused, like the night owl, by the brightness of the true light.

SERMON 74

On the Thief[1]

1. Since we made mention yesterday of the thief, let us see who this thief is who on the cross not only obtains the pardon of his sins from the Lord but even has bestowed on him the beauty of paradise, so that he who had been condemned to punishment on account of his crimes is brought to glory on account of his faith, and the cross that he bore is for him not so much a condemnation to suffering as an occasion for salvation. For the one crucified on the cross he believed to be Christ the Lord, and therefore, having the companionship of His suffering, he is granted His companionship in paradise. Blessed indeed is the thief who obtains the heavenly kingdom while he endures punishment! See the guilty one for whom, as it is said, being condemned was a timely thing! For he would not have come to glory if he had not been handed over to punishment.

Let us see, then, why one who is guilty of such misdeeds is so quickly promised paradise by the Savior while others with their many tears and frequent fasting only barely obtain the remission of their sins. The reason why, brethren, is significant and many-faceted. In the first place, this thief was so quickly converted by the fervor of his faith that he despised present suffering and prayed for future pardon, and he believed that it would be more beneficial to him to make a request with respect to eternal judgment than to petition concerning temporal punishment. For, remembering his misdeeds and acting penitently, he began to be anxious for what he hoped rather than to feel what he suffered. For, once believing in Christ, he would have been quite able to petition concerning present punishment, except that he had given more thought to the future. And then it is more meritorious from the point of view of grace that he believed in Christ the Lord on the cross; and the suffering, which constitutes a stumbling block for others, served to increase his faith. For the suffering of the cross was a stumbling block to many, as the Apostle says: *But we preach Christ crucified, a stumbling block indeed to the Jews and foolishness to the Gentiles.*[2]

2. Rightly, then, does he merit paradise who considered the cross of Christ to be not a stumbling block but power, for the same Apostle says: *to those Jews who have been called, Christ the power of God and the wisdom of God.*[3] Rightly indeed does the Lord also give paradise to him because on the gibbet of the cross he confesses the one whom Judas Iscariot had sold in the garden.[4] This is a remarkable thing: the thief confesses the one whom the disciple denied. This is a remarkable thing, I say: the thief honors the one who suffers, while Judas betrayed the one who kissed him. Flattering words of peace are peddled by the one and the wounds of the cross are preached by the other, for he says: *Remember me, Lord, when you come in your kingdom.*[5]

3. This is truly the full devotion of faith, that pardon is asked from His power when the blood pouring forth from the Lord's wounds is discerned; that His divinity is the more honored when His humility is seen; that kingly deference is extended to Him when He is thought to have been given over to death. For this faithful thief did not believe that the one who he proclaimed was about to reign was going to die; he does not consider that the one who he confesses is about to exercise dominion in the heavens will have to be subject to the underworld; he does not think that the one from whom he asks for freedom will be detained in the nether regions. Although he sees His gaping wounds and observes His blood pouring forth, nonetheless he believes Him to be God whom he does not recognize as guilty and acknowledges Him to be righteous whom he does not think of as a sinner. For he says to that other complaining thief: *We indeed are receiving what is due our deeds, but this man has done nothing wrong.*[6] He understood that Christ[7] received these blows because of others' sins and that He sustained these wounds because of others' crimes, and he knew that the wounds on the body of Christ were not Christ's wounds but the thief's; therefore, after he recognized his own wounds on Christ's body, he began to love all the more. For the prophet says: *For he bears our infirmities and suffers pain on our account. Yet we esteemed Him to be stricken. By His wounding we have been healed.*[8] The thief, hanging on the cross, loves the Lord more, then, when he sees His wounds. This is a remarkable thing: the thief on the cross loves Christ more than Judas loved Him at the supper; the one trips up his master through food[9] while the other believes his

Lord through suffering, as the prophet says: *He who ate my bread spread out deceit against me.*[10] This thief knew, then, that all the Lord's suffering occurred of His own volition and that it was in His power either to hand over His life to death or to return again to life, as the Lord Himself says: *I have power to lay down my life and I have power to take it up again.*[11] So much did he judge Christ free from the laws of the nether regions, though, that he asked that he too might be freed from them.

Sermon 75

A Sequel[1]

1. Your love[2] remembers, brethren, that I gave the reason why the thief of long standing, condemned after having confessed his great crimes and misdeeds, could be promised paradise on the very gibbet and was so quickly saved that grace overtook his sins before punishment did, and he began to glory in his afflictions instead of suffering from them. For, having been promised paradise, he does not suffer torture.[3] Christ says to Peter: *You cannot follow me now, but you will follow afterwards,*[4] and to this man it is said: *Today you will be with me in paradise.*[5] The one is put off as being overhasty, but the other is invited as a companion; the prize is still reserved for the one, but the other is already loved in fellowship. *You cannot follow me now,* He says. It is impossible for Peter to follow the Lord, but it is already easy for the thief to be with the Lord. *Today,* he says, *you will be with me in paradise.* He is not put off until some other season, he is not held back until some other day. Paradise received the thief at the very hour that it received the Lord. One suffered for the sake of the salvation of all, but the gate of immortality is opened to both alike.

It is faith that offers this great glory to the thief, for it is faith that covers over sins,[6] overcomes crimes, and makes thieves innocent. However great may be the guilt of the wrongdoers, still the grace of faith is greater, for it means more to have believed in Christ than to have done wrong in the world, and it counts for more[7] to have hoped for pardon from the Lord than to have contracted guilt from the world. For just as faithlessness makes a criminal, so does faith perfect one who is innocent. Judas, after he lost the faith, lost the innocence of the apostleship. He became guilty of every crime after he denied the Lord of every virtue.[8] Just as deserting Christ suffices for the wickedness of the one, so does believing in the Lord suffice for the innocence of the other. Faith, then, makes thieves innocent and faithlessness makes apostles criminals.

2. There was, therefore, a great and excellent faith in that thief. Clearly it is a great and admirable faith which believed that the crucified Christ was being glorified more than punished. For this is the shape that all salvation takes—that the Savior should be recognized as the Lord of majesty when He is seen to be crucified and subject to humiliation. Hence the Apostle says: *If they had known, they would never have crucified the Lord of majesty.*[9] This, I say, is an excellent faith, to believe that Christ on the cross is God and not a wrongdoer. Therefore that thief was justified while the Jews insulted the Savior on the gibbet and said to Him as if He were a criminal: *Free yourself if you are able.*[10] But he, certain of Christ's[11] divinity and sure of His good will, asks instead to be freed himself. There was a great faith in that thief, I say, and one which was comparable to that of the holy apostles; indeed, it preceded theirs. For he who preceded with respect to devotion preceded with respect to the prize, for the thief came to paradise before the apostles did. Peter follows the Lord and this man accompanies Him. But the Lord gives him a reward according to faith and merit, for, as we read, all the disciples were afraid during the Savior's suffering, and all left Him just when He was betrayed.[12] It happened as it was written: *I shall strike the shepherd and the sheep of the flock will be scattered.*[13]

3. Peter, having been warned, was unable to maintain his faith.[14] He succumbed as often as he was warned not to fall, and unless the Lord had set a kind of limit of three denials for him he would perhaps have denied Him more frequently had he been questioned more frequently.[15] For the Savior's suffering brought such a fear upon the disciples that the maidservant destroyed what Christ had predicted beforehand to the apostle, and the faithlessness induced by the portress was more powerful than the apostle's precaution. It is no good portress who admits Peter into the high priest's house so as to cut him

off[16] from the Savior's faith. Wickedly did Eve deceive Adam,[17] wickedly did the portress let Peter in.[18] The one cut off from paradise, the other from Christ; the one deceived her husband by her persuasion, the other entrapped the apostle by her questioning; the one incited Adam to transgression, the other compelled Peter to a denial; and in both cases the same sex, performing the office of portress, cuts off from life and locks in death.[19]

SERMON 76

A Sequel[1]

1. We have said, brethren, that the portress deceived Peter in a manner similar to Eve, and that as a woman entrapped Adam so also a woman cheated the apostle. For this sex is accustomed to deception: in the portress the devil recognized the vehicle of his lie; he was used to attacking faithful men through nothing else than a woman.[2] In one instance he overcomes Adam through Eve, in another he vanquishes Peter through the portress. For, as we read, the devil was in the paradise of delights, and he was not absent either, as we know, from the praetorium of the Jews; in the one place Satan was nearby as a snake, and in the other the serpent incited Judas. There is consequently the same kind of deceit in the case of Peter as there was in the case of Adam, since there is the same kind of command. For both received a command from the Lord: Adam, that he should not touch, the apostle, that he should not deny; the one, that he should not take from the tree of knowledge, the other, that he should not bypass the cross of wisdom. But in their transgression each of them neglects the precept in like manner: the one tastes what is not permitted, the other speaks what is not fitting. And yet Peter's denial is less severe than Adam's misdeed, for the apostle is more quickly aided than the first-formed man: God looks for the one at eventide as he wanders, while the Lord rebukes the other at cockcrow as he makes his denial; the naked Adam, guilty of the deed, was ashamed, while Peter, corrected, was conscious of what he said and lamented; the one hastens, like a

person caught in the act, to a hiding place, while the other, like a person who has been reproved, breaks into tears. It is said to Adam as to one hiding and concealing himself from the Divinity: *Adam, where are you?*[3] Not that Adam would have been able to conceal himself from the gaze of the Lord, but that no place is safe or sure for the sinful conscience as long as it fears being caught. The Lord looked at Peter and, with his eyes opened, corrected his fault. Rightly does He correct with His eyes, since it is written: *The eyes of the Lord are upon the righteous, and His ears toward their prayers.*[4]

2. Therefore Peter broke into tears; he does not pray at all in words. For I find that he wept, but I do not find that he spoke; I read of his tears, but I do not read of his apology. Clearly it is right that Peter wept and was silent, since what is not accustomed to be excused is usually wept over, and what is indefensible can be washed away. For a tear cleanses what the voice is abashed to acknowledge. Tears, then, have equally to do with shame and salvation; they do not blush to make a request, and they obtain what they ask for. Tears, I say, are a kind of silent prayers: they do not ask for pardon but they merit it; they give no reason and they receive mercy. In fact, prayers of tears are more beneficial than those of words, since in making its prayer the word can err, but a tear never errs; for sometimes a word does not make the whole matter plain, but a tear always manifests the state of one's mind. And for this reason Peter does not use words, by which he had erred, sinned, and given up his faith, lest he not be believed when he make confession because this is what he had used for his denial. Hence he prefers to weep over his case rather than to speak of it, and to confess by tears what he had denied by voice.

3. But I also believe that Peter was silent lest by asking quickly for pardon he offend by shamelessness rather than obtain what he requested. For the one who asks with modesty usually wins pardon more quickly. With respect to every blameworthy action, then, there is to be weeping beforehand; this is how prayer is to be made. From this example we know how to heal our sins. See, the apostle's denial did not harm us at all, and his correction was very profitable. Let us imitate him as he speaks in another place. For when he is asked a third time by the Lord: *Simon, do you love me?* he replies a third time: *Lord, you know that I love you;* and the Lord says a third time: *Feed my sheep.*[5] These words served to make up for the former fault, for the one who

had denied the Lord three times confesses Him three times, and as often as he had contracted guilt by sinning he seeks grace by loving.[6] See, then, how much weeping profited Peter: before he wept he fell, and after he wept he was elected; he who before his tears was a wrongdoer was received as a shepherd after his tears, and he who at first did not rule himself accepted rule over others.

SERMON 77

A Sequel[1]

1. Last Sunday we showed that Saint Peter proceeded along his erring ways during the Savior's suffering and that after he denied the Lord he was better.[2] For he became more faithful after he wept over the faith that he had lost, and for that reason he gained back a greater grace than he lost: like a good shepherd he accepted the charge of protecting the sheep,[3] so that he who had previously been weak to himself would now become the foundation for all,[4] and the very person who had faltered when tested by questioning would strengthen others with the unwavering character of his faith. On account of the firmness of his faithfulness he is called the rock of the churches, as the Lord says: *You are Peter, and upon this rock I will build my Church.*[5] He is called a rock because he will be the first to lay the foundations of the faith among the nations and so that, like an immovable stone, he might hold fast the fabric and the structure of the whole Christian endeavor. Because of his faithfulness, therefore, Peter is called a rock, as the Apostle says: *And they drank from the spiritual rock that was following them, and the rock was Christ.*[6] Rightly does he who merits fellowship in deed merit fellowship also in name, for in the same house Peter laid the foundation and Peter does the planting, and the Lord gives the increase and the Lord provides for the watering.[7]

2. Peter, therefore, profits from his temptations, has cause for joy in his tears, and grows in his trials. Thus in the sea, as the audacious wayfarer steps out upon the waves, he falters in his stride but gains strength in his love, he is endangered in body but does not waver in

devotion, his feet go under but he is supported by the hand of Christ.[8] Faith supported the one whom the water was causing to sink, and the Savior's love strengthened the one whom the violence of the waters threw into dismay. For Peter walked on the sea more with love than with his feet, since he did not see where he might put down his feet, but he did see where he could fix his love. For when he was in the boat he gazed upon the Lord and, drawn by His love, stepped upon the sea; he does not think about the heavy waves or the flowing currents, and as long as he pays heed to Christ he does not notice the elements. He believes that faith can find a solid foothold even amidst the waves. Although the sea is tossed by billows and the waters are shaken by winds, still Peter's path, which leads to the Lord, is not disturbed. Peter walks upon the waters, then, and under his feet the yielding liquid does not give way. We read in the Old Testament that the children of Israel walked through the Red Sea on dry paths and that, for the safety of those proceeding, the water was transformed into a kind of solid mass lest it slip back.[9] How much better this, when, as Peter walks, the waves are neither transformed nor moved, and the water is neither solidified nor does it flee away! Better, I say, is this, when the very waves that toss also provide support, when the flood that drowns also acts as a servant. In the one case nature abandoned its course so that the people of Israel might be carried through the sea, while in the other Peter is carried on the waters and the streams do not abandon their course.

3. The apostle, then, audacious wayfarer, sets out upon a new kind of path; now he mounts the mass of the arching flood, now he comes down the hollow of the subsiding wave, and amidst the waters of the sea he continues on his upward and downward journey. But when he is struck by the winds and disquieted by the storms he begins to fear what he had put trust in, and immediately the flood slips out from under him and the waters withdraw, and thereupon the path fades away from the one from whom faith is fading away. Then, calling upon the Lord Jesus, he prays to be saved, and the Savior rescues the man who has taken His hand and rebukes him, saying: *You of little faith, why have you doubted?*[10] That is to say, why are you of such little faith that, having begun to walk upon the sea in trust, you are not crossing it in perseverance? For it is written: *The one who perseveres to the end will be saved.*[11] But as long as you hesitate and doubt you have

lost the path upon which you had entered. Why, I say, are you of such little faith that with that faith you do not arrive at the end of the journey? Understand, therefore, that your trust carried you upon the sea and that your lack of trust made you sink. Consequently, brethren, Saint Peter, as he wavers, sinks, and is imperiled, comes thus to the Lord, showing us that one does not hasten to Christ except through dangers. For there are many diabolical billows in this world of temptations and many shipwrecks, from which we can be freed if the Savior extends His hand to those who cry out. Let us not cease, then to cry out to the Lord, and He will not refuse us the accustomed help.

SERMON 78

A Preface,
and On the Lord's Body[1]

1. Yesterday, beloved brethren, I believe that you were considerably pleased with the sermons of our lord and brother, the bishop[2] who was present here and who spoke with such ease on divine matters that his preaching was redolent of the grace of the priesthood,[3] the eloquence of a public speaker, and the learning of a teacher. Nor is it strange if he who holds the primatial honor in the episcopate[4] also has the primatial eloquence in preaching, so that in flowing words he might commend God's virtues, bringing them forth from within his holy breast. And therefore I know that my littleness will be less pleasing to your ears than usual, for who would be content to drink from a rivulet when he could draw water from fountains? For the earth is unable to absorb a drizzle after a heavy downpour has soaked it. Thus your love,[5] therefore, drenched in the eloquence of the holy bishop,[6] will not tolerate the uncultivated style of my preaching. For although a man may be learned and an accomplished speaker, he will seem ill-spoken if he begins to talk in the presence of someone better. Nonetheless this embarrassing situation[7] has its consolation, for there is nothing disgraceful in a comparison with the high priest[8] that would offend the lowliest priest,[9] especially since the distinguished companionship of the blessed can help me. For if David

proclaims that one person may become holy through fellowship with another person who is holy when he says: *With the holy I shall be holy*,[10] why, then, although I am unskilled and a sinner, would one not suppose that I could become a preacher of the Lord's virtues in the company of such masters?

2. Therefore, since our most blessed brother has elaborated the praises of the holy apostles with great eloquence, we ought also to preach on the burial of the Lord Himself, so that, as we see[11] the members of a single body[12] attentively cared for, the whole body might likewise be adorned with preaching.

Let us see, then, what happens to the Lord's body after it is taken down from the cross. Joseph of Arimathea, a righteous man, as the Evangelist says, took it and buried it in his new tomb, in which no one had ever been laid.[13] Blessed, therefore, is the body of the Lord Christ, which in birth comes forth from a virgin's womb and in death is placed in the grave of a righteous man! Clearly blessed is this body, which virginity brought forth and righteousness held! Joseph's grave held Him incorrupt, just as Mary's womb preserved Him inviolate. In the one He is not touched by a man's impurity, in the other He is not hurt by death's corruption, in every aspect holiness is conferred upon that blessed body, and in every aspect virginity. A new womb conceived Him, a new grave enclosed Him. The Lord's is the womb, then, and it is virginal, and virginal is the sepulcher. Or should I not rather say that the sepulcher itself is a womb? There is, in fact, no small similarity. For just as the Lord came forth living from His mother's womb, so also He rose living from Joseph's sepulcher; and just as then He was born from the womb in order to preach, so also now He has been reborn from the sepulcher in order to evangelize. But the latter birth is more glorious than the former. For the former begot a mortal body, whereas the latter brought forth an immortal one; after the former birth He descends to hell, whereas after the latter He returns to the heavens. The latter birth is more religious than the former. For the former kept the Lord of the whole world locked in the womb for nine months, whereas the latter held Him in the bowels of the grave for only three days; the former offered hope to all rather slowly, whereas the latter raised up salvation for all quite speedily.

SERMON 79

A Rebuke to the People [1]

Since, brethren, I have never ceased to rebuke you with fatherly concern, I am amazed that you have made no progress for all my admonitions, and I grieve that my frequent preaching does not set you aright by some increase of salvation but that it restrains you, as it were, by the pain of witness. For the bishop's [2] preaching to the people is a corrective for those who are to be saved but a witness against those who are to be judged. We bear witness to them before the day of judgment as to what awaits them in that judgment so that they may be without excuse then and may be accused of sins and held liable for contempt. For this reason I would also like to keep silent occasionally and to spare you, but I prefer to give you an account of your arrogance than to subject myself to a sentence of negligence. For I have discovered, brethren, that during my absence so few of you came to church, so very few of you were present, that it was as if you had gone off together with me; it was as if, since I was taken away by things that needed attending to, the same obligation dragged you along with me. We are equally absent from God's house, then, but there is this difference: obligation causes me to be absent, but choice you. Do you not know that even if I am away from the church, nonetheless Christ, who is everywhere, is not away from His Church? You come to church, brother, and you do not find the bishop [3] there, but if you come in faith you find there the Savior, the bishop of bishops. [4] For a Christian who only goes to church when the bishop is present seems to have attended not so much for divine as for human reasons and not to have fulfilled the obligation of a God-fearing Christian so much as to have acted obsequiously like a false friend.

But why do I reproach you when you can convict me with a word? For I am convicted when, in this regard, I see that the clerics are more negligent than you. How can I convict sons when I cannot convict brothers? Or with what assurance may I be angered with layfolk when I keep silent for shame before my confreres? However, brethren, I am not speaking of everyone. There are, to be sure, some devoted persons, and others who are negligent. I name no one: let everyone's conscience speak for itself.

SERMON 80

A Discourse after the Rebuke[1]

1. Perhaps my preaching last Sunday was somewhat unpleasant because I visited many of you harshly with the severity of the teaching authority and took up not what would flatter a number of you but what would make you sad. Truly, this is of no concern to me, for I rejoice in the knowledge that the disciple's sadness is the master's joy. For the hearer profits when the preacher proclaims what is harsh, and salvation is begotten for a person when the sadness of correction is pressed upon him. As the blessed Apostle says: *What is sadness according to God brings about a lasting salvation.*[2] Justifiably, therefore, do I rejoice, since I bring about salvation when I reprove. Although my son is grieved on account of the roughness of my speech, nonetheless I am made happy because I know that he profits by the grief. The holy Apostle says: *But who is the son whom his father does not beat?*[3] For a father does not always kiss his son but also sometimes chastises him. When one who is loved is chastised, therefore, a pious act is exercised in his regard, for love has its wounds as well, which are all the sweeter for the harshness of their infliction. For a religious chastisement is sweeter than easy forgiveness, which is why the prophet says: *Sweeter are the wounds of a friend than the freely offered kisses of an enemy.*[4]

2. Therefore, brethren, since after the many beneficial words of my rebuke I believe that you have derived profit from the kind intention of my observations, let us take up some things from the sacred writings. For just as a well that does not supply its customary water is stirred up with sticks and thus is found to be more abundant, and muddy water is produced from it at first in order that purer water may follow, so also, then, your holiness[5] had indeed been irritated by

the harshness of the sermon, but it has become more devout by the sweetness of piety. Perhaps your souls retained some trace of agitation, but already purity in its fullness flows forth from your actions.

Let us see, then, what the Lord means when He says to His disciples: *But what do you call me?*[6] It is not as one who is ignorant that the Lord asks what the people and the disciples thought of Him, but, as one who knew the minds of all, He wished to manifest the faith of certain individuals so that they would proclaim with their mouth what they believed in their heart.[7] For some believed that the Lord was Elijah, and others Jeremiah, and still others John the Baptist; Peter alone confesses that Christ is the Son of God.[8] There are, to be sure, levels of faith, and one who believes more faithfully confesses more devoutly.

3. On account of this faithfulness Peter is told: *Blessed are you, Simon bar Jonah, because flesh and blood have not revealed this to you but my Father who is in heaven. And I say to you: You are Peter, and upon this rock I will build my Church.*[9] Although he used to be called Simon, then, he is named Peter on account of his faithfulness. We read what the Apostle says of the Lord Himself: *They drank from the spiritual rock, but the rock was Christ.*[10] Rightly, then, inasmuch as Christ is a rock, is Simon named Peter, in order that he who shared with the Lord in faith might be at one with the Lord as well in the Lord's name—that just as a Christian is so called from Christ, the apostle Peter would similarly receive his name from Christ the rock. But we cannot disapprove of the opinion of the people who thought that the Lord was one of the prophets.[11] For perhaps some thought that the Savior was like Elijah because Elijah, like the Savior, ascended to the heavens.[12] But Christ is not like Elijah, for the one is snatched up to the heavens and the other is returning to them; the one, like a weak man, is carried in a fiery chariot, and the other, like God, is borne by His own strength; the one is conducted like a man, and the other ascends like a Savior; the one follows the angels who are leading him, and the other precedes the angels who are accompanying Him. And the same angels, returning to the earth from the Lord, the Savior, said to the apostles: *Men of Galilee, why do you stand looking towards heaven? This is Jesus, who has been taken from you; He will come in the same way as you saw Him going to heaven.*[13]

SERMON 81

On the Fasts of the Ninevites[1]

1. We read in the prophets that, when a divinely ordained destruction threatened the city of Nineveh and the time for its overthrow according to the sentence of God drew near, those dwelling in it had no defense but to reject their abundant repasts and take up constant fasting and, setting aside the desire for wealth, clothe themselves in the humility of poverty. Thus, as a result, they would obtain a remedy from the place whence doom threatened them—that is to say, by abstaining they would soften the wrath of the Divinity, which they had provoked by dissipation, and their humility would alleviate the offense for which their pride had been responsible. For it is said that in that tribulation the king himself, laying aside the imperial purple and banishing royal pomp, girded his limbs in a coarse garment and rolled about in sackcloth for days and nights. What a wise king, who knew how to overcome what endangered him! For with virtue he overcame his foes, with humility he conquered God. Clearly this was a wise king, who understood what weapons to use at such a time, for when men lie in wait for him he takes up weapons of war, but when God is angered with him he seizes the weapons of righteousness.[2] What a wise king, I say, who for the well-being of his citizens confesses himself to be a sinner rather than a king! For he heeds not that he is a king when he fears God, the king of all, nor is he mindful of his power when he recognizes the power of the Divinity. He heeds not that he is a king, then, when he lays down the purple and takes off his crown, but he puts on a coarse garment and sackcloth, observes constant fasting, and abides in prayer. This is a remarkable thing: while unmindful of his kingship over human beings he begins to be a king of righteousness.

2. This devout prince, then, did not lose his empire but changed it. Previously he held a rule of military discipline, but now he obtains a rule of heavenly teachings.[3] No, I say, he did not lose his empire because, whether by sword or by righteousness, he is the first to watch over the well-being of his citizens. Clearly he is the first to keep watch because, in order that the whole city might fast, the king

first decreed hunger for himself, and for the well-being of all he went hungry before any of his soldiers did. For it was necessary that he who had been more powerful than everyone else should become more devout than everyone else. Therefore by his own example he makes ready an army of religion that is outfitted not with weapons but with devotion alone. He commands each sex and every age to abstain from daily meals. Numbers are added to the religious army since the devotion is such that even infants are obliged to enlist, for in a cause of this sort it is held to be a pious act to deny food to children as well. For the satisfaction of sinners was not enough to appease God unless the innocence of children also lamented the sins of their elders, and youth washed away its own misdeeds with others' tears.[4]

3. But there is no one, brethren, who does not realize that all these things were done as a warning for us,[5] so that as often as we are oppressed by tribulations we might run to these defenses, that when the adversary threatens or the enemy is before our eyes we might fast and conquer. Indeed, men are accustomed to send ambassadors to neighboring peoples for help whenever they undergo some unavoidable difficulty. Let us—which is better—send an embassy to God by our fasts, let us beg help from Him, let us betake ourselves to Him with heart and prayers. For they did not seek help by asking anywhere else but demanded it with their stomachs by fasting. Why should a person ask from someone else when he is able to find what he is looking for within himself? For the closer we are to God, the further our adversaries are driven from us. Therefore it behooves us to be very near to God, since the prophet says: *Behold, those who part from you will perish.*[6] If those who are far from God will perish, certainly those who are very near will be saved. But we cannot be very near to God unless we approach Him with fasting, prayers, and almsgiving, for God is Himself merciful, empty of food,[7] and holy, and thus whoever wants to be very near to God must imitate what God is.

4. The entire city of the Ninevites, then, fasted in its tribulation. I said the entire city, for we read that not only the old, the young, and infants fasted but even cattle. This is a remarkable thing, that one whom a sinful condition does not fetter fasts for a city's sin. Wherefore we also, brethren, bearing the burdens of the times, should all fast as well and call down God's mercy by the abstinence of all. For

how can it be that Christians do not do for their own salvation what the cattle did for the salvation of human beings? Is this not to be more senseless than a beast, not to fast when a fast has been decreed for one by the bishop?[8] Is he not a beast who does not understand what threatens him, what hangs over him? And indeed a beast, when it sees them, turns aside from pitfalls and bewares of precipices, but you do not want to turn aside from the danger that you discern by fasting. For it is a kind of audacity to eat when you should be fasting and to rejoice when you should be lamenting. The Apostle says of this audacity (God keep us from it!): *Let us eat and drink, for tomorrow we shall die.*[9] Therefore let us fast constantly, brethren, so that we might be able to overcome our foes with prayers and abstinence.

SERMON 82

A Sequel[1]

1. Last Sunday we said that the Ninevites merited divine mercy by their abstinence when they were in tribulation and freed their city from danger by fasting, and that they were so wise that they did not protect themselves with others' help but saved themselves through their own devotion. For they did not immediately give up hope of their salvation when they heard from the prophet that they would be destroyed along with their city, but they armed themselves all the more with religious deeds as the ruin that was announced drew near. Nor did they abandon their city that was about to be destroyed; instead they stayed in it, knowing that what was hurt by the sins of the citizens would be saved by the prayers of the citizens and that religious devotion would bring safety to that upon which an evil life had brought doom. For it was right that what had endured sinners should have them as its defenders, since ruin befalls a city for no other reason than the sins of its citizens.

2. Cease from sinning, then, and the city will not perish! Why do you flee your native land?[2] Get away from your sins instead if you wish to be saved! If you cease from sinning the enemy has been conquered. The divine Scripture says to Abraham that one's native

land can be saved through ten righteous men.[3] Therefore, if there are ten righteous men who can save their native land, those who abandon it are indeed unrighteous, and if the ones obtain grace on account of their presence, necessarily the others are considered criminal on account of their desertion. Clearly a son who deserts his mother when she is in danger is unjust and impious, for one's native land is a sweet mother, so to speak, who has begotten you, nurtured you, and, so that you might be able to flee, enriched you.[4] For if there were no abundant supply of wealth at your disposal you would not have the wherewithal for your flight. Therefore, led by avarice and fearing to lose your riches, you do not hesitate to be disrespectful to your mother. Hence we understand that you have more regard for your money than you do for your salvation. Tell me, O good citizen, why are you getting ready to flee? Why are you leaving your native land? Do you perhaps fear captivity? †Pardon me,† [5] do you not understand? Do you not know that the first captivity is not to see your native land, and that to undergo the hostile exile of wandering is more burdensome than any other evil? A person who commits some crime is often sentenced to a penalty of this sort: he is driven from his native land and confined to unknown regions. This evil, then, which is a frequent punishment incurred by a condemned person, you are preparing for yourself of your own choice. But let us suppose that you are stouthearted and able to bear the distress of wandering with equanimity. Tell me, how freely will you live among strangers? When you begin to speak, will someone not object: "Why is this fellow in exile?[6] Why has this fugitive come? Is he trying to oppress our nation too as he oppressed his own native land?" Thus you will be straitened, thus you will be thrown into confusion, so that you will doubt your freedom and fear that you will never find anyone in that place to defend your liberty. Believe me: in a foreign country you will hear exactly what you said to others in your own country. I do not want to tell you this, but, although you may be rich in your native land and enjoy many things, as soon as you leave your home you shall be reduced to begging and be impoverished.

3. The Lord says to Abraham, then, that a city can be saved through ten righteous men. You do not think well of yourselves, therefore, Christian people, if you do not believe that among such as us there are ten righteous men to save the city. For in leaving your

native land you declare that there are not in it ten persons by whose merits it might be saved. I fear, however, that when all the righteous have been left behind in it, only you who are deserting it may be found unrighteous. But I do not want you to be preoccupied by the number of ten righteous men. We read concerning the destruction of the Sodomites that Lot alone, by his own merits, saved a city and that the grace of a single person had more effect for salvation than the sins of many had for ruin.[7] For, insignificant as it was, Segor is pardoned on account of its hospitality towards the one who fled from Sodom.[8] If a city is forgiven on account of a righteous host, all the more is one's native land pardoned on account of a righteous citizen.

SERMON 83

That One Who Fears God Should Not Fear the Barbarians, and On Holy Elisha[1]

1. I remember having frequently said that we should not fear any warlike disturbances nor be frightened at any great multitude of foes since, as the Lord says, *The one who is in us is greater than the one who is in this world;*[2] that is to say, Christ is more powerful to protect His servants than the devil is to provoke our enemies. For although this same devil collects mobs for himself and arms them with cruel rage, nonetheless they are easily destroyed because the Savior surrounds His people with superior auxiliaries, as the prophet says: *The angel of the Lord comes round about those who fear him, and he will save them.*[3] If the angel of the Lord snatches those who fear him from dangers, then one who fears the Savior cannot fear the barbarians, nor can one who observes the precepts of Christ be afraid of the onslaught of the foe. These are our weapons, with which the Savior has outfitted us: prayer, mercy, and fasting. For fasting is a surer protection than a rampart, mercy saves more easily than pillage, and prayer wounds from a greater distance than an arrow, for an arrow only strikes the person of the adversary at close range, while a prayer even wounds an enemy who is far away.[4]

2. Thus, when the king of Syria wanted to capture holy Elisha the

prophet and subject him to his power and had surrounded him with many warriors and troops, he was not terrified or disturbed but said to the servant who brought him the information: *Do not fear, for there are more on our side than on theirs.*[5] O the faith of the holy prophet! He does not fear the adversaries whom he sees because he knows that angels are with Him in whom he believes; he is not afraid of earthly plots because he knows that heavenly auxiliaries are present to him. *There are more on our side,* he says, *than on theirs.* What a remarkable thing! There are more defenders from heaven merited by holiness than there are attackers on earth produced by wickedness. See the merit of blessedness! The prophet already speaks of a multitude while his servant is still uncertain of salvation. How much more do spiritual eyes discern than fleshly ones! The one perceives a throng of warriors and the other catches sight of a sign of protection. How great is the divine mercy! A benefit is conferred upon human beings and it is not seen, those in danger obtain help and they do not know it. For this is the kindness of the Savior, that He should intervene for the sake of salvation and not let Himself be seen, that He should be sensed through His benefits and not be discerned through sight.

3. Hence he errs who thinks that, when he has waged a war successfully, he has overcome by his own power. For he ought to know that adversaries are conquered more by merits than by strength and are overcome not so much by power as by holiness, just as holy Elisha overcame his foes not by arms but by prayer. For when he said to his servant, in order to drive out his fear, that there were more defenders present, but his fear could not be removed, then he prayed to the Lord and said: *Lord, open his eyes that he may see! And his eyes were opened and he saw, and behold, there was a whole mountain full of horsemen,*[6] and so forth. The prayer of the prophet, then, opened his servant's eyes. It is not to be wondered at if prayer, which opened heaven for an army to come, opened his eyes so that he could see the army. It is not to be wondered at, I say, if he who promises new auxiliaries inserts new eyes. Or why would not he who furnished an army of angels produce an army of seers? Why, I say, would not he who penetrated the darkness of the clouds by his merits cleanse dullness of vision by his prayer? Necessarily, then, with this deed holy Elisha offered safety to his frightened servant, to whom he had already given clearness of vision, and from the one from whom he had removed

blindness he removed fearfulness of heart; bestowing a double gift on him, he dismissed his fear and freed his sight. He began to fear less after he merited to see more, for he merited both peace and sight at the same time.

4. On the mountains, then, warriors are discerned. It appears that they whose coming is first observed on the mountains have truly descended from heaven. The very nearness of the places meant that those descending from heaven could not help but set their feet on the heights of the nearby mountains. Then Elisha prayed and struck the whole enemy army with blindness. It is not to be wondered at if he who bestowed clearness of vision on his attendant brought blindness upon his adversaries, and if he who offers vision to his servant takes away the sight of his foes. Where are those who say that the weapons of men can do more than the prayers of the saints? Look, one prayer of Elisha inflicted a wound on a whole army, and by the merits of a single prophet the entire foe was led captive. What troops of kings, what mob of soldiers has carried off such a victory as to cut down the foe while from among themselves no one falls? This is the true, this the bloodless victory, when the adversary is conquered in such a way that none of the conquerors is hurt.

SERMON 84

A Sequel[1]

1. It may perhaps seem remarkable that, when we were describing the grace of holy Elisha a few days ago, we said that troops descended from heaven in his defense, that warriors, horsemen, and chariots were divinely present to him, and that even a fiery chariot stood near him. This is, to be sure, a great thing, but it is not to be marveled at in the holy man. For what is there remarkable if he merits help from heaven, he whose soul is always in heaven, as the apostle Paul says: *But our way of life is in heaven?*[2] If, then, our way of life is in heaven, the way of life of the heavenly beings can also be with us; that is to say, we who live the life of the angels may justifiably merit their companionship. For among those who live in holy fashion there is a

certain bond, union, and relationship, nor is it a question of whether they dwell in heaven or on earth or whether their state is angelic or human, so long as there is in them the same life and holiness. For way of life joins those whom nature separates, and although they are divided by different bodies they are linked by the same deeds. And therefore it happens that the saints, holding fast to one another by a kind of companionship, are not absent from one another, and sometimes angels come to earth and sometimes human beings are brought to the heavens, and, by a change for the better, those whose life is in common begin to have elements of living in common.[3]

But suppose someone says: "We have frequently heard that angels have come down to human beings. We also want to know when human beings have gone to heaven." The response is clear and it is right before our eyes. Was not Elijah, Elisha's master, snatched up to heaven by angels and did he not go up in a fiery chariot like a conqueror in a kind of triumph?[4] For he was a conqueror not of barbarian nations but of worldly pleasures, inasmuch as depraved habits are more bitter enemies than a destructive foe, and nowadays we should understand that a wicked foe can more easily be conquered than wicked habits.

2. Angels bring Elijah to heaven, then, and angels watch over Elisha on earth. What is there to wonder at if angels, who carried away the master, protected the disciple? And what is noteworthy in the fact that the deference that they showed to the father they also manifested to the son? For he is the spiritual son of Elijah, he is the inheritor of his holiness. Justifiably is Elisha called the spiritual son of Elijah because when he went up to heaven he left a double spirit of his grace to him. For when Elisha was given the right to ask for whatever he wanted before Elijah would be taken from him, he asked that a double portion of Elijah might be in him.[5] Then Elijah said: *What you have asked is hard, but so it shall be for you.*[6] O precious inheritance in which the inheritor is left more than is possessed and the one who receives obtains more than the giver owned! Clearly this is a precious inheritance that is doubled by a kind of meritorious interest when it is transferred from father to son. Elijah, therefore, left a double portion to Elisha, although he himself had a single spirit of holiness. In a marvelous way, then, Elijah left more grace on earth than he carried with him to heaven, and although he is transported whole in body to

the heights, yet with his son there remains a greater degree of holiness.

3. What should we say of the merits of Elisha? This, first of all, is praiseworthy—that he wished to outdo his father in grace, asking that more be given him than he knew that the one who possessed it had. He is, to be sure, covetous in his request but deserving in his merits. For while he demands from his father more than he had, he made him stand out by his own merits more than he was able.[7] For this same Elisha came to Jericho after the ascension of his master and was asked by the townspeople to remain in that city.[8] And when they said to him: *The town is in a good location, but the waters are bad and sterile,*[9] he ordered a clay vessel to be given him and, going to the source of the waters, he threw the salt that was kept in it into the waters, saying: *Thus says the Lord: I have cleansed the waters; neither death nor sterility shall come from them. And the waters have been cleansed up until this day.*[10] See how great, then, are the merits of Elisha! His first stay in his children's city results in much fruitfulness, because in doing away with the sterility of the waters he makes many people the object of his benefaction. For in accomplishing this Elisha did not cleanse a single person or offer healing to a single household, but he restored the people of the whole city. For if he had done this later the city would have remained without an inhabitant; everyone would have grown old, afflicted with sterility. Therefore Elisha cleansed the people as well when he cleansed the waters, and in blessing the spring of waters he showed favor to the spring, as it were, of souls. For as, by his blessing, water came forth from the earth's hidden channels, so also healthy offspring came forth from the hidden organs of the womb. For Elisha blessed not only those streams alone that were contained in the bowels of the springs, but also those that were eventually going to flow later and were still concentrated in the earth's damp soil. Hence Scripture says that Elisha gave a blessing at the source of the waters so that the prophet's sanctifying act might seize the water as it distilled, before the bosom of the spring concealed it.[11]

4. Therefore, since the holy apostle Paul says that *these things happened to them as a figure,*[12] let us see what the true meaning is of this figure—that is to say, what that city is which suffers sterility and what the vessel means and also why sprinkled salt should confer health. In the same apostle we read that this is said of the Church:

Rejoice, you sterile one who do not bear; break forth and shout, you who do not beget.[13] The Church, then, is that sterile city which, because of the bad condition of the waters before the coming of Christ (that is to say, because of the sacrilege of the Gentile peoples), was unable to conceive children for God in its sterility.[14] But when Christ came, taking on a human body like a clay vessel,[15] He cleansed the bad condition of the waters; that is to say, He cut off the sacrileges of the peoples, and immediately the Church, which used to be sterile, began to be fruitful. Hence the Apostle says: *Rejoice, you sterile one.* From this moment the Church, which used to be sterile, begot more children than the Synagogue bore, which used to be fruitful. And we recognize without difficulty what the sprinkled salt is that acted as a remedy, for the Lord says to His apostles: *You are the salt of the earth.*[16] If the apostles are compared to salt, then, the figure is well rounded out: just as the salt poured from the vessel brought healing to the waters at that time, so also now the apostles sent by the Savior bring healing to all the peoples so that they may begin to bring forth the offspring of the virtues, since the sterility of the vices has been removed.

SERMON 85

On Warlike Disturbances[1]

1. Perhaps you are anxious, brethren, at the fact that we hear constantly of the tumult of wars and the onslaughts of battles, and perhaps your love[2] is still more anxious inasmuch as these are taking place in our times. But this is the reason: the closer we are to the destruction of the world, the closer we are to the kingdom of the Savior. For the Lord Himself says: *In the last days nation will rise against nation and kingdom against kingdom. But when you see wars and earthquakes and famines, know that the kingdom of God is at hand.*[3] This nearness of wars, then, demonstrates to us rather that Christ is near. Therefore I must not be afraid of the approaching adversary, since by these signs I understand instead that the Savior is approach-

ing, for although the one induces a temporal fear, yet the other will bring an eternal salvation. The same Lord, however, is powerful both to drive from us fear of the foes and to bestow on us His own presence.

2. By these warlike disturbances, then, the destruction of the world is somehow signified, for this unrest precedes the future judgment of God. But it is a kind of warning judgment of God to see what you should fear, so that you may understand that you should fear what is still to come, for in being careful about what we see we are made more careful about those things for which we hope. But one who is wise is instructed by these earthly events as to how he must avoid the coming judgment of the world. For, as he perceives how, in this universal confusion, the leading men prepare for safety by building ramparts, he himself is warned as to how to prepare a defense for Christian souls in the future destruction of the world. Seeing that the gates of the city are fortified, we ought first to fortify the gates of righteousness in ourselves, for there are gates of righteousness, about which the holy prophet said: *Open to me the gates of righteousness,*[4] and so forth. But the city gate can be secured only if the gate of righteousness in ourselves is first made secure; otherwise it is of no help to secure the walls with bulwarks while rousing God's anger with sins. The one is built of iron, stones, and spikes; let the other be armed with mercy, innocence, and chastity. The one is guarded with a large number of spears; let the other be defended with frequent prayers. And for the complete protection of cities the ensigns of princes usually stand before the gates, but let the ensign of the Savior[5] stand before the gates of our souls.

3. Therefore, brethren, let us arm ourselves with heavenly weapons for the coming judgment of the world: let us gird on the breastplate of faith, protect ourselves with the helmet of salvation, and defend ourselves with the word of God as with a spiritual sword.[6] For the one who is arrayed with these weapons does not fear present disturbance and is not afraid of future judgment, since holy David, protected with this devotion, slew the very strong and armed Goliath without weapons and struck down the warlike man, girt about with defenses on all sides, by the strength of his faith alone.[7] For although holy David did not put on a helmet, strap on a shield, or use a lance, he

slew Goliath. He slew him, however, not with an iron spear but with a spiritual sword, for although he appeared weaponless in the eyes of human beings, yet he was adequately armed with divine grace. But the spiritual sword itself was not a sword, since it was not by the sword but by a stone that Goliath died when he was struck down. We read in the Scriptures that Christ is figuratively designated by the word "stone," as the prophet says: *The stone that the builders rejected has become the head of the corner.*[8] Therefore, when Goliath is struck by a stone, he is struck down by the power of Christ. And in what part of the body is he struck? On the forehead, for when the sacrilegious man is struck, there Christ was absent, and where his end comes upon him, there the sign of salvation is not to be found. For although Goliath was protected by weapons on all sides, still his forehead was exposed to death because it did not carry the Savior's seal, and therefore he is slain in the spot where he is found to be bare of God's grace.[9]

But there is no one who does not realize that this took place in figure.[10] For David had also put on armor beforehand but, since he was so heavy and awkward in it that he could hardly walk, he removed it at once, signifying that the weapons of this world are vain and superfluous things and that the person who chooses to involve himself in them will have no unimpeded road to heaven, since he will be too heavy and encumbered to walk.[11] At the same time this teaches us that victory is not to be hoped for from arms alone but is to be prayed for in the name of the Savior.

SERMON 86

A Sequel[1]

1. Your love[2] remembers that last Sunday we preached that by good actions and constant prayers we may open to ourselves the gates of righteousness and that by frequent almsgiving we may fortify ourselves as with a rampart of mercy. For to resist by almsgiving and to struggle by fasting are indeed an impregnable wall against the

adversary. For although the enemy's weapons may be powerful, nonetheless these weapons of the Savior are stronger. If anyone is armed with them, even though he appear defenseless in the eyes of human beings, he is nonetheless adequately armed because the most high Divinity is guarding him. In tribulation, then, it is good to pray, to fast, to sing psalms, and to be merciful,[3] for by these weapons, as we have mentioned in the example of David against Goliath,[4] Christians are accustomed to conquer their adversaries; by these arms they are accustomed to guard the bulwarks of the city. For the holy prophet says: *Unless the Lord guard the city, those who guard it keep watch in vain.*[5] He keeps watch in vain, therefore, who thinks that he is defending the city by his own attentiveness when he himself does not have the arms of faith. Clearly he labors in vain who judges that he is able to make someone else safe when he himself is bereft of the grace of God. The Lord says in the Gospel: *Physician, heal yourself.*[6] What is meant by this example is that you, man, must look out for your own salvation first, so that you may be able to provide for the salvation of many. Moreover, when I see you feeble and weak and bereft of the divine assistance, I not only have no confidence in the protection of the city that you provide but I even fear lest your foolhardiness throw the city into confusion. The city is protected, therefore, when it is God Himself, rather, who guards it. But God guards it—as it is written—when those dwelling in it are all temperate and serious Christians and Catholics, for it must needs be that God would save the city in which He finds what He might preserve[7] of His own precepts. But the Lord does not preserve that city where there is wantonness, faithlessness, and blasphemy, lest it be not so much the city that is preserved as the sins that are in it.

2. Therefore the one who prepares a defense for a city in the name of the Lord is the one who truly makes its citizens secure. But whoever tries to construct a defense for a city apart from the grace of God seems to prepare a den for himself similar to a foxes' hole. For is he not like a fox in a hole,[8] which is constantly digging the earth and not at all looking at heaven? For the Lord says, as we have just now heard read: *The foxes have holes and the birds of heaven have nests where they may rest, but the Son of Man has nowhere to lay His head.*[9] Let us carefully inquire what meaning this phrase may have. For the Lord

was not speaking of that particular animal but of people who are always clever and shrewd and always acting like a fox: while they deceitfully seize what belongs to others they are digging a hole of perdition for themselves. And therefore the head of Christ, which is God,[10] cannot find a dwelling in them because they themselves dwell in places that are buried in the earth.

3. But no one doubts that the heretics in particular are comparable to foxes.[11] For they are like crafty, troublesome, and daring foxes; where they perceive quiet, there they insinuate the madness[12] of their fickleness; where they discover watchfulness, from there they disperse in their crafty guile. For as the animal of which we are speaking is always deceitful, always untrustworthy, and can never change its clever ways, so also every heretic is always deceitful and always untrustworthy and, although he might seem to speak with you in a straightforward way, it is his words that he alters but not his character; in his speech he gives promise of temperance, but from his heart he draws out madness.[13] The fox deceives with its tail, while the heretic cheats with his tongue; the fox feigns gentleness among the animals so that it may seize them, while the heretic gives promise of moderation among human beings so that he may harm them; the one plays a game beforehand in order to slay, while the other speaks flattery first in order to ruin. It is customary with the fox always to lie in wait for a hen and its chicks, so that if one of them should go off some distance from its mother it might be seized as its prey. So also the heretic always lies in wait for mother Church[14] and her children, so that if perchance he should find one somewhat negligent he might ensnare him with his madness. But that the Church is rightly compared to a hen we read in the Gospel, when the Lord says to Jerusalem: *Jerusalem, how often have I wished to gather your children as a hen gathers its chicks under its wings.*[15] And rightly is a hen compared to the Church, for as it not only cares for its own children but also receives strange ones who come, so also a hen not only cares for those whom it itself has hatched but also nourishes strangers that have been placed near it.[16] Therefore, brethren, let us arm ourselves throughout this week with fasts, prayers, and vigils so that, when the mercy of God comes upon us, we may both hold back the savagery of the barbarians and render ineffectual the snares of the heretics.

SERMON 88

On John the Baptist[1]

1. Last Sunday, when we were asking pardon for our silence, we said that even if the bishops[2] were silent about the salvation of all, the Gospel teaching would not be silent, and that the divine words would make up for their silence.[3] For the divine Scripture always speaks and cries out, as it is written of John: *I am the voice of one crying in the desert.*[4] For John did not only cry out at the time when he announced the Lord, the Savior, to the Pharisees and said: *Prepare the way of the Lord, make straight the paths of our God,*[5] but he also cries out today among us, striking the desert places of our sins with the thunder of his voice, and although he has fallen asleep in a martyr's holy death, still his voice lives. For he also says to us today: *Prepare the way of the Lord, make straight His paths.* The divine Scripture, then, always cries out and speaks; hence God also says to Cain: *The voice of your brother's blood cries out to me.*[6] Blood, to be sure, has no voice, but innocent blood that has been spilled is said to cry out not by words but by its very existence[7] and to make demands of the Lord not with eloquent discourse but with anger over the crime committed—not to accuse the wrongdoer with words so much as to bind him by the accusation of his own conscience. For although the evil deed may perhaps be excused if it is talkatively explained away, it cannot be excused if it is made present to the conscience, for in silence and without contradiction the wrongdoer's conscience always convicts and judges him.[8]

2. Today, therefore, John cries out and says: *Prepare the way of the Lord, make straight,* and so forth. We are ordered, then, to prepare the way of the Lord—not a highway, namely, but a pure faith. For the Lord does not proceed along an earthly path but sets out in the recesses of the mind. If, therefore, there is on this way any unevenness of character, any rough unkindness, any filthy habit, we are ordered to clean it, to make it level, and to arrange it so that, when He comes, the Lord may not find in us anything that would make Him stumble but would instead discover a way that was clean because of chastity, easily traversable because of faith, and lofty because of almsgiving. And that the Lord is used to setting out on such a road the

prophet mentions when he says: *Make a road for Him who ascends over the setting sun; the Lord is His name.*[9]

3. But let us see what road John, who orders that a way be prepared for the Lord, himself prepares for the Savior. Clearly he arranged and laid out his own pathway everywhere for the coming Christ, for, indeed, he was given to fasting, humble, frugal, and virginal. All these virtues of his the Evangelist describes when he says: *But John had a garment of camel hair, and there was a leather belt around his waist, and his food was locusts and wild honey.*[10] What greater humility was there in the prophet than, disdaining soft clothing, to wear the harshness of hair? What more devout faith than, girt about with a belt, always to be ready for every serviceable act? What more noble abstinence than, despising the pleasures of this life, to feed on whirring locusts and wild honey? Since all these things were of use to the prophet, I think that there was something prophetic in them. For indeed, inasmuch as the precursor of Christ had a garment sewn out of the harshness of camels, what else does this mean but that Christ Himself, who was to come, would use the covering of a human body that had been made thick with the harshness of sins and that He would Himself, as if girt in the skin of a most unclean beast (that is, of the Gentile people), bear its deformity?[11] And what else does a leather belt show but this frail flesh of ours,[12] which before Christ's coming was mastered by vices but after His coming would be constrained to virtue, and which previously grew fat through wantonness but would now become thin through abstinence?

4. And we read how blessed his death was—that a dancer,[13] the daughter of a king, should ask for his head in consequence of that enemy, sensual pleasure.[14] What is there to wonder at if a dancer kills a prophet? We know that wantonness is always the enemy of righteousness and that wickedness persecutes the truth incessantly. In this deed a great mystery is contained, for in fact this dancer must be compared to the Synagogue, which kills Christ while it behaves wantonly. That this dancer is the Synagogue the Lord tells the Jews: *We sang for you and you did not dance.*[15] And it is evident why John's head should have been removed from his body. John, as is known from the Scriptures, was an image of the law, but we read of the Lord that *the head of a man is Christ.*[16] When John's head is removed from his body, then, Christ is in a certain way separated from the Jews, the

practitioners of the law, for without the Savior there was left them a law that was lifeless and truncated.[17] From the moment when they began to be without a head the Jews have been utterly ignorant of divine matters.

5. He makes a road for the Lord, then, who, among the other virtues of continence, does not go outside the bounds of matrimony nor sully the prescribed limit of marriage by an adulterous union. For there are some who, when they have married wives in lawful fashion, associate with concubines contrary to the divine law, not realizing that by acting against marriage they have bound themselves by their own fetters. For one who marries a wife in lawful fashion professes that he will not act against the law. Consequently one who ignores his promise by taking an adulteress to himself declares himself guilty. But suppose someone says: "I have no wife; therefore I have taken a little serving girl for myself." Hear what the Scripture says to Abraham: *Drive out the slave and her son! For the son of the slave shall not be heir with the son of the free woman.*[18] If, therefore, the son of the slave is not an heir, neither is he a son. Why, then, is such a union sought, whose offspring can be an heir in terms neither of succession nor of blood? For one who does not have the right of birth cannot have a participation in inheritance either. Why, I say, is such concubinage sought, from which are born not the children of matrimony but witnesses to adultery? Why are such children conceived, who are not an honor to their father but a shame? Scripture says: *The children of adulterers,*[19] and so forth. Your companion,[20] then, if she is endowed with such character that she merits your company, should also merit the name of wife. Offer your concubine liberty and the name of wife, therefore, so as not to be an adulterer but rather a husband.[21]

6. But that Christian also makes a road for the Lord who offers Him the faithful service of his profession and guards the chastity that he has promised as much in mind as in body. For there are many who, while intending a single life, are unable to be single but seek concubinage for themselves—and that among the brethren! For you find a Christian monk who does not endure a brother but more willingly endures a sister, who does not hearken to his senior who advises beneficial things but hearkens to a young woman who laughingly says unbecoming things, whose soul cannot be incorrupt even if his body is incorrupt.[22]

And that cleric also makes a road for the Lord who lives according to the gospel and submits to the bishop in all things. For some, since they are less submissive, act in an annoying way when they are reproached by their seniors and say: "The bishop[23] is very angry; he should be more patient." Listen, then, excellent cleric! Do you demand patience of the bishop and not demand discipline of yourself? Do you not know that it has been granted to me to make a reproach occasionally for the sake of salvation, but that you have never been conceded the right to sin? For the Apostle says: *Rebuke when convenient and inconvenient, reproach.*[24] Be submissive to the bishop in all things, then, if you wish him to be mild in all things.

SERMON 89

A Consoling Discourse to the People[1]

After these several days, brethren, I should preach something richer and refresh you with a sweet sermon, having returned from such a swarm of bishops.[2] Rightly have I said "a swarm of bishops," since like the bee they produce delightful honey from the blossoms of the divine Scriptures, and whatever pertains to the medicine of souls they make by the skill of their mouth. Justifiably are bishops compared to bees because, like the bee, they display bodily chastity, offer the bread of heavenly life, and exercise the sting of the law. For they are pure in order to sanctify, sweet in order to refresh, and severe in order to punish. Clearly they are to be compared to bees who are kept, as it were, in a kind of beehive by the grace of mother Church.[3] In it they produce many swarms of Christians from the one swarm of the Savior, arranging little cells of different merits by their most sweet preaching.

SERMON 91

A Warning That the End of the World Is at Hand, and That Idols Should Be Removed[1]

1. And you yourselves know, brethren, that I shall not cease to admonish you frequently and anxiously in many sermons and to dis-

pense the care of the priestly ministry[2] day and night. I do not regret doing this, to be sure, since I am fulfilling the duty of my office and giving back with interest, as it were, the responsibility that has been imposed. Yet it upsets me that these same sermons of mine charm your ears and do not penetrate your hearts; they warm you outwardly but do not nourish you inwardly, because if they moved your inmost being your zeal would in fact anticipate my sermon. Hence, when you lessen and weaken the fruit of your works you somehow curb the impetus of my preaching. For what use is there in speaking much to people from whom you receive not even a little in return? What use is there in scattering an abundance of seeds when the infertile earth does not receive them?[3]

2. Yet silence is not to be kept because it must rather be pressed upon the unfruitful that the end of the world is at hand, the day of judgment is near, the fires of Gehenna are burning, and each of us will have to give an account of his deeds and his life—not only of his own life, however, but also of the lives of those subject to him. Therefore I grieve because, even if your own sins did not hurt you, still the crimes of your household will bind you fast. For, apart from a few religious people, hardly anyone's field is unpolluted by idols, hardly any property is kept free from the cult of demons. Everywhere the Christian eye is offended, everywhere the devout mind is assailed; wherever you turn you see either the altars of the devil or the profane auguries of the pagans or the heads of animals fixed to boundary posts (although the person who sees these things occurring on his property and does not correct them is headless, for truly he is headless whose dimmed eyes—as if they were those of a beast that has been struck down—are preoccupied with wicked intent).[4] You should know that whoever is not adversely affected by such an offense is himself a participant in the offense. What householder will knowingly accept services of this sort from his laborers, which he realizes are offered to him with polluted hands? How will he enjoy first fruits that he surmises were consecrated to demons before they were to the Lord? Let us be equally solicitous, then, of ourselves and of our household. And since holy Quadragesima is at hand, let us call the pagans to Christianity and the catechumens to baptism.

SERMON 92

On the Watchman Who Is Set over the Children of Israel[1]

1. Sometimes, brethren, when we preach, our sermon seems rather harsh to many, and what we speak about as a rule is taken by some as if it were produced out of a hard strictness. For they say: "How severely and bitterly the bishop[2] has preached!"—not knowing that for bishops[3] speaking is more a matter of obligation than of desire. Speaking, I say, is more a matter of obligation—not because the desire to preach the truth is lacking but because the silence that comes from not speaking is driven away by the punishment of the law.[4] We are obligated inasmuch as we are afraid, and thus we are compelled by what we can do more than by what we wish to do; and we call fearful things to the attention of others inasmuch as we ourselves tremble for our own salvation. This, then, is the preacher's situation—that he should not be silent with respect to the sins of another if he wishes to avoid sinning himself, and that he should correct his brother by reproving him so that he may not destroy what is priestly in himself.[5] But if he wishes to dissemble, to be silent, and to conceal, his silence fails to correct the other person, and by not preaching he also condemns himself.

Consequently it is better to correct the sinner by rebuking him than to accept the sinner's misdeeds by keeping quiet. This is the position in which we have been placed: if we told sinners that their crimes were not their own, the guilt of their crimes would also implicate us. For this is in fact what the Lord says through the prophet: *And you, son of man, you I have given as a watchman to the house of Israel, and you shall hear the word from my mouth. When I say to the sinner: You shall die the death, and you do not speak so that the impious may beware of his way, the wicked himself shall die in his own wickedness, but I will require his blood from your hand,*[6] and so forth. Clearly these words are plain and obvious. They soil the watchman with criminal blood when he keeps silence and they are not satisfied that the evildoer's own evil-doing condemns him unless they also incriminate the one who was unwilling to rebuke the evil in question. See, then, how great the iniquity of the sinner is! The sinner himself sins and the bishop[7] is convicted; he kills himself by his own sins and his blood is required from the hand of the bishop.[8] There must be speaking and crying out, then, lest that same sinner accuse our silence on the day of judgment and the one who now feigns participation in holiness be charged then as a companion in error.

2. *And you, son of man,* He says, *you I have given as a watchman to the house of Israel.* What is a watchman? A watchman is one who, while standing, as it were, on a lofty pinnacle, looks out on the populace around him so that no enemy might fall unexpectedly upon it but so that, as he keeps careful watch, the citizens might retain the sweetness of peace. If he should suddenly see something hostile, he lets it be known at once, he proclaims it without cease, both so that the city might be prepared for the danger and so that the enemy, once detected, might flee. Otherwise, if the watchman is careless or silent or negligent while the enemy attacks, the consequence is that the unprepared people are seized and the enemy overcomes them and rages uncontrollably. And therefore the whole guilt is ascribed to the one who was unwilling to speak so as to save the many but preferred to be silent so that he himself would perish with the many. These watchmen who have been established by the Lord, then—who do we say that they are if not the most blessed bishops?[9] Having been set, as it were, on a kind of lofty pinnacle of wisdom, they look out over a distance for oncoming evils for the sake of the people's safety and, while still far away, they survey future distress not with the sight of the fleshly eye but with the vision of spiritual prudence. Therefore they cannot be silent but are compelled to cry out, lest by their silence the enemy, the devil, invade Christ's flock. For look, we foresee the day of judgment coming, and already in our very thought we sense the punishment of sin. And so we announce to each person that he should turn away from the path of his wickedness: to the drunken that he should pursue temperance, because drunkenness' companion is that enemy wantonness; and to the avaricious that he should give away his money, lest in holding onto it he seem to possess wealth not to use it but to worship it, for what a person loves he worships, protects, and, so to speak, venerates. Beware, then, avaricious one, lest the little chests on your table turn into an idolatrous temple for you because

you do not make use of them like a master but guard their contents like a slave.[10]

SERMON 93

On What Is Written: Lift Up Your Voice Like a Trumpet and Tell My People of Their Sins[1]

1. Yesterday we discoursed about the obligation that weighs upon us of not being silent and, lest we expose ourselves to danger from outside, we assert that we must rise up to preach with an outcry. For we must cry out in church lest we cry out in punishment, since the Lord speaks thus through the prophet: *And cry out forcefully and do not be sparing; lift up your voice like a trumpet and tell my people of their sins.*[2] We are commanded, then, to cry out and to cry out forcefully and not to spare our voice lest we lose our salvation. *And do not be sparing,* He says. That is, do not pass over the sinner's wickedness by keeping silent and by being considerate of his shame but inconsiderate of his well-being, for by keeping silent you have made worse the wounds that you ought to have healed by crying out. We are commanded, then, to cry out and, lest someone say that he did not hear or that the bishop's[3] voice was inaudible to him, we are ordered to cry out forcefully. And if perhaps this should not be enough He adds: *Lift up your voice like a trumpet.* We know that a trumpet is usually not so much heard as dreaded; it is not so much accustomed to bring pleasure as to inspire fear. A trumpet is necessary for sinners: it not only penetrates their ears but should strike their heart as well; it should not delight with its melody but chastise when it has been heard; the vigorous it should encourage to righteousness, while the cowardly it should turn from their crimes. For just as in battle the trumpet disconcerts the mind of the frightened soldier and kindles the spirit of the brave, so also the priestly trumpet brings low the mind of the sinner and strengthens the spirit of the saint, and with one and the same sound it encourages the one to be stronger in virtue and strikes fear in the other so that he will be more hesitant to sin. For it is the

nature of the trumpet to destroy the works of sinners and confirm the deeds of saints.[4]

2. The walls of Jericho fell down on account of the priestly trumpets because they contained within themselves a sinful people.[5] A battering ram did not strike it nor did a machine of war storm it, but—what is remarkable—the terror of the priestly sound brought it down. The walls that had stood impervious to iron collapsed at the sacred voice of the trumpets. Who would not be amazed that, when the sound had been made, stones were broken to pieces, foundations were shattered by the noise, and everything collapsed in such a way that, although the conquerors did not injure their own forces, nonetheless among the enemy nothing remained standing? But although no one touched those walls, still they were taken from without at the sound of the righteous while sinners dwelled within. For this reason, then, they gave way, lest they offer resistance to the ones or somehow protect the others. To the righteous they opened a path and to the faithless they denied protection.

Therefore, brethren, if the sound of the priestly voice was so powerful at that time, such that its blast in the air announced a certain confusion, how much more do we believe that that priestly voice is living now, which shows forth something magnificent when it speaks Christ in words! ⟨. . .⟩[6] should give way before the authority of the Savior when even the elements gave way at the sounding air? Or how could feeling creatures resist when even unfeeling ones were unable to endure the sacred dread? For we believe that hearts can more easily be softened than rocks at the words of the priests and that sins can be forgiven in a shorter time than those stones were split asunder.[7] For the voice of the Spirit, when it comes, destroys the stain of sin more easily than it breaks apart a tangible fortification of rock.

SERMON 94

A Sequel[1]

1. Last Sunday we said that the walls of Jericho were laid waste by the priestly[2] trumpets[3] and that, contrary to order and nature, an unfeeling thing gave way before the sacred sounds with a kind of

dread of the threat, and everything so collapsed at the loud noise that the most solid fortifications fell to the ground and the sinful people remained without protection. The one occurred lest resistance be offered for any amount of time, the other so that they would be the more easily captured.

But we have said that all these things were done then in symbol,[4] for we believe that the priestly trumpets of that age were nothing other than the preaching of the priests of this age, by which we do not cease to announce, with a dreadful sound, something harsh to sinners, to speak of what is dismal, and to strike the ears of evildoers with, as it were, a threatening roar, since no one can resist the sacred sounds and no one can gainsay them. For how could feeling creatures not tremble at the word of God when at that time even unfeeling ones were shaken? And how could human hardheartedness resist what a stone fortification could not withstand? For just as, when the stone walls were destroyed, the clash of the trumpets reached the people within, so also now, when evil thoughts have been destroyed, the preaching of the priests penetrates to the bare parts of the soul, for the soul is found bare before the word of God when its every evil deed is destroyed. And that the soul is bare before God the holy Apostle says: *But all things are bare and uncovered to His eyes.*[5] In this regard, before the soul knows God and accepts the truth of the faith it veils itself, so to speak, under superstitious works and surrounds itself with something like a wall of perversity, such that it might seem to be able to remain impregnable within the fortifications of its own evil-doing. But when the sacred sound thunders, its rashness is overthrown, its thinking is destroyed, and all the defenses of its superstitions break asunder in such a way that, remaining unprotected, as it is written, *the word of God might penetrate even to the division of its spirit and its inmost parts.*[6] Just as the ring of the sacred sound destroyed, captured, and took vengeance on a hardhearted people then, so also now the priestly preaching subjugates, captures, and takes vengeance on a sinful people. For thus says the blessed Apostle: *The weapons of our warfare are not fleshly, but they have divine power for the destruction of strongholds, destroying thoughts and capturing every height that lifts itself up against the knowledge of God, ready,* he says, *to punish every disobedience.*[7] See, then, if on the tongue of the priests there are not, according to the Apostle's saying, some weapons of words by which vain thought is destroyed, puffed-up pride is captured, and the hardheartedness of disobedience is punished.

2. But what was done then to the city of Jericho, as we have said, was done in symbol, since now this very thing happens in reality. For we read that at that time the priests circled the aforementioned city continuously for seven days and that, although a band of armed men was unable to take it, it was overthrown by the sound of trumpets coming from all sides[8]—of trumpets, I say, not played by a rough soldier but sounded by a consecrated priest.[9] Who would not fear a person's trumpet if he did not fear his sword? After seven days, therefore, the walls that were circled fell at the priestly trumpets; we read that in seven days the works of this world were completed.[10] You see, then, that with this number seven it is not so much one city that is destroyed by the priests as the wickedness of the whole world that is destroyed. For just as in the naming of a single city the condition of the whole world is symbolized,[11] so also the course of seven days indicates the space of seven thousand years during which the trumpets of priestly preaching announce destruction to the world and threaten judgment, as it is written: *For the world will also perish and all the things that are in the world, but the one who does the will of the Lord endures for ever.*[12]

SERMON 95

On Zacchaeus[1]

It has been my frequent wish, beloved brethren, to preach on the parable from this section of the Gospel and to speak of the grace of the wealthy Zacchaeus in words of great eloquence and to be abundant in praise of him, since he was free-giving for his own salvation. For who would not praise a person who was able to give his own wealth to himself and to acquire everlasting dominion for himself by owning temporal property?[2] He gave his wealth, I say, to himself, because what we possess is another's if we do not use it properly for salvation;[3] for whatever seems to be mine will not be mine when

I depart from the world if it is kept from being useful to me in the world.

It has been my wish, then, to preach on Zacchaeus' wealth and grace—that of a rich person, clearly, and of one for ever rich, because he merited to be richer to Christ than to the world, and he was wealthier in the possession of faith than in temporal goods. Zacchaeus must be praised, then, because although the rich are excluded from the glory of the heavenly kingdom (as the Lord says: *It is easier for a camel to pass through the eye of a needle than for one who is rich to enter the kingdom of heaven*[4]), he hastened to enter into the kingdom of heaven by means of those very riches and to pass through that strait and narrow needle's eye with the twisted mass of his body. What is a ruinous hindrance to others was profitable to his salvation.

But do not be surprised that I should speak of the deformed members of a camel in a human being: in a human being the camel's deformity is a question not of bodily but of spiritual disfigurement, not of awkward bearing but of base heart, for just as a camel is ungainly because of its disproportioned members, so also a human being is deformed because of the harshness of his sins. This is what the Lord means when He says: *It is easier for a camel to pass through the eye of a needle than for one who is rich to enter the kingdom of heaven.* That is to say that it is difficult for a sinner to pass through that hard and narrow way of heavenly life[5]—one that is poor and mean—with the deformity of sins. It is most necessary for one who wishes to pass from a hulking and base ungainliness to the exalted substance of that purity to simplify and mortify his way of life. Unless he does this he stumbles against the narrow gate of heaven like a burdened and deformed animal.[6]

Zacchaeus must be praised, therefore—he whose riches were unable to keep him from the royal threshold. He is greatly to be praised because his riches brought him to the threshold of the kingdom. Hence we understand that wealth is not a hindrance but a help to attaining the glory of Christ if, while yet possessing it, we do not squander it on wantonness but give it away for the sake of salvation, for there is no crime in possessions but in those who do not know how to use possessions.[7] For wealth is a temptation to vice for the foolish, but for the wise it is a help to virtue; to the ones an opportunity for salvation is given, by the others a stumbling block of perdition is acquired.

SERMON 96

A Sequel[1]

I believe that all the rich are rejoicing in last Sunday's sermon and that they are happy to whom Zacchaeus opened the heavenly portal which had been closed to them on account of their possessions. For he opened the heavenly portal when he taught them to come to the kingdom by that very thing which kept them from the kingdom; that is to say that property, which was a reproach to them to their destruction, would be of use to their salvation. Zacchaeus, therefore, bestowed a great deal on the rich inasmuch as he saw to it that they would possess their wealth for ever and that those who were never poor here would not be beggars in the future, but that by a kind of lucrative exchange they would receive great things for little ones, heavenly things for earthly, and everlasting things for temporal. Clearly it is a lucrative exchange not to wish to have what you possess so that you might be able to obtain what you do not have, and to make a sacrifice by letting go of your money sometimes so that you might have the advantage of possessing grace for ever.[2]

Zacchaeus, then, although he was a publican and by the deceit of usury sought great wealth by loaning out money, was suddenly converted to such an extent upon seeing Christ that he sought spiritual grace with a greater desire than he had sought worldly money. He was converted to such an extent, I say, that, looking at his former deeds, he himself condemned his deceitful acts and, on the verge of correcting himself, he first corrected his awareness of desire.[3] For he said: *Behold, I give half my goods to the poor, and if I have taken anything away from anyone I return it fourfold.*[4]

Suppose someone should say: "Why would a holy man, seeing the Savior before him, have given a half to the poor and not everything, since it is written: *If you wish to be perfect, sell all that you have and give to the poor, and come, follow me?*"[5] But in fact you will notice that he followed to the utmost because he gave not half but everything, for if you take away other people's property from Zacchaeus, nothing remains to him. This righteous man, in order that his liberality might be acceptable, knew how to distribute justly—that is, by returning what was not his. For with God it is a welcome alms that comes from one's own property and is not given from ill-gotten booty, for regarding generosity to the poor it is not spoils but gifts that are sought. What kind of a present, moreover, is that which one person takes with joy but which another gives up with tears, over which one is joyful and another sighs? Hence I know not how much the grace of the taker would help you, but the plaint of the one groaning burdens you greatly. For although you give what is your own, you offer a better alms if you return what is another's. Seeing this, holy Zacchaeus returned what he had taken away so that what he gave would be acceptable, for he said: *If I have taken anything away from anyone I return it fourfold.* See how often he made amends for the one time that he had sinned! He was a good lender, knowing that he would make a profit if he restored with multiple interest the money that he had taken with interest. He should be a model for all of us, and a special model for this world's lenders. But unfortunately there are many who do not imitate his grace but imitate his usury: they know how to seize things but are utterly unaware of how to restore them. And while he spontaneously returned fourfold what he took, they do not restore once what they have seized, even when they are compelled; they prefer to lose what is theirs at law than to restore what is others' by making a settlement.[6]

SERMON 98

On the Kalends of January[1]

1. Well indeed has it been disposed by a provident God that the Lord Christ should have been born amidst the festivals of the Gentiles and that amidst gloomy and superstitious error the splendor of the true light[2] should shine. Thus people might see that the righteousness of pure divinity has gleamed forth upon their empty super-

stitions and might forget their past sacrileges and not cultivate future ones. For what wise person, who understands the sacrament of the Lord's birthday,[3] would not condemn the drunkenness of the Saturnalia and turn away from the excess of the kalends, and what person desiring to have partnership with Christ would not refuse to be a partner with the world? For this is the essence of the divine cult, that whoever wishes to be associated with the vanity of the Gentiles cannot have union with the truth of the saints, for the blessed Apostle says: *What portion does righteousness have with wickedness? Or what fellowship is there of light with darkness?*[4] That is to say, a Christian cannot both practice the wantonness of wickedness and possess the gentle God of righteousness. For there are many who, following the custom of the ancient superstition of vanity, observe the day of the kalends as the highest festival and desire joy in such a way that they have sadness instead. For to so great an extent do they behave riotously and give themselves to wine and feasting that a person who had been chaste and temperate the whole year through is drunken and polluted that day; and unless he has done this he thinks that he has let the holiday go by, not realizing that on account of a holiday such as this he has let his salvation go by.

2. But what sort of thing is this—that, rising early, everybody goes out into the street with a little gift (that is, with a new year's gift) and, when he is about to greet a friend, greets him with a present before he does with a kiss, offering his lips to the other's lips while placing his hand in the other's hand? He does not return a sign of love but perform an office of avarice, with one and the same action embracing his friend and deceiving him. Judge for yourselves how venal this kiss is, for the more dearly it is purchased the more base it is considered. Before gold[5] how many of the better sort of people are judged unworthy of a kiss! After gold has shone in the hand it is booty and not favor that makes them worthy. But how unjust this is in its very wickedness—that an inferior is expected to make a gift to his better and that one who perhaps borrows in order to give is forced to give to someone who is rich! Yet they call this generosity new year's giving, although more prompt[6] ⟨. . .⟩.[7] A poor wretch, I say, is forced to give what he does not have, and to make the gift he must abandon his obedient sons.[8] Those who are wealthy, however, are also free-giving in their generosity, yet neither are they themselves unstained by sin.

For a wealthy person who would have disdained to give a beggar a denarius gives a solidus[9] to someone who is rich, and on the kalends someone who came to church on the Lord's birthday empty-handed and without anything hastens to his friend's house laden with gold. You see, then, that present flattery counts for more in the eyes of many than does a future reward: they prefer the kiss of their betters to the glory of the Savior. This kiss ought not to be called a kiss because it is venal, for Judas Iscariot kissed the Lord with just such a kiss, but in doing this he sought to betray Him.[10]

3. But what sort of thing is this—that, after a day has elapsed, those as it were who are beginning to live go outside the city, just as they do at the start of the year, so as to gather auspices and search for omens, from which they calculate for themselves the prosperity or the misfortune of the whole year?[11] Although these things are silly and laughable, for them they are also useless and harmful, for they have no prosperity so long as they are deceived by auguries, and they are always sad whenever they think that these things may happen while others are aware of them.[12] This they also add to their evil deeds, that, returning home after taking the auspices, they carry little branches in their hands for an omen. Thus they go back burdened to their dwelling, not understanding—wretched people!—that they go back burdened not indeed with a bundle of gifts but with a pile of sins.

SERMON 99

On the Birth of the Lord, the Savior[1]

1. What holy John the Baptist says of the Lord, the Savior, is true: *He must increase, but I must decrease,*[2] since this is demonstrated first in the seasons themselves. For look, at the birth of Christ the day increases, and at the birth of John it decreases; as the one comes forth the light advances, and as the other is born it is diminished. For in a certain way the ministering seasons themselves undergo a loss in their parts when the servant is born, but when the Lord is born they make a gain. Clearly the day progresses when the Savior of the world comes

forth, but it declines when the last prophet is brought to life, for it is written: *The law and the prophets were until John.*[3] And therefore it was necessary that the observance of the law should be dimmed when the grace of the gospel shone, and that the prophecy of the Old Testament should cease when the glory of the New Testament followed in its place. At the birth of the Lord, therefore, the day advances. There is nothing marvelous if that day advances on which the new sun of justice[4] flashes forth. There is nothing marvelous if that day advances which the most radiant light of truth illuminates, for the Evangelist says of Christ the Lord: *He was the true light that enlightens everyone.*[5] Therefore, if He was the true light that enlightens humankind, why should He not enlighten the world as well? And so the very day that brought forth light for the human race shone beforehand with the brilliance of the same light, and when the periods of its nights had been brought to a close it scattered the darkness through the gleaming of the Lord's light. For the length of the nights had taken up the whole day, but on the very shortest day the coming of the Lord—who in His rising as it were scatters the darkness of the sins of the human race—shone forth in such a way that on the day of His birth He both cut off the darkness of gloom and in one and the same rising brought in light to human beings and to days alike. Hence there is nothing marvelous if that day increases which is clothed with a double radiance of brilliance.

2. But let us pursue how the Lord, the Savior, increases and John the Baptist diminishes. We said previously that John was in fact an image of the law and the prophets. It was necessary, then, that the law should fade as the gospel shone forth and that the Jewish people should decrease as the Christian people arose. For who doubts that from the birth of the Lord the assembly of the Synagogue has been emptied and the peoples of the Church have been multiplied, that in a wonderful manner Christ daily increases by way of the Christians and John decreases by way of the Jews, and that the ones shine with the radiance of the Lord's day and the others labor under the gloom of night? For, in a certain way, a long night lay heavily upon the Jews, which is why they said of the Savior's death: *His blood be upon us and upon our children.*[6] Clearly they were covered by the long darkness of night, which is why they tried to slay the day of truth.

3. But that we might be able to demonstrate more manifestly what

we are saying, let us briefly discuss both births. For look, when Christ is born the angels rejoice, the shepherds keep watch, the Magi come, and the star goes before,[7] and all the most beautiful things in heaven and on earth are offered to the Lord Himself. For to Him glory is offered by the angels, brightness by the star, devotion by the Magi,[8] simplicity by the shepherds, and, since all these things were to exist for Him alone, they all therefore render service to the newborn. When John is conceived, however, Zechariah is struck dumb, the high priest becomes silent, and Elizabeth his mother is hidden,[9] indicating after his birth the silence of the law, the termination of the priesthood, and the eclipse of the Synagogue. There is no doubt that John, who took away the use of his father's voice when he was conceived, took away the righteousness of the law from the Pharisees when he was born. The Lord always increases, then, and John the Baptist decreases. He does not decrease because he is wanting in merits, but, inasmuch as the glory of the Savior is augmented daily, his own seems to grow less.

4. John is called a lamp by the Lord when he says: *He was a burning lamp.*[10] Lamplight is dimmed, then, when the sunlight shines, and it suffers a kind of eclipse in its brightness when it is overcome by the radiance of a brighter light. For what wise person needs a lamp in the sun? It may not be extinguished, to be sure, but it is not considered necessary. That is to say, who would come to John's baptism of repentance[11] when he could be saved by the Savior's baptism? Not, to be sure, that the one is demeaned, but the other is judged more beneficial and necessary because in it the remission of sins is bestowed.

SERMON 100

On Holy Epiphany[1]

1. The Gospel mentions, as we have just heard read, that the Lord came to the Jordan for the sake of baptism and that He wished to be consecrated by the heavenly mysteries in that same river.[2] We should not be astonished that the Lord and master of baptism itself did this,

since He said: *Whoever does thus and teaches thus shall be called very great in the kingdom of heaven.*[3] He wished, therefore, to do first what He ordered should be done by all, so that the good teacher[4] would not so much suggest His teaching in words as carry it out in actions and would strengthen our faith in deed and understanding alike. That[5] all this happened today is clear because we can gather its truth from reason itself. For reason demands that after the day of the Lord's birth—during the same season, despite the intervening years—this feast should follow, which feast should itself also, I think, be called a birthday. For then He was born to human beings, but on this day He was reborn in the sacraments;[6] then He was brought forth by a virgin, but on this day He was generated by a mystery. For the Lord arranged that the festivals of human beings should not be too far separated from one another. Thus in a single season those who rejoiced over the newborn on earth might exult in the one sanctified from heaven, and those who possessed the virgin's offspring through the angels' proclamation might hold fast the Son of God through the heavens' witness, so that people would be certain that He whom the virgin bore and the Divinity acknowledged was the Son of God. Extraordinary births merit extraordinary attentions: in the one, when He is born as a man, Mary His mother nourishes Him at her breast; in the other, when He is begotten in mystery, God His Father overshadows Him with His voice, saying: *For this is my Son, in whom I am well pleased; hear Him.*[7] The mother, then, caresses the tender child in her bosom, the Father ministers to His loving Son with His testimony; the mother, I say, holds Him up to be adored by the Magi,[8] the Father manifests Him to be worshiped by the Gentiles.

2. He is held, then, by His mother at her breast when He is born, but His Father unceasingly extends the warmth of His breast to Him, for we read that He always reposes in the Father's bosom, as the Evangelist says: *No one has ever seen God except the only-begotten Son, who is in the Father's bosom.*[9] Willingly, therefore, does the Lord repose in the bosom of the saints—which is why He chose the breast of John the Evangelist[10]—so that they might rest in Him.[11] But the bosom upon which Christ finds rest is not furnished by the corporeal breast nor is it covered with splendid clothing, but it is composed of the practice of the heavenly virtues. In John the Evangelist the bosom for Christ was faith, in God His Father it is divinity, and in Mary His

mother virginity. Where there is a dwelling for the virtues, there is a bosom for Christ; where He finds the lodging of the heavenly commandments, there He lays His head.[12] Therefore He says to sinners and to the faithless: *The foxes have holes and the birds of heaven have nests, but the Son of Man has nowhere to lay His head.*[13]

3. The Lord Jesus, then, came today to baptism, and He wanted His holy body to be washed with water. Perhaps someone should say: "Why did one who is holy want to be baptized?" Listen, then! Christ is baptized not that He might be sanctified by the waters but that He Himself might sanctify the waters and purify with His own purification the streams that He touches.[14] For Christ's consecration is greater than that of the element. For when the Savior is washed all water is cleansed for our baptism, and the source is purified so that the grace of the washing might be ministered to the people who would follow after. Christ underwent baptism first, then, so that after Him the Christian people might confidently follow. I understand that this is a mystery, for thus also the pillar of fire went first through the Red Sea so that the children of Israel might follow on a tranquil path, and it went through the waters first in order to prepare the way for those coming after it.[15] What took place, as the Apostle says, was the mystery of baptism.[16] Clearly this was a kind of baptism, where a cloud covered the people and water carried them. But the same Christ the Lord who did all these things now goes through baptism before the Christian people in the pillar of His body—He who at that time went through the sea before the children of Israel in the pillar of fire.[17] This, I say, is the column which at that time offered light to the eyes of those who followed and now ministers light to the hearts of those who believe, which then made firm a watery path in the waves and now strengthens the traces of faith in the washing. Through this faith—as was the case with the children of Israel—the one who walks calmly will not fear Egypt in pursuit.[18]

SERMON 101

A Sequel on the Same Holy Day[1]

1. We ought to exult, dearest brethren, because feasts follow upon feasts and joys are piled upon joys.[1a] For look, our hearts are still

leaping from the solemnity of the Lord's birthday[2] and already we glory in the festival of holy Epiphany. We ought, therefore, to give thanks to the Lord who frequently visits us and often rejoices us; He seeks us out the more so that He may bless us the more. Although, then, the Gentiles foolishly rejoice with numerous feasts on account of the diversity of their gods, yet the visitation of the one God offers us more festivals than the superstitious presumption of their many demons offers them. For as we have overcome them by the truth of religion, so we have overcome them by the number of feasts.[3]

2. Hence we look today to the joys of Epiphany. Someone might ask how this word is to be interpreted because the Greek word "epiphany" means "to appear" in Latin. Therefore, because the Savior first appeared in the world at that time, this day has been called Epiphany from that same word. But let us ask how He appeared. It is not that He was not in the world before, since the world was made through Him, but that then for the first time God, who is Christ, shone in the hearts of believers by signs and wonders, and radiant faith came into people's darkened consciences. Although God is everywhere, then, and maintains all things, yet since He was not seen before, He is said not to have appeared. But He appeared not so much for the eyes of human beings as for their salvation, for even though He was first seen by fleshly eyes when He was born of the virgin, still He did not appear because the eye of faith did not as yet recognize His power. Hence it is said to the Jews by the prophet: *Seeing you will see and will not see;*[4] that is, the Savior whom they discerned with their fleshly eyes they did not see in a spiritual light.[5] For after He manifested His divinity with miracles, appearing as it were freshly and unexpectedly to human minds, He filled the eyes of the heart, so to speak, so that the intellect might recognize what sight did not. Thus it happens that by faith we contemplate Christ, whom we have never seen, but the Jews, who gazed upon Him with their eyes and touched Him with their hands,[6] today do not see Him.

3. Let us inquire, then, what sign He performed in order to manifest His divinity to the people. This is said to have been His first miracle—that He changed water into wine.[7] Clearly this is a great sign and one sufficient for believing the majesty of God, for who would not be amazed at elements transformed into something other

than they were? For no one can change nature except the one who is Lord of nature. From this one must believe that a mortal human being can be transformed into immortality, when a base substance has been transformed into a precious substance. For, listener, I do not want you to notice only the names of wine and water, but if you wish to ascertain the power look at the virtue of the things, for by this deed something very lofty is pointed out. When the Lord converts water into wine, He does this not so that drunkenness may not be wanting to the banqueters but so that eternity may be the lot of believers. For, since Christ came into the world not that He might provide supplies for feasters but that He might obtain salvation for human beings, neither did He do so in order to fill water jars with a pleasant-smelling substance but in order to water souls with the grace of the Holy Spirit. Therefore, when from that base water He wished the feasters to savor the taste of an excellent wine, He wished rather for believers to savor from this base flesh the taste of a heavenly resurrection. In this sign, in fact, the whole mystery of the resurrection is contained, for the turning of water that is base, lackluster, and cold into wine that is precious, red, and fiery, signifies that the substance of the human person—base in its condition, lackluster in its weakness, and cold in its dying—is to be changed into the glory of the resurrection, which is precious in its eternity, bright-hued in its grace, and fiery with the Spirit of deathlessness.[8]

It is proper to believe, therefore, that the Lord wished to do this so that through this earthly sign the future heavenly mystery would already be seen then by the wise. For if it is truly marvelous that what was lacking to those at table was made up for by the wine, how much more marvelous it is that life which has been drained dry has been restored to human beings! And if it is a glorious thing to change water into wine, how much more glorious it is to change sins into righteousness and to temper behavior rather than goblets! I dare say that those water jars serve that precious substance not only to that banquet but to the whole world; indeed, they serve us better. For it is well known that they drew drunkenness from those vessels, but we draw righteousness; that they received a goblet of wine, but we take the cup of salvation;[9] and, if it is permitted to speak thus, that what they drank was passing, but that what we have received abides.

SERMON 102

A Sequel on the Same[1]

1. Even if bodily weakness occasionally dulls the power of our speech, nonetheless we are made stronger by your eager devotion, for the more eagerly you listen the more willingly we preach, and the ability to speak is given to us when you prepare your hearing to understand. For who would not try to cast the seed of the heavenly word where the fertile earth of a pure heart would receive it? Who, I say, would not wish to place the Savior's word where concern for earthly riches would not choke it but the power of spiritual instruction would nourish it?[2]

2. Therefore, brethren, since on holy Epiphany we have exulted upon seeing the miracles of the Savior, we ought to do what the disciples of that time did then. But I have said that we have seen now what once took place; we have seen it clearly and we do see it daily. For those miracles of Christ do not exist so that they may fall into neglect because they happened long ago but so that they may increase in grace, not so that they may be buried in forgetfulness but so that they may be renewed in strength. For as far as the power of God is concerned, there is nothing that is abolished or past, but by reason of His majesty all things are present to Him; to Him all time is today, which is why the holy prophet says: *Before your eyes a thousand years are as one day.*[3] If all the time of the ages is one day to the Lord, on the same day that the Savior worked wonders for our fathers He also worked wonders for us. We also, then, like our ancestors, have seen the Lord's wonders when we have regarded them with an awe equal to theirs. Like them, we also have tasted from the same water jars, since they drank a goblet of wine from them, but we took the cup of salvation.[4]

3. Having seen the Lord's sign, then, we should do what those who went before us did, for if the same divine grace has shone in us the same devout faith ought also to be in us. For the Evangelist says of the Lord when He had performed this miracle: *And He manifested His glory, and His disciples believed in Him.*[5] Therefore we ought to believe as the apostles believed then. Suppose someone says: "We are

Christians too; we believe in the Lord, the Savior." But it is necessary to believe in deed and not in word, not with the tongue but with the heart, lest it also be said to us: *This people honors me with their lips, but their heart is far from me.*[6]

SERMON 103

A Sequel on the Same[1]

1. Your holiness[2] remembers our last sermon, brethren, in which we spoke of how the blessed apostles, having seen one miracle (that is, when water was changed into wine by the Savior), immediately believed in Him, for thus the Evangelist says of the Lord: *And He manifested His glory, and His disciples believed in Him.*[3] This deed was not written down only so that the glory of faith of those among whom this took place might be manifested but also for the sake of us who are aroused to the glory of believing by the same example of devotion. For what Christ accomplished He accomplished not only for those whom He had around Him then but also for us who were to follow afterwards, so that although our ancestors preceded us in time, yet they would not go before in the grace of the signs. For the same power that was exhibited to them in present wonders has been preserved for us in a treasury in written form so that the written page might offer us what history showed them—indeed, so that whatever is repeated to us suggestively in the mirror of the Scriptures might take place among us, and so that we might see in a spiritual light the power of the Lord which they discerned with their fleshly eyes.[4]

2. *And,* it says, *He manifested His glory, and His disciples believed in Him.* Well does the servants' devotion follow upon their master's power, and what the teacher teaches in deed the disciples transcribe in their heart. For see, the power of the one who acts is manifested, and the manifest faith of the believers is preached. Clearly the faith of the apostles, which believed in the Savior's omnipotence after having seen one sign, should be preached. And while the apostles are marveling at the water changed into wine, they themselves in similar fashion are converted from every sinful impurity, and in the likeness of the

wondrous deed they are brought over from the base superstition of the Gentiles to the precious devotion of believers. And as the water turned into wine is seasoned with savor, redness, and warmth, so also whatever there was in them that was insipid received the savor of knowledge, whatever was lackluster took on the hue of grace, and whatever was cold glowed with the warmth of immortality.[5]

3. Therefore the faith of the apostles, which was spoken of in the words of the Gospel, should be glorified so that what redounded to their praise might also serve us as an example. It would be all the worse if their praiseworthiness should abide but their example not move us. The more recent we are in terms of time, the worse we are in terms of merit, for they believed in the Lord as soon as they had seen one sign, but we still doubt after having received the wonders of so many benefits. We doubt, I say, because we love present things and do not believe in future ones; we love riches in the world and hesitate to accept them from Christ; we are carried away by immoderate anger and do not fear the judgment of retribution. But whoever knows what is written—*You will be judged by the same judgment by which you have judged*[6]—is without doubt mild, moderate, and gentle, and he persuades with kindness rather than compels with severity. He is a friend to mercy, at home with pardon, so that in frequently bestowing it he may always receive it from the Lord, since it should be the part of the wise ruler to bear earthly honors in such a way that he may acquire the honor of heavenly dignity.[7]

SERMON 105

On the Feast of Saint Alexander[1]

1. Although we admire with due reverence all the blessed martyrs that antiquity gives us, yet we ought especially to receive Saints Alexander, Martyrius, and Sisinius, who suffered in our time, with a wholehearted veneration. For in some way we have a greater affection for those with whom we have personally been acquainted than for those about whom history teaches us.[2] For that the ones were martyrs we know from reading, but the others from seeing with our

eyes; we learn of the suffering of the ones from their reputation, but the agony of the others we seize by the testimony of our sight. Consequently I owe a greater love where seeing urges my belief than where reputation encourages my faith. I owe a greater love, I say, where I am compelled by what I have seen to believe devoutly even what I have not seen. For although some things seemed impossible to me when I heard of them, I began to believe that they were possible when I saw similar things accomplished. For this reason, then, the suffering of our times has been given us—to confer grace in the present and to strengthen faith with respect to the past. We should, therefore, receive the above-mentioned blessed men with a whole-hearted veneration: first, because they have deigned to illumine our own lifetimes with their precious blood; next, because, being in the presence of the Lord, they have given us no small sign, showing us what sort of faith there was in the Christians of our age, in whose company the martyrs merited to live;[3] and third, because they were of such a holy life that they found the crown of martyrdom in a time of peace. For, since no vengeful ruler oppressed them and no sacrilegious tyrant pursued them, it was not public persecution but Christian devotion that made them confessors.

2. For when, while building a church in the region of Anaunia[4] at their own expense, they were presiding at its holy altar (since one of them functioned as a deacon and two as clerics), and the people of that region, among whom the Christian name had not been known before, wanted to pollute every place with the customary sacrilege that they call a lustrum,[5] and the holy men were reproaching them, pointing out their errors and convicting them with a reasoned reproof, they—drunken more with rage than with wine—seized them and wounded them with such cruel blows that one of them, half-dead after his many torments, awaited his death with longing and experienced it. For when the church building had been destroyed, they constructed a pyre from its beams and gave the blessed bodies over to the flames. Truly blessed bodies, which the deadly fire did not take to the punishment of the idol but the holy flame received for the repose of the house of the Lord! Truly blessed flame, which received the martyrs not in order to consume them by its fatal heat but to keep them from sacrilegious hands! In such a burning the flesh of the blessed was not cremated but consecrated. What the Apostle says applies to this suf-

fering: *He will be saved, but as it were by fire.*[6] For they were saved when they were completely consumed by the fire of a reverent confession. This, then, is the full reason for their suffering, brethren—that by it the death-devoted holy men might urge others to be like them. And their exhortation has been so successful that, as they departed from the world, their faith prevailed over all the localities of that region. Thus where Christ once suffered persecution in three martyrs,[7] now He rejoices in the many Christian people of that place.

SERMON 106

A Sequel[1]

1. A few days ago, when we were very festively celebrating the anniversary[2] of Saints Alexander, Martyrius, and Sisinius, what we especially praised in their suffering was that they merited to be martyrs while resisting sacrilegious persons and that they obtained the palm of righteousness while speaking against their superstitions. For they were not condemned to death by these people because they were Christians, but rather they were seized for punishment because the sacrilegious were being rebuked for not being Christians and devout persons. In a time of peace, then, when no vengeful ruler was acting oppressively, it was not public persecution but religious devotion that made martyrs of the holy men. For, desiring to provide for the salvation of the many, they did not fear to place their own well-being in jeopardy.[3] When they noticed that in their region the Gentiles were polluting[4] every place with their defiled circular movements (the customary sacrilege that they call a lustrum[5]) and were sullying the innocent and those who were absent by reason of their connivance[6] if not by reason of their agreement (since connivance sullies one who has, by dissimulating, as it were, let something happen that he could have prevented from happening had he spoken against it)—when the blessed men discerned these things, then, they rebuked them firmly and reproached them in faith, and they brought it about that they made themselves martyrs and made their persecutors Christians.

2. Therefore, brethren, since we have an example, let us imitate

the holy men, if not by a martyr's suffering, then certainly by fulfilling the responsibilities of Christianity.[7] And since we have heard that
the lustrum is accustomed to be celebrated by a few sacrilegious
persons, by the example of the saints let us rebuke the impious and
reproach the errant, for the portion of martyrdom is to do what the
martyrs did. But if we see these things and are silent, if we let them be
without speaking, then we make ourselves guilty by tacit assent even
if not by the commission of the crime. For, as hindering the sacrilegious makes righteous the one who speaks out against them, so also
pretending that you do not see what you do see sullies the one who
keeps silence.[8] Many pitiable people are in the habit of saying: "I
don't know; I didn't order it; it's none of my business; it has nothing
to do with me." But this is, as I have said, what a pitiable or anxious
person declares, denying that he ordered something to happen that he
was unwilling to order not to happen. The evil, indeed, that ordinarily occurs when it is not restrained is admitted. "It's none of my
business," he says. You are in error and you do not know it. Do you
not know that God's affairs are the affairs of all and that the sin of one
is avenged in the many? Just as many are made holy by the holiness of
one,[9] so also many are polluted by the sacrilege of one. Therefore the
evil that you know about, even though it is perpetrated by someone
else, touches you inasmuch as you are indisputably aware of it.

But I do not know, brethren, why it is that we carry out the
commandments of God so negligently and that everyone carefully
obeys what worldly princes order. All keep their rules vigilantly, but
when God commands we are asleep to His commands! How often has
this same God ordered that the sacrilegious idols be destroyed, and
never do we wish to be careful in this regard! We are consistently
negligent and consistently disdainful. Afterwards some imperial
command gives us a warning. See what a detraction from the Divinity
is this inflation of human power! And how shall we be judged when
we are made to live so religiously not out of devotion but out of fear?
Good Christian princes, indeed, go so far as to promulgate laws for
the sake of religion,[10] but the administrators do not enforce them
competently. Therefore, when a prince has been deposed by reason
of guilt the administrator remains answerable; if he executes the law
precisely he is absolved of sin and, because of the well-being[11] of the
many, will be endowed with an eternal reward.[12]

SERMON 107

On Removing Idols from One's Possessions[1]

1. A few days ago I admonished your charity,[2] brethren, that as devout and holy people you should remove every idolatrous pollution from your possessions and wipe out the entire Gentile error from your fields, for it is not lawful for you who have Christ in your hearts to have the antichrist in your houses or for your servants to worship the devil in shrines while you adore God in church. Nor should anyone consider himself excused, saying: "I didn't order this to take place, I didn't command it," for whoever realizes that a sacrilege is being committed on his property and does not forbid it from taking place has himself ordered it in a certain way: by keeping silence and by not complaining he has given assent to the one offering sacrifice.[3] The blessed Apostle says that not only those who perform the deed are criminal but also those who assent to the ones who perform the deed.[4] Therefore, brother, when you see your farmhand sacrificing and do not forbid him from making his offering, you sin—if not by having provided the wherewithal, then by having permitted the liberty. If it is not your command that is criminal, still your will is blameworthy, for in your silence you are pleased with what your farmhand is doing, since if he did not do it you would perhaps be displeased. When an underling sacrifices he sins not merely in his own regard but also implicates his landlord who does not forbid him, and he would certainly not have sinned if he had forbidden him.

2. Idolatry, then, is a great evil: it pollutes those who practice it, it pollutes those who live nearby, it pollutes those who see it; it penetrates to its ministers, it penetrates to those who are aware of it, it penetrates to those who say nothing. The landlord is contaminated by the farmhand who makes the offering. He is unable not to be polluted when he takes food that the sacrilegious farmer has cultivated, the bloodstained earth has brought forth, and a foul storehouse has preserved, for everything that has been contaminated there, where the devil dwells, is abominable—in houses, in fields, in the country.[5] Nothing is free of evil where everything is touched by evil. When you go into your storeroom you discover dried-up turf altars in it and

dead coals—a worthy sacrifice for demons, since a dead spirit is
entreated with dead things. And if you go out to the fields you notice
wooden altars and stone images—appropriate for a mystery in which
unfeeling gods are ministered to on rotten altars. When you rise early
and see your farmhand suffering from a hangover, you should know
that, as they say, he is either a devotee of Diana[6] or a soothsayer,[7] for
an insane spirit is accustomed to having a mad priest. Such a priest
prepares himself with wine for his goddess' wounds, and since he is
drunk the wretch does not feel his own pain.[8] But they do this not
only from intemperance but also according to plan, so that they may
be less troubled by their wounds on succumbing to the drunkenness
of wine. Vain indeed is the soothsayer who thinks to add to piety
with cruelty. And how merciful is such a god to others when he is so
bloodthirsty to his own priests?

Let us briefly describe the appearance of a soothsayer of this kind.
His head is unkempt, with long hair, his breast is bare, his legs are half
hidden by a mantle, and, like a gladiator, he carries a sword in his
hands and is prepared to fight. Indeed, he is worse than a gladiator
because, while the one is obliged to struggle with someone else, he is
compelled to fight with himself; the one seeks out another's vitals, but
he tears his own members to pieces; and, if it may be said, the
gladiator's trainer urges the one to cruelty but the demon urges the
other. Judge whether this man, wearing this garb and bloodied with
this carnage, is a gladiator or a priest. Therefore, as the public crime
of the gladiators has been abolished by the religious devotion of the
princes,[9] so ought also these gladiators of madness to be removed
from our households by a Christian concern.

SERMON 108

A Sequel[1]

We believe that you have made no little progress as a result of last
Sunday's sermon, since with our preaching we cleansed your hearts
from every contamination of idols. For our hearts are purified when
our conscience is not kept polluted by the devil's filth, and one who

does not tolerate the practice of sacrileges on his property does not have a polluted conscience. But one who knows that sacrifices are being made to idols in his field and does not forbid it is touched by an abominable pollution even if he is away in the city, and although it is his farmhand who stands at the altars the horrible contamination turns back upon the landlord, for he is made a participant in this, if not in agreement, then certainly in knowledge.[2] We believe that you have made progress, then, when you restrain the sacrilegious cult in your possessions, for we say that the possession of the Christian—that is, of one who is clean—should be clean. But Solomon says: *A precious possession is the clean man.*[3] If, therefore, the one who is clean is compared to a very precious possession, of how much greater worth is that possession if it is uncorrupt, pure, and not debased by any contagion of the devil! But we should know why one who is clean is said to be a precious possession: not bodily frailty but integral goodness makes him precious, and the Lord deigns to possess him on account of that very purity of mind, as the prophet says in the person of the saints. . . .

SERMON 110

On the Anniversary of the Holy Apostles Peter and Paul[1]

1. The season urges us, brethren, to speak on the Gospel lesson that has just been read, in which the Lord said to Peter, who is still in his boat: *Do not be afraid; henceforth you shall give life to human beings.*[2] From this phrase we can understand the sacrament[3] of the whole reading. For why was it that, when the disciples were astonished at the boats that returned after the catch of fish, the Savior did not promise Peter what He knew but pledged something that He did not know at all? That is to say, why in the very boat in which He was did He provide an abundance of human beings to be given life in place of fish flopping about, when, of course, human beings are not ordinarily given life on a boat but transported, nor comforted on a vessel but anxious about its journey? Notice, then, that this boat is not a boat that is given to Peter to be piloted; rather it is the Church, which is

committed to the apostle to be governed.[4] For this is the vessel that is accustomed not to kill but to give life to those borne along by the storms of this world as if by waves, for just as a little boat holds the dying fish that have been brought up from the deep, so also the vessel of the Church gives life to human beings who have been freed from turmoil.[5] Within itself, I say, the Church gives life to those who are half-dead, as it were. This is what the expression "to give life" signifies, for nothing is given life but what had shortly before been without life. It is said that Peter will give life to people who are, so to speak, wounded by the storms of the world and suffocated by the billows of this age, so that whoever was astonished at the boat that returned with a quantity of fish flopping about ought to be more astonished at the Church loaded with a multitude of living persons.

2. The entire content of this lesson bears a mystical meaning, for a little before, when sitting in the boat, the Lord said to Peter: *Go out into the deep and let down your net for the catch.*[6] He is not, indeed, teaching him how to cast out his fishing gear but how to let down the words of preaching into the deep. Paul also penetrated this deep with the net of his mouth when he said: *O the depth of the riches of the wisdom and the knowledge of God!*[7] He is not teaching him, I say, how to catch fish with a net but how to collect human beings by faith, for faith does on earth what a net does in the waters. Just as a net does not let what it holds slip out, neither does faith permit those whom it gathers to go astray, but as the one brings what it has caught in its bosom, so to say, to the boat, so the other brings those whom it has gathered in its breast, so to say, to peace. That you may understand that the Lord was speaking of spiritual fishing, however, Peter says: *Teacher, laboring through the whole night we have caught nothing, but at your word I shall let down the nets.*[8] It is as if he were saying: Since through the whole night our fishing has brought us nothing and we have been laboring in vain, now I shall not fish with fishing gear but with grace, not with the diligence acquired by skill but with the perseverance acquired by devotion. *At your word,* he says, *I shall let down the nets.* We read that the word is the Lord, the Savior, as the Evangelist says: *In the beginning was the Word, and the Word was God.*[9] When Peter lets down the nets at the word, therefore, he is in fact letting down teachings in Christ,[10] and when he unfolds[11] the tightly-woven and well-ordered nets at the behest of the master he is

really laying out words in the name of the Savior in a fitting and clear fashion; by these he is able to save not creatures but souls. *Laboring through the whole night,* he says, *we have caught nothing.* Peter, who beforehand was unable to see in order to make a catch, enduring darkness without Christ, had indeed labored through the whole night, but when the Savior's light shone upon him the darkness scattered and by faith he began to discern in the deep what he could not see with his eyes. Peter clearly endured the night until the day, which is Christ, became present to him. Hence the apostle Paul also says: *The night has passed, but the day has drawn near*[12]—Jesus Christ our Lord, who lives and reigns for ever. Amen.[13]

SERMON III

On Holy Quadragesima[1]

1. Your holiness[2] recalls that a few days ago we said that by the observance of holy Quadragesima a kind of restoration of the human race is brought about, and that by this most sacred season our frail condition is renewed. For our frailty is renewed when Christ mercifully re-establishes the grace of immortality that Adam had sinfully lost; and what the one had sinned against, contrary to the prohibition, by eating,[3] the other justifies by fasting according to the commandment.[4] This is the whole reason for Christianity and for the faith— that what had perished should be saved, that what had wandered should be called back,[5] and that what had already died should be reborn. It should be reborn anew, I say, not born, since the offense of the first begetting became the occasion for the second birth, and the grace of the justification of the one is the result of the criminal deed of the other, for it would not have been necessary for a person to be reborn anew if what had existed had not perished.

2. But suppose someone says: "God was able to forgive the human being the sins that had been contracted through Adam and to bestow upon him the grace of immortality in such a way that it would not have been necessary for him to be reborn anew." Listen, then, and understand the reason. God, as we know, is truthful and just, and He

cannot ever deceive. When, therefore, He had formed Adam and had set down for him a law of this kind in paradise—that he should never taste of the tree of the knowledge of good and evil, but that on the day he tasted it he would die the death[6]—the man, although bound by this command, disregarded the command, went against the law, and in his wickedness sought the death that God had foretold. Therefore, as we have said, because it is impossible for the statutes of the divinity to be overthrown and because the human person had fallen into the trap of the law, it did not behoove him to be forgiven without another birth. Because the series of precepts was not able to be fulfilled, he wished the human person to be reborn and to become, so to speak, something else. And because the sentence of the law could not be changed, the person given over to the law was changed,[7] so that, in one and the same person, what his condition straitened grace would likewise set free, while the old man made amends in harshness, the new one would increase in goodness; and, seeing that the precept retained its force in the human person, another reckoning of the precept would liberate him. For whoever is reborn has exhausted the conditions of the first birth and receives the beginning of a second birth. Whoever is reborn, I say, has ceased being what he had been and has begun to be what he was not; the old man has died and the one who is to be has been renewed. How good, then, is our Lord! He sets down the law in such a way that He does not leave out mercy; He is merciful in such a way that He does not violate the statutes of the law; as one who is just He has carried out the sentence, and as one who is merciful He has granted pardon. For that we should die is the command of the first decree, but that we should rise is the gift of the benefaction that followed.

3. Therefore, brethren—I speak to you catechumens—hasten to the grace of the second birth so that Adam may be ended in you and Christ may begin, so that death may be annulled and life may take its place, so that the harsh sentence may be abolished and the grace of renewal may follow upon it. For the judge's harshness ceased because, with the coming of the renewal, the sentence was abolished. But unless our old man has been changed the punishment of the precept pursues the new person, nor will anyone be able to avoid the condition of death who has not taken refuge with the author[8] of that condition. For the Lord Christ says: *Unless you believe that I am he,*

you shall die in your sins.[9] But we believe Christ if we faithfully clothe ourselves with His grace. What He says is true: *Unless one is reborn of water and the Holy Spirit,*[10] and so forth. Let us, then, be clothed with the Lord[11]—as much with grace as with His commandments. For death will not hold them when it sees Adam with Christ, who is life.[12] Let us observe His commandments above all, I say, and especially the fast days of Quadragesima. For there are many who, when this most sacred number of fasting is announced to them, violate the divinely ordained season by eating during some weeks, not understanding that by eating contrary to the prohibition they are guilty of no less a crime than was Adam, who ate contrary to the prohibition.[13] But if the suffering of Christ redeemed that crime, who will redeem those who are criminals after the time of the Lord's suffering?[14]

APPENDIX

SERMON 7

On the Anniversary of Saint Eusebius, Bishop of Vercelli[1]

1. It is futile to wish to add anything to the praise of the holy martyr Eusebius, for he excels as a teacher of such ineffable doctrines that his merits can more easily be known by deeds than they can be explained by words. To the extent that one's consciousness retains something of him, speech does not succeed in expressing it. Therefore his deeds should not be embellished with words but touched upon briefly in a few sentences. This is especially true since we know that we must not adorn with words what we see is already adorned with virtues,[2] inasmuch as the Apostle says that *the kingdom of God consists not in word but in virtue.*[3] Therefore it is futile to wish to add anything to his merits, particularly for me, since I am ignorant of history, unaccomplished in the sacred writings, and unskilled in priestly functions. My holy predecessors, however, would have been able to preach these things, being more habituated and having a more proven experience as well as a clearer doctrine. I speak especially of my lord and father the blessed Exuperantius, who ministered to him in the priesthood,[4] was his companion in martyrdom, his partner in labor, and in whose face we believe that we can also see Saint Eusebius and gaze upon the image of his goodness as if in a kind of mirror.[5] It is easy to understand what sort of a master he was when we see what sort of a disciple he had. But since the glory of a like confession of faith attends him, he prefers not to answer the paternal praise lest he seem to be vaunting his own merits equally.

2. What, then, shall I say of the glory of the martyr Eusebius, whose whole people is that glory? And when Scripture says that *a wise*

son is his father's glory,[6] how many glories are his who rejoices in the wisdom and devotion of such sons! For in Christ Jesus he himself begot us through the gospel.[7] Consequently, whatever there is of virtue and grace in this holy people is traceable to the teaching of Saint Eusebius. This purity has flowed in streams, as it were, from this most unsullied fountain of virtues. For since he abounded in the vigor of chastity he established a foundation for virgins; because he gloried in the deprivations of abstinence he introduced the hard servitude of the monks; because he was endowed with charming speech he drew the love of all his people to God; because he shone in the administration of the episcopal office he left many of his disciples as the heirs of his priesthood. Although some leave treasures of gold and silver to their children, no one has left them richer than has Saint Eusebius, since indeed they have all stood out as either priests or martyrs. To say nothing of other matters, what is especially wonderful is that in this holy church he established those who were clerics as monks and had the priestly offices contained by the same interior disciplines by which matchless chastity is also preserved, so that there would be in these men both the contempt of material things and the exactitude of Levites. Thus if you saw the monastery's little beds you would think them the equal of Oriental ones,[8] and if you observed the clergy's devotion you would rejoice as if you had seen the angel hosts.

3. But I do not think that this should be passed over in silence, namely, that when the hateful perfidy of the Arians had thrown all of Italy into tumult, along with the rest of the world, and the priests of this plague had taken captive the simplicity of the martyr Saint Dionysius and had enchained him by his signature, Eusebius cleverly freed him from their hands.[9] For as the holy Apostle says: *I became a Jew to the Jews in order to win the Jews,*[10] so also Saint Eusebius feigned that he was a heretic before the heretics in order to snatch his son from heresy. For he said that he agreed to their perfidy and that it pleased him that they had placed Dionysius before themselves in the signing, but that he was greatly disturbed that they had put his son before him. "You," he told them, "who say that the Son of God cannot be equal to God the Father, why have you placed my son before me?" Swayed by this reasoning they immediately erased Saint Dionysius' signature and offered the first place for signing to the blessed Eusebius. Upbraiding them and laughing at them he said: "I

will not pollute myself with your crimes nor permit my son to participate with you." Therefore, when the Gospel says that in this generation the children of darkness are more astute than the children of
light,[11] see how here a son of light has been found who is more astute
than the darkness itself.[12]

4. Then, greatly angered that their wickedness had thus been
mocked at, through the ruler Constantius they distressed him with
new sufferings. And after many injustices had been committed by this
plague from the East,[13] they sent him in chains into exile, where he
suffered so greatly that he obtained the unconquerable glory of martyrdom. For it is said that among other kinds of sufferings he endured
this torture when he was being interrogated by the Arians and he
refused to join in their perfidy: he was dragged headfirst down a steep
stairway all the way to the bottom; when he was brought back up
again he was interrogated anew, and when he gave the same response
he suffered the same thing; thus repeated torture of this kind followed
upon repeated interrogation. In this suffering of the martyr Saint
Eusebius, although his head was crushed, his body battered, and his
limbs broken, still the spirit of his faith remained unconquered. For
the more the Arian perfidy mutilated him bodily, so much the more
did Catholic integrity revive him spiritually. Indeed, we can say that
in his dream Jacob prophesied this ascent and descent of stairs;[14] just
as he saw that ladder going from down below all the way up to
heaven, so also on it Eusebius mounted to heaven and the Arians went
down to hell. Hence, brethren, I think that Saint Eusebius is to be
numbered in the choir of the Maccabean martyrs, since they endured
a martyrdom in each member of their bodies,[15] while he confessed the
Lord by the suffering of his whole body. And I do not think that those
whom one day has united in martyrdom are unequal in grace.[16]

SERMON 8

On the Deposition or Anniversary of the Same Saint Eusebius[1]

1. We celebrate the deposition of Saint Eusebius today. What is a
deposition? It is not indeed what is provided for corpses that are to be

buried in the ground at the hands of clerics; it is, rather, that by which a person who is free of the chains of the body and about to go to heaven lays down his earthly body. This itself is clearly a deposition —when we cast off desire, cease from doing evil, stop sinning, and lay down whatever is too heavy for salvation and is, so to speak, a worthless bundle of trouble. This day, therefore, is a very great celebration because it is truly the highest festivity for the saints when they are unburdened of vices and flourish in righteousness. Hence the very day of deposition is called a birthday because then we are liberated from our sins and born into the freedom of the Savior.[2]

2. But let us see how gloriously Saint Eusebius came to this day of deposition. For it is said that shortly before the time of his departure he had a vision in which he saw himself flying from one mountain to another on the kalends of August.[3] This was interpreted as a kind of prophesy that on this day he would leave his body. In this regard I do not know what is more wonderful—that he merited to know the time of his departure or that he was able to know what grace would abide after that departure. Holy David says: *Lord, make known to me my end and the number of my days*, and so forth.[4] See how what the prophet desired the martyr received; the one obtains the knowledge that the other pleads for, except that, saving the faith, I would say that much more was obtained. For the one asks to know the end, while the other knows what is to happen after the end; the one is unacquainted with what is lacking up to his death, while the other adds what remains after his death.

3. And so, on that day, the martyr Eusebius sees himself flying. As we know, nothing is able to fly except what is pure, light, and subtle, the soundness of which is not hindered by excess, nor its promptness ⟨. . .⟩,[5] nor its swiftness burdened by weight. But I say that something which flies is burdened not so much by the weight of its members as by the heaviness of sins. Consequently I think that among birds themselves the dove flies more swiftly than nearly all the others because it unites swiftness and innocence. Holy David, when he wished to fly with purity of mind, desired the wings of no other living thing than a dove when he said: *Who will give me wings like a dove, and I shall fly away and be at rest?*[6] For he understood that the higher

places are more easily penetrated by simplicity of mind than by light-
ness of wings.

On this day, then, Saint Eusebius flew. We may appreciate his
innocence from his having taken flight and judge his purity from the
altitude. For, like a dove living in the house of God, he assumed
spiritual wings and rested on a mountain. And although he said that he
was flying from mountain to mountain, nonetheless I take it to mean
that in the flying itself there was a greater rest. For what else is flying
from mountain to mountain than hastening from the Savior's grace to
the Father's glory? They themselves are the mountains, as the prophet
says: *A mountain from a mountain without the hands of dividers*[7]—that
is to say, the Son who comes from the Father without the admixture
of anything created.[8]

SERMON 14

On the Anniversary of the Martyrs[1]

1. It is worthy and fitting, brethren, that after the gladness of the
blessed Pasch, which we have celebrated in the Church, we should
bring our joys to the holy martyrs and announce to them the glory of
the Lord's resurrection, they who are partakers of the Lord's passion.
For they who are companions in suffering ought also to be sharers in
gladness. Thus it is that the blessed Apostle says: *If you share His
sufferings you will also share His resurrection.*[2] *If we have endured,* he
says, *we shall also reign with Him.*[3] Those who have borne evils for
Christ's sake, then, ought also to have glory with Christ. Let us
announce, I say, the grace of the Lord's Pasch to the holy martyrs, so
that as we preach that the gates of His sepulcher were opened, their
graves might also be opened; and as we say that His dead body
suddenly came alive as warm blood flowed through His veins, their
limbs long cold might also be warmed with the warmth of immortality. For the same cause that raised up the Lord also raises up the
martyrs. As they have experienced the path of His suffering, so they
will also experience that of His life; for so it is written in the psalm:

You have made known to me the paths of life.[4] This, indeed, is said of the person of the Savior in the resurrection[5]—of Him who, when after His death He returned from the depths to the heights, began to make known the path of life, which previously had been unknown. The path of life was unknown before Christ because until then it had never been trodden upon by anyone who had risen from the dead. But when the Lord rose, that path, now known, was worn smooth by the feet of a multitude, about whom the holy Evangelist says: *The bodies of many of the saints rose with Him and entered into the holy city.*[6] Hence, when the Lord says in His own resurrection: *You have made known to me the paths of life,* we also are able to say to the Lord: "You have made known to us the paths of life." For He who has shown us the way to life has Himself made known to us the paths of life. He made the paths of life known to me when he taught me faith, mercy, justice, and chastity; by these roads one arrives at salvation. And although in the dissolution of our body the shadow of death encompasses us, nonetheless life does not desert its own steps, and by the power of Christ we walk swiftly in the midst of the very laws of hell. This is why the holy prophet says: *And if I should walk in the midst of the shadow of death I shall fear no evils, for you are with me.*[7] The Lord says this more clearly when He speaks of the one who is faithful: *But whoever believes in me shall not die, and although he die he shall live.*[8]

2. Therefore, brethren, let us bestow the glory of the Lord's Pasch on the holy martyrs. Let us bestow it, I say, and although they know everything better, yet let us preach to them how He rose to the heavens from the depths of the sepulcher, and let them reveal to us how He returned to the sepulcher from the depths of hell. Let them make known to us, I say, how warmth insinuated itself into a body already lifeless and cold, how the spirit entered it, blood flowed in, and the pulse of its original vigor quickened the icy veins with its moisture. Let them make known to us, I say, how the unbound bundle of sinews returned to its previous state in a body that had decayed, and how the life-giving spirit restored the silent harmony of the internal organs to its old tone.[9] Let the bishops[10] preach, then, what wonders the Savior did in the heavens after His resurrection, and let the martyrs reveal what refreshment has been given to the departed even in death.

SERMON 45

On the Day of Holy Epiphany[1]

1. Today the true sun has arisen upon the world, today light has gone out into the shadows of this age. God has become a man so that man might become God.[2] The Lord took the form of a slave[3] so that the slave might be turned into a master. The inhabiter and founder of the heavens lived on earth so that the human person, the earth-dweller,[4] might travel to heaven. O day more lightsome than all the sun! O time more hoped for than all the centuries! What the angels were waiting for, what the seraphim and cherubim and the mysteries of heaven did not know—this has been revealed in our time. What they saw through a glass[5] and in mere semblance we perceive in reality. The one who spoke to the Israelite people through Isaiah the prophet and the other prophets now speaks to us through the Son.[6] See what a difference there is between the Old Testament and the New! In the one He spoke through a cloud,[7] but now He speaks to us in utter clarity. In the one God was seen in a bush,[8] but in the other God is born of a virgin.[9] In the one He was a fire consuming the people's sins, but in the other He is a man forgiving the people's sins—indeed, a master pardoning His slaves, for no one but God alone can forgive sins.[10]

2. Whether the Lord Jesus was born today or baptized today (different opinions are given by people, and in the variety of traditions there is a meaning for us),[11] it is clear that, whether today He was born of a virgin or reborn in baptism, His birth both of flesh and of spirit profits us. Both are my mystery, both are useful to me. The Son of God had no need to be born and to be baptized, for He had not committed any sin that needed to be forgiven Him in baptism, but His humiliation is our exaltation, His cross our victory, and His gibbet our triumph. With joy let us take this sign on our shoulders, let us bear the banners of victory, let us bear such an imperial banner, indeed, on our foreheads![12] When the devil sees this sign on our doorposts[13] he trembles.[14] Those who are not afraid of gilded temples are afraid of the cross, and those who disdain regal scepters and the

purple and the banquets of the Caesars stand in fear of the meanness and the fasts of the Christian. In Ezekiel the prophet, when the angel who had been sent had slain everyone and the slaughter had begun at the holy places, only they remained unharmed whom he had signed with the letter tau—that is, with the mark of the cross.[15]

3. Let us rejoice, then, dearest brethren, and let us lift holy hands[16] to heaven in the form of a cross. When the demons see us thus armed they will be cast down. When Moses' hands were lifted up Amalek was conquered; when they came down a little he grew strong.[17] The sail yards of ships and the ends of the sail yards move about in the form of our cross.[18] The very birds, too, when they are borne to the heights and fly through the air, imitate the cross with their wings outstretched.[19] Trophies themselves are crosses,[20] and so are adorned victories of triumphs. These we ought to have not only on our foreheads but also on our souls so that, thus armed, we may trample upon the asp and the basilisk,[21] in Christ Jesus, to whom be glory forever.

SERMON 46

*Again, On the Day of Epiphany,
and On the Gospel Where the Lord Was Baptized,
and On Psalm 28*[1]

SERMON 47

*On What Is Written in the Gospel:
The Land of a Certain Rich Man Brought Forth Abundant Fruit*[1]

SERMON 61B

On the Birthday of the Lord, the Savior[1]

1. Last Sunday we admonished your love,[2] brethren, about the coming of this day when we said that we celebrate the birth of the Lord today with the world as witness. For the world bears witness

since it itself is reborn when Christ is born. It is reborn when it is rescued from the profound darkness of its nights by a kind of birth of light. It is reborn, I say, when its waning comes to an end and brightness is restored. And therefore it behooves us to call the rising[3] of Christ, in more complete fashion, a rising of the world, for on this day He rises up for the salvation of all things: He rises up on this day as a light for the world, as resurrection for the dead, and as life for those subject to death, and thus today is not so much the birthday of the Savior as it is of salvation.

2. Christ, the salvation of all things, then, is born—He who the prophets testified is the king of the nations.[4] He is born of a virgin, as Isaiah declares when he says: *Behold, a virgin shall conceive and bear a son, and they shall call His name Emmanuel, which means God with us.*[5] The manner of His birth proves the truth about the Lord: a virgin conceived without knowing a man; her belly was filled, having been touched by no embrace; and her chaste womb received the Holy Spirit, whom her pure members preserved and her unsullied body carried. Behold the miracle of the mother of the Lord! She is a virgin when she conceives, a virgin when she brings forth, a virgin after birth. What glorious virginity! What splendid fruitfulness! The world's goodness is born and there is no pain of childbirth. The womb is emptied, a child is brought forth, and still virginity is not violated. For it was fitting that, when God was born, the value of chastity should increase, and that one who was untouched should not be violated by His coming—He who came to heal what was injured —and that bodily purity should not be harmed by Him who bestows virginity on those who have been baptized and had formerly been unchaste. The child who has been born, then, is placed in a crib. This is God's first dwelling place, and the ruler of heaven does not disdain these straitened circumstances—He whose home was the virginal womb. Clearly Mary was a fit habitation for Christ not because of the nature of her body but because of the grace of her virginity.

When, therefore, Mary has unburdened herself of her happy burden, the joyful one, who is ignorant of wifeliness, experiences motherhood, and she who knows no husband is glorious in her offspring. And she marvels at the child whom she has begotten, since she is certain of having received the Holy Spirit, nor is she frightened because she brought forth out of wedlock, since she has the testimony of her offspring and her virginity at her disposal. The offspring points to God as the father, the virginity dispels the suspicion of dubiousness. On the one hand the Divinity bears witness to the virginity, and on the other the mystery bears witness to the nature.[6] The Divinity bears witness, I say, to the virginal birth, for, according to the Gospel announcement, in order for Christ to be conceived Mary is filled with the grace of the Holy Spirit and is overshadowed by the power of God the Father, just as was told her: *The Holy Spirit shall come upon you and the power of the Most High shall overshadow you, and therefore what will be born of you shall be called holy, the Son of God.*[7]

3. At the birth of the Savior, then, there was fulfilled that divine sentence which says: *Every word shall stand with two or three witnesses.*[8] For see, the Word of God is born with the Trinity as witness. For indeed, in the womb of holy Mary—when the Holy Spirit comes upon her, when the Most High overshadows her, when Christ is begotten—there is implied a confession of faith in Him. For it was fitting that the mother who was about to bring forth salvation for the peoples should first corroborate the mystery of the Trinity in her own bowels, and that we should understand that, before the birth of the Savior, the sacrament of faith[9] had been corroborated, since Mary, in a mystery, bore a priest in the sanctuary of her womb.[10] Now all that was to be of benefit in the world proceeded from her womb— God, priest, and victim: God because of the resurrection, priest because of the offering, and victim because of the suffering. All this we acknowledge in Christ, for He is God because He returned to the Father, high priest because He offered Himself, and victim because He was slain for our sake. Mary's womb, therefore, I would say was not a womb but a temple. Clearly a temple is a place where whatever is holy in heaven dwells. Indeed, the place where a mystery is established by the Divinity, as in a hidden tabernacle, should be considered superior to the heavens, inasmuch as by it many attain to heaven.[11] Clearly Mary's womb ought to be considered superior to the heavens because she sent the Son of God back to heaven more glorious than when He had descended from heaven. For from the one He came in order to suffer, while from the other He returned in order to reign; from the one He descended humbly among humankind, while from the other He ascended gloriously to the Father. Clearly the temple of

the body is better than that of heaven. For when Christ resides in the latter He is awesome, when in the former gentle; in the latter He is invisible, in the former visible and palpable; in the latter He avenges sins, in the former forgives them; in the latter He employs a judge's power, in the former encourages with a brother's love. And therefore it is good for us to adore Him when He invites us so that we need not fear Him when He judges us.

SERMON 61C

Given after the Birthday of the Lord, the Savior[1]

1. The joy of the Lord's birthday, brethren, still resounds in our hearts,[2] and they yearn for the heavenly festival and its unceasing delights. For although the day of the sacred rites passes on, yet the rites' sanctifying power remains with us, and just as the Savior grows with each day from the time of His birth,[3] so also the love of His faith grows in us and increases both in age and in salvation. For the Lord grows in age in His own regard, but He advances in holiness for our sake—not that Christ's holiness, which is eternal and perfect, advances; rather, it is said to advance when it causes faith to increase in us. For after His birth Christ, although an infant in terms of body, is nonetheless God in terms of majesty.

2. The delights of the Lord's festival, then, still move us deeply within. They move us, encouraging us to break into speech for very joy, so that we also might say what the angels said at the birth of Christ: *Glory to God in the highest and on earth peace to men of good will*.[4] See what the angels said: they did not say "peace to men," as if to just anybody whomsoever, but *to men of good will*, so that we might realize that Christ's peace is not a human thing but is related to virtue. For not generation but desire merits this, not human depravity but Christian goodness. It is not conferred on all but offered to the approved, not given to be spread abroad but proposed as something to be chosen. The peace of Christ, then, is for the one who believes that Christ is the author of peace, the peace of Christ is for the one who has no sins battling in him, the peace of Christ is for those whose

desire is not polluted by the blood of idols. For it is fitting that a stainless desire should possess the Savior whom an immaculate virginity begot. And just as Mary bore Him inviolate, so also our soul should watch over Him unspotted, for Mary was a kind of image of our souls,[5] and just as Christ looked for virginity in His mother, so He also demands integrity in our interior disposition. A virgin with respect to sin, the soul conceives and brings forth the Savior as it preaches, and it watches over Him as it follows the commandments, for faith holds fast the one who has been conceived, confession announces the one who has been brought forth, and care watches over the one who has been born.

3. Let us continue to rejoice, then, over the festival of Him whose birth the angels' brightness proclaims, the shepherds' simplicity seeks, and the Magi's devotion venerates.[6] For in Christ the angels' grace honors God, the shepherds' innocence the lamb, and the Magi's veneration the priest. Clearly the Magi's veneration proves that Christ is a priest, since the whole mystery is corroborated by their gifts. They offered the Savior what, as far as in them lay, they considered to be most beautiful—gold, incense, and myrrh: gold for royal power, myrrh for the resurrection, and incense for propitiation.[7] By gold power is shown, by myrrh incorruption is signified, and by incense the high priesthood is indicated. For it was not without meaning that the Magi came to the Lord with these gifts. Finding Christ in a curiosity that was prompted by their superstition, they brought Him who was to rule over all things the signs of the elements—gold, by which earthly things are conquered; incense, by which heavenly beings are said to be placated; and myrrh, with which the lower regions are seasoned. In this they showed that after the birth of Christ none of these things was necessary, because on account of Christ victory would be established on earth, propitiation in the heavens, and peace in the lower regions. The Magi in their curiosity, then, learn from the birth of the Lord that they must no longer be curious, and in this their magic art was of use to them—that they should realize that it could no longer be of use to them.[8] Then, abandoning their former cult because of Him, they set out on another road—both of return and of life. For the star led the Magi, before they saw Christ, to worship as the superstitious do, but after they saw

the Lord and believed, faith called them back to their homeland as religious men.

4. Therefore, brethren, let us also, who have come from the pagans, imitate those Magi. Before Christ was known it was possible for us to go astray, but since Christ has been recognized we must take care lest pagan credulity divert us from the same road by which we came. For there are many Christians who, after having accepted the faith, get overwhelmed in their former vanities and, although they celebrate the joys of the Lord's birthday with us, celebrate the drunken banquets of the kalends with the pagans;[9] although with us they receive the blessing of God, with them they observe the superstitious omens. It is tragic that the Magi disdained their auguries and that Christians practice divination, that the ones laid down the knowledge of their art and that the others are unwilling to put aside the wantonness of their ways.

SERMON 87

On the Centurion's Slave in the Gospel
on the Occasion of the Dedication of a Basilica[1]

1. We read in the holy Gospel,[2] when the slave of a certain centurion who was very dear to him was laboring under the serious illness of paralysis and the centurion asked the Savior by way of the elders of the Jews to cure his sufferings (for he was, as Scripture says, at the point of death), that, among other things, the Jews said to the Lord in order to commend him the more: *It is right that you should help him, for he loves our nation, and he himself has built us a synagogue.*[3] If, then, one who has built a synagogue is commended to the Lord, how much more commendable is one who has built a church! And if one who has been responsible for a den of irreligion merits grace, how much more grace does one merit who has prepared a dwelling for religion! And if one who has constructed a place where Christ is always denied is visited with heavenly mercy, how much more to be visited is one who has built a tabernacle where Christ is daily

preached! For in the centurion it was not the work that he had done that the Lord approved but the spirit in which he accomplished it. For if he solicitously built a synagogue at a time when there were as yet no Christians, it is understood that he would all the more solicitously have built a church had there in fact been Christians. But he still preaches Christ even though he builds a synagogue, for in this very work he warns the Pharisees that they must accept the Savior, and he shows that it was for this reason especially that he built the tabernacle, namely, that they might speak the glory of the Lord in manifold fashion.[4] For if the founder of the synagogue believes in Christ, all the more should the frequenter of that synagogue believe.

2. The centurion, then, is justified because of a work that is fragile and earthly. Clearly to be justified is that most illustrious and provident man,[5] our comes,[6] because of a work that is enduring and heavenly. As this comes is higher in dignity than the centurion, so also must he be more fervent in faith. It is a wise man and a devout comes who soldiers as much in peace for the Savior as he soldiers in war for the emperor and who, as much as he hastens to seize captives out of the hands of the foe, hastens all the more to free from sacrilege those who have been captured by the devil. In the one case he slays enemies of an earthly kind, in the other he presses against the adversaries of the heavenly Lord; in the one case he overcomes barbarians, in the other demons. It is a wise man, I say, who, like the emperor's comes, wishes to be Christ's comes as well. For by acting well and religiously he desires his dignity to be enduring, according to what is written in the prophet: *And you, O good kings,*[7] and so forth.

3. Therefore, when the centurion asked the Lord to snatch the sick man from death, and when the Lord wanted to go to the centurion's house where the slave was lying ill, the centurion said: *Lord, I am not worthy that you should enter under my roof.*[8] The centurion makes excuses, then, and calls himself unworthy lest the Lord enter under his roof. Behold how worthy is our comes, under whose roof the Savior enters today! Let us see what favor this excuse of the centurion wins, inasmuch as he says: *Lord, I am not worthy that you should enter under my roof, but only say a word and he will be healed.*[9] O Christian faith, you that are used to accomplishing everything with humility! See how the devout centurion becomes worthier to receive health[10] as he confesses that he is unworthy, and in considering his

dwelling contemptible he has made it the more honorable and acceptable. It was a man of great and perfect faith who, when he recognized
that Christ was Lord of the heavens, feared that the narrow confines
of his lodging might not contain Him. Therefore, since the centurion
is opposed to it, the Lord does not go to his house, but the Lord's
healing goes; the Savior does not visit the sick man, but the Savior's
health visits him.

4. But what shall I say of our brothers, the holy men Vitalianus and
Marianus?[11] I know that they seek glory not from human beings but
from God alone. Yet, even if I should be silent, their very works
speak their praise, for to their praise pertains whatever we have
praised in others a little while ago. Even if many have constructed this
tabernacle, nonetheless these have produced it out of their own re-
sources †and the other by his co-operation.† [12] But with what re-
sources, since in the world they are ordinary and insignificant? With
those, namely, about which the Apostle says: *with an abundance of
faith and with the riches of simplicity*.[13] For to the saints poverty is
itself always rich. Hence I believe that these blessed men built this
church no less by their prayers than by financial contributions, for it
was fitting that Christ's work should increase more by prayers than
by blocks of stone. They spent their whole substance upon the construction of this edifice, and certainly nothing is lacking to them.
Clearly a poverty that both expends all and possesses all[14] is, as we
have said, rich and wealthy. This is also the case with that widow who
was blessed by God, about whom the Lord says in the Gospel: *This
poor widow put in more than anyone else, for all these contributed to
God's service from their abundance, but she put in all that she had to
live on*.[15]

SERMON 90

On the Heretics Who Deal in Sins[1]

1. Beloved brethren, we should always remember and have before
our eyes the fact that the Lord Jesus Christ came from heaven to earth
for this reason—to bestow eternal life on us. Therefore, although He

was the Son of God, He preferred to become a son of man so that He might make us, who were men, sons of God. For not on account of this present life, which is short, perishable, and mortal, was such a divine mystery effected, but on account of that which is enduring and everlasting. For God was not going to offer us a long life, full of toil, labor, and need, lest He offer us not so much a long life as constant evils. For this alone seems to be a remedy for it—that it is short. Hence also the Apostle says: *If for this life only we hope in Christ, we are more wretched than anyone else.*[2] Therefore Christ is not to be hoped in for this life only, in which the bad can do more than the good, in which those who are more evil are happier and those who lead a more criminal life live more prosperously. For what good does this life have? Honors, riches, and health, although they are passing, are obtained not by merit but fortuitously. For we see that it is not goodness but power[3] that has given so many people titles of honor. How many people have acquired wealth not because they inherited it from their parents but because they seized it in bloody fashion! How many people are powerful because of their family connections, and are not governed by the mercy of God but fatten themselves on the blood of cattle![4] These things, then, because they are temporal and of no value, are offered to anybody anywhere without regard to merit and at random, because they are given not as rewards but as temptations.[5]

2. We, therefore, to whom eternal life is promised, should always possess and seek after eternal goods—that is to say, faith, righteousness, and charity. For these good things arouse opposition and, although these gifts cannot be bestowed by human beings, they are still frequently taken away by evil people. Therefore we must be careful and provident with respect to the good of faith, and in order to protect it we must always be armed with inner devotion and not quickly give credence to flattering falsehoods. For the enemy is accustomed to creep in under the guise of peace; that is to say, a heretic insinuates himself under the title of Christian, carrying Christ in his mouth in order to deceive simple people but bearing the devil in his heart; and indeed he confesses Him with his tongue but blasphemes Him in his mind. From this person, then, one must turn away immediately, and one should not be linked with him in any way whatsoever. For how can someone who is the Lord's enemy be the friend of His servants? Nor should we be astonished that heretics of

this sort have begun to wander about in our own region, for the treacherous wolf always follows after the flock of sheep; the deceitful devil
always attacks the Christian assembly. Indeed, this occurs for a beneficial end, so that, by being more careful, the sheep might not leave the
flock nor the Christian abandon the Church. Hence the Apostle also
says: *Heresies must exist so that those who are approved among you might be
made manifest.*[6] It is as if he had said: There must be a struggle of faith
among Christians so that victory might be certain for the approved.

3. But let us set aside their blasphemies for the time being and refute
their precepts for living. Those who are set over them, whom they call
priests,[7] are said to have this kind of command—that if any layperson
confesses to having committed a crime he should not tell him: "Do
penance, mourn what you have done, weep over your sins," but he
should say: "For this crime give a certain amount to me and you will be
forgiven." It is indeed a vain and foolish priest[8] who, when he takes
plunder, thinks that Christ forgives the sin. He does not know that the
Savior is used to forgiving sins and that for a misdeed He looks for
precious tears and not for a great sum of money. Hence He Himself
says: *You have freely received; give freely.*[9] And Peter, when he had sinned
by denying the Lord three times, did not merit pardon because of his
gifts but obtained it by his tears, for the Evangelist says of him: *He wept
most bitterly.*[10] You see, I say, that with Christ value is measured not in
gifts but in tears. Pardon is quickly obtained in proportion to how
mournfully guilt is wept over. The priest[11] takes the gifts, then, and by a
kind of bargain he promises the Savior's forgiveness. What a foolish
smoothing-over, in which it is said that the one who has given more to
the priest[12] has sinned less against the Lord! With teachers of this sort
the rich are always innocent and the poor are always criminal. How can a
poor person, who has nothing to offer for his sin, make satisfaction for his
misdeed?

SERMON 97

On the Birthday of the Lord[1]

1. By what grace or with what praises I should preach today on the
Lord's birthday I am utterly ignorant, for on such a festival human

speech is insufficient to proclaim God's greatness. If Christ was praised by the voice of angels when He was born, with what voice must He be praised now that He reigns? For our celebration surpasses the festival of that time, since then they were amazed at the Lord who had merely been born, but we should look up to the one who was born as one both risen and reigning. The praise of this season, then, ought to be more eloquent inasmuch as its wonders are greater. But since human frailty cannot put forth a worthy sermon, let us betake ourselves to the praises of the angels. And because we cannot equal them in merit, let us be linked in devotion; that is to say, on the same festival let us exult with the same words as they did, saying: *Glory to God in the highest and on earth peace to men of good will.*[2] Clearly these are worthy and proper words which, at the birth of Christ, both pay God honor in the heavens and bestow peace upon men on earth.[3] Before the coming of the Savior neither did the heavenly places offer reverence nor the earth possess repose. But see what these words say: *Peace to men of good will*—not to any men whomsoever but *to men of good will*, so that you may understand that the peace of Christ is not something owed but something merited, for it is not condition that merits it but desire.

2. With these words, then, the angels exulted on that night when shepherds keeping watch over their flock learned first, before anyone else, of the Lord's birth.[4] They knew of the Savior's birth first, before all the others, because the angels announced it. It is no wonder that shepherds were able to know of the world's redemption before rulers, for the angels made their announcement not to kings or judges but to countryfolk. It is not to be wondered at, then, if innocence merited to know the grace of Christ before power did and simple country manners merited to recognize the truth before proud dominion. For what the shepherds recognized the rulers were unable to recognize; hence the blessed Apostle says: *What none of the rulers of this age recognized,*[5] and so forth. At the birth of Christ, therefore, the angels rejoiced together with the shepherds, giving God high glory, for in close and even joined choruses, so to speak, they preached the glory of God.

Hence I also believe that the same angels rejoice in a like bond of joy with us on the same festival of this same Lord, for those who are used to addressing shepherds because of Christ's birth are unable not to search out the bishops[6] on account of the joy of this same Christ, since what they spoke to them then as they kept watch over their flock in the dead of night they were signifying as a mystery for this era. By that deed this was indicated: the flock is the people, the night is the world, and the shepherds are the bishops[7] who, watching over their flock with unceasing solicitude for the sake of Christ, are not abandoned by the angels.

3. Today, then, the Lord was born according to the flesh in such hiddenness and such silence that the world was completely unaware of His birth. The world was unaware because He was both born without the knowledge of a father and conceived outside the order of nature, for Joseph recognized a son whom he did not beget and Mary brought forth one whom she did not conceive in a sexual way. Thus the Lord was born, then, so that no one would suspect His future birth or believe it or perceive it. How would they believe that this would be when they hardly believe what happened after? That the Savior would thus hiddenly and secretly descend into a virgin the prophet David had already prophesied beforehand when he said: *He will descend like rain upon fleece.*[8] For what takes place with such silence and so noiselessly as a shower upon a fleece of wool? It strikes no one's ears with its sound, it sprinkles no one's body with the damp of spattered moisture, but without disturbing anyone it completely absorbs throughout itself the whole shower that has poured down, not knowing a particular course but by its firm softness offering many courses; and what seems to be resistant because of its density is open because of its fineness.[9]

Rightly, then, do we compare Mary to fleece—she who conceived the Lord in such a way that she absorbed Him with her whole body; nor did she undergo a rending of that same body, but she was tender in submission and firm in chastity. Rightly, I say, is Mary compared to fleece—she from whose offspring saving garments are woven for the people. Clearly Mary is fleece since from her tender womb came forth the lamb who Himself, bearing His mother's wool (that is, flesh), covers the wounds of all peoples with a soft fleece. For every wound of sin is covered with the wool of Christ, tended by the blood of Christ, and, so that it may receive health, clothed in the garment of Christ.[10]

SERMON 104

On the Canaanite Woman[1]

. . . Rightly, however, can we call Moses and the prophets crumbs because the Savior Himself is the whole loaf of bread, according to what He says of Himself: *I am the bread that has come down from heaven.*[2] When the Canaanite woman asked to be refreshed with this bread the Lord said to her: *It is not good to take the children's bread and throw it to the dogs*[3]—that is, to the Gentiles. Understanding this mystery she responds, saying: *But, Lord, the dogs also eat their masters' crumbs.*[4] Marveling at her faith, the Savior immediately presented her daughter with the medicine of perfect health. Thus this great woman finds the bread of salvation while asking for crumbs of faith, and she is filled with the children's food while desiring the dogs' scraps. O blessed wounds, which keep eternal sorrow from us! O abundant crumbs, which fend off everlasting hunger! For whoever kisses the Savior's wounds with his mouth will himself no longer sorrow; whoever takes the crumbs of His bread will not suffer everlasting famine.

SERMON 109[1]

. . . He receives. Some He casts down into the depths, others He raises up to heaven. For some He provides a fall for their ruin, for others He works a resurrection for their glory. Thus it is written in the Gospel where holy Simeon says to Mary: *Behold, He is set for the ruin and the rising of many.*[2] For the person who falls away from Christ is the one who, ignoring the pathway while he wanders about, stumbles against His commandments. The person who rises in the Lord is the one who, fearing His precepts, raises himself up from his sins to virtue. This is how the heretic suffers ruin on the journey, ignoring the path of true religion, while the Catholic proceeds without hindrance, for he travels to salvation on the straight way of faith.

NOTES

LIST OF ABBREVIATIONS

AC	Antike und Christentum (Münster 1929–1950)
ActaSS	Acta sanctorum (Paris *et alibi* 1863–)
ACW	Ancient Christian Writers (Westminster, Md.–London–New York–Paramus, N.J.–Mahwah, N.J. 1946–)
Callewaert	C. Callewaert, "Le carême à Turin au Ve siècle d'après s. Maxime," *Sacris erudiri* (The Hague 1940; repr. 1962) 517–28
CCL	Corpus christianorum, series latina (Turnhout 1953–)
DACL	Dictionnaire d'archéologie chrétienne et de liturgie (Paris 1907–1953)
Daniélou	J. Daniélou, *The Bible and the Liturgy* (Notre Dame 1956)
DHGE	Dictionnaire d'histoire et de géographie ecclésiastiques (Paris 1912–)
DS	Dictionnaire de spiritualité (Paris 1932–)
DTC	Dictionnaire de théologie catholique (Paris 1903–1950)
FC	The Fathers of the Church (New York–Washington 1947–)
Fitzgerald	A. Fitzgerald, "The Relationship of Maximus of Turin to Rome and Milan: A Study of Penance and Pardon at the Turn of the Fifth Century," *Augustinianum* 27 (1987) 465–86.
GCS	Die griechischen christlichen Schriftsteller der ersten drei Jahrhunderte (Leipzig 1897–)
JAC	Jahrbuch für Antike und Christentum (Münster 1958–)

JLW	Jahrbuch für Liturgiewissenschaft (Münster 1921–1941)
Kyriakon	*Kyriakon: Festschrift Johannes Quasten,* ed. P. Granfield and J. A. Jungmann (Münster 1970).
LTK	Lexikon für Theologie und Kirche (2nd ed., Freiburg 1957–1967)
MG	Patrologia graeca, ed. J. P. Migne (Paris 1857–1866)
Miscellanea Lercaro	*Miscellanea liturgica in onore di S. E. il Card. Giacomo Lercaro* (Rome 1966)
ML	Patrologia latina, ed. J. P. Migne (Paris 1844–1855) with supplementary volumes
PWK	Pauly-Wissowa-Kroll, Realencyclopädie der classischen Altertumswissenschaft (Stuttgart 1893–)
RAC	Reallexikon für Antike und Christentum (Stuttgart 1950–)
Rahner, *Myths*	H. Rahner, *Greek Myths and Christian Mystery,* tr. B. Battershaw (New York 1963)
Rahner, *Symbole*	H. Rahner, *Symbole der Kirche: Die Ekklesiologie der Väter* (Salzburg 1964)
Ramsey	B. Ramsey, "Almsgiving in the Latin Church: The Late Fourth and Early Fifth Centuries," *Theological Studies* 43 (1982) 226–59
SC	Sources chrétiennes (Paris 1941–)
SCA	Studies in Christian Antiquity (Washington 1941–)
SP	Studia patristica (Berlin 1957–)
VC	Vigiliae christianae (Amsterdam 1947–)

INTRODUCTION

1. Cf. *Itinerarium Egeriae* 25.1; *Const. apost.* 2.57.9; Jerome, *Hom. de nativ. Dom.*, *ad fin.*, for instances of priests preaching in the East at this time, and Augustine, *Ep.* 41.1, for the West.

2. Cf. Possidius, *V. s. Augustini* 4.

3. Canon 16 of the Council of Nicaea permitted the ordination of someone from another diocese with the permission of the bishop of that person's diocese.

4. Cf. M. Schanz, C. Hosius, G. Krüger, *Geschichte der römischen Litteratur* 4.2 (Munich 1920) 536.

5. Cf. CCL 23.xxxiii n. 1.

6. Cf. Caesar Baronius, *Annales ecclesiastici* 6 (Rome 1607) 128–29, 267.

7. Cf. ML 57.129.

8. Cf. the contributions made in this regard by F. Savio, *Gli antichi vescovi d'Italia dalle origini al 1300, descritti per regioni: Il Piemonte* (Turin 1898) 286–93; C. Benna, "San Massimo, vescovo di Torino," *Riv. dioces. Torinese* 2 (1934) 48–50, 62–67, 102–9; P. Bongiovanni, *S. Massimo vescovo di Torino e il suo pensiero teologico* (diss. Pontif. Athen. Sales., Turin 1952) 26–27.

9. Cf. CCL 23.xxxi–xxxii.

10. Cf. B. Czapla, *Gennadius als Litterarhistoriker* (Münster 1898) 205–9, 211. Ironically, Czapla, following Baronius, considers that Gennadius erred with respect to Maximus.

11. This argument is not conclusive of itself, however, inasmuch as some of the writers are out of the chronological order: cf. Czapla 206.

12. Cf. Sermons 26.4, 56.3, and 58.3.

13. Sermons 54, 67, and 68.

13a. Cf. Sermon 18 n. 1.

14. For this section I have relied exclusively on Mutzenbecher in CCL 23.xvi ff.

15. Mutzenbecher's criteria for judging the individual sermons are given in some detail in her article "Bestimmung der echten Sermones des Maximus Taurinensis," *Sacris erudiri* 12 (1961) 197–293.

16. CCL 23.444.

17. A. Olivar, "Preparación y improvisación en la predicación patrística," *Kyriakon* 2.754–55.

18. *Ibid.* 753–54.

19. *Ibid.* 755.

20. *vir in divinis scripturis satis intentus et ad docendam ex tempore plebem sufficiens.*

21. Sermons 30, 63.1–2, 91.2, 106.2, 107, and 108.

22. Cf. n. 12 above.

23. Sermons 29.4, 41.5, 58.3, 73.5, and 86.3.

24. Sermons 3.2, 23, 32.2, and 79.

25. Sermon 3.1–2.

26. Sermon 42.1.

27. Sermons 79 and 91.

28. Cf. Sermons 72–73 and 81–86.

29. Cf. Sermon 50 n. 1.

30. *De cat. rud.* 15.23.

31. Sermons 6.2, 15.2, 21.2, 30.3, 39.1, 53.2, 67.2, 84.1, 96, 100.3, 102.3, and 111.2.

32. Sermon 42.1.

33. Sermon 30.2.

34. Sermon 50.1.

35. Cf. Sermon 37 n. 1.

36. Cf. Sermon 57 n. 1.

37. Cf. Sermon 44 n. 17.

38. A. Hamman, ed., *The Paschal Mystery*, tr. T. Halton (New York 1969) 190.

39. Cf. Sermon 39 n. 5.

40. H.-I. Marrou, *Saint Augustin et la fin de la culture antique* (Paris 1938) 480.

41. *De doct. christ.* 2.6.7–8; cf. *Ep.* 55.21.

41a. A. Grillmeier mentions Maximus as a typical example of popular Western Christological preaching in the fifth century: "He did not further christological doctrine or christological formulas. His illustrations were of a popular character. He finds images in which to celebrate Christ and his work everywhere: in the cosmos, in ancient sagas (Odysseus tied to the mast, an idea which Jerome also knows), and in the cultural life of his time. In this way he makes the theological picture of Christ into the sort of colourful mosaic which is loved by a popular audience. Of course, even the great theologians do not disdain popular expression like this, as, say, Ambrose shows us" (*Christ in Christian Tradition* 1: *From the Apostolic Age to Chalcedon* [*AD 451*], tr. J. Bowden [2nd ed. Atlanta 1975] 393).

42. Sermon 86.3.
43. Sermon 2.2.
44. Sermons 20.5 and 33.6.
45. Sermons 50A.3–4, 75.3, and 76.1.
46. *S. Massimo di Torino: Sermoni* (Alba 1975).
47. M. C. Conroy, *Imagery in the Sermons of Maximus, Bishop of Turin* (Washington, D.C. 1965).

SERMON I

1. *Natale,* here rendered as anniversary, may also be translated as birthday. The day of a martyr's death was referred to as his or her birthday since at least the middle of the second century: cf. *Mart. Pol.* 18.3. For a comprehensive discussion of this point cf. A. C. Rush, *Death and Burial in Christian Antiquity,* SCA 1 (1941) 72–87. In these sermons, however, *natalis* has consistently been rendered as anniversary, unless it refers to the day of a person's physical birth. In the case of Sts. Peter and Paul, in any event, it is not an anniversary of death that is being celebrated, since the exact date of their death was unknown, but rather the anniversary of the translation of both their remains on June 29, 258, from the original burial place to a new location along the Appian Way. Cf. J. P. Kirsch, "Die 'memoria apostolorum' an der Appischen Strasse zu Rom und die liturgische Festfeier des 29. Juni," JLW 3 (1923) 33–50.

1a. On the image of the Church as a school cf. Augustine, *Enarr. in ps.* 126.3, where, however, Christ is the teacher.

2. Cf. Luke 11.52. On the symbolism of the key cf. also Sermons 43.2 and 52.4.

3. Col. 2.3.

4. On this and what follows cf. also Sermon 9.2. On the equality in heaven of Peter and Paul, mentioned in a polemical context cf. also Tertullian, *De praescript. haer.* 24. For a similar idea, with respect to St. Eusebius and the Maccabees cf. Sermon 7.4 *ad fin.*

5. Cf. Sermon 44.1: ". . . there should be an equal celebration of those things whose holiness is equal."

6. In early Christian symbolism the West was considered inferior to the East. This is alluded to in Cyril of Jerusalem, *Cat. myst.* 1.4, 9: the East is the realm of the rising sun, which is associated with Christ, and hence of light and blessedness, and paradise had been in the East; but the West is the realm of the setting sun and hence of darkness, and thus it is associated with Satan. On the symbolism of the East, cf. F. J. Dölger, *Die Sonne der Gerechtigkeit und der Schwarze* (Münster 1918) *passim,* esp. 1–48. There must have been some self-consciousness in Maximus' congregation about being Western, because he also seeks to dilute the effects of this symbolism in Sermon 13.2.

7. Maximus' view here that Christ's sufferings were sufficient for the salvation of the human race and that the sufferings of the martyrs have only an exemplary value stands in contrast to the thesis advanced by Origen in *Exhort. ad mart.* 30, 50. There Origen says that the sufferings of the martyrs, like those of Christ, have a role to play in the salvation of the world. On this issue cf. W. Rordorf, "La 'diaconie' des martyrs selon Origène," *Epektasis: Mélanges patristiques offerts au Card. J. Daniélou,* ed. J. Fontaine and C. Kannengiesser (Paris 1972) 395–402, where martyrdom is shown to be analogous to the Eucharist in the mind of Origen. But there is a hint of Origen's point of view in Sermon 3.3, where Maximus speaks of the martyrs as "victims . . . on our behalf." On the martyrs as examples, cf. Sermons 12.1, 16.2–3, 105.1, 106.2.

8. On this and what follows cf. *Actus Petri* 31–32; cf. also Sermon 31.3.

9. Cf. *Passio apost. Petri et Pauli* 60–62.

SERMON 2

1. On the term "anniversary" and on the feast of Sts. Peter and Paul cf. Sermon 1 n. 1.

2. Cf. Acts 10.9–13.

3. Acts 10.13.

4. Acts 3.6.

5. Cf. 1 Kings 17.6.

6. The raven had a bad reputation in both pagan and Christian antiquity because of its hoarse cry and its blackness, among other things: cf. Ovid, *Metam.* 2.541–542 and the references in DACL 3.2.2912–13.

7. On Peter as hungry, in the same setting, because of the Jews' lack of faith cf. also Jerome, *Ep.* 125.2. On Jesus as hungry and thirsty for the salvation of others cf. Sermons 22.2 and 66.4.

8. With its Plotinian themes of purgation and ascent, this is a brief but classical description of mystical prayer and the phenomena that accompany it; it recalls the longer and famous description of the vision at Ostia in Augustine, *Conf.* 9.10.23–24.

9. On this imagery cf. Augustine, *C. Faustum* 12.15, where the vessel shown to Peter is likened to Noah's ark, which also contained all sorts of animals symbolizing all nations.

10. Cf. Eph. 5.27.

11. Cf. Rev. 19.8. On the excellence of linen in pagan and Christian antiquity cf. J. Quasten, "The Garment of Immortality: A Study of the 'Accipe vestem candidam,' " *Miscellanea Lercaro* 1.391–401; W. J. Burghardt, "Cyril of Alexandria on 'Wool and Linen,' " *Traditio* 2 (1944) 484–86. There is an unusual exception to this view in Cassian, *Inst.* 3.3, where it is said without explanation that linen symbolizes death.

12. Cf. Acts 10.

13. Cf. Heb. 3.14.

14. Cf. John 11.25.

15. Cf. Ambrose, *Exp. evang. sec. Luc.* 7.4.

16. Phil. 1.23.

17. Phil. 1.21.

18. 1 Tim. 5.6.

SERMON 3

1. The occasion for the recriminatory tone of this sermon was the insufficient attendance at the celebration of the feast of Sts. Peter and Paul, mentioned in §2, which must have occurred in the week preceding the Sunday before the present sermon was preached. Attendance at such celebrations, in addition to the Sunday liturgy, seems to have been considered obligatory. For similar recriminatory words on the occasion of the same feast cf. Leo the Great (?), Sermon 84.

2. *sacerdotum*, which is also used in §2. Although *sacerdos* can be used of a priest as well, doubtless bishops are intended here, since at this period they were still carrying out almost exclusively the task of preaching that is being spoken of (although cf. Introduction n. 1 for references to the preaching of priests). On the term *sacerdos* cf. DACL 15.1.240–42. On the bishop as the ordinary preacher cf. Sermon 92 n. 4.

3. The term *sacramentum*, employed here in the plural to refer to the Scriptures, has a very broad usage in the patristic era. In whatever context it is used, however, it indicates an event, thing, or person that is somehow productive of grace. Cf. DTC 14.1.493–95.

4. Cf. Matt. 7.6.

5. Cf. Matt. 13.45–46.

6. Heb. 12.6.

7. On the martyrs as victims for others cf. Sermon 1 n. 7.

8. Luke 10.16.

SERMON 4

1. On the term "anniversary" cf. Sermon 1 n. 1. St. Laurence was a Roman deacon who suffered in the persecution of Valerian in 258. His feast has been kept on August 10 since the earliest times. Laurence was probably beheaded, and the death by roasting that is

attributed to him seems to be legendary: cf. P. Franchi de' Cavalieri, "S. Lorenzo e il supplizio della graticola," *Römische Quartalschrift* 14 (1900) 159–76.

2. *dilectionem vestram*. Such forms of address were common in sermons, and they are often employed by Maximus. On their use in letters, which was comparable, cf. M. B. O'Brien, *Titles of Address in Christian Latin Epistolography to 543 A. D.* (Diss., Catholic University of America, Washington, D.C. 1930).

3. Luke 12.49.

4. Luke 24.18 gives the name of only one of the two disciples —Cleopas. The name Ammaus is probably taken by a process of association from Emmaus, the name of the village to which the two were going. For other attempts to denominate this unknown disciple cf. B. M. Metzger, "Names for the Nameless in the New Testament," *Kyriakon* 1.96–97.

5. Luke 24.32.

6. It is a commonplace in early Christian literature that the martyr does not feel the torture intended for him because of his closeness to Christ: cf. *Mart. Pol.* 2.2–3; Eusebius, *Hist. eccl.* 5.1.56. Prudentius, *Peristeph.* 2.360 ff. is very clear about the fact that Laurence endured his tortuous death with superhuman fortitude and calm. In general, on the martyr's inability to feel pain, cf. H. Delehaye, *Les passions des martyrs et les genres littéraires* (Brussels 1921) 287–89.

7. *ut mors et non desit ad supplicium et desit ad finem.*

8. Cf. Dan. 3.19–24.

9. Ps. 26.2.

10. The point is that the reins, or kidneys, were understood to be the seat of the emotions and hence of attraction to the world; thus Augustine, *Enarr. in ps.* 25, serm. 2.7., identifies reins with pleasures.

SERMON 5

1. On the term "birthday" cf. Sermon 1 n. 1. John the Baptist's physical birth, with which the present sermon is concerned, was celebrated on June 24 in the West from about the beginning of the

fifth century. The anniversary of his death on August 29 did not appear in the West as a feast until the sixth century. Cf. LTK 5.1087.

2. Cf. Matt. 14.3–12.

3. Cf. Luke 1.13–17.

4. Luke 1.13.

5. Luke 1.24.

6. Cf. Luke 1.8–20, 26–38.

7. Cf. Luke 1.20.

8. Luke 1.44.

9. Jer. 1.5.

10. Cf. Matt. 14.3.

11. The allusion is perhaps to Matt. 11.2–6, although this passage does not say that John preached Christ but only that he sent his disciples to Christ to see if He were the one "who is to come."

SERMON 6

1. On the term "birthday" cf. Sermon 1 n. 1; and on the celebration of this feast cf. Sermon 5 n. 1.

2. Cf. Luke 1.62–64.

3. Cf. Luke 1.20.

4. In fact, according to Luke 1.63, Zechariah first wrote John's name, and only after that was his tongue loosed.

5. Mark 1.2.

6. Mark 1.3.

7. John 1.23.

8. Matt. 11.11.

9. Gal. 4.4.

10. *ne dominus extra veritatem videretur esse condicionis humanae,* i.e. let the Lord not seem to share the human condition in a way that does not accord with the fact of His divinity. Perhaps a criticism of the Arians is being made here.

SERMON 9

1. On the term "anniversary" and on the feast of Sts. Peter and Paul cf. Sermon 1 n. 1.

2. Ps. 19.4.

3. Cf. Acts 3.1–11.

4. Acts 3.6.

5. Matt. 16.18.

6. Cf. Acts 9.15.

7. On the image of the vessel that does not empty cf. 1 Kings 17.14–16. For the related image of the Scriptures as a stream that never runs dry cf. Ephrem, *In Diatessaron* 1.19.

8. On this and what follows cf. Sermon 1.2.

9. *dominicae devotionis.*

10. Cf. *Passio apost. Petri et Pauli* 60.

11. Cf. *Passio Pauli apost.* 16.

12. 1 Cor. 3.2.

13. Exod. 3.8; 13.5.

14. *candidior,* which could also be translated as "clearer" or "more splendid," but which requires this translation in order to play out the image of milk. Cf. Sermon 30.1 and n. 3.

15. On the image of maternal breasts in patristic literature cf. RAC 2.661–64, where this particular usage, however, is not given. The closest approximation is the image of the Church's breasts, which signify the two Testaments: cf. Augustine, *In ep. ad Parth.* 3.1, cited *ibid.* 663.

The progress of the imagery here is worthy of note. Paul's neck is said to have streamed forth with milk. Then there is a suggestion of Pauline maternity in his nourishing the Corinthians with milk. Finally, it is specifically Paul's epistles that are qualified in maternal terms.

16. 1 Cor. 15.50.

SERMON 10

1. On the term "anniversary" cf. Sermon 1 n. 1. St. Cyprian was bishop of Carthage from 249 to 258. He died Sept. 14, 258, in the persecution of Valerian.

2. *natali.* On the use of this term in a context such as this cf. RAC 9.240-42.

3. On the pressing of grapes as an image of martyrdom cf. also Augustine, *Enarr. in ps.* 8.3, where it is said that wine presses customarily have symbolic reference to martyrdom.

4. Ps. 23.5. Martyrdom is associated with the image of the cup in Matt. 20.22-23 par., Matt. 26.27-28 par., Matt. 26.39 par., and John 18.11, and in patristic literature as early as the middle of the second century in *Mart. Pol.* 14.2. On this last cf. T. Baumeister, *Die Anfänge der Theologie des Martyriums* (Münster 1980) 299-300. Origen develops this image in *Exhort. ad. mart.* 28-29, where he quotes some of the same scriptural passages that Maximus himself does. Inebriation is also associated with martyrdom: cf. Tertullian, *Scorpiace* 12.11; Jerome, *Ep.* 44; Augustine, *Enarr. in ps.* 35.14; Rabbula, *Hymn to the Martyrs,* in *Early Christian Prayers,* ed. A. Hamman, tr. W. Mitchell (Chicago 1961) 184-85.

5. Matt. 26.39.

6. Ps. 116.13.

7. On the image of Christ hanging on the cross as a grape or cluster of grapes on a vine cf. also Ambrose, *Exp. evang. sec. Luc.* 5.81; *De fide* 1.20.135. On the image of Christ as a grape or grape cluster, such as it appears here and in the following few lines, in ancient Syrian literature, where it seems to have been quite popular, cf. R. Murray, *Symbols of Church and Kingdom: A Study in Early Syriac Tradition* (Cambridge, Eng. 1975) 113-29. On the same theme in early Christian art cf. O. Nussbaum, "Die grosse Traube Christus," JAC 6 (1963) 136-43; L. Eckhart, " 'Die grosse Traube Christus': Ein römerzeitliches Grabrelief aus dem nördlichen Wienerwald," JAC 19 (1976) 173-98.

8. Cf. Num. 13.2-25. On the image of Christ as a grape cluster in this particular context cf. Gregory of Nyssa, *V. Moysis* 2.268, and the numerous references cited in Gregory of Nyssa, *The Life of Moses,*

tr. A. J. Malherbe and E. Ferguson (New York 1978) 190 n. 378, to which may be added Jerome, *Ep.* 108.11; Augustine, *Enarr. in ps.* 8.2. Caesarius of Arles, Sermon 107.3–4, is reminiscent of Maximus from here until the end of the sermon.

9. Ps. 69.23.

SERMON 11

1. The present sermon seems to follow on the preceding one.

2. On the term "anniversary" cf. Sermon 1 n. 1.

3. On the use of the oxymoron *sobria ebrietas*, "sober intoxication," which entered Christian literature by way of Origen, cf. J. Quasten, "Sobria ebrietas in Ambrosius De sacramentis," *Miscellanea liturgica in honorem L. Cuniberti Mohlberg* (Rome 1948) 1.117–25. On the association of wine with martyrdom cf. Sermon 10 nn. 3–4.

4. *Qui enim inebriatur caelesti gratia, exsobriatur sarcina peccatorum*—a pun difficult of translation.

5. Cf. Acts 2.1–13. On the image of sober intoxication in this context cf. also Paulinus of Nola, *Carm.* 27.105–6.

6. Perhaps the practices of a pagan cult or even of a heterodox Christian group are intended here. Ecstasy (*elatione aliqua*) tended to have a bad reputation in many circles because of associations with Montanism and pagan and heretical enthusiastic movements, although it was seen as legitimate in others. In any case one must distinguish between external manifestations of ecstasy, which were particularly subject to suspicion, and more interior forms. Cf. DS 4.2087–2113; R. Knox, *Enthusiasm: A Chapter in the History of Religion* (Oxford 1950) 1–70. Speaking in tongues seems to have been unknown in the Church at this time: cf. DS 9.225.

7. Isa. 5.7.

8. Gal. 3.7.

9. Isa. 5.2.

10. For another description of the crowning with thorns as a glorious event cf. Hilary, *In Matt.* 33.3. The first iconographic representation of this, on a mid-fourth-century "Passion" sarcophagus in the Pio Cristiano Museum of the Vatican, depicts well the

ambivalent symbolic character of the event, which Maximus suggests here. The crowning with thorns is one of a series of panels concerned with Christ's suffering and death, but it portrays the occurrence as if it were the garlanding of a victor rather than an act of punishment.

11. Zech. 12.10; John 19.37.
12. Cf. Matt. 13.7.
13. Cf. Matt. 13.22.
14. 1 Cor. 7.32–33.
15. Gen. 3.18.

SERMON 12

1. On the term "anniversary" here and in the first sentence cf. Sermon 1 n. 1. Sts. Octavus, Adventus, and Solutor, whose feast is celebrated on November 20, were martyrs claimed by Turin: cf. Socii Bollandiani, *Bibliotheca hagiographica latina A-I* (Brussels 1898–99) 16. C. Benna, "San Massimo, vescovo di Torino," *Riv. dioces. Torinese* 2 (1934) 142–45, claims rather daringly, according to Mutzenbecher, that these were bishops of Turin who preceded Maximus: cf. CCL 23.40. On the link between Christian towns of late antiquity and their patron saints cf. P. Brown, *The Cult of the Saints: Its Rise and Function in Latin Christianity* (Chicago 1981) 61 ff. Paulinus of Nola, *Carm.* 19.1 ff., speaks at considerable length on this link and gives numerous examples. The most famous of all such saintly patrons are Peter and Paul in Rome. In Maximus' time local saints are just beginning to be seen as intercessors and personages having the power of *grands seigneurs*.

2. On the martyrs as examples cf. Sermon 1 n. 7.

3. The allusion is to the custom of burying the dead in proximity to the remains of the saints: cf. Augustine, *De cura pro mort. gerenda* passim.

4. Cf. Eph. 5.14.
5. Matt. 16.18.
6. Exorcisms were relatively frequent occurrences at the graves

of the saints in late antiquity and were, of course, signs of the saints' power: cf. Brown 106–13.

   7. Cf. Ps. 68.18.

SERMON 13A

1. *Extravagans.* By this time in the West, at least four events could be commemorated in the single feast of the Epiphany on January 6: the birth of Christ, the adoration of the Magi, the baptism of Christ, and the miracle of Cana. Of these Maximus seems to know only the last two; the allusion to the Magi in Sermon 100.1, which is an Epiphany sermon, is in connection with the birth of Christ rather than with the celebration of the Epiphany itself. (The spurious Sermon 45.2, however, mentions the commemoration of the birth of Christ at Epiphany.) In fact Maximus gives the impression that the celebration of the miracle of Cana used to be for him the unique aspect of the feast, since in Sermon 64.1 he speaks of "some" who also commemorated the baptism of the Lord; but in Sermon 65.1 he affirms that he celebrates both mysteries on the same day, and Sermons 13A and B and 100 indicate this as well. In his emphasis on the baptism of Christ and the miracle of Cana, to the exclusion of the adoration of the Magi, Maximus runs counter to the Western practice of his time, which stressed instead the event of the Magi: cf. Augustine, Sermons 199–204; Leo, Sermons 31–38. Cf. B. Botte, *Les origines de la Noël et de l'Epiphanie* (Louvain 1932; repr. 1961); H. Frank, "Zur Geschichte von Weihnachten und Epiphanie," JLW 12 (1932) 145–55, and 13 (1935) 1–38; A. Mutzenbecher, "Der Festinhalt von Weihnachten und Epiphanie in den echten *Sermones* des Maximus Taurinensis," SP 5 (1962) 109–16. (Both Botte and Frank are somewhat hampered by the lack of a critical edition of Maximus.)

   The present sermon is devoted to the baptism of Christ: cf. Matt. 3.13–17 par. On the patristic view of the necessity for Christ to have been baptized cf. R. L. Wilken, "The Interpretation of the Baptism of Jesus in the Later Fathers," SP 11 (1972) 268–77, in which the patristic exegesis of Christ's baptism is explained to be usually an attempt to justify baptismal practices in the early Church. On the baptismal symbolism of the Jordan cf. Daniélou 99–113. On baptism in general in this and the following two sermons cf. G. Langgärtner, "Die Taufe bei Maximus von Turin," *Zeichen des Glaubens: Studien zur Taufe und Firmung. Balthasar Fischer zum 60. Geburtstag,* ed. H. auf der Maur and B. Kleinheyer (Zurich-Freiburg 1972) 72–76.

The relative significance of the feasts of Christmas and Epiphany, at least at Turin in Maximus' time, is well illustrated in §§1–2 of the present sermon, where every effort is made to show that Christ's baptism is an event superior to His birth; even Mary and the Jordan are compared, to the detriment of the former. (For other comparisons made to the disadvantage of Mary cf. Sermons 38.4 and 78.2, where Christ's tomb is said to be better than Mary's womb, and Sermon 39.1 *ad fin.,* where it is suggested that Joseph of Arimathea is in some way superior to Mary.) On Epiphany as a greater event than Christmas cf. also Ps.-Augustine, Sermon 135.2 (PL 39.2012), cited in Frank 13.32. It is possible, however, that the emphasis given Epiphany is merely a rhetorical device.

Finally, for a general commentary on this and Maximus' other Epiphany sermons cf. I. Biffi, "Teologia e spiritualità del 'Dies beatissimae epyfaniae' in S. Massimo di Torino," *Ambrosio* 40 (1964) 517–44.

2. On this and the following few lines cf. Sermons 65.3 and 100.1.

3. On the term "sacrament" in general cf. Sermon 3 n. 3. On the sacramental theology of Maximus' Epiphany sermons in particular, where Christ appears as a kind of *Ursakrament,* cf. P. Visentin, " 'Christus ipse est sacramentum' in S. Massimo di Torino," *Miscellanea Lercaro* 2.27–51.

4. Cf. Luke 1.35.

5. Cf. *ibid.*

6. Matt. 3.17.

7. Some apocryphal literature speaks, if not of Joseph being absent at the birth of Christ, at least of his having been unaware of the event or unable to witness it: cf. *Protoevang. Iac.* 19.2; *Ascensio Isaiae* 11.8–10. The theme is taken up in the ancient iconography of the Nativity, where Joseph is frequently portrayed as looking away or being asleep. Joseph's detachment from what is occurring is meant to indicate that he is not the real father of Christ.

8. Cf. Matt. 13.55.

9. On the image of God as a workman (*faber*) in Western thought, cf. E. R. Curtius, *European Literature and the Latin Middle Ages*, tr. W. R. Trask (New York 1953) 544–46.

10. Cf. Luke 1.51–52.

11. Cf. Matt. 3.10.

12. That Christ cleansed the waters of the Jordan, and thus ultimately of the world, at his baptism is an idea that dates to at least the beginning of the second century: cf. Ignatius, *Eph.* 18.2. There are references contemporary with Maximus in Jerome, *Ep.* 108.12; *Dial. contra Lucif.* 6; Paulinus of Nola, *Carm.* 27.48–50. An attempt to explain this in a physical-mystical way occurs in Sermon 13B.2, where it is said that the waters of the Jordan, blessed by their contact with Christ, flowed back to their source so that the source itself would be blessed.

SERMON 13B

1. *Extravagans.* The present sermon seems to follow on the preceding one. On the feast of Epiphany cf. Sermon 13A n. 1.

2. *vestra sanctitas:* cf. Sermon 4 n. 2.

3. On the term "sacrament" here and elsewhere in the sermon, cf. Sermons 3 n. 3 and 13A n. 3.

4. Col. 2.9.

5. John 1.16.

6. Matt. 3.14–15.

7. The notion of a material substance like water having a spiritual effect appears already at the end of the second century in Tertullian, *De bapt.* 7. It is developed by later Fathers such as Gregory of Nyssa in *Or. cat.* 33 ff.

8. Ps. 114.3.

9. *In baptismate enim Christi retrorsum Iordanes non aquis conversus est sed sacramentis.*

10. On the consecration of the waters at Christ's baptism cf. Sermon 13A n. 12.

SERMON 13

1. The present sermon seems to follow on the preceding one. In this sermon, which is addressed primarily (if not necessarily exclusively) to catechumens, the baptism of Christ is seen as an image or figure of the baptism of the Christian and, in a comparison that appears daring, although not atypical for Maximus, the baptism of the latter is shown to be a superior event.

2. The mystique of the Jordan and of the East apparently had some hold on Maximus' congregation. On the symbolism of East and West cf. Sermon 1 n. 6. On the Jordan in particular as pre-eminent among rivers cf. Origen, *In Ioann.* 6.47.245; Gregory of Nyssa, *In diem luminum* (MG 46.592–93).

3. On the term "sacrament," cf. Sermons 3 n. 3 and 13A n. 3.

4. Matt. 3.15.

5. Cf. Rom. 9.5.

6. Matt. 3.15.

7. Matt. 5.17.

SERMON 15

1. On the term "anniversary" cf. Sermon 1 n. 1. Sts. Cantus, Cantianus, and Cantianilla, whose feast is celebrated on May 31, suffered at Aquileia in the persecution of Diocletian at the end of the third century. Cantus and Cantianus were brothers, and Cantianilla was their sister. For the acta of their martyrdom cf. Acta SS, Maii t. 7.421–22. Their relics were eventually translated to Grado, near Aquileia: cf. DACL 6.2.1449–53. Maximus has transformed the martyrs' flight from persecution into a triumphal journey to their death, perhaps because he was embarrassed that they should have fled. Flight in time of persecution, however, was recommended: cf. Matt 10.23; *Mart. Pol.* 5.1. Tertullian, *De fuga in persec.*, constitutes an unusual exception to this recommendation.

2. Cf. Ps. 133.1.

3. I.e., whose limbs had been quickened in the same womb.

4. Maximus compares the vehicle of escape of the three martyrs to the victor's carriage in a Roman triumph, which is particularly described as being high: cf. PWK 2e Reihe, 7.1.503.

5. Cf. 2 Kings 2.11. A comparison with Elijah, whether directly or by way of allusion, is a commonplace in hagiography: cf. Athanasius, *V. s. Antonii* 91; Theodoret of Cyrrhus, *Hist. relig.* 17.6; Gregory the Great, *Dial.* 2.8.

6. Cf. John 8.12.

7. Heb. 12.29.

SERMON 16

1. On the term "anniversary" cf. Sermon 1 n. 1. The saints in question are martyrs: cf. §§2–3. But whether this is a general sermon on martyrdom or one that refers to particular martyrs we cannot tell.

2. The pre-eminence of deeds over words on the part of the preacher is a commonplace in early Christian literature: cf. Augustine, *De doct. christ.* 4.27.59; Julianus Pomerius, *De vita contemplativa* 1.17; Gregory the Great, *Reg. past.* 2.3. From this Maximus goes on to develop the theme of the superior didactic quality of the martyrs' deeds, an idea that had its roots, among other places, in Stoic philosophy: cf. Baumeister 266 ff.

3. Matt. 5.19.

4. On the martyrs as examples cf. Sermon 1 n. 7.

5. *oculorum autem historia semper inspicitur.*

6. Ps. 51.4.

7. Rev. 6.9–10.

8. Gen. 4.10.

9. Cf. Sermon 88.1.

SERMON 17

1. Acts 4.32. The nostalgia for and glorification of the Church of the Acts of the Apostles, which characterizes §1 of the present sermon, is not uncommon at this period in the West: cf. Augustine,

Enarr. in ps. 44.28. The idea of a decline from the ideals of the apostolic Church, which appears in §§2–3, exists already by the middle of the third century: cf. Cyprian, *De lapsis* 6; *De unit. cath. eccl.* 25–26. For similar sentiments in Maximus' own time cf. Jerome, *V. Malchi* 1; Cassian, *Conlat.* 18.5; and Sermon 103.3.

2. The idea is ancient in Christian thought: cf. *Didache* 4.8; *Ep. Barn.* 19.8. Cf. also Maximus' contemporary Chromatius, Sermon 1.7, where Acts 4.32 is also cited: "Why would those who share heavenly goods not have earthly goods in common as well?"

3. Acts 4.32.

4. *Ibid.*

5. Acts 4.34.

6. Acts 4.34–35.

7. 1 Cor. 11.21.

8. Cf. Prov. 11.24.

9. *sacerdotum:* cf. Sermon 3 n. 2. On the right of asylum in Christian antiquity cf. DACL 4.2.1551–65; RAC 1.840–44.

10. This seems to be a conflation of 2 Tim. 3.1 and Matt. 24.12. Caesarius of Arles, Sermon 71.1–2, is reminiscent of this and what follows, up to the end of the present sermon.

11. 1 Tim. 6.18.

12. 1 Cor. 1.5.

13. Gen. 4.7.

14. Cf. Acts 5.1–6.

15. Acts 5.4.

16. *quid censemus de eo qui non vult reddere quod alius repromisit?* The sense of this is obscure. Perhaps, from what the following sentence says, Maximus means promises made by a sponsor on behalf of a candidate for baptism, particularly if the candidate were an infant. These would have been promises to live out the Christian life virtuously.

17. The reference to strangers and foreigners (*hospites sive peregrini*) suggests that Turin was regularly host to such or that they had temporarily sought refuge there in order to escape some unnamed turmoil.

Sermon 18

1. The present sermon seems to follow on the preceding one. §3 suggests some recent civil disturbances in which property belonging to Roman citizens had been pillaged by barbarians and then sold to other persons. §2, indeed, speaks of children taken in slavery. It is against the buyers, who knowingly or unknowingly purchased such property or slaves, that Maximus inveighs. For an attempt to date this sermon to the fall or winter of 408, based upon legislation issued in December of that year which touched upon the redemption of slaves sold by barbarians, cf. O. Maenchen-Helfen, "The Date of Maximus of Turin's Sermo XVIII," VC 18 (1964) 114–15.

2. *dilectio vestra:* cf. Sermon 4 n. 2.
3. Prov. 22.10.
4. Cf. Ambrose, *Exp. in ps. 118.* 18.7.
5. 1 Tim. 6.10.
6. Cf. Wisd. 15.12.
7. On the early Church's attitude to usury cf. Sermon 96 n. 6.
8. Maximus is perhaps aware of Paulinus of Nola, *Carm.* 18.219 ff., which tells at length the story of a poor farmer whose yoke of oxen has been stolen, only to be recovered later through the intercession of St. Felix.
9. *in hospitio tuo.*
10. Lev. 22.8.
11. *pellito*, i.e. one who wears skins or furs, a common designation for a barbarian: cf. Maenchen-Helfen 115.

Sermon 19

1. Luke 17.24; cf. Luke 17.34. From the middle of §2 until the middle of §3 is reminiscent of Ambrose, *Exp. evang. sec. Luc.* 8.46–47.
2. The mention of daily churchgoing may be an allusion either to the celebration of the hours or to the Eucharist.

3. Luke 17.24.

4. Luke 17.34–35.

5. Cf. Matt. 24.3–28.

6. The image of Christ coming in brilliance to drive away shadows and darkness has paschal resonances: cf. Ps.-Hippolytus, *Hom. pasch.* 1.1 (SC 27.117); Gaudentius, Sermon 1 (PL 20.843–45).

7. On the image of the body as a bed for the soul cf. Origen, *Comm. in Cant. cant.* 3.2 (GCS Orig. 8.175); Ambrose, *Exp. evang. sec. Luc.* 5.14.

8. Ps. 41.3.

9. Matt. 9.6.

10. On the two men in the field symbolizing Jews and Gentiles cf. also Paulinus of Nola, *Ep.* 11.6. Ambrose, *Exp. evang. sec. Luc.* 8.52, merely says that they represent two peoples, one of which believes and one of which does not.

SERMON 20

1. The present sermon seems to follow on the preceding one. The imagery of the millstones and of the women who are grinding seems to depend on Ambrose, *Exp. evang. sec. Luc.* 8.48 and 52; the same imagery appears in Ambrose, *De Cain et Abel* 1.8.30, and in Paulinus of Nola, *Ep.* 11.6. In Ambrose, *De poen.* 1.15.82, the mill symbolizes the Church in the act of softening the letter of the law with a mystical interpretation. On the millstone imagery, which is most developed in Maximus, cf. H. de Lubac, *The Sources of Revelation*, tr. L. O'Neill (New York 1968) 131.

For §5 cf. also Sermon 33.6.

2. Luke 17.34.

3. Luke 17.35.

4. Matt. 5.17.

5. *hoc est legem primum hominibus constitutam, deinde ad perfectum evangelium confirmatam.*

6. Ps. 14.3.

7. Rom. 4.15.

8. Ezek. 1.16.

9. 1 Cor. 3.2.
10. Heb. 5.14.
11. Ps. 51.17.
12. 2 Thess. 3.1.
13. Isa. 1.13.
14. Matt. 16.6.
15. Cf. Exod. 31.18.
16. On the aimlessness involved in turning a millstone cf. Sermon 48.4.

Sermon 21

1. Hospitality, also the subject of Sermon 34, was an extremely important practice in antiquity, and the spiritual benefits that come with receiving guests, some of which Maximus enumerates here, would by no means have been considered exaggerated. The example of Abraham appears already in the late first century in Clement, *1 Cor.* 10.7. On hospitality in general cf. RAC 8.1061–1123. The appeal in §2 to provide quarters for bishops perhaps refers to a council that was being held in Turin. Although there may have been others, we know for certain of only one council having taken place in Turin in the fourth or fifth centuries—on Sept. 22, 398: cf. the references in CCL 23.xxxiv. Possibly the present sermon may be dated to this time. Sermon 78.1 also seems to point to a council, which may be the same one.
2. Cf. Gen. 18.1–5.
3. Matt. 10.41.
4. John 1.12.
5. The image of the heart as a guesthouse for Christ may derive from Rev. 3.20: "Behold, I stand at the door and knock. . . ."
6. Ps. 18.25. The use of this part of Ps. 18 occurs also in Sermon 78.1. As these are the only two sermons in which it is cited (although it is alluded to in Sermon 106.2), we have greater reason for believing in their relationship.
7. *sacerdotibus:* cf. Sermon 3 n. 2. The claims made for the holiness of the bishops in this section either represent an attempt by

Maximus to make the Torinesi more willing to receive them or perhaps bear witness to an aura of sacredness that was beginning to surround them. This latter is typical of the East at this time, if not of the West: cf. Chrysostom, *De sacerd.* 3.4; Gregory of Nazianzen, *Or.* 2 *passim*, esp. 95–99 (applies to priests, but a fortiori to bishops).

    8. *episcopum.*

    9. Cf. John 8.39.

    10. *sacerdotibus.*

    11. *episcopos.*

    12. forgiven . . . was given: *donentur . . . donatus est.*

    13. Cf. Gen. 18.9–15.

    14. *sacerdotibus.* The notion of the bishop representing Christ appears for the first time in Ignatius, *Trall.* 2.1. The present phrase is somewhat reminiscent of Cyprian, *Ep.* 61.3, where a bishop's return to his city is likened to Christ's return in glory.

SERMON 22

    1. It seems that the Gospel of the Samaritan woman (John 4.5–42), now read on the second Sunday of Lent in the Ambrosian rite, was read on that Sunday already in the time of Ambrose: cf. H. Frank, "Das mailändische Kirchenjahr in den Werken des hl. Ambrosius," *Pastor bonus* 52 (1941) 44–45. Since Turin was within the ambit of Ambrosian influence, and since the present sermon also stresses almsgiving, which was a typical Lenten theme, it makes sense to see this as a Lenten discourse, most likely held on the second Sunday. On the penitential aspect of the sermon cf. Fitzgerald 473–5.

    2. Sir. 3.30.

    3. Almsgiving is frequently considered as an exchange of material or temporal for spiritual or eternal goods: cf. Ramsey 247–48.

    4. Luke 11.41.

    5. Almsgiving was always believed to have the power to remit sins: cf. Ramsey 241–47.

    6. Ps. 36.9.

    7. Cf. John 4.5–42.

    8. John 4.13.

9. The reference to Christ's having feigned (*simulat*) His thirst and having been unable to drink is undoubtedly to be taken in a rhetorical way, rather than as having Docetist undertones such as may be found in Clement of Alexandria, *Strom.* 6.9.71, where it is said that Christ ate and drank not because He needed to but in order to prove His humanity to His disciples. Cf. also Sermon 51.1. But contrast Ambrose, *De fide* 5.4.53; Augustine, Sermon 78.6 ("the source descended so that He might thirst").

10. Cf. Sermons 2.2 (with n. 7) and 66.4.

11. Prov. 30.20.

SERMON 22A

1. *Extravagans.* The present sermon seems to follow on the preceding one, which would make it a Lenten discourse as well. On the penitential aspect of the sermon cf. Fitzgerald 474–5.

2. *vestra dilectio:* cf. Sermon 4 n. 2.

3. Cf. John 4.5–42.

4. Cf. Prov. 30.20.

5. 1 Cor. 6.16.

6. Undoubtedly basing himself on John 4.6 ("It was about the sixth hour"), Maximus seems to suggest here that there were six millennia before the coming of Christ. The more usual understanding, however, was that there were five millennia before the Incarnation and that the sixth millennium was the age of the Church: cf. Augustine, *Tract. in Ioann.* 15.9, commenting on the same verse. Cf. also Sermon 94 n. 12.

7. Cf. Eph. 5.26.

8. On the Samaritan woman as an image of the Church cf. Augustine, *Tract. in Ioann.* 15.10: "an image of the Church, not already justified but about to be justified." A prostitute as a type of the Church was not unheard of; the prostitute Rahab in Jos. 2 was understood in this sense by the end of the second century, as we see in Irenaeus, *Adv. haer.* 4.20.12. Cf. J. Daniélou, *From Shadows to Reality: Studies in the Biblical Typology of the Fathers,* tr. W. Hibberd (Westminster, Md. 1960) 244–60. The prostitute of Hos. 1.2 is sometimes

likewise understood: cf. Irenaeus, *Adv. haer.* 4.20.12; Origen, *In Iesu Nave* 3.4; Hilary, *Tract. myst.* 2.1.

9. Sir. 3.30.

10. John 4.14.

11. On the term "sacrament" cf. Sermon 3 n. 3.

12. Luke 11.41.

13. The comparison of almsgiving with baptism is already made by the middle of the third century: cf. Origen, *In Deut.* 2.4; Cyprian, *De opere et eleem.* 2. Maximus daringly but typically suggests that almsgiving is more indulgent than baptism: cf. Ramsey 242–43. There is a remarkably similar comparison made between baptism and the gift of tears in John Climacus; *Scala paradisi* 7 (MG 88.804). Maximus' comparison of almsgiving with a fountain is somewhat paralleled in Chrysostom, *Hom. in Act. Apost.* 22.3.

SERMON 23

1. The present sermon seems to be in fact only the beginning of a sermon, the rest of which is lost.

2. On the term "sacrament" cf. Sermon 3 n. 3.

3. *sacramentorum die,* which seems to indicate a Sunday, although it could also mean any day on which the Eucharist was celebrated.

SERMON 24

1. On St. Laurence cf. Sermon 4 n. 1. §§1, 2, and the beginning of §3 are reminiscent of Ambrose, *Exp. evang. sec. Luc.* 7.175–79; where Maximus speaks of Laurence, however, Ambrose mentions the martyrs Felix, Nabor, and Victor. If Sermon 25 is a true sequel, as it seems to be, the beginning of §1 would indicate that the present sermon is a Sunday discourse utilizing the example of Laurence rather than a homily for his feast.

2. Luke 13.18–19.

3. Luke 17.6.
4. Cf. Sermon 4.1 and n. 4.
5. Luke 24.32.
6. Cf. Eph. 4.15; Col. 1.18.
7. 2 Cor. 2.15.
8. The comparison between a mustard seed and a person suffering (in this case Job) is also made in Gregory the Great, *Moralia in Iob, praef.* 2.6.
9. Cf. Sermon 4.1 and n. 6.

SERMON 25

1. The present sermon seems to follow on the preceding one. Most of the sermon, from near the beginning of §2 until the conclusion, is reminiscent of Ambrose, *Exp. evang. sec. Luc.* 7.180–82 and 185.
2. Luke 13.18.
3. Cf. Ambrose, *Exp. evang. sec. Luc.* 7.177.
4. John 16.20.
5. Hair occasionally symbolizes superfluity: cf. Augustine, *Tract. in Ioann.* 50.7. Hence to shave off hair can imply disposing of superfluity, i.e. wealth. Shearing sheep is an image with the same meaning: cf. Ambrose, *Exp. in ps. 118* 16.24; Paulinus of Nola, *Ep.* 11.9. Perhaps Maximus has this imagery in mind. He is possibly also alluding to the baptismal ceremony, since those who went down into the font did so naked and specifically without wearing precious ornaments: cf. Hippolytus, *Trad. apost.* 21.
6. Luke 13.19.
7. On the image of Christ as a tree cf. RAC 2.25–27. In the last sentence of the sermon, though, the tree has taken on some of the aspects associated with the cross, i.e. protection and shade: cf. Ps.-Hippolytus, *Hom. pasch.* 51 (SC 27.177).
8. Cf. Matt. 14.13–21.
9. John 12.24.
10. John 9.28.
11. Exod. 12.8 and 11.

12. Matt. 19.21.

13. Cf. Matt. 10.10.

14. Cf. Luke 23.50–53 and John 19.40–41.

15. On the common image of the soul or the heart as a garden cf. Tertullian, *Adv. Marc.* 4.30.2; Macarius, *Hom. Spir.* 28.2–3 (MG 34.712); Gregory the Great, *Dial.* 2.3. The related image of the soul or the heart as an object of husbandry is developed at considerable length in Philo, *De agric.* 2.8–5.25; cf. also Origen, *In Luc.* 11.2; Cassian, *Conlat.* 1.22.

16. The apostles are compared to branches in the same context in Hilary, *In Matth.* 13.4.

Sermon 26

1. Matt. 22.21. This sermon is evidence of the total acceptance that the military profession enjoyed in the Church in Maximus' time, although there was an important distinction made between having that profession and abusing it. There is considerable debate as to whether and to what extent the pre-Constantinian Church countenanced Christians holding military office. For a strongly negative view on the question cf. J.-M. Hornus, *It Is Not Lawful for Me to Fight: Early Christian Attitudes toward War, Violence and the State,* tr. A. Kreider and O. Coburn (Scottsdale, Pa. 1980). On the other hand, for a classic position that sees the earliest Church as having been fundamentally tolerant of the military profession, within certain boundaries and with some exceptions (e.g., Tertullian), cf. A. Harnack, *Militia Christi: The Christian Religion and the Military in the First Three Centuries,* tr. D. McI. Gracie (Philadelphia 1981) 65–104. There is a brief summary of the debate on this issue between the time that Harnack's book first appeared in 1905 and the publication of the translation on pp. 9–21. With respect to the post-Constantinian Church, however, there is no doubt from the sources that soldiering was an acceptable profession. For relevant texts and commentary cf. L. J. Swift, *The Early Fathers on War and Military Service* (Wilmington, Del. 1983).

2. *militiae cingulo detinentur.* The belt was a sign of military service: cf. DACL 2.2.2779–83.

3. common weal . . . private property: *rem publicam . . . rem familiarem.*

4. Cf. Ambrose, *Exp. evang. sec. Luc.* 2.77.

5. Cf. *ibid.*

6. Luke 3.12–13.

7. Matt. 22.21.

8. deceived . . . seized: *decepisse . . . deceperint.*

9. *Vidua autem, si qua fuerit, aut sic iniuriis excitatur ut nubat, aut si voluerit in castitatis permanere proposito, dando munera in sua facultate vix permanet.* The sense is unclear, but Maximus seems to say that widows are threatened by two alternatives: they are either forced into marriage, which would mean that they would lose control of their property, or, while remaining unmarried, find themselves obliged to make substantial gifts in order to protect themselves, which also implies a loss of property.

10. Luke 3.14.

11. *militibus protectoribus cunctisque rectoribus.*

12. *et nulla iam causa possit esse sine causa.* The sense is unclear, but the present translation is ventured.

13. 2 Tim. 2.4.

14. The belt also serves as a symbol of chastity: cf. Cassian, *Inst.* 1.11.

15. Luke 12.35.

16. 2 Tim. 2.3.

17. 2 Cor. 1.22.

18. Maximus may be alluding here to the Arians known as Macedonians or Pneumatomachians, who denied the divinity of the Holy Spirit.

19. For a brilliant portrait of just such a greedy flattering cleric cf. Jerome, *Ep.* 22.28. For a warning against clerical avarice cf. Ambrose, *De off. min.* 3.6.37–44. The problem was so severe that the Emperor Valentinian decreed in 370 that ecclesiastics and those who professed celibacy might not inherit the property of widows and orphans: cf. *Const. Valentiniani Imp. ad Damasum* (ML 13.575).

SERMON 27

1. The present sermon seems to follow on the preceding one.

2. *sacerdotalis ministerii:* cf. Sermon 3 n. 2. Forms of *sacerdos* and *sacerdotalis* are used throughout.

3. On almsgiving as an exchange cf. Sermon 22 n. 3.

4. Cf. Matt. 25.34–40.

5. The theme of the intercessory power of the poor on behalf of their benefactors occurs frequently in patristic literature. The most ancient witness to it is the mid-second-century *Pastor Herm.*, sim. 2, which speaks of the mutual dependence of rich and poor: the poor are dependent on the rich for material support, but the rich are dependent on the poor for their prayers. Cf. Ramsey 247–49.

6. Matt. 25.26–27.

7. The metaphor is mixed here.

8. Gal. 6.8.

9. capital bearing interest . . . fundamental principle of salvation: *de capite sortis . . . de capite salutis.* On the early Church's negative attitude to usury cf. Sermon 96 n. 6.

10. Col. 2.14.

11. Cf. Matt. 5.25–26.

12. Cf. Ambrose, *De Tobia* 13.43.

13. Cf. Heb. 13.17. The words in question are those of the Gospel.

14. Cf. Sermon 28.1 *ad fin.*

SERMON 28

1. Isa. 1.22. The present sermon seems to follow on the preceding one. Maximus' interpretation of the verse in question touches upon three areas: priestly morality (§2), Christology (§3), and the relationship between the Church and the Synagogue (§3). Another Christological interpretation may be found in Athanasius, *De decretis* 10; *Ad episc. Aegypti* 17; *C. Arianos* 2.80 and 3.35. Most frequently, however, the watering of the wine spoken of here is taken to mean a

dilution of the Scriptures, whether by pleasure-seekers (cf. Basil, *In Esaiam, ad loc.*), preachers currying popularity (cf. Gregory Nazianzen, *Or.* 2.46), heretics (cf. Jerome, *In Esaiam, ad loc.*), or Jews (cf. Irenaeus, *Adv. haer.* 4.12.1; Cyril of Alexandria, *In Esaiam, ad loc.;* Theodoret of Cyrrhus, *In Esaiam, ad loc.*).

    2. *sacerdotalem:* cf. Sermon 3 n. 2.

    3. *redemptio.*

    4. Cf. Heb. 13.17.

    5. *sacerdotes.*

    6. Cf. Sermon 27.2 *ad fin.*

    7. *administratio sacerdotum.*

    8. Hag. 1.9.

    9. *sacerdos.*

    10. *pontificatus officio.*

    11. John 10.33.

    12. John 8.41.

    13. Cf. Matt. 9.17.

    14. On the inferiority of water in comparison with wine cf. Sermons 101.3 and 103.2; Gregory Nazianzen, *Or.* 2.46; Jerome, *C. Ioann. Hieros.* 32; Cassian, *De incarn. Dom.* 7.3.

    15. Cf. Gal. 4.24.

    16. Gen. 21.10.

    17. Reading *sed aquam solam qua,* as Mutzenbecher suggests, instead of *aquarum solam qua.*

    18. Is this perhaps an allusion to a liturgical practice of the church of Turin, otherwise unknown, namely that water was not added to the wine in the celebration of the Eucharist, or is it only a rhetorical device? For the classic account of the symbolism of mixing water with wine in this context cf. Cyprian, *Ep.* 63.13.

    19. Cf. John 2.1–11.

SERMON 29

    1. Ps. 22 in the Hebrew enumeration.

    2. Ps. 22.1.

    3. Cf. Rom. 7.14.

4. Cf. 1 Cor. 2.13.
5. Cf. Mal. 4.2.
6. Ps. 101.8.
7. Cf. Eph. 3.17.
8. Wisd. 5.6.
9. Cf. John 20.1 and 11–18.
10. Ps. 30.5.
11. Ps. 22.1.
12. *adsumpti hominis,* i.e. Christ in His human nature. For the use of *assumptus homo* and related terms in the Fathers cf. Grillmeier, *Christ in Christian Tradition* 1, esp. 144, 350, 385–88, 399, 406, 432. Of Latin contemporaries of Maximus, cf. esp. Cassian, *Conlat.* 7.22, 9.34; Aponius, *In Cant. cant.* 5, 12 (MLSuppl. 1.887, 1020). To quote briefly W. Kasper, *Jesus the Christ,* tr. V. Green (New York 1976) 240: the *homo assumptus* theory "holds that the Logos assumed not just a complete human nature, but a complete human being." The danger in *homo assumptus* Christology was the making of Christ's human nature a human person, which was not intended by the Fathers. Maximus clearly employs the terminology to distinguish between Christ's passible humanity and His impassible divinity. Cf. also Sermon 37.4.
13. Cf. Isa. 53.9.
14. Cf. Isa. 53.12.
15. Cf. Rom. 14.8.
16. Cf. Isa. 53.10.
17. This unusual reading is very close to the one that appears in the fifth- or sixth-century Codex Bezae (D) for Matt. 27.46 and Mark 15.34, which seems like an attempt to Hebraize the more Aramaic reading that most of the ancient manuscripts of the Gospels have. Cf. H. B. Swete, *The Gospel according to St. Mark* (3rd ed. London 1927) 385–86 nn. 34–35. I am grateful to Lorraine Caza, C.N.D., for alerting me to this and to some of the information contained in n. 22 *infra.*
18. Ps. 22.1; Matt. 27.46.
19. Ps. 22.6.
20. What Maximus is referring to here is unknown.
21. Cf. 1 Sam. 24.14; 26.20.
22. For the use of this odd comparison cf. also Origen, *In Luc.* 14.8; Augustine, *Enarr. in ps. 21,* serm. 2.7; Chromatius, *Tract. in*

Matt. 2.5. Note also the midrash on the Psalm, which likens the children of Israel to a worm: "Like a worm whose only resource is its mouth, so the children of Israel have no resource other than the prayers of their mouths" (*The Midrash on Psalms,* tr. W. G. Braude [New Haven 1959] 1.315–16). On the notion that worms are begotten without intercourse cf. Pliny, *Hist. nat.* 10.68. In the present sermon the image develops so that by the end of §3 the worm symbolizes not only the virgin-born Jesus but the eschatological judge as well. This follows roughly the pattern set by Origen, *In Exod.* 7.8.

23. Cf. Exod. 16.20.

24. The more usual comparison is of Christ and manna, as in Gregory of Nyssa, *V. Moysis* 2.139–40. But Maximus' image is somewhat confused: in the following sentence Mary is said to produce a food—manna, as it were, itself bringing forth manna. Thus Christ also appears here as manna.

25. John 6.53.

26. 1 Cor. 11.29.

27. For a similar meaning for these worms cf. Sermon 50.3; Origen, *In Exod.* 7.6.

28. John 5.22.

29. Isa. 66.24.

30. Ps. 22.18.

31. Cf. John 19.23–24.

32. *Christi domini . . . sacramentum,* i.e. Christ Himself. On the term "sacrament" here cf. Sermons 3 n. 3 and 13A n. 3.

33. Cf. Matt. 26.50.

34. I.e., Scripture.

35. Reading *ait* instead of *it,* as given by Mutzenbecher.

36. On the symbolism of Christ's seamless garment in patristic literature cf. M. Aubineau, "La tunique sans couture du Christ," *Kyriakon* 1.100–127. Maximus' use of the symbol as referring to Christ's heavenly wisdom is rather unusual, although basically, in opposing the unity characteristic of Christ to the division characteristic of human nature, it bespeaks the tradition. The final sentence of the sermon, which compares the seamless garment (and the other garment) to the Church, is still more in keeping with the tradition, which most frequently saw that garment in terms of ecclesial unity: cf. Aubineau 120 n. 138.

37. Although Maximus remarks that human wisdom is inferior to divine, he nonetheless does not demean human learning or the pedagogy of his day. Contrast Augustine in *Conf.* 1.16.25–18.29; *De disciplina christ.* 11.12. On the other hand, C. Chaffin, "Civic Values in Maximus of Turin and His Contemporaries," *Forma Futuri: Studi in onore del Card. M. Pellegrino* (Turin 1975) 1041, suggests that this is in fact a deprecating reference to human learning.

38. John 7.15.

39. John 7.16.

40. Ps. 45.9.

SERMON 30

1. §3 of the present sermon recalls Ambrose, *Hex.* 4.8.31. For a commentary on the eclipse in question cf. F. K. Ginzel, *Spezieller Kanon der Sonnen- und Mondfinsternisse für das Ländergebiet der klassischen Altertumswissenschaften und den Zeitraum von 900 vor Chr. bis 600 nach Chr.* (Berlin 1899) 219–21. Ginzel lists 12 eclipses of the moon in the period from 383 to 412 that would seem to correspond to Maximus' description, and he suggests that those of December 17, 400 and November 4, 412 are "besonders beachtenswert." On the early Christian symbolism of the moon cf. Rahner, *Myths* 154–76; *idem, Symbole* 91–173. To this may be added Augustine, *Ep.* 55.5–15, which includes a justification for using the heavenly bodies to symbolize divine realities.

2. 1 Cor. 9.7.

3. *candore*, i.e. splendor or whiteness, hence a wordplay that is lost in translation.

4. Mutzenbecher suggests that this is a reference to Sermons 17–18.

5. The custom of howling at the moon in its eclipse is a pagan survival. It is also mentioned, along with the blowing of trumpets and the ringing of bells, in Caesarius of Arles, Sermons 13.5 and 52.3.

6. Sir. 27.11.

7. Ps. 72.5.

8. Rom. 8.22.

9. Rom. 8.21.
10. Rom. 8.20.
11. Ps. 89.37.

SERMON 31

1. The present sermon seems to follow on the preceding one. The whole sermon recalls Ambrose, *Hex.* 4.2.7, 4.7.29–30, 4.8.32–33.

2. Reading *illis* instead of *illi.*

3. Cf. Virgil, *Georg.* 3.337.

4. Phil. 2.6–7.

5. Cf. Mal. 4.2.

6. This is the most common meaning for sun and moon in relation to one another in early Christian literature: cf. Rahner, *Myths* 89–176.

7. Gal. 2.20.

8. Rom. 8.29.

9. For the idea that those who have persecuted the Church may also one day become ardent members of the Church cf. also Augustine, *De civ. Dei* 1.35.

10. *eam,* lit. it; the words "the Church" have been supplied by the translator for the sake of clarity.

11. Cf. Exod. 7.11–12; 2 Tim. 3.8. Jambres is the name of the second of the magicians. On the common notion that the Church existed in Old Testament times, which Maximus alludes to here, cf. Irenaeus, *Adv. haer.* 4.25.1; Origen, *Comm. in Cant. cant.* 2.8 (GCS Orig. 8.157).

12. The song of Christ, *Christi canticum,* is perhaps to be understood as the song that *is* Christ: cf. Clement of Alexandria, *Protrep.* 1 (where Christ is depicted as the new song, opposed to the songs of the pagan cults); Paulinus of Nola, *Carm.* 20.28–61.

13. Cf. Acts 13.6–11. Here the magician is not called Simon but Bar-Jesus or Elymas.

14. Cf. Matt. 16.18.

15. Cf. *Actus Petri* 32; cf. also Sermon 1.3.

SERMON 32

1. Matt. 19.24. §2 indicates that this sermon was given shortly after Epiphany. Maximus' interpretation of Matt. 19.24 is harder and more literal than that of most of his Latin contemporaries, who try to find a way for the camel, symbolizing a rich person, to get through the needle's eye. Thus Ambrose, *Exp. evang. sec. Luc.* 8.70–72; Paulinus of Nola, *Ep.* 29.2–3. Augustine in particular allegorizes to a remarkable extent: the camel signifies Christ, and the eye of the needle suffering; thus the camel, Christ, who has endured suffering, has gone through the eye of the needle, and the rich need not despair of passing through it themselves: cf. *Quaest. evang.* 2.47. It is against this kind of interpretation that Pelagius (or his disciple) inveighs when he remarks in *De divitiis* 18.10 (MLSuppl. 1.1411) that the very people who customarily treat the Old Testament allegorically and the New Testament literally suddenly take an allegorical approach when a New Testament passage speaks about the evils of wealth.

2. Matt. 19.23a, 24.

3. On the image of the camel cf. Sermons 48; 88.3; 95. The camel commonly symbolizes some sort of moral disorder: cf. Origen, *In Gen.* 10.2; Novatian, *De cibis iudaicis* 3.14; Basil, *Hex.* 8.1; Gregory the Great, *Moralia in Iob* 1.15.21–22.

4. Matt. 7.14.

5. 1 Kings 20.11.

6. Cf. Mark 10.42.

7. Cf. Matt. 8.12.

SERMON 33

1. Luke 13.20–21. §§2–5 recall Ambrose, *Exp. evang. sec. Luc.* 7.187. For §6 cf. also Sermon 20.5. The present sermon may well have been addressed primarily to catechumens. This is suggested first by the reference both to catechumens and to the *traditio symboli* in §5. The mention of progress having been made at the beginning of §2

also implies persons who are growing in the knowledge of Christian truths, and these could very likely be catechumens. Finally, §§3–6 teach a basic Christology and ecclesiology such as might have been directed to beginners.

2. This seems to indicate that Maximus was not a native of Turin. The opening words are very reminiscent of Novatian, *De bono pudicitiae* 1.1.

3. Cf. Acts 20:18 and 20.

4. Cf. Phil. 1.18.

5. Heb. 12.11.

6. Luke 13.20–21.

7. Cf. Rom. 7.14.

8. John 12.24–25.

9. This and what follows is an example of what may be called the "physico-mystical" theology of redemption, which emphasizes the solidarity between Christ and the rest of humankind and the salvific effect that this solidarity has on the human race. Irenaeus develops this theology at some length, as in *Adv. haer.* 2.22.4, where he speaks of Christ having passed through every stage of human life in order to sanctify it; cf. also Gregory Nazianzen, *Or.* 30.21 (where the same imagery of Christ as leaven in the dough of humanity is used); Gregory of Nyssa, *Or. cat.* 16 and 32.

10. This may be a reminiscence of *Didache* 9.4.

11. Eph. 5.30.

12. Matt. 24.41.

13. The symbol spoken of here is the creed, which was "handed on" when it was taught to the catechumens. This act of handing on or teaching was known as the *traditio symboli*. Cf. *Itinerarium Egeriae* 46.

14. Rom. 10.2.

15. Matt. 16.6.

16. Matt. 27.25.

17. On the aimlessness involved in turning a millstone cf. Sermon 48.4.

SERMON 34

1. On hospitality cf. Sermon 21, with n. 1. §1 is reminiscent of Ambrose, *Exp. evang. sec. Luc.* 6.66 and 7.64, and for §2 cf. *ibid.* 6.67.

2. *sanctitas vestra:* cf. Sermon 4 n. 2.

3. Matt. 10:11.

4. Cf. Matt. 10:12.

5. *diem exitus nostri,* i.e. the day of our death.

6. This is perhaps an allusion to the custom, especially practiced in the Middle East, of taking in a stranger for three days and treating him during that time with elaborate hospitality; after that period, however, he would be obliged to work for his keep if he chose to stay: cf. *Didache* 12.2–3.

7. The image of the Church as a house where hospitality is offered and of Christ as the host is unusual. In the sentences immediately following, this image seems to be transformed into one in which both Christ and the Church, similar to a husband and wife, act as hosts.

8. Cf. John 13.3–5.

9. This is perhaps an allusion either to a liturgical reading of John 13.1 ff. or to a foot-washing ceremony that had occurred in the recent past; this latter would in all likelihood have been connected with a rite of baptism, as was the case in Milan: cf. Ambrose, *De sacr.* 3.1.7. On foot washing and baptism cf. RAC 8.765–68.

10. Cf. John 7.38.

11. Matt. 6.24.

12. John 6.68–69.

SERMON 35

1. On the observance of Quadragesima, or Lent, in Turin in the time of Maximus cf. Callewaert *passim;* and on its baptismal content in particular, cf. Langgärtner, "Die Taufe bei Maximus von Turin" 76–80. Callewaert is unfortunately hampered in not having had a critical edition of the sermons. From §§3–4, where baptism is re-

ferred to as a forthcoming event, it appears that the present sermon was addressed primarily, if not necessarily exclusively, to catechumens. On the penitential aspect of the sermon cf. Fitzgerald 470–72.

2. 2 Cor. 6.2; Isa. 49.8.

3. 2 Cor. 6.2.

4. Deut. 32.39. On the image of Christ as physician, which is very common, cf. R. Arbesmann, "The Concept of 'Christus medicus' in St. Augustine," *Traditio* 10 (1954) 1–28; DS 10.891–901.

5. Col. 3.3.

6. Rom. 6.4.

7. Deut. 32.39.

8. Cf. Acts 9.1–19.

9. Cf. Sermon 50.2.

10. Cf. 1 Kings 19.8.

11. Cf. 1 Kings 17.1.

12. Cf. 1 Kings 18.41–45.

13. Cf. 1 Cor. 10.6.

14. A scriptural justification for the 40-day period of fasting, which was introduced in the first half of the fourth century, is common: cf. RAC 7.515.

15. Cf. Sermon 52.2.

16. Cf. Exod. 24.18; 31.18; Deut. 9.9–11.

17. Cf. Sermon 81.3 *ad fin.* The idea of fasting as somehow relating the faster to the Divinity is a commonplace in both pagan and early Christian literature: cf. R. Arbesmann, "Fasting and Prophecy in Pagan and Christian Antiquity," *Traditio* 7 (1949–51) 1–71. But the notion that one will be made close to God because God Himself fasts—or is empty of food—is unusual, although it is quite understandable; it is reminiscent of the recommendation of virginity based upon the divine virginity in Gregory of Nyssa, *De virg.* 1–2; Ambrose, *De virginibus* 1.5.21.

18. Exod. 33.11.

19. Cf. Matt. 4.2–4. But Christ's fast in the desert did not take place immediately before His resurrection, as is suggested here.

20. The *itaqua* in Mutzenbecher appears to be a misprint for *itaque.*

21. Cf. Matt. 16.18.

SERMON 36

1. The present sermon seems to follow on the preceding one. On the observance of Quadragesima in Turin, cf. Sermon 35 n. 1. On the penitential aspect of the sermon cf. Fitzgerald 471–2.

2. Isa. 58.5–6.

3. Keeping vigil and visiting the martyrs' graves were customs associated with fasting: cf. Jerome, *Ep.* 22.17.

4. On the days when fasting was observed it was the custom to abstain from food until late afternoon or sunset: cf. RAC 7.506–7.

5. Luke 6.38.

6. Cf. Gal. 3.27.

7. On the rich treating their animals better than they do their fellow human beings cf. also Ambrose, *De Nabuthae* 13.56; Gaudentius, Sermon 13; Chrysostom, *In ep. ad Heb.* 11.3.

8. The meditative reading of Scripture was another custom associated with fasting: cf. Jerome, *Ep.* 22.17, where the implication is that fasting sharpens one's mental faculties. In the following sentence the possibility of illiteracy is supposed, and a conversation with a holy person on a religious topic is offered as a substitute. On the practice of meditative Scripture reading cf. B. Smalley, *The Study of the Bible in the Middle Ages* (3rd ed. Oxford 1983) 26–36; DS 9.470–81. Cf. also Sermon 66.4 *ad fin.*

9. The alternative was to fast without giving to the poor what one had not eaten, a possibility that is spoken of in §2 *ad fin.* and §4 *ad fin.* of the present sermon. The custom of fasting to which Maximus refers is first mentioned in Christian literature in *Pastor Herm.*, sim. 5.3.7.

10. On the mutual dependence of rich and poor cf. Sermon 27 n. 5.

11. On the false fasting of monks cf. Jerome, *Ep.* 22.34.3.

SERMON 37

1. This may be the first of a series of four sermons, concluding with 39A. Assuming that this is so, the following placement within the liturgical year is proposed for them: Based on the reference to

"today . . . the cross has snatched . . ." in §2, the present sermon would have been preached during the day on Holy Saturday; this is possible if one understands "today" in a somewhat broader context, i.e. as applying to a period of time rather than to an individual day. Sermon 38, which begins with a mention of "yesterday" (*hesterna die*) in reference to the time of the previous sermon, would have been preached on Easter Sunday itself. Sermon 39, with its mention of "last Sunday's sermon" (*prioris dominicae praedicationis*) at the beginning of §1, both demands that Sermon 38 have been given on a Sunday—namely Easter—and suggests that 39 was given, then, on the Sunday after Easter. Finally, Sermon 39A, which starts by speaking of the previous sermon having been delivered "a very few days ago" (*ante dies paucissimos*), would have been preached during the week after the octave of Easter.

On the episode of Ulysses and the Sirens, which is developed into a Christian symbol in the course of this sermon, cf. Homer, *Od.* 12.39–54, 166–200; Ambrose, *Exp. evang. sec. Luc.* 4.2–3. For a lengthy commentary on the relevant imagery, cf. Rahner, *Myths* 328–86; *idem, Symbole* 239–71. In the latter, 266–67, Rahner observes that, whereas previously the Fathers had used Ulysses as a symbol of the individual Christian, Maximus is the first to see in the pagan hero an image of Christ Himself. To the iconography mentioned in the former work there may be added a small fourth-century bronze from Asia Minor (?), currently in the Virginia Museum of Fine Arts in Richmond, Virginia (with accession no. 67.20), which depicts Ulysses bound to the mast of a ship, while atop the mast a dove, supposedly representing the Holy Spirit, is perched. Rahner's use of archeological evidence, however, should be checked against T. Klauser, "Studien zur Entstehungsgeschichte der christlichen Kunst VI: 15: Das Sirenenabenteuer des Odysseus—ein Motiv der christlichen Grabkunst?" JAC 6 (1963) 71–100.

2. *salutis*, i.e. well-being or salvation.
3. port . . . death: *portum . . . exitium*.
4. *dulce naufragium*, lit. sweet shipwreck.
5. *crucis arbor. Arbor* also means mast. The parallel between cross and mast is made explicit later in §2. The use of this imagery dates at least to Justin, *1 Apol.* 55, and it is very common in the Fathers. Cf. Rahner, *Myths* 371–86.

6. In passing here from pagan myth to Christian reality (cf. also
§3), Maximus seems to express a certain distance from the myth that
he had so willingly employed in the previous section, and thus he
manifests in classic fashion the ambivalence that characterizes the
Fathers' approach to the legends that they appropriated for Christian
use. In *Epp.* 16.7 and 23.30, Paulinus of Nola also utilizes the Ulysses
episode, but in *Ep.* 49.9 he rejects all such recourse to pagan myth:
"We have our own ships, so that we can more worthily give examples
that are true and our own."

7. Luke 23.43.

8. *naufragia,* lit. shipwrecks.

9. Cf. Num. 21.6–9.

10. John 3.14.

11. Cf. Gen. 3. The contrast between the tree of the knowledge
of good and evil and the tree of the cross is a commonplace in patristic
literature and appears already by the middle of the second century in
Justin, *Dial. c. Tryph.* 86.

12. Cf. Rom. 6.6.

13. *per hominem quem suscepit:* cf. Sermon 29 n. 12.

14. Luke 10.19.

SERMON 38

1. The present sermon seems to follow on the preceding one:
cf. Sermon 37 n. 1. For §4 cf. also Sermon 78.2.

2. On the term "sacrament" here and later in the sermon cf.
Sermon 3 n. 3.

3. On the parallel between cross and mast cf. Sermon 37 n. 5.

4. On the power of the sign of the cross over the devil cf.
Athanasius, *V. s. Antonii* 35, 53, 80 and ACW 10.110–11 n. 53. On
the protective power of the sign of the cross in general cf. F. J.
Dölger, "Beiträge zur Geschichte des Kreuzzeichens VI: 11: Tutela
salutis," JAC 6 (1963) 7–18.

5. The parallel between cross and plow dates at least to Justin, *1
Apol.* 55. On the symbolism of the plow cf. J. Daniélou, *Primitive
Christian Symbols,* tr. D. Attwater (London 1964) 89–101, esp. 97.

6. The idea that the image of the cross may be found in the arrangement of the universe is suggested in Eph. 3.18 and in Justin, *1 Apol.* 60, and it is developed in Irenaeus, *Demonstr.* 34. Thereafter it is found with some frequency. Cf. Dölger, "Beiträge zur Geschichte des Kreuzzeichens IX: 37: Die kreuzförmige Ausbreitung des Logos im Weltall. Das Kreuz der Feldmesser und die Ausbreitung der Weltseele in Chi-Form," JAC 10 (1967) 23–29.

7. Cf. 1 Tim. 2.8.

8. That the prayer stance of the Christian is reminiscent of Christ on the cross is mentioned already in Tertullian, *De orat.* 14.

9. Exod. 17.11. Moses' outstretched arms, often used by the Fathers as a type of the cross, appear as such in the first half of the second century in *Ep. Barn.* 12; Justin, *Dial. c. Tryph.* 90.

10. Cf. Luke 23.50–53.

11. Mary's womb and the sepulcher are briefly compared in Augustine, *De fide et symbolo* 5.11 and *De Trin.* 4.5.9, while Origen links Christ's virginal conception and His burial in *C. Celsum* 2.69. For other comparisons in Maximus made to Mary's detriment, as it were, cf. Sermon 13A n. 1.

SERMON 39

1. The present sermon seems to follow on the preceding one: cf. Sermon 37 n. 1. Parts of §§2–4 are reminiscent of Ambrose, *Exp. evang. sec. Luc.* 10.140–42, and for part of §4 cf. *ibid.* 10.162.

2. Maximus suggests here that he is unaware of the idea that Mary conceived Christ in her heart or soul before she did so in her womb: cf. Augustine, *De s. virg.* 3; Leo the Great, Sermon 21.1.

3. Cf. Luke 1.26–38; 2.6–7; 23.50–53.

4. This suggests that Joseph's righteousness is superior to Mary's having been called by the angel. For other comparisons detrimental to Mary cf. Sermon 13A n. 1.

5. Ps. 5.9. Maximus uses this verse in an entirely different way than it was originally intended: he finds a positive mystical meaning in the Psalmist's complaint about his enemies. Ambrose's use of the same verse in *Exp. evang. sec. Luc.* 10.141 is more in keeping with the

original intent; cf. also Jerome, *Tract. de ps.* 5.11; Augustine, *Enarr. in ps.* 5.12. Cf. p. 9.

6. On the term "sacrament" here and later cf. Sermon 3 n. 3.
7. 1 Cor. 11.25–26.
8. I.e., the sepulcher.
9. 2 Cor. 6.11.
10. Cf. Matt. 8.20.
11. Cf. John 11.25.
12. I.e., Christ.
13. Luke 24.5.
14. John 20.15.
15. Luke 23.43.
16. Col. 3.1.

SERMON 39A

1. *Extravagans.* The present sermon seems to follow on the preceding one: cf. Sermon 37 n. 1. Much of §3 is reminiscent of Ambrose, *Exp. evang. sec. Luc.* 10.159–60.
2. Cf. *ibid.* 10.161.
3. John 20.17.
4. *auditum.*
5. Maximus' interpretation of John 20.17 is shared by other Fathers: cf. the question posed in Paulinus of Nola, *Ep.* 50.16, which is answered in Augustine, *Ep.* 149.32; also Jerome, *Hom. in Ioann.* 1.1–14 (CCL 78.523).
6. John 14.10. Cf. Ambrose, *Exp. evang. sec. Luc.* 10.158.
7. This is one of Maximus' rare "narrowly theological" statements; perhaps the Arians are being aimed at here.
8. John 3.13.
9. Luke 24.5.
10. Cf. Ambrose, *Exp. evang. sec. Luc.* 10.155.
11. John 14.9.
12. John 1.1.
13. Col. 3.1.
14. Col. 3.2.

15. 2 Cor. 5.16.
16. Acts 7.60.

SERMON 40

1. Ps. 110.1. On the significance of this psalm verse with respect to the ascension of Christ in patristic thought cf. P. Beskow,
Rex gloriae: The Kingship of Christ in the Early Church, tr. E. J. Sharpe
(Stockholm 1962) 131–35. Mutzenbecher notes that the present sermon, as well as Sermons 44 and 56, indicate that both the ascension
and Pentecost were celebrated on the same day in Turin. On this
liturgical custom, which had an Eastern provenance and for which we
have no other witnesses in the West, cf. R. Cabié, *La Pentecôte:
L'évolution de la cinquantaine pascale au cours des cinq premiers siècles*
(Tournai 1965) 127–42, esp. 138–42. Maximus shows confusion in
regard to when this double event actually occurred and hence was to
be celebrated: in Sermon 44.1 he suggests 50 days after Easter, but in
56.1, 40 days after. In the latter sermon, however, we must be dealing
with either a slip of the tongue on Maximus' part or a copyist's error,
since Pentecost would certainly never have been celebrated on a
Thursday.

In general on Maximus' preaching during the Pentecost season cf.
I. Biffi and P. Re, "La cinquantina pasquale nella predicazione di S.
Massimo," *Ambrosio* 40 (1964) 324–33.

§§2–3 of the present sermon are interesting for their development
of the image of Christ sitting and standing. Sitting ordinarily indicates Christ's royal function, standing his priestly office: cf. Beskow
131. In Maximus they signify, respectively, judgeship and advocacy.

2. The mention of fasting on the Saturday preceding Pentecost
Sunday, as Mutzenbecher remarks, contradicts what is said in Sermon
44.1–2, i.e. that no fast was proclaimed during the whole period from
Easter to Pentecost. Cabié 141–42 suggests that the custom of fasting
may have been dropped in the interval between the preaching of
Sermons 40 and 44, but this is, as he acknowledges, "une solution de
désespoir."

3. John 16.7 and 14.16–17.

4. Ps. 110.1.

5. Here is a rare "narrowly theological" statement by Maximus; probably he has the Arians in mind.

6. Cf. Matt. 25.33.

7. Rev. 14.4.

8. Acts 7.56.

9. John 4.24.

10. 1 John 2.1.

SERMON 41

1. Matt. 8.20. §§4–5 recall Ambrose, *Exp. evang. sec. Luc.* 7.30–31. For §§4–5 cf. also Sermon 86.2–3. Taking off from Matt. 8.19–22, Maximus speaks of the two men in question in a way that seems hardly justified by the very meager evidence of the Gospel. But other Fathers also exercise a harsh judgment against the man who volunteers to follow Christ: cf. Tertullian, *Adv. Marc.* 4.23.9–10; Hilary, *In Matt.* 7.8–10; Ambrose, *De poen.* 2.5.29; Augustine, *C. Faustum* 22.48.

2. *vestra dilectio:* cf. Sermon 4 n. 2.

3. Matt. 8.22.

4. *iste*, which adds to the tone of disdain.

5. Matt. 8.20.

6. Cf. Acts 10.34.

7. Prov. 17.28.

8. Matt. 7.21.

9. Matt. 8.21.

10. Ps. 45.10.

11. Matt. 10.37.

12. Cf. Tob. 2.3.

13. Augustine, *De civ. Dei* 1.12–13, remarks that burial of the dead is fundamentally unnecessary but is nonetheless a sign of honor and a token of belief in the resurrection of the body. On the importance that the early Christians attached to the burial of the dead, cf. RAC 2.208–9.

14. Matt. 8.19.

15. John 13.36.

16. Cf. John 13.37–38.

17. *ancillulae*, the diminutive of *ancilla*, which emphasizes the extent of Peter's fall after his having made his proud assertion.

18. Cf. Matt. 26.69–75.

19. Cf. Sermon 75.3.

20. Origen, *Comm. in Cant. cant.* 3.16 (GCS Orig. 8.235–41), speaks at length on the symbolism of the fox, which is invariably an image of evil, and in one place he refers to foxes as teachers of heretical dogmas, a comparison that Maximus makes in §5. Cf. also JAC 16 (1973) 168–78.

21. To what heretics Maximus is referring in this section is unknown.

22. Matt. 23.37. There follows a phrase deleted by Mutzenbecher, which makes no sense in the context: *Sed sicut Samson ardentes faces vulpibus religavit.*

23. Cf. Judg. 15.4–5.

24. Cf. Matt. 10.16.

Sermon 42

1. Mark 4.25; Luke 7.32. §§4–5 recall Ambrose, *Exp. evang. sec. Luc.* 6.5 and 9. The dancing imagery contained there and reflected in the present sermon occurs elsewhere in Ambrose (*De Isaac* 4.31; *Exp. in ps.* 118.6.6), and he appears to have borrowed it ultimately from Hippolytus, *In Cant. cant.* 11. Nonetheless Ambrose condemns the actual practice of dancing: *De virginibus* 3.6.27. On early Christianity's antipathy to dancing cf. J. Quasten, *Music and Worship in Pagan and Christian Antiquity*, tr. B. Ramsey (Washington 1983) 174–77. For §5 cf. also Sermon 65.3.

2. On the term "sacrament" cf. Sermon 3 n. 3.

3. The word is spoken of here as analogous to the Eucharist, particularly the cup. The image is pursued for several lines. It is more usual to speak of the word—whether the scriptural word or that which is preached—in terms of food (especially bread) that is eaten than as a cup that is drunk: cf. Origen, *In Gen.* 12.5; Hilary, *In Matt.*

27.1; Augustine, *Enarr. in ps. 36*, serm. 3.5. This is in turn derived in large part from Deut. 8.3 and Matt. 4.4. But for a comparison of word and cup, or rather the blood of Christ, cf. Origen, *Series commentariorum in Matt.* 85 (MG 13.1734).

    4. *caritati vestrae:* cf. Sermon 4 n. 2.

    5. *episcopum.*

    6. The sense, which becomes clearer in the following lines, seems to be that one who dies does not thereby remove himself from judgment, as if he had conquered immediately or immediately been annihilated.

    7. Logion 38, in A. Resch, *Agrapha: Ausserkanonische Schriftfragmente* (Leipzig 1906; repr. Darmstadt 1967) 315–16. Resch seems not to have known of Maximus' use of this agraphon.

    8. Mark 4.25.

    9. On almsgiving as an exchange cf. Sermon 22 n. 3.

    10. Cf. 1 Tim. 6.18.

    11. *quod virgo debeat permanere.* Literally this is of course impossible: one who has ceased the practice of virginity cannot return to it, although he or she can return to chastity. Cf. Jerome, *Ep.* 22.5.2: "Although God can do all things, He cannot restore a virgin after her fall."

    12. 1 Cor. 2.14.

    13. Luke 7.32.

    14. John 3.29. The marriage of the Church to Christ, referred to here, is an idea associated with the feast of the Epiphany, and it appears as such in Sermon 65.3. On the Syrian origin of the image cf. H. Frank, "Hodie caelesti sponso iuncta est ecclesia," *Vom christlichen Mysterium: Gesammelte Arbeiten zum Gedächtnis von Odo Casel,* ed. A. Mayer et al. (Düsseldorf 1951) 192–226, esp. 210–11; Murray, *Symbols of Church and Kingdom* 131–42.

    15. Cf. 2 Sam. 6.14.

    16. *praevidebat enim in spiritu Mariam de germine suo Christi thalamo sociandam:* cf. Sermon 65 n. 14.

    17. Ps. 19.5.

    18. On the mystical significance of David's dancing cf. also Gregory Nazianzen, *Orat.* 5.35.

19. On the comparison of Mary and the ark of the covenant cf. Augustine, *Enarr. in ps.* 131.15.

SERMON 43

1. Mark 3.1–6. Much of §4 recalls Ambrose, *Exp. evang. sec. Luc.* 5.39–40.

2. Mark 3.5.

3. Cf. Gen. 2.7.

4. On the reason for the existence of the hand expressed in a similar way cf. Gregory of Nyssa, *De opif. hom.* 8.

5. Luke 11.52.

6. Matt. 16.19. On the symbolism of the key cf. also Sermons 1.1 and 52.

7. Cf. Exod. 31.18.

8. Cf. Exod. 16.1–35.

9. Cf. Exod. 7.11–12; 2 Tim. 3.8. Cf. Sermon 31 n. 10.

10. Exod. 4.6.

11. Cf. Gen. 3.1–19.

12. Cf. Gen. 1.27.

13. Mark 3.5.

14. Sir. 4.31.

15. On the hand as a symbol of good works cf. Jerome, *Tract. in Marci evang.* 1.13–31 (CCL 78.469); Augustine, *Enarr. in ps.* 142.15.

SERMON 44

1. On the celebration of Pentecost cf. Sermon 40 n. 1.

2. *sanctitas vestra:* cf. Sermon 4 n. 2.

3. Cf. Sermon 40 n. 2.

4. The custom of standing during Pentecost, as opposed to kneeling or prostrating oneself, is already mentioned at the end of

the second century: cf. *Acta Pauli* (ed. Schmidt 26); Tertullian, *De corona* 3.

    5. Cf. Mal. 4.2.

    6. "The day of the Lord" was the more ancient name for Sunday, but the symbolism of the sun was so easily attached to the person of Christ that it made the new name, "the day of the sun," at least as popular: cf. Rahner, *Myths* 103–9; W. Rordorf, *Sunday*, tr. A. A. K. Graham (Philadelphia 1968) 274–93.

    7. Cf. Ambrose, *Exp. evang. sec. Luc.* 8.25.

    8. Cf. Sermon 40 n. 1.

    9. Cf. Sermon 1.2: "I think that those who have suffered equally are equal in merits. . . ."

    10. Luke 5.34.

    11. Luke 5.35.

    12. Ps. 69.3.

    13. Acts 1.9.

    14. Phil. 3.20.

    15. John 1.5.

    16. Luke 9.35.

    17. *gremio*, i.e. lap or bosom, usually understood in a maternal sense. The image, which recalls medieval (and later) representations of the Father receiving the dead Christ in his arms, the most famous of which is perhaps Dürer's woodcut "Der Gnadenstuhl in den Wolken," is a remarkable one at this period.

    18. Luke 1.35.

    19. Cf. Exod. 13.21–22.

    20. Ps. 105.39.

    21. The reference to the most usual day for the administration of baptism in the ancient Church—Easter—is followed by a mention of the day when, according to Maximus, the apostles were baptized. Perhaps Maximus is responding here to a concern that seems to have exercised some early Christians as to whether, when, and how the apostles were baptized: cf. H. A. Echle, "The Baptism of the Apostles," *Traditio* 3 (1945) 365–68. To the many references listed there add Ephrem, *In Diatessaron* 5.15, where it is said that the apostles were baptized by the word of Christ.

22. Acts 1.5.

23. Acts 2.1–3.

SERMON 48

1. Matt. 18.1. Much of §4 is reminiscent of Ambrose, *Exp. evang. sec. Luc.* 8.61–64.

2. *ministris ac sacerdotibus:* cf. Sermon 3 n. 2.

3. Matt. 18.4.

4. Rom. 12.10.

5. Matt. 7.14.

6. Matt. 19.24.

7. On the image of the camel cf. Sermons 32.1 (with n. 3); 88.3; 95.

8. The reference is to baptism; the descent into the font was done in nudity. Baptismal nudity was often associated with the nudity of Adam and Eve in paradise: cf. Cyril of Jerusalem, *Cat. myst.* 2.2; Chrysostom, *Cat.* Papadopoulos-Kerameus 3.28. With this theme of original innocence Maximus links the idea of being denuded of wealth. The whole concludes with a reflection on nudity and unlawful desire.

9. On the image of those who embrace voluntary poverty as being naked and unencumbered cf. Paulinus, *V. Ambrosii* 38; Jerome, *Ep.* 145.

10. Cf. Job 1.21.

11. Matt. 19.21.

12. *nuda virtus:* cf. Ambrose, *De Isaac* 6.55.

13. Maximus takes a hard line here: cf. Sermon 32 n. 1.

14. Cf. Gen. 3.7–24.

14a. On the angels clothed in glory cf. also Hilary, *In Matt.* 5.11.

15. Matt. 18.6.

16. 1 Cor. 14.20.

17. On the image of the millstone cf. Sermons 20.5 (with n. 1) and 33.6.

18. Cf. Acts 17.23.

19. Cf. Acts 17.24.

20. Here the sea of Matt. 18.6, the place of punishment for those who scandalize the innocent, has been transformed into an eschatalogical flood.

SERMON 49

1. Cf. Luke 4.38–5.4. §§2–4 are reminiscent of Ambrose, *Exp. evang. sec. Luc.* 4.68–71.

2. Cf. Exod. 14.21–29.

3. John 5.46.

4. Cf. Sermon 110.1. The identification of Peter's boat with the Church, a commonplace in patristic literature, is already made by Tertullian, *De bapt.* 12.6–7. Cf. Rahner, *Symbole* 473–503, for its use throughout patristic literature.

5. Matt. 4.19.

6. Rom. 11.33.

7. Luke 5.4.

8. Matt. 16.17.

9. *terrenum*, lit. earthly.

10. Luke 4.22.

11. Cf. Matt. 12.34.

12. Matt. 16.17.

13. Matt. 12.34.

14. Matt. 16.18.

15. Cf. Gen. 7–8.

16. The comparison of the Church with Noah's ark, based on 1 Pet. 3.20–21, dates at least to the end of the second century: cf. Tertullian, *De idol.* 24; *De bapt.* 8.4. Cf. Rahner, *Symbole* 504–47.

17. Cf. Gen. 8.10–11.

18. John 16.22.

19. On the term "sacrament" cf. Sermon 3 n. 3.

20. Cf. Matt. 8.23–25.

SERMON 50

1. On the observance of Quadragesima in Turin, cf. Sermon 35 n. 1. On the custom of interrupting the time of fasting in Lent, against which Maximus inveighs throughout this sermon, cf. Callewaert 524–25. Callewaert remarks that it was a practice in several places to relax the rigor of the fast occasionally during Lent: cf. Peter Chrysologus, Sermon 166; Socrates, *Hist. eccl.* 5.22; Sozomen, *Hist. eccl.* 7.19. Maximus emphasizes that the fast should be unbroken also in Sermons 67.1, 69.3–4, 111.3. But, as Callewaert notes on p. 522, the fast would certainly not have been kept in any event on Sundays in Lent; this would have been contrary to the most ancient observance of the Lord's Day, already mentioned in Tertullian, *De cor.* 3 (cf. RAC 7.508–9). For his unremitting insistence on fasting in a rather external way, Maximus may perhaps be compared unfavorably with other Fathers, such as Augustine in Sermons 205–10.

2. Quinquagesima is the name for the 50-day period from Easter Sunday until Pentecost Sunday. On the use of the term cf. Cabié 78. When Maximus speaks of observing in Quinquagesima what should be observed in Quadragesima, he is referring to fasting, which was not customary in Quinquagesima: cf. Sermon 44.1–2.

3. Cf. Matt. 4.2.

4. Cf. Sermon 69.3 *ad fin.*

5. *episcopo.* May we infer from this sentence that the bishop used to give the kiss of peace to a relatively large number of people? On the ancient practice of the kiss of peace, which is alluded to here in what must be a unique manner in patristic literature, cf. DACL 2.1.117–30. It is interesting to note that Tertullian refers to the custom that some persons had of omitting the kiss when they were fasting: cf. *De orat.* 18.

6. Reading *reprobet* instead of *reprobent.*

7. Cf. Sermon 35, n. 14.

8. Cf. Gen. 7.17–20.

9. Cf. 1 Pet. 3.20–21.

10. The reference to baptism as enlightenment, which is very

common, dates at least to the middle of the second century: cf. Justin, *1 Apol.* 61.

11. Cf. Sermon 35.2 *ad fin.*
12. Cf. Exod. 16.35.
13. On the term "sacrament" here and later cf. Sermon 3 n. 3.
14. *jejunium*, or fasting.
15. Cf. Exod. 16.20.
16. For a similar meaning for these worms cf. Sermon 29.3.

SERMON 50A

1. *Extravagans.* The present sermon seems to follow on the preceding one. §§2–3 recall Ambrose, *Exp. evang. sec. Luc.* 4.6–7. On the observance of Quadragesima in Turin cf. Sermon 35 n. 1.

2. *vestra dilectio:* cf. Sermon 4 n. 2.

3. On the image of Christ as physician cf. Sermon 35 n. 4.

4. Cf. Matt. 4.1–2.

4a. Adam's sin is occasionally characterized in terms of gluttony: cf. Philoxenus of Mabbug, *Hom.* 10 (SC 44.366).

5. Cf. 1 Cor. 15.45.

6. Cf. Rom. 5.12–19.

7. The same kind of connection with respect to Adam and Eve, that loss of virginity followed eating, is made by Jerome, *C. Iovinianum* 2.15. That Adam and Eve were unmarried and virgins before the Fall was commonly held: cf. Jerome, *ibid.* 1.16; Gregory of Nyssa, *De virg.* 12.4; Chrysostom, *De virg.* 14.5. Augustine's view, in *De civ. Dei* 14.10, that they were married in paradise, even though it is unclear whether he believed that they ever had intercourse there, is exceptional. Note that in Maximus such intercourse would have been considered a "shameful sin."

8. Cf. 1 Cor. 15.47.

9. Cf. Gen. 2.7.

10. Cf. Matt. 1.18. A parallel between Mary and the earth, such as is drawn here, appears already in Irenaeus, *Adv. haer.* 3.21.10; Tertullian, *Adv. Iudaeos* 13; *De carne Christi* 17. Cf. C. G. Jung, *Psychological Types,* tr. H. G. Baynes, rev. R. F. C. Hull (Princeton

1974) 233–34, where attention is directed to the probable origin of the parallel.

11. Cf. Luke 3.22, 38.

12. Cf. Ambrose, *Exp. evang. sec. Luc.* 3.49.

13. Such antifeminism was relatively common in the patristic period: cf. RAC 8.241–60, esp. 258–60. For texts and commentary on the place of women cf. E. A. Clark, *Women in the Early Church* (Wilmington 1983).

14. This is remarkably similar to the picture of the ideal monk in the desert as described in Jerome, *Ep.* 14.10.3.

15. Ps. 63.2.

SERMON 51

1. Cf. Matt. 4.1–4. The present sermon seems to follow on the preceding one. §§1–2 are reminiscent of Ambrose, *Exp. evang. sec. Luc.* 4.16 and 18–20, and for §3 cf. *ibid.* 4.20. On the observance of Quadragesima in Turin cf. Sermon 35 n. 1.

2. *vestra dilectio:* cf. Sermon 4 n. 2.

3. Matt. 4.3.

4. The rather common idea of the deception of the devil with respect to Christ dates to at least the beginning of the second century: cf. Ignatius, *Eph.* 19.1. On Christ feigning hunger and thirst, cf. Sermon 22.2 and n. 9.

5. Reading *qui* instead of *quia*.

6. Cf. Exod. 17.4–6.

7. 1 Cor. 10.4.

8. Matt. 4.4.

9. John 1.1.

10. John 6.41.

11. Ps. 104.15.

12. Cf. Gen. 25.29–34.

13. John 13.26–27.

14. On reading and fasting cf. Sermon 36 n. 8.

15. John 6.64.

SERMON 52

1. The present sermon does not necessarily follow on the preceding one. On the observance of Quadragesima in Turin cf. Sermon 35 n. 1.

2. Cf. 1 Kings 17.1; 18.41–46; 19.8.

3. *conpetentibus*, i.e. the catechumens who were undergoing immediate preparation for baptism: cf. RAC 3.266–68.

4. On baptism as enlightenment cf. Sermon 50 n. 10.

5. Cf. Sermon 35.4.

6. On the term "sacrament" cf. Sermon 3 n. 3.

7. *conpetentibus:* cf. n. 3 above.

8. Acts 7.56.

9. Matt. 16.19. On the symbolism of the key that follows cf. also Sermons 1.1 and 43.2.

10. Cf. Matt. 14.28–31. But Peter was afraid!

11. Cf. Matt. 16.18–19.

12. That the symbol, or creed, was composed by the twelve apostles, each of whom contributed an article, is an idea that first appears at the end of the fourth century in the anonymous North Italian *Explanatio symboli ad initiandos* (ML 17.1155–60). On this legend cf. J. N. D. Kelly, *Early Christian Creeds* (3rd ed. New York 1972) 1–6.

SERMON 53

1. This sermon, delivered in the presence of the newly baptized (cf. the references to neophytes in §1), was probably given on Easter morning at the conclusion of the rites of initiation. There is an English translation in A. Hamman, ed., *The Paschal Mystery*, tr. T. Halton (New York 1969) 191–93.

2. Cf. Ps. 118.24.

3. Cf. Luke 23.39–43.

4. Cf. Matt. 27.52–53.

5. Cf. Ps. 118.24. For brief references to the resurrection of the

universe in Christ, here developed at some length, cf. Ambrose, *De excessu frat.* 2.102; Asterius, Sermons 11.3 and 20.6; an anonymous Arian sermon 1.3 (SC 146.60). On the related notion of the participation of nature in the Resurrection cf. Sermon 56.1 and n. 3.

6. Cf. Ps. 118.24.
7. Rom. 13.12.
8. John 1.9.
9. Isa. 9.2.
10. Ps. 89.29.
11. Ps. 19.2.
12. Sir. 24.6.
13. John 1.5.
14. Cf. Luke 23.44–45.
15. Cf. Matt. 8.12; 22.13; 25.30.

SERMON 54

1. The present sermon does not necessarily follow on the preceding one, although it could have been given that same Easter day in the evening. There is an English translation in Hamman 193–95. Much of §1 and all of §2 recalls Ambrose, *Exp. evang. sec. Luc.* 8.57–58.

2. Cf. 1 Cor. 12.27.
3. Cf. John 5.24.
4. Cf. Jerome, *Ep.* 78.1.
5. Cf. Matt. 5.39–44.
6. Cf. Augustine, *Conf.* 1.7.11 ("Thus the weakness of infant limbs is sinless, not the soul of infants"); Cassian, *Inst.* 7.3.
7. Wisd. 4.8–9.
8. Matt. 18.3.
9. John 3.5.
10. Isa. 9.6.
11. Cf. 1 Pet. 2.23.
12. Luke 23.24.
13. Matt. 16.24.

SERMON 55

1. The present sermon seems to follow on the preceding one.

2. *sanctitas vestra:* cf. Sermon 4, n. 2.

3. I.e., baptism.

4. Col. 3.9–10.

5. Ps. 103.5.

6. Cf. Ambrose, *Exp. evang. sec. Luc.* 8.56.

7. On the eagle as an image of immortality and renewal and hence as a particularly appropriate symbol for baptism cf. RAC 1.91–92.

8. There is doubtless an allusion here to the newly baptized putting on a white garment after their baptism, which they wore for a week and which symbolized their new life. On this custom cf. Cyril of Jerusalem, *Cat. myst.* 4.8; Ambrose, *De myst.* 7.34.

9. On the eagle as a symbol of Christ, cf. Sermon 56.2; RAC 1.92.

10. Ps. 28.7.

11. Isa. 11.1.

12. On the image of Christ as a flower, although not necessarily in the same context, cf. Tertullian, *De cor.* 15; Origen, *In Cant. cant.* 2.6; Ambrose, *De Isaac* 4.30. The image is developed at length in Sermon 56.1; cf. also Sermon 66.4.

SERMON 56

1. The present sermon seems to follow on the preceding one. On the feast of Pentecost cf. Sermon 40 n. 1.

2. Cf. John 19.41.

3. The participation of all of nature in the Resurrection is a common theme in patristic literature: cf. Ps.-Augustine, Sermon 164.2 (ML 39.2067); Chromatius, Sermon 17.3. It seems linked to the oft-used apologetic argument that what occurs in nature is a foreshadowing of what will occur in the resurrection of the body. Thus, as nature passes from winter to spring, so also the human body

will experience its own springtime after having passed through the winter of death: cf. Minucius Felix, *Oct.* 34.11–12 and ACW 39.354–55 n. 578. On the related notion that spring is the most fitting season in which the Resurrection could have taken place and could be commemorated, cf. Daniélou 288–92. On another related notion, that of the resurrection of the universe in Christ, cf. Sermon 53.1 and n. 5.

4. John 12.24–25.

5. Cf. Sermon 40 n. 1.

6. *sanctitas vestra:* cf. Sermon 4 n. 2.

7. Cf. Ps. 103.5.

8. On the eagle as a symbol of Christ cf. Sermon 55.2 and n. 9.

9. Ps. 68.18; Eph. 4.8.

10. On this cf. Appianus, *De bello punico* 9.66.

11. Cf. Ps. 110.1.

12. Cf. Acts 2.4–11.

13. Ps. 19.3.

14. Cf. Sermon 40.2.

15. The heretics referred to here are probably Arians, with their view of the inferiority of the Son to the Father.

SERMON 57

1. §1 and the beginning of §2 are reminiscent of Ambrose, *Exp. evang. sec. Luc.* 10.97–98, and for much of §3 cf. *ibid.* 10.100.

Extended references to Susanna in patristic literature are rather rare. She is a type of the Church in Hippolytus, *In Dan.* 1.14, and is alluded to as a type of Christ in Ambrose, *De Nabuthae* 11.46. She also appears as a type of Christ, as is the case in the present sermon, in a fourth-century mural in the Arcosolium of Celerina in the Catacomb of Praetextatus. The mural in question depicts Susanna as a lamb standing between two wolves. The lamb is, of course, primarily and almost exclusively associated with Christ, the Lamb of God, and this would certainly be understood as a representation of Christ between his persecutors were it not for the fact that SVSANNA is clearly printed above the lamb's head.

2. *praesidem.*

3. Cf. Matt. 27.12–14.
4. Ps. 51.4.
5. Matt. 27.24.
6. *salutem*, translated as life also in the following two instances.
7. Cf. Matt. 10.38.
8. Cf. Dan. 13.1–64.
9. Dan. 13.46.
10. Cf. Matt. 27.24.

SERMON 58

1. Cf. Dan. 13.1–64; Matt. 27.12–14. The present sermon seems to follow on the preceding one. Much of §2 recalls Ambrose, *Exp. evang. sec. Luc.* 10.93–94. On Susanna as a type of Christ cf. Sermon 57 n. 1.

2. *praeses*, as also in §2.

3. *pseudopraesbyteri*, which also means pseudo elders. Maximus refers to the men who accused Susanna as both *seniores* and *praesbyteri*.

4. *pseudoepiscopus*.

5. *episcopus*, a form of which is used in §3.

6. Ps. 109.8; Acts 1.20.

7. Cf. Matt. 27.3–10.

8. Matt. 27.4.

9. The same sentiment occurs in Sermon 88.1 *ad fin.*

10. Tit. 3.10–11.

11. This last phrase suggests that the heretics to whom Maximus is referring are Arians.

SERMON 59

1. The present sermon may follow on the preceding one. Much of §§2–3 recalls Ambrose, *Exp. evang. sec. Luc.* 10.95.

2. *dilectio vestra:* cf. Sermon 4 n. 2.

3. Cf. Matt. 27.3–10.
4. *salutem.*
5. 1 Pet. 1.18–19.
6. John 3.17.
7. Ps. 2.8.
8. Cf. Matt. 13.38.
9. Gen. 2.7.
10. 2 Cor. 3.18.
11. Rom. 9.20–21.
12. 2 Cor. 5.6. The common theme of the Christian life as a traveling through or a sojourning in a foreign land is found in patristic literature already at the end of the first century in Clement, *1 Cor.*, inscrip., and very frequently thereafter. For instances of its elaboration cf. Jerome, *Tract. de ps.* 83.5ff; Augustine, *De doct. christ.* 1.4.4; Cassian, *Conlat.* 9.18.
13. Rom. 6.4.
14. On baptism as a return to infancy cf. Sermons 54–55.

SERMON 60

1. On the feast of Christmas, celebrated on December 25, cf. Botte, *Les origines de la Noël et de l'Epiphanie* passim, esp. 59–67. On Maximus' understanding of the feast cf. Mutzenbecher, "Der Festinhalt von Weihnachten und Epiphanie in den echten *Sermones* des Maximus Taurinensis" 109–16.
2. On the celebration of imperial birthdays in late antiquity cf. RAC 9.222–23.
3. Isa. 64.4; 1 Cor. 2.9.
4. Cf. Matt. 22.11–13.
5. Cf. Sermon 61A.3.
6. Reading *consumatur* instead of *consummet.*
7. On the efficacy of prayer as dependent on almsgiving, which is a commonplace in patristic literature, cf. Ramsey 246.
8. Cf. Matt. 6.13.
9. Cf. Sermon 17.1 with n. 2.
10. On the term "sacrament" cf. Sermon 3 n. 3.

11. This phrase does not seem to exist as such in the Scriptures, although it is reminiscent of Isa. 52.5.

12. This phrase does not seem to exist in the Scriptures either.

13. On the intercessory power of the poor on behalf of their benefactors cf. Sermon 27 n. 5.

14. 2 Cor. 1.11.

15. Rom. 15.16.

SERMON 61

1. The present sermon may follow on the preceding one. Much of §§2 and 4 is reminiscent of Ambrose, *Exp. evang. sec. Luc.* 5.111–12, 115. On the feast of Christmas cf. Sermon 60 n. 1.

2. Sir. 3.30. On almsgiving as capable of forgiving sin cf. Sermon 22 n. 5.

3. Matt. 11.12.

3a. On the kingdom of heaven as Christ Himself cf. also Cyprian, *De orat. dom.* 13. This is but one of numerous interpretations of the kingdom in patristic literature. It is also understood as the end of this age: cf. Tertullian, *De orat.* 5; as a life of virtue: cf. Origen, *De orat.* 25.1; as contemplation: cf. Evagrius (formerly attributed to Basil), *Ep.* 8.12; as the Holy Spirit: cf. Gregory of Nyssa, *De orat. dom.* 3; as faithful Christians: cf. Augustine, Sermon 57.5.5.

4. The explanatory phrase is the translator's. *Cogi* means both to be forced and to be condensed.

5. Luke 1.33.

6. Matt. 11.12.

7. Cf. John 14.6.

8. exercise control over . . . kingdom: *regnare . . . regnum.*

9. Cf. Gal. 4.4.

10. Matt. 21.31.

11. Cf. Gen. 49.27. For the same connection drawn between Matt. 11.12 and this verse cf. Rufinus, *De bened. patriarch.* 2.29.

12. Matt. 15.24.

13. Matt. 28.13.

14. Eph. 5.14.

SERMON 61A

1. *Extravagans.* On the feast of Christmas cf. Sermon 60 n. 1. The first sentence of the present sermon, which speaks of "the extreme conclusion of the cycle of days" (*dierum extrema conclusio*) having already occurred, suggests that this sermon was preached in the few days between the winter solstice and Christmas.
2. Cf. Rom. 8.19.
3. Cf. Sermon 62 n. 1.
4. Cf. Mal. 4.2.
5. Mark 9.3. Sins are spoken of as filthy garments for the first time in patristic literature in Justin, *Dial. c. Tryph.* 116.
6. Ps. 45.8.
7. Cf. Sermon 60.4.
8. Luke 11.41. On almsgiving as capable of forgiving sin cf. Sermon 22 n. 5.

SERMON 62

1. Much of §4 recalls Ambrose, *Exp. evang. sec. Luc.* 3.2. On the feast of Christmas cf. Sermon 60 n. 1.

The extensive use of solar imagery in the present sermon is occasioned by the fact that Christmas is celebrated shortly after the winter solstice. So emphatic is the comparison in §2 between Christ the new sun and the old sun, the heavenly sphere, that we may well see in this sermon a polemic against a sun worship that continued to exist in northern Italy at this period. For a similar polemic, cf. Jerome, *Tract. de ps.* 148.3; Leo the Great, Sermons 22.6 and 27.4. On Christ as the sun in Christian antiquity cf. F. J. Dölger, *Sol salutis* (Münster 1925). One of the oldest pictorial representations of Christ that we possess is on a late-third-century mosaic from the tomb of the Julii in the necropolis under St. Peter's Basilica in Rome, where he appears as Helios, the sun god. On the image of the sun specifically in relation to Christmas cf. Rahner, *Myths* 145–54.

2. Such a designation for the winter solstice was not unknown

to the pagans, quite apart from Christian influence: cf. Ovid, *Fasti*, 1.163; Censorinus, *De die natali* 2. I am grateful to Prof. Agnes Michels for these references.

3. Eph. 1.10.

4. Cf. Matt. 27.45.

5. Cf. Matt. 2.9. This allusion indicates that, rather than associating the event of the Magi with Epiphany (cf. Sermon 13A n. 1), Maximus does so with Christmas: cf. Sermons 99.3 and 100.1 *ad fin.*

6. Cf. Luke 2.8–20.

7. Cf. Rev. 21.5.

8. Cf. Jos. 10.12–13.

9. Cf. Rom. 8.20–21.

10. Joel 2.31.

11. Mal. 4.2.

12. Wisd. 5.6.

13. Jer. 7.25.

14. Cf. Matt. 5.45.

15. Cf. Rom. 8.21.

16. Ps. 132.17.

17. John 5.35.

18. Luke 3.16.

19. John 3.30.

20. Cf. Mark 1.4.

20a. The words in question do not necessarily imply an immaculate conception for Mary. They simply mean that, as the result of a divine gift, she was immaculate before bearing Christ. In fact, Maximus seems to use "immaculate" here exclusively in terms of Mary's having begotten Christ virginally, as the following lines suggest, rather than in terms of her being completely sinless. On the doctrine of Mary's immaculate conception in the patristic era previous to the Council of Ephesus (431), when Maximus was preaching, cf. DTC 7.1.872–93.

21. On the notion of the Father begetting the Son virginally cf. also Gregory of Nyssa, *De virg.* 2.

22. Matt. 13.55.

23. Cf. Gen. 6.14–16.

24. Cf. Exod. 33.7.

25. Cf. Exod. 25.10–16.

26. Cf. 1 Kings 6.

27. Matt. 3.10.

28. On the image of God as a workman (*faber*) cf. Sermon 13A n. 9.

SERMON 63

1. The present sermon, according to §2, was given on the day after the kalends. On the pagan celebration of the kalends of January, the first day of the new year, cf. Sermon 98, which speaks at greater length of certain pagan practices, and PWK 10.2.1562–64. On the Christian observance, cf. ACW 15.219–20 n. 16. Because of the nature of the day a sermon given on the kalends of January was frequently an occasion to attack pagan customs: cf. Augustine, Sermons 197–98.

2. I.e., the Eucharist.

3. goal . . . hopelessness: *ratio . . . desperatio.*

4. 2 Cor. 6.14–16.

5. Cf. 2 Cor. 6.16.

6. Matt. 6.24.

7. Cf. Virgil, *Aen.* 8.357–58. That the gods were originally human beings was a charge frequently made by the early Christians. With regard to Janus in particular in this respect cf. Minucius Felix, *Oct.* 23.10–11.

8. Gal. 4.10–11.

9. I.e., to celebrate the pagan rites.

10. On this passage cf. p. 10.

SERMON 64

1. The whole sermon recalls Ambrose, *Exp. evang. sec. Luc.* 2.83 and 92–94. On the feast of Epiphany cf. Sermon 13A n. 1.

2. Cf. John 2.1–11.

3. Cf. Matt. 3.13–17.

4. On the term "sacrament" here and later cf. Sermons 3 n. 3 and 13A n. 3.

5. Isa. 53.9.

6. Words supplied by the translator.

7. John 1.29.

8. John 1.1.

9. Matt. 10.16.

10. Ps. 55.6.

11. Cf. Gen. 8.11.

12. Ps. 114.3.

13. Cf. 2 Kings 2.8.

SERMON 65

1. Much of §3 recalls Ambrose, *Exp. evang. sec. Luc.* 6.5–9. On the feast of the Epiphany cf. Sermon 13A n. 1. For §3 cf. also Sermon 42.5, and for the image of dancing there, cf. Sermon 42 n. 1. The present sermon is primarily addressed to catechumens.

2. Cf. John 2.1–11.

3. Cf. Matt. 3.13–17.

4. *divinitatis sapore:* lit., by a taste of the Divinity.

5. Cf. Matt. 9.17.

6. 2 Cor. 2.15.

7. The baptismal imagery of water and wine here appears as resurrectional imagery in Sermons 101.3 and 103.2; in all cases, however, the idea is fundamentally the same inasmuch as baptism is itself a type of resurrection.

8. Maximus is alluding to the custom, often opposed in the ancient Church, of putting off baptism for as long a time as possible, sometimes until one's deathbed. Opposition is voiced in canon 12 of the Synod of Neocaesarea, which forbade ordination to the priesthood to persons baptized on their sickbed; Basil, *In sanct. bapt.;* Gregory of Nyssa, *Adv. eos qui differunt bapt.* Some delay is defended, however, in Tertullian, *De bapt.* 18, where it is argued that younger people cannot adhere to the baptismal vows as well as older people.

9. John 3.5.

10. savor . . . wisdom: *saporis . . . sapientiam.*

11. *vota.*

12. John 3.29. On the marriage of the Church to Christ cf. Sermon 42 n. 14.

13. Cf. 2 Sam. 6.14.

14. *praevidebat enim in spiritu per Mariam de germine suo ecclesiam Christi thalamo sociandam:* cf. Sermon 42 n. 16.

15. Ps. 19.5.

SERMON 66

1. On the observance of Quadragesima in Turin cf. Sermon 35 n. 1. §1 of the present sermon picks up themes that appear particularly in Sermon 50 and suggests that this may have followed that one, although not necessarily immediately.

2. *sacerdotum.* The next two instances are also forms of *sacerdos:* cf. Sermon 3 n. 3.

3. Cf. Luke 10.16.

4. The idea of nature participating in a liturgical season, which is pursued here, is not unusual, although it is more common to find the image developed with reference to Easter: cf. Sermon 56.1 and n. 3. In fact the nature imagery in the present sermon, with its emphasis on new life, is fundamentally paschal.

5. *episcopus.*

6. Gen. 3.18.

7. 2 Cor. 2.15.

8. Cf. Matt. 4.2.

9. Is. 11.1. On the image of Christ as a flower cf. Sermons 55.2 (with n. 12) and 56.1.

10. shoot . . . virginal: *virga . . . virgo:* cf. Ambrose, *Exp. evang. sec. Luc.* 2.24.

11. Cf. Matt. 4.2.

12. Cf. Sermons 2.2 (with n. 7) and 22.2; Hilary, *In Matt.* 3.2; Ambrose, *Exp. evang. sec. Luc.* 4.16; Jerome, *Tract. in Marci evang.* 11.11–14 (CCL 78.488).

13. Cf. Ambrose, *Exp. evang. sec. Luc.* 2.72.

14. On reading and fasting cf. Sermon 36 n. 8.

SERMON 67

1. For §4 cf. Jerome, *Ep.* 78.7. This letter of Jerome is in turn inspired by Origen, *In Num.* 27, where the idea of the Hebrew journey in the desert as a type of the Christian pilgrimage originated.

2. Cf. Matt. 4.2.

3. Reading *conplere* instead of *conplecti.*

4. On maintaining an unbroken fast in Quadragesima cf. Sermon 50 n. 1.

5. Maximus anticipates a reasonable question here. Having probed the symbolism of the number 40 "last year," he answers it by proceeding to show why the number 42 also has a deeper meaning. From this and the following sermon we learn that Lent in fifth-century Turin extended over the full course of the six weeks preceding Easter Sunday, including Good Friday and Holy Saturday, which had been the ancient paschal fast. On the anomaly of a Quadragesima (i.e., 40-day period) consisting in 42 days cf. Callewaert 525–28.

6. Cf. Num. 33.1–49. Mutzenbecher remarks that one would expect years, rather than days, to be spoken of here.

7. Cf. Jerome, *Ep.* 78.2.

8. Rom. 10.15; Isa. 52.7.

9. 1 Tim. 5.10.

10. Ps. 114.3.

11. On baptism as a return to infancy cf. Sermons 54–55.

12. Cf. Jerome, *Ep.* 78.2.

13. *aestum,* i.e. heat or tossing.

14. Cf. Exod. 15.23–25.

15. On the term "sacrament" cf. Sermon 3 n. 3.

16. Cf. 1 Cor. 10.6.

17. That the wood thrown into the waters of Marah symbolizes the cross is an image dating at least to Justin, *Dial. c. Tryph.* 86. Origen is the first to relate the bitter waters to the Old Testament law: cf. *In Exod.* 7.1.

18. Exod. 21.24.
19. Ps. 119.103.
20. Matt. 5.39–40.
21. 2 Cor. 3.6.
22. *Ibid.*

SERMON 68

1. The present sermon seems to follow on the preceding one. For §§2–4 cf. Jerome, *Ep.* 78.8 (and Sermon 67, with n. 1), and for much of §3 cf. Ambrose, *Exp. evang. sec. Luc.* 9.11.

2. Cf. Num. 33.1–49.

3. Cf. Exod. 16.13–36.

4. Cf. Exod. 14.21–29.

5. Cf. Jos. 3.14–17; Ps. 114.3.

6. Cf. Exod. 15.23–25.

7. Cf. Exod. 15.27.

8. On the palm as a symbol of victory and martyrdom cf. DACL 13.1.947–50; and on palm symbolism in general cf. Daniélou, *Primitive Christian Symbols* 1–24.

9. Cf. John 12.12–15.

10. Cf. Matt. 21.7–8.

11. Rev. 5.5.

12. Ps. 92.12.

13. Ps. 68.26.

14. On the term "sacrament" cf. Sermon 3 n. 3. The 12 springs of Elim are commonly understood as symbols of the twelve apostles: cf. Tertullian, *Adv. Marc.* 4.13; Hilary, *Tract. myst.* 1.37; Augustine, *C. Faust.* 12.30.

15. Cf. Luke 10.1. On the 70 palm trees as types of the 70 disciples cf. also Origen, *In Exod.* 7.3; Hilary, *Tract. myst.* 1.37.

16. Cf. Luke 10.17.

Sermon 69

1. The present sermon seems to follow on the preceding one.
2. Cf. Num. 33.1–49 and Sermon 67 n. 1.
3. posts . . . stand: *stationes . . . stantes.*
4. The comparison of Satan and Pharaoh dates from the second half of the second century: cf. Melito of Sardis, *Hom. pasch.* 67.
5. 2 Cor. 12.10.
6. Matt. 17.20.
7. On maintaining an unbroken fast in Quadragesima cf. Sermon 50 n. 1.
8. Cf. Matt. 4.1–11.
9. 1 John 2.6.
10. Cf. Sermon 50.1.
11. Cf. 1 Sam. 14.24–46.
12. Prov. 5.3–4.

Sermon 70

1. The present sermon does not necessarily follow on the preceding one.
2. Cf. Matt. 4.1–11.
3. Matt. 4.5–6.
4. Cf. Ambrose, *Exp. evang. sec. Luc.* 4.23.
5. On the term "sacrament" cf. Sermon 3 n. 3.
6. Ps. 104.3. There is an untranslatable play on words here: *pinna* means either pinnacle or wing.
7. *alacrem*, i.e. either swift or glad.
8. On wing imagery in general and on the common theme of the flight of the soul in pagan, Jewish, and Christian literature cf. RAC 8.29–65.
9. Ps. 55.6.
10. 2 Cor. 6.16.
11. Matt. 4.7.
12. On God turning His face away from the sinner cf. Ps. 51.9.

13. Isa. 50.2.
14. Matt. 10.30.
15. Cf. John 10.11.
16. Cf. Luke 15.4–5.
17. I.e., on the shoulders of the Lord.

SERMON 71

1. It is hard to place the present sermon in the Church year. The references to fasting in both summer and winter in §2 indicate that it might have been given at almost any time, since local churches usually followed their own customs with regard to fasting: cf. RAC 7.519–24. This is probably not a Lenten sermon, however, or the season would almost certainly have been mentioned.

2. *sacerdoti*, a form of which is used in the following lines as well: cf. Sermon 3 n. 2.

3. The notion of the indispensable complementarity of union with Christ and union with the bishop is emphasized throughout the letters of Ignatius of Antioch; cf. also Cyprian, *De eccl. cath. unitate* 17.

4. Cf. Phil. 3.19.

5. Gen. 3.19.

6. Matt. 8.12.

7. 2 Cor. 9.7.

8. On almsgiving as an exchange cf. Sermon 22 n. 3.

9. 1 Tim. 6.17.

10. Cf. *ibid.*

10a. The solidus was a gold coin established by Constantine; it was current for several centuries and there were 72 to a pound of gold. Cf. PWK, 2. Reihe, 3.1.920–26 and also Sermon 98 n. 9.

11. That the value of precious metals is arbitrary is an idea that appears already in Aristotle, *Pol.* 1.3.14–16; *Nic. eth.* 5.5.11.

SERMON 72

1. §2 of the present sermon alludes to barbarian invasions, or at least incursions. Mutzenbecher, CCL 23.xxxv n. 1, suggests four possible times during which it and several other sermons in the collection might have been preached: 393, when the usurper Eugenius invaded Italy; 401–2, when Alaric conquered Piedmont; 406, when Radagaisus did the same; or 411, when the Visigoths passed from Italy to Gaul under the leadership of Athaulf. These dates presuppose, however, that Maximus died before 423, since there was also considerable barbarian activity after 423.

2. Cf. Mic. 2.10.

3. Cf. Ambrose, *De Cain et Abel* 2.9.35.

4. Job 7.1.

5. Maximus seems to be the only witness to *piraterium* also meaning *experimentum,* or experience.

6. Matt. 10.28. These few lines bear a close resemblance to what Augustine says in similar circumstances in *De civ. Dei* 1.10 ff.

7. Reading *quam* instead of *qui.*

8. Job 2.10.

9. This sentence suggests two customary times for prayer—on rising and before retiring: cf. Sermon 73 n. 1.

10. The custom of prayer at mealtimes is first mentioned in patristic literature in Clement of Alexandria, *Paed.* 2.4.44.1; *Strom.* 7.7.49; Tertullian, *De orat.* 25.

SERMON 73

1. The present sermon seems to follow on the preceding one. For dating cf. Sermon 72 n. 1.

§§2–5 bear witness to the custom of praying on rising, before retiring, and in the course of the night. By the end of the second century prayer at the first two times is spoken of as obligatory in Tertullian, *De orat.* 25. Mention is made of prayer at midnight, in addition to the two other times, in the early third century in Hippolytus, *Trad. ap.* 41. Cf. also Sermon 72.3; P. F. Bradshaw, *Daily Prayer in the Early Church* (London 1981) 1–71.

2. Mal. 1.6.

3. 1 Cor. 10.31.

4. *Dum enim nescit homo, ubi suum adversarium persequatur, quam volens praestare noluit, praestat invitans.* Maximus seems to mean that night provides a protection for the sleeper from one who is pursuing him, and that because of the darkness the pursuer is obliged to discontinue, whether he wants to or not. The sentence is somewhat confusing because Maximus refers to the sleeper as an enemy, whereas one would expect the pursuer to be denominated as such.

5. Acts 17.28. The sign of the Savior and the sign of Christ spoken of in this section may refer to the sign of the cross or, more likely, simply to Christ Himself.

6. On the birds praising their Creator with song cf. Ambrose, *Hex.* 5.12.36, which Maximus seems to recall in this section and the next. The idea of the praise of irrational creation for its God is common in Jewish and Christian literature: cf. Dan. 3.51–90; Tertullian, *De orat.* 29; Hippolytus, *Trad. ap.* 41.

7. shepherd . . . feeds: *pastorem . . . pascit.* The play on words, which is the justification for Maximus to speak of birds having a shepherd, is untranslatable.

8. Matt. 6.26 and 28.

9. On the image of the owl that follows cf. Ambrose, *Hex.* 5.24.86, which Maximus seems to recall. That the owl is primarily a negative symbol is a notion shared by most ancient Christian authors who discuss the matter, whereas among the pagans it was more an ambivalent symbol: cf. RAC 6.890–900. But cf. also Paulinus of Nola, *Ep.* 40.7, where it represents the repentant sinner.

10. Pss. 133.16; 82.5.

Sermon 74

1. Cf. Luke 23.40–43. The previous sermon mentioned at the beginning of §1 is unknown. On the penitential aspect of the present sermon cf. Fitzgerald 478–9, 484–5.

2. 1 Cor. 1.23.

3. 1 Cor. 1.24.

4. Cf. Matt. 26.47–50.

5. Luke 23.42.

6. Luke 23.41.

7. Here and in two further instances the word "Christ" or "Christ's" has been supplied by the translator for the sake of clarification.

8. Isa. 53.4–5.

9. Cf. Matt. 26.20–25.

10. Ps. 41.9.

11. John 10.18.

SERMON 75

1. Cf. Luke 23.40–43. The present sermon seems to follow on the preceding one. On the penitential aspect of the sermon cf. Fitzgerald 484–5.

2. *vestra dilectio:* cf. Sermon 4 n. 2.

3. Perhaps Maximus is suggesting that the thief enjoyed an obliviousness of pain that was commonly attributed to the martyrs: cf. Sermon 4 n. 6.

4. John 13.36.

5. Luke 23.43.

6. Cf. 1 Pet. 4.8.

7. *plenioris est meriti.*

8. A similar title occurs in Ambrose, *De fide* 3.7.52, where Christ is called the principle of every virtue.

9. 1 Cor. 2.8.

10. Matt. 27.40.

11. *Eius,* his, has been rendered here as "Christ's" for the sake of clarity.

12. Cf. Matt. 26.56.

13. Zech. 13.7.

14. Cf. Matt. 26.34 and 69–75.

15. Cf. Sermon 41.3 *ad fin.*

16. admits . . . cuts him off: *includit . . . excludat.*
17. Cf. Gen. 3.6.
18. Cf. Ambrose, *Exp. evang. sec. Luc.* 10.75. Deceive . . . let
. . . in: *induxit . . . introduxit.*
19. On antifeminism in the early Church cf. Sermon 50A n. 13.

SERMON 76

1. The present sermon, for which cf. Gen. 3.1–10 and Matt.
26.69–75, seems to follow on the previous one. §§2–3 are concerned
with the expression of contrition through weeping, a common theme
in patristic literature. Perhaps the most famous examples of this are
Jerome, *Ep.* 22.30.4–5, and Augustine, *Conf.* 8.12.28. Another instance occurs in Sermon 90.3. In general cf. DS 9.290–96, esp.
295–96. On the penitential aspect of the sermon and its relation to
Ambrose's view of Peter's repentance cf. Fitzgerald 481–5.
2. On antifeminism in the early Church cf. Sermon 50A n. 13.
3. Gen. 3.9.
4. Ps. 34.15.
5. John 21.17.
6. On the common theme of Peter's threefold confession as a
compensation for his threefold denial cf. Ambrose, *De fide* 5, prol. 2;
Augustine, *Enarr. in ps.* 37.17.

SERMON 77

1. The present sermon seems to follow on the preceding one.
Some chronological confusion is apparent here: after having spoken
of Peter's denial of Christ and his subsequent contrition, Maximus
goes on to speak of Peter's walking on the waters—an event that
came before the denial—as if it had followed it and as if the faith
strengthened by his tears had made this miracle possible. The solution
perhaps lies in that Maximus is confusing Matt. 14.28–31 (the narrative in which Peter walks on the water) and John 21.6 (where Peter

jumps into the water and swims to the Lord on the shore, an occurrence that did in fact come after his denial). This solution is rendered more probable by the fact that Maximus refers to John 21.15–17 at the beginning of the sermon, which recounts an event closely related, from the chronological point of view, to that narrated in John 21.6. On the penitential aspect of the sermon cf. Fitzgerald 484–5.

   2. Cf. Matt. 26.69–75.
   3. Cf. John 21.15–17.
   4. Cf. Luke 22.32.
   5. Matt. 16.18.
   6. 1 Cor. 10.4. Cf. also Sermon 80.3.
   7. Cf. 1 Cor. 3.6.
   8. Cf. Matt. 14.28–31.
   9. Cf. Exod. 14.15–22.
 10. Matt. 14.31.
 11. Matt. 10.22.

SERMON 78

   1. On a possible date and setting for this sermon cf. Sermon 21 n. 1. For the second paragraph of §2 cf. also Sermon 38.4 and n. 11.
   The whole of §1 consists in a self-deprecating comparison with the unnamed prelate (who, if the date of the sermon is 398, might have been Simplicianus, bishop of Milan), which is, of course, a classic way of gaining a congregation's sympathy. For other examples of self-deprecation cf. Sermon 7.1; Ambrose, *De off. min.* 1.1.1–4; *De virginibus* 1.1.1–4; Sulpicius Severus, *V.s. Martini,* praef.
   2. *episcopi.*
   3. *sacerdotii:* cf. Sermon 3 n. 2.
   4. *in pontificio primatus honorem.*
   5. *vestra dilectio:* cf. Sermon 4 n. 2.
   6. *sacerdotis.*
   7. *ista confusio.*
   8. *summi sacerdotis.*
   9. *minimum sacerdotem.*
 10. Ps. 18.25: cf. Sermon 21 n. 6.

11. Reading *videmus* instead of *videmur*.
12. Cf. 1 Cor. 12.27.
13. Cf. Luke 23.50–53.

SERMON 79

1. The rebuke to the laity in the first paragraph is balanced by a rebuke to the clergy in the second. Evidently many of the clergy too had neglected to come to church in Maximus' absence.

2. *sacerdotis:* cf. Sermon 3 n. 2.

3. *episcopum,* forms of which are used in the following lines.

4. Christ is referred to as a bishop for the first time in 1 Pet. 2.24; in patristic literature in Clement, *1 Cor.* 59.3, and shortly thereafter in Ignatius, *Poly.,* inscrip., where He shares the title with God the Father.

SERMON 80

1. The present sermon does not necessarily follow on the preceding one. In fact the reference in §2 to "the many beneficial words of my rebuke" suggests a longer sermon than 79.

2. 2 Cor. 7.10.

3. Heb. 12.7.

4. Prov. 27.6.

5. *sanctitas vestra:* cf. Sermon 4 n. 2.

6. Matt. 16.15.

7. Cf. Rom. 10.9.

8. Cf. Matt. 16.13–16.

9. Matt. 16.17–18.

10. 1 Cor. 10.4. Cf. also Sermon 77.1.

11. For this and what immediately follows cf. Ambrose, *Exp. evang. sec. Luc.* 6.93 and 96–97.

12. 2 Kings 2.11; Acts 1.9.

13. Acts 1.11.

SERMON 81

1. On possible dates for the present sermon, which recalls Jon. 3.3–10, cf. Sermon 73 n. 1.

2. Cf. 2 Cor. 6.7.

3. discipline . . . teachings: *disciplinae . . . disciplinarum.*

4. In fact there is no specific mention made of children fasting in the scriptural account, and perhaps Maximus is justifying such a practice in Turin. Jerome, *Ep.* 107.10, suggests that a young girl named Paula should learn to fast, but he speaks strongly against immoderate fasting for "those of tender years." Paula is an unusual case in any event, since she was being raised as an ascetic. On the idea of youthful innocence being more capable of earning the divine mercy cf. Quasten, *Music and Worship in Pagan and Christian Antiquity* 88–89; and, for pagan testimony in this regard, H. Herter, "Das unschuldige Kind," JAC 4 (1961) 153–54.

5. Cf. 1 Cor. 10.11.

6. Ps. 73.27.

7. *ieiunus.* On God as fasting and on fasting as relating the faster to God cf. Sermon 35.4 and n. 17.

8. *sacerdote:* cf. Sermon 3 n. 2.

9. 1 Cor. 15.32.

SERMON 82

1. The present sermon, which also recalls Jon. 3.3–10, seems to follow on the preceding one. On possible dates for it cf. Sermon 72 n. 1. Maximus' efforts here are directed to preventing flight from Turin during a time of distress, and to this end he both plays on his congregation's patriotic sense, which was a formidable quality in the ancient world, and depicts for it the hardship of a life lived in exile. For a commentary on this sermon cf. Chaffin, "Civic Values in Maximus of Turin and His Contemporaries" 1041–53.

2. *patriam,* rendered throughout as native land.

3. Cf. Gen. 18.32.

4. On the comparison of one's birthplace with one's mother cf. Virgil, *Aen.* 3.96; Livy 5.54.2. On Rome itself as mother cf. Claudian, 3 *Cons. Stil.* 175; Rutilius Namatianus, *De reditu suo* 2.60.

5. Mutzenbecher gives no reason for distinguishing this phrase.

6. Reading *exulat* instead of *exultat*.

7. Cf. Gen. 19.20–22.

8. I.e., Lot.

Sermon 83

1. On possible dates for the present sermon, cf. Sermon 72 n. 1. §§2–4 recall 2 Kings 6.13–20.

2. 1 John 4.4.

3. Ps. 34.7.

4. On the triple practice of prayer, almsgiving (here referred to as mercy), and fasting, first mentioned in Christian literature in Matt. 6.2–18 and then in the mid-second century in *2 Clem.* 16.4, cf. Ramsey 244–46. Prayers are compared to darts, but in a different context, in Augustine, *Ep.* 130.20.

5. 2 Kings 6.16.

6. 2 Kings 6.17.

Sermon 84

1. The present sermon, which initially recalls 2 Kings 6.13–20, seems to follow on the preceding one. On possible dates for it cf. Sermon 72 n. 1.

2. Phil. 3.20.

3. This rather remarkable passage on the communion of the saints on earth and the angels in heaven is in some way reminiscent of Sermon 17.1, where Maximus speaks of sharing property as a result

of sharing faith. For a similar striking passage on the intercourse of angels and saints, living and dead, cf. Origen, *De orat.* 31.5.

4. Cf. 2 Kings 2.11.

5. Cf. 2 Kings 2.9–10.

6. 2 Kings 2.10.

7. *Dum enim a patre plus exigit quam habebat, fecit eum meritis suis plus praestare quam poterat.* The meaning seems to be that because of his great works Elisha brought more glory to Elijah by what he himself accomplished than Elijah himself was capable of.

8. Cf. 2 Kings 2.19–22.

9. 2 Kings 2.19.

10. 2 Kings 2.21–22.

11. *prius . . . quam sinus fontis includeret.* The meaning seems to be: before the spring returned into the earth.

12. 1 Cor. 10.6.

13. Gal. 4.27; Isa. 54.1.

14. In these words and what follows Maximus identifies the Gentiles who lived before the coming of Christ with the Church. More usual in patristic literature is the identification of the Old Testament people with the Church: cf. Augustine, *De bapt.* 1.15.23–16.25. Maximus, however, is enabled in this way to draw a still greater contrast between Church and Synagogue.

The sterility of the Church, which later becomes fruitful, is a common theme in the Fathers; frequently, as is the case here in Maximus, this situation is contrasted with that of the Synagogue, which had been fruitful and now is sterile. In her sterility and later fruitfulness Rachel (Gen. 29.31 ff.) is seen as an image of the Church, while Leah, Jacob's unloved first wife (*ibid.*), is likewise often understood to be an image of the Synagogue: cf. Justin, *Dial. c. Tryph.* 134; Cyprian, *Testim.* 1.20; Hilary, *In Matt.* 1.7 (with no reference to Leah); Jerome, *Ep.* 123.13.

15. On the human body as a clay vessel cf. 2 Cor. 4.7; Ambrose, *De Sp. sancto* 1.14.147. In both Ambrose, who compares the human body to the water jars of Judg. 7.16, and Maximus the body appears as considerably extrinsic to the soul. On Christ's body in particular as a clay vessel cf. Jerome, *Ep.* 84.8.

16. Matt. 5.13.

Sermon 85

1. On dating the present sermon cf. Sermon 72 n. 1.

2. *dilectionem vestram:* cf. Sermon 4 n. 2.

3. Luke 21.10 and 31, with the insertion of some words from vv. 9 and 11. Maximus' interpretation of v. 31 here—which stresses the approach of Christ, the end of the world, and the consequent joy of the Christian—seems to be unique at this time: cf. A. Lauras, "Le commentaire patristique de Lc. 21.25–33," SP 7 (1966) 507.

4. Ps. 118.19.

5. *signum salvatoris:* cf. n. 9 below and Sermon 45.2 for similar imagery.

6. Cf. Eph. 6.14–17.

7. Cf. 1 Sam. 17.38–51.

8. Ps. 118.22.

9. The *signum salutis* and the *signaculum salvatoris*—the sign of salvation and the seal of the Savior—refer to the baptismal seal, the signing of the cross on the forehead of the baptizand, which took place during the course of the baptismal ceremonies; this was considered to have protective qualities. Cf. F. J. Dölger, *Sphragis* (Paderborn 1911); Daniélou 54–69.

10. Cf. 1 Cor. 10.6.

11. On the image of the Christian ascetic as a lightly armed soldier, common at this time, cf. Jerome, *V. S. Hilarionis* 3; Paulinus, *V. Ambrosii* 38; Peter Chrysologus, Sermon 28.1.

Sermon 86

1. The present sermon seems to follow on the preceding one. On possible dates for it cf. Sermon 72 n. 1. For §§2–3 cf. Sermon 41.4–5. The heretics referred to in §3 are unknown.

2. *vestra dilectio:* cf. Sermon 4 n. 2.

3. On the triple practice of prayer, fasting, and almsgiving (here referred to as mercy) cf. Sermon 83 n. 4.

4. Cf. 1 Sam. 17.38–51.

5. Ps. 127.1.

6. Luke 4.23.

7. save . . . preserve: *conservet . . . reservet.*

8. Reading *in fovea* instead of *in eo fovea.*

9. Matt. 8.20.

10. Cf. 1 Cor. 11.3.

11. On the symbolism of the fox cf. Sermon 41 n. 20.

12. *rabiem,* which is translated in the same way elsewhere in the sermon. It may refer to the madness both of humans and of animals.

13. gives promise . . . draws out: *promittit . . . depromit.*

14. On the image of the Church as a mother cf. J. C. Plumpe, *Mater ecclesia: An Inquiry into the Concept of the Church as Mother in Early Christianity* (SCA 5; 1943).

15. Matt. 23.37.

16. Based on Matt. 23.37 par., the hen is more usually seen as an image of Christ, particularly in Augustine: cf. Augustine, *Enarr. in ps.* 58.10 and 90, serm. 1.5; *Tract. in Ioann.* 15.7. On the hen as an image of the Church cf. Rabanus Maurus, *De universo* 8.6 (PL 111.248).

SERMON 88

1. The latter half of §3 is reminiscent of Ambrose, *Exp. evang. sec. Luc.* 2.69–70.

2. *sacerdotibus,* forms of which are also used in §6, except in the one instance noted: cf. Sermon 3 n. 2.

3. The previous sermon, preached "last Sunday," cannot be placed.

4. John 1.23.

5. Matt. 3.3.

6. Gen. 4.10.

7. Cf. Sermon 16.3.

8. Cf. Sermon 58.2 *ad fin.*

9. Ps. 68.4.

10. Matt. 3.4.

11. On the camel's deformity cf. also Sermons 32.1 (with n. 3),

88.3, 95. On the camel as an image of the Gentiles cf. Hilary, *In Matt.* 19.11. Christ is Himself compared with a camel in Augustine, *Quaest. evang.* 2.47 (cf. Maximus, Sermon 32 n. 1); *Enarr. in ps.* 110.6; Sermon Caillau-Saint-Yves II.19.5 (MLSuppl. 2.438).

12. Leather, obtained from a mortal animal, symbolizes mortality: cf. Gregory of Nyssa, *V. Moysis* 2.22; Jerome, *Ep.* 23.4; Augustine, *Enarr. in ps.* 103, serm. 1.8. The idea is ultimately a Pythagorean one: cf. J. Quasten, "A Pythagorean Idea in Jerome," *Amer. Jour. of Philology* 63 (1942) 207–15.

13. *psaltria*, which is used in the following case as well.

14. Cf. Matt. 14.6–11.

15. Luke 7.32.

16. 1 Cor. 11.3.

17. On John's decapitation as an image of the Jews' separation from Christ cf. Origen, *In Matt.* 10.22; Jerome, *In Matt.* 14.11.

18. Gen. 21.10.

19. Wisd. 3.16.

20. *mulier.*

21. Maximus' first argument against an unmarried man who takes a concubine is that the offspring of such a union would have no right to inherit, which is a declaration consonant with Roman law: cf. *Cod. Theod.* 4.6.8, which, however, made it possible for illegitimate children to inherit if they were actually included in a will. From there Maximus goes on to argue further that these offspring would be "the children of adulterers" —a false statement, strictly speaking, if neither parent were married.

22. Maximus is perhaps alluding here to the practice of virgins of both sexes living together in what was professedly a spiritual relationship. The women involved in such a situation were called variously *agapetae, syneisaktoi,* and *virgines subintroductae.* The custom, which seems to have had its roots in the second century, was repeatedly denounced by the official Church. Cf. DACL 10.2.1881–88.

23. *episcopus.*

24. 2 Tim. 4.2.

SERMON 89

1. This brief sermon, which must only be a fragment, alludes to a council that was held elsewhere than at Turin. On this council we have no further information.

On the bee imagery cf. Ambrose, *Hexam.* 5.21.67-72, and, in general, RAC 2.274-82.

2. *sacerdotum,* a form of which is also used in the following instance: cf. Sermon 3 n. 2.

3. On the image of the Church as mother cf. Sermon 86 n. 14.

SERMON 91

1. *Extravagans.* The present sermon was given before Quadragesima: cf. §2 *ad fin.* The concerns of §2 find fuller expression in Sermons 106-8. For a discussion of the responsibilities of Christian landlords vis-à-vis their pagan farmers, with their pagan practices, cf. F. J. Dölger, "Christliche Grundbesitzer und heidnische Landarbeiter: Ein Ausschnitt aus der religiösen Auseinandersetzung des vierten und fünften Jahrhunderts," AC 6.4 (1950) 297-320, most of which deals with Maximus.

2. *ministerii sacerdotalis:* cf. Sermon 3 n. 3.

3. Cf. Matt. 13.3-7.

4. *vere enim sine capite est cuius velut caesi pecudis morientia lumina prava dispositione versantur.* On keeping silent in this respect cf. also Sermons 106.2, 107.1, and 108.

SERMON 92

1. *Extravagans.* Cf. Ezek. 3.17.

2. *episcopus.*

3. *sacerdotibus:* cf. Sermon 3 n. 2.

4. Augustine, Sermon Frang. 2.4 and 8, expresses similar sentiments on the office of preaching. At this time preaching was still a peculiarly episcopal function, although priests were gradually coming to exercise it too: cf. Introduction n. 1 and B. Cooke, *Ministry to Word and Sacraments* (Philadelphia 1976) 254-73.

5. *ut in se possit non perdere sacerdotem.*

6. Ezek. 3.17-18. These verses (as well as Ezek. 33.1-9) are

NOTES   349

interpreted in the same way as Maximus does in the following lines
by Jerome, *In Hiez., ad loc.* (where they are applied to either bishops
or priests) and by Gregory the Great, *Hom. in Hiez., ad loc.*

7. *sacerdos.*

8. *episcopi.*

9. *sacerdotes.*

10. On avarice as idolatry cf. Zeno of Verona, *Tract.* 1.14.2.4–
4.7 (CCL 22.57–58); Ambrosiaster, *In ep. ad Eph.* 5.5; *In ep. ad Colos.*
3.5. And on the avaricious person as a slave to his wealth cf. Ambrose,
De Nabuthae 12.51–52, 14.58, 15.63.

SERMON 93

1. *Extravagans.* Is. 58.1. The present sermon seems to follow
on the preceding one.

2. Isa. 58.1.

3. *sacerdotis:* cf. Sermon 3 n. 2. Forms of *sacerdos* and *sacerdotalis*
are used throughout.

4. A somewhat similar significance is given to the trumpet already in Origen, *In Ierem.* 5.16. It is "a sublime noise, spurring on the
hearer, preparing him for the war against the passions, for the war
against the assaults of the adversary powers, preparing him for the
heavenly feasts." Cf. also *idem, In Iesu Nave* 7.1, where the trumpets
of Jos. 6.20 are images of the teaching and preaching of the apostles.

5. Cf. Jos. 6.20.

6. A lacuna that, as Mutzenbecher suggests, may be supplied for
from Sermon 94.1.

7. forgiven . . . broken apart: *resolvi . . . resoluta.*

SERMON 94

1. *Extravagans.* The present sermon seems to follow on the
preceding one.

2. *sacerdotalibus:* cf. Sermon 3 n. 2. Forms of *sacerdos* and *sacer-*

dotalis are used throughout and rendered as "priest" and "priestly," except in the one instance noted.

3. Cf. Jos. 6.20.

4. Cf. 1 Cor. 10.6.

5. Heb. 4.13.

6. Heb. 4.12.

7. 2 Cor. 10.4–6.

8. Cf. Jos. 6.8–20.

9. *sacratus pontifex.*

10. Cf. Gen. 1.3–22.

11. Jericho, both in its Old Testament and its New Testament (Luke 10.30) context, is commonly understood as a figure of this world: cf. Origen, *In Iesu Nave* 6.4; Ambrose, *Exp. evang. sec. Luc.* 7.73; Jerome, *Tract. de ps.* 136 (CCL 78.296).

12. 1 John 2.17. Maximus suggests that the seven days of Gen. 1.1—2.3 represent the seven millennia for which the world will exist and during which the work of salvation can be accomplished. The more usual interpretation, however, was that there were six millennia corresponding to six days of creation. The seventh day, having been a day of rest, was ordinarily a figure either of the kingdom of the saints on earth, which would endure for a thousand years (thus the chiliasts: cf. Justin, *Dial. c. Tryph.* 80–81), or a type of heavenly blessedness (thus Augustine, *De civ. Dei* 22.30). In neither case would there be preaching announcing judgment and threatening destruction in the seventh millennium. Maximus is perhaps the only Father to suggest such a scheme. Cf. also Sermon 22A.2 and n. 6. On this issue cf. A. Luneau, *L'histoire du salut chez les Pères de l'église: La doctrine des âges du monde* (Paris 1964); Luneau, however, does not mention Maximus.

Sermon 95

1. *Extravagans.* Zacchaeus (Luke 19.1–10) is occasionally used as an example to show that it is possible for someone who is rich to be saved, despite Matt. 19.24: cf. Ambrosiaster, *Quaest. ex Novo Test., pars* 2a.27; Jerome, *Ep.* 79.3. Several Old Testament personages also

serve in this capacity: cf. Jerome, *Ep.* 79.2. In this respect Abraham, not mentioned by Jerome, is a prime example: cf. Paulinus of Nola, *Ep.* 13.20. Joseph of Arimathea is another such: cf. Ambrosiaster, *ibid.* In the present sermon, which seems to owe something to Ambrose, *Exp. evang. sec. Luc.* 8.84–85, Maximus gives the impression that he is mitigating to a certain extent the strong stand against wealth that he had taken in Sermons 32 and 48.2 (cf. Sermon 32 n. 1). In Sermon 96, however, which is a sequel, he declares that Zacchaeus in fact gives away all that he owns, thus observing Matt. 19.21 to the letter. Others also say that Zacchaeus divests himself of all his wealth: cf. Jerome, *In Matt.* 19.23; Peter Chrysologus, Sermon 54.

    2. dominion . . . property: *dominio . . . dominatum.* On almsgiving as an exchange cf. Sermon 22 n. 3.

    3. *salutem,* which may mean either salvation or well-being. If salvation, then it refers to the salvation of the almsgiver; if well-being, then the well-being of the one receiving the alms. Augustine, *Ep.* 153.26, expresses the same idea, which is a common theme in patristic literature: "What is lawfully possessed does not belong to someone else; but what is lawfully possessed is justly possessed, and what is justly possessed is well possessed. Therefore what is badly possessed belongs to someone else; but a person possesses a thing badly when he uses it badly."

    4. Matt. 19.24.

    5. Cf. Matt. 7.14.

    6. On the image of the camel cf. Sermons 32.1; 48.2; 88.3.

    7. This last distinction was an important one in Maximus' time: cf. Ambrose, *De Noe* 2.3; Jerome, *In Esaiam* 11.6–9; Augustine, Sermon 72.3.4; Cassian, *Conlat.* 6.3.

SERMON 96

    1. *Extravagans.* The present sermon, which seems to follow on the previous one, continues to develop the theme of Zacchaeus (Luke 19.1–10) and also recalls Ambrose, *Exp. evang. sec. Luc.* 8.84–85. Cf. Sermon 95 n. 1.

    2. On almsgiving as an exchange cf. Sermon 22 n. 3.

3. *et emendaturus concupiscentiae emendaret primitus conscientiam.* The phrase is a difficult one. Mutzenbecher suggests that *concupiscentiae* is a dative that goes with *emendaturus,* which would make the phrase read: on the verge of correcting his desire, he first corrected his conscience.

4. Luke 19.8.

5. Matt. 19.21.

6. On the image of almsgiving as a "pious usury," based on Prov. 19.17 ("The one who is kind to the poor lends to the Lord, and He will repay him for his deed"), cf. Ramsey 229. On the negative attitude of the early Church in general to usury cf. S. Giet, "De saint Basile à saint Ambroise: La condamnation du prêt à intérêt au IVe siècle," *Rech. de sc. rel.* 32 (1944) 95–128; R. P. Maloney, "The Teaching of the Fathers on Usury: An Historical Study on the Development of Christian Thinking," VC 27 (1973) 241–65.

SERMON 98

1. *Extravagans.* On the observance of the kalends of January cf. Sermon 63, with n. 1.

2. Cf. John 1.9.

3. On the term "sacrament" cf. Sermon 3 n. 3.

4. 2 Cor. 6.14.

5. I.e., has been given.

6. new year's giving . . . prompt (?): *strenas . . . strenuum.*

7. There is a lacuna here.

8. The reference would seem to be to someone who finds himself obliged to sell his sons as slaves in order to provide a new year's gift—almost surely an exaggeration. Yet the image of a man who must sell his sons to escape from debt is not unknown in patristic literature: cf. Basil, *Hom.* 12.4; Ambrose, *De Nabuthae* 5.21.

9. The value of the denarius and the solidus, the latter of which was invariably minted in gold, fluctuated in relation to one another, depending on whether the denarius was silver or bronze. By the beginning of the fifth century there were as many as 6800 denarii to one solidus. Cf. PWK 9.1.212.

10. Cf. Matt. 26.48–49.

11. Prof. Agnes Michels has drawn my attention to the custom of taking one's annual vows for the emperor on January 3, when auspices were also taken by private individuals; hence the mention of one day having elapsed from the start of the year. Cf. A. Degrassi, *Inscriptiones Italiae* 13.2: *Fasti anni Numani et Juliani* (Rome 1963) 388–91.

12. *tristitiam semper habent dum rememoratione[m] [h]ominum sunt solliciti ne contingant.* The phrase is a difficult one, and the translator owes thanks to William Conlan, O.P., for his help.

SERMON 99

1. *Extravagans.* On the feast of Christmas cf. Sermon 60 n. 1.
2. John 3.30.
3. Luke 16.16.
4. Mal. 4.2.
5. John 1.9.
6. Matt. 27.25.
7. Cf. Matt. 2.1–12; Luke 2.8–20.
8. Cf. Sermon 62 n. 3.
9. Cf. Luke 1.8–25.
10. John 5.35.
11. Cf. Mark 1.4.

SERMON 100

1. *Extravagans.* On the feast of the Epiphany cf. Sermon 13A n. 1.
2. Cf. Matt. 3.13–17.
3. Matt. 5.19.
4. Cf. Mark 10.17.
5. On this and the following few lines cf. Sermons 13A.1 and 65.3.

6. On the term "sacrament" cf. Sermons 3 n. 3 and 13A n. 3.

7. Matt. 3.17.

8. Cf. Sermon 62 n. 3.

9. John 1.18.

10. John 13.23.

11. On the rest of the Lord and His saints in one another cf. also Augustine, *Conf.* 13.36.51–37.52.

12. The breast is the seat of the virtues and hence an appropriate resting place for Christ, but it is also the seat of the vices: cf. RAC 2.655–56.

13. Matt. 8.20.

14. On the notion of Christ sanctifying the waters of the Jordan cf. Sermon 13A n. 12.

15. Cf. Exod. 13.21–22.

16. Cf. 1 Cor. 10.1–2.

17. A quasi identification of Christ and the pillar of fire is made toward the end of the second century in Melito of Sardis, *Hom. pasch.* 84.

18. Cf. Exod. 14.5–9.

SERMON 101

1. *Extravagans.* The present sermon does not necessarily follow on the preceding one.

1a. This sentence is reminiscent of Athanasius, *Ep.* 5.1.

2. Cf. Sermon 61C.1.

3. By this time the number of Christian feasts would indeed probably have surpassed the number of pagan ones, particularly if the celebration of Sunday were taken into account. On the outnumbering of pagan by Christian feasts in an apologetic context cf. Tertullian, *De idolol.* 14 *ad fin.*

4. Isa. 6.9.

5. Cf. Sermon 103.1.

6. Cf. 1 John 1.1.

7. Cf. John 2.1–11.

8. For a similar use of this image cf. Sermons 65.2 and 103.2;

Jerome, *C. Ioann. Hieros.* 32. The present is a rare instance in patristic literature of the transformation of the water into wine signifying a transformation from mortality into immortality. More usually the water and wine symbolize the Old and New Testaments respectively. Cf. H. de Lubac, *Exégèse médiévale: Les quatre sens de l'Ecriture* (Aubier 1959) 1.1.343–49, esp. 344 n. 6, where the present sermon is ascribed to Ps.-Ambrose.

    9. Ps. 116.13. Cf. Sermon 102.2.

SERMON 102

    1. *Extravagans.* The present sermon does not necessarily follow on the preceding one.

    2. Cf. Matt. 13.4–23.

    3. Ps. 90.4.

    4. Cf. Ps. 116.13. Cf. Sermon 101.3.

    5. John 2.11.

    6. Matt. 15.8; Isa. 29.13.

SERMON 103

    1. *Extravagans.* The present sermon may follow on the preceding one. The pessimism of §3 is somewhat similar to that in Sermon 17.2–3 (cf. n. 1).

    2. *sanctitas vestra:* cf. Sermon 4 n. 2.

    3. John 2.11.

    4. Cf. Sermon 101.2.

    5. For a similar use of this image cf. Sermons 65.2 and 101.3 (with n. 8).

    6. Matt. 7.2.

    7. The intent of this final phrase is obscure.

SERMON 105

1. *Extravagans.* On Alexander, Martyrius, and Sisinius, who died May 29, 397, cf. LTK 9.799. The present sermon and the following one, as well as *Epp.* 1–2 of Vigilius of Trent, are the primary sources for their martyrdom. The accounts of Maximus and Vigilius are considerably dissimilar: Vigilius says that the martyrs died simply as a result of pagan persecution, but Maximus emphasizes that there was no persecution and that they provoked their own death by rebuking the pagans for their practice of the lustrum. On the discrepancies and the reasons for them cf. C. E. Chaffin, "The Martyrs of the Val di Non: An Examination of Contemporary Reactions," SP 10 (1970) 263–69. Chaffin suggests that this and the following three sermons are concerned to force Christian landowners to deal with the practice of the pagan cults on their lands; in this regard cf. also Sermon 91, with n. 1.

2. What this means is uncertain. Inasmuch as the three martyrs were active in Milan under Ambrose, only to be sent later by him to Bishop Vigilius of Trent, it may be that Maximus himself knew them while they were at Milan. Otherwise he is perhaps suggesting that he is acquainted with them by reputation, since they could only have been relatively recently deceased when this sermon was preached. On the apparent references to Maximus having been an eyewitness of the martyrdom, with the conclusions that have been drawn from this, cf. p. 2.

3. On the martyrs as examples cf. Sermon 1 n. 7.

4. I.e., the Val di Non in the Tyrol.

5. The lustrum was a ceremony of purification that often involved a procession of sacred objects. Although it would originally have taken place at five-year intervals in Rome, by the end of the fourth century it might have occurred with greater frequency or at least certainly as the need arose: cf. PWK 13.2.2040–59, esp. 2055–59.

6. 1 Cor. 3.15.

7. On the notion of Christ suffering in the martyrs cf. Eusebius,

Hist. eccl. 5.1.23; Melito of Sardis, *Hom. pasch.* 69; Paulinus of Nola, *Ep.* 38.3.

SERMON 106

1. *Extravagans.* The present sermon follows on the preceding one. On the saints in question cf. Sermon 105 n. 1. For the concerns expressed in this and the following two sermons cf. also Sermon 91, with n. 1.

2. On the term "anniversary" cf. Sermon 1 n. 1.

3. salvation . . . well-being: *saluti . . . salutis.*

4. Reading *polluere* instead of *pollueret.*

5. Cf. Sermon 105 n. 5.

6. *coniventia.* On this term, which Maximus immediately defines, cf. Chaffin 267–68.

7. On the martyrs as examples cf. Sermon 1 n. 7. The idea of imitating the martyrs, which is alluded to here and briefly developed a few lines later ("the portion of martyrdom is to do what the martyrs did"), is one that becomes prevalent as the time of the persecutions draws to a close, and it shows to what extent martyrdom has become the norm of holiness for the Christian. By the same token it also shows that that level of holiness is now attainable by the nonmartyr, which is a theme increasingly in evidence from the beginning of the fourth century: cf. Methodius, *Symposium* 7.3; Ambrose, *Ep.* 63.70; Peter Chrysologus, Sermon 128. The monk in particular is the successor of the martyr: cf. E. E. Malone, *The Monk and the Martyr* (SCA 12; 1950).

8. On keeping silent in this regard cf. also Sermons 91.2, 107.1, and 108.

9. Cf. Ps. 18.26.

10. Beginning with the so-called "Edict of Milan" in 313, laws were regularly promulgated to promote Christianity, especially during the reigns of Gratian and Theodosius (378–95). Cf. in particular *Cod. Theod.* 16.1.2 and 16.10.10, which record edicts of 380 and 391 respectively that required all citizens to embrace Christianity or face

certain sanctions, thus effectively prohibiting the pagan cult. But paganism could not be completely destroyed, as the present sermon indicates.

11. *salute,* which may also be rendered as "salvation."

12. Whether this last phrase refers to an actual incident is unknown.

SERMON 107

1. *Extravagans.* The present sermon follows on the preceding one. The reference at the end of §2 to the abolition of gladiatorial combat is too vague to help in a close dating of this or related sermons. For a commentary on §2 cf. Dölger, "Christliche Grundbesitzer und heidnische Landarbeiter" 306–20.

2. *caritatem vestram:* cf. Sermon 4 n. 2.

3. On keeping silent in this regard cf. also Sermons 91.2, 106.2, and 108.

4. Cf. Rom. 1.32.

5. On the question of eating food involved in idol worship cf. 1 Cor. 8.1–13, 10.23–33; Augustine, *Ep.* 47.3–4 and 6.

6. *dianaticus,* i.e., either a devotee of Diana or a person who has succumbed to moon madness: cf. Dölger, "Christliche Grundbesitzer" 313–16.

7. *aruspex.*

8. The allusion here and later may be to the rite of self-flagellation practiced by the galli or archigalli, the priests of Cybele: cf. Apuleius, *Metam.* 8.173. But since no mention is made of castration, the most striking practice of the galli and something that Maximus would almost certainly have spoken of, perhaps these are not galli but the adherents of another cult that carried out self-mutilation of one kind or another. On the galli in general cf. RAC 8.984–1034, esp. 1028–31 for the Christian judgment.

9. Gladiatorial combat was forbidden as a punishment for criminals by Constantine in a letter to the praetorian prefect of the Orient in the year 325: cf. *Cod. Theod.* 15.12.1. Subsequent legislation oc-

curred, however, and perhaps Maximus is referring here to the closing of the gladiatorial schools by Honorius in 399. Cf. RAC 11.27–28 and 40–44.

SERMON 108

1. *Extravagans.* The present sermon, which is in fact only a fragment, follows on the preceding one. On the concerns expressed in this and the preceding three sermons cf. Sermon 91, with n. 1.

2. On keeping silent in this regard cf. also Sermons 91.2, 106.2, and 107.1.

3. Prov. 12.27.

SERMON 110

1. *Extravagans.* On the term "anniversary" and on the feast of Sts. Peter and Paul cf. Sermon 1 n. 1.

2. Luke 5.10.

3. On the term "sacrament" cf. Sermon 3 n. 3.

4. On the identification of Peter's boat and the Church cf. Sermon 49.2 and n. 4.

5. *turbine,* lit. whirlpool.

6. Luke 5.4.

7. Rom. 11.33.

8. Luke 5.5.

9. John 1.1.

10. Cf. Ambrose, *Exp. evang. sec. Luc.* 4.72. On Peter's fishing as an image of his teaching and preaching cf. Rahner, *Symbole* 483.

11. *explicat,* which also means "expounds"—hence an untranslatable play on words.

12. Rom. 13.12.

13. According to Mutzenbecher, the final words seem to have been added to the original text.

SERMON III

1. *Extravagans.* This sermon was directed primarily, although not necessarily exclusively, to catechumens, as §3 indicates.

2. *sanctitas vestra:* cf. Sermon 4 n. 2.

3. Cf. Gen. 3.1–7.

4. Cf. Matt. 4.2.

5. Cf. Matt. 18.11–12.

6. Cf. Gen. 2.17.

7. Cf. Ambrose, *Exp. evang. sec. Luc.* 4.7. On the idea that the immutability of the divine sentence demanded the Incarnation cf. also Athanasius, *De incarn.* 6–7.

8. Reading *auctorem* instead of *auctoritatem.*

9. John 8.24.

10. John 3.5.

11. Cf. Gal. 3.27.

12. Cf. John 14.6.

13. On maintaining an unbroken fast in Quadragesima cf. Sermon 50 n. 1.

14. This sentence is reminiscent of Heb. 6.4–6.

APPENDIX

SERMON 7

1. Spurious. On the term "anniversary" cf. Sermon 1 n. 1. On St. Eusebius of Vercelli, whose death day, along with the feast of the Maccabees (cf. §4 ad fin.), was celebrated on August 1, cf. DHGE 15.1477–83. Eusebius did indeed suffer under the Arians, as he himself relates in a letter to Patrophilus (CCL 9.106–9), but this was quite unlike the suffering described in the present sermon, and he

survived to die a peaceful death in 371. Much of what is contained in this sermon must be considered legendary.

2. *virtutibus*.

3. 1 Cor. 4.20. *Virtute,* rendered here as "virtue" on account of the allusion to virtue in the previous clause, may also be translated as "power."

4. *sacerdotio.* This and related words used throughout seem to refer sometimes to the priesthood and sometimes to the episcopate: cf. Sermon 3 n. 3.

5. Cf. Wisd. 7.26. Of this Exuperantius nothing more is known.

6. Prov. 10.1.

7. Cf. 1 Cor. 4.15.

8. This phrase alludes to the fact that Western monasticism took its inspiration from the East.

9. This Dionysius is undoubtedly the bishop of Milan who seems to have signed a condemnation of Athanasius in 355, which he later retracted under the influence of Eusebius. He suffered exile with Eusebius and died in Armenia. Cf. DHGE 14.263. That Eusebius would have been thought to call the bishop of Milan his son, as he does later in §3, is an indication of the great esteem that Eusebius himself enjoyed.

10. 1 Cor. 9.20.

11. Cf. Luke 16.8.

12. The narration and justification of Eusebius' deceptive act (which is probably legendary in any event) has many parallels in Eastern patristic literature but fewer in the West. This particular passage is discussed in L. Thomassin, *Traité de la vérité et du mensonge* (Paris 1691) 179–82. In general cf. B. Ramsey, "Two Traditions on Lying and Deception in the Ancient Church," *Thomist* 49 (1985) 504–33.

13. On account of the Arian heresy it would appear that the East, where it originated, was sometimes demeaned in Western eyes: cf. Jerome, *Ep.* 15.1.

14. Cf. Gen. 28.12.

15. Cf. 2 Mac. 7.1–41.

16. Cf. Sermon 1.2 and n. 4.

SERMON 8

1. Spurious. On the term "anniversary" cf. Sermon 1 n. 1. On the term "deposition" (*depositio*) used in the sense of anniversary rather than burial cf. C. Lambot, "Critique interne et sermons de s. Augustin," SP 1 (1957) 121. On St. Eusebius cf. Sermon 7 n. 1.

2. On the day of death as a birthday cf. Sermon 1 n. 1.

3. I.e., the first day of August. Dreams or visions prophetic of a martyr's death are not uncommon in patristic literature: cf. *Mart. Pol.* 5.2; *Passio ss. Perp. et Felic., passim;* Pontius, *V. C. Cypriani* 12.

4. Ps. 39.4.

5. There is a lacuna here.

6. Ps. 55.6.

7. Dan. 2.34.

8. This interpretation is perhaps addressed to the Arians, from whom Eusebius had suffered.

SERMON 14

1. Doubtful. On the term "anniversary" cf. Sermon 1 n. 1. The beginning of §1 indicates that this sermon was preached shortly after Easter. It is known that a feast of all the martyrs, celebrated on the Friday after Easter, found its way from Syria to the West. Perhaps this is an early indication of this. Cf. M. Righetti, *Manuale di storia liturgica* (Milan 1955) 2.356.

2. 2 Cor. 1.7.

3. 2 Tim. 2.12.

4. Ps. 16.11.

5. Cf. Acts 2.28–31.

6. Matt. 27.52–53.

7. Ps. 23.4.

8. John 11.25.

9. On the human body as a musical instrument cf. Tertullian, *De bapt.* 8; Basil, *Hom. in ps.* 29.1.

10. *sacerdotes:* cf. Sermon 3 n. 3.

SERMON 45

1. Spurious. On the feast of Epiphany cf. Sermon 13A n. 1.

2. This is a classic statement of the doctrine of the divinization of the human person: cf. Athanasius, *De incarn.* 54, where it appears in equally succinct form, and DS 3.1376–98 for the patristic teaching in general.

3. Cf. Phil. 2.7.

4. *colonus terrae.*

5. Cf. 1 Cor. 13.12.

6. Cf. Heb. 1.1–2.

7. Cf. Exod. 24.15–18.

8. Cf. Exod. 3.2.

9. The parallel between the burning bush that was not consumed by the flames and Mary, whose virginity was not destroyed in childbirth, seems to have been introduced toward the end of the fourth century by Gregory of Nyssa: cf. *V. Moysis* 2.21; *In diem nat. Christi* (MG 46.1136). Cf. Gregory of Nyssa, *The Life of Moses*, tr. A. J. Malherbe and E. Ferguson (New York 1978) 159–60 n. 28.

10. Cf. Luke 5.21.

11. On the different traditions as to what was celebrated on Epiphany cf. Sermon 13A n. 1.

12. The reference is most likely to the *signaculum* or sign of the cross received at baptism: cf. Sermon 85.2 and n. 8 for similar imperial imagery. Otherwise it may refer simply to the signing with the cross as an apotropaic act, as the following lines suggest.

13. Cf. Exod. 12.21–23.

14. On the devil's fear of the sign of the cross cf. Sermon 38 n. 4.

15. Cf. Ezek. 9.4–6.

16. Cf. 1 Tim. 2.8.

17. Cf. Exod. 17.11. On Moses' outstretched arms as a type of the cross cf. Sermon 38 n. 9.

18. On the parallel between cross and mast cf. Sermon 37 n. 5.
19. On birds in flight imitating a cross cf. Tertullian, *De orat.* 29.
20. On the Roman trophy as a cross cf. Justin, *1 Apol.* 55.
21. Cf. Ps. 91.13.

SERMON 46

1. This is a sermon of Jerome, under the same title. The text is in CCL 78.530–32. An English translation is in FC 57.229–31.

SERMON 47

1. Luke 12.16. This is a sermon of Basil of Caesarea, translated by Rufinus. The Greek text of Basil is in MG 31.261–77, and the Latin translation of Rufinus is in MG 31.1744–53. There is an English translation in W. Shewring, *Rich and Poor in Christian Tradition* (London 1948) 51–62.

SERMON 61B

1. Doubtful. *Extravagans.* On the feast of Christmas cf. Sermon 60 n. 1, and on the solar imagery of §1 cf. Sermon 62 n. 1.

Mutzenbecher ascribes from the beginning of the sermon until "which means God with us" at the beginning of §2 to Maximus, and she thinks that from about "Mary's womb, therefore, I would say" in §3 until the end of the sermon can perhaps be ascribed to Maximus. The rest of the sermon may have been drawn from the source that Cassian in *De incarn. Dom.* 7.25.2 identifies with Ambrose. On Ambrose's Mariology, which the present sermon seems to reproduce in part, cf. F. H. Dudden, *The Life and Times of St. Ambrose* (Oxford 1935) 2.599–601. If the final section of the sermon, with its glorification of Mary, is in fact by Maximus, it should be contrasted with Sermons 13A.1-2, 38.4, 39.1, and 78.2, where Mary appears somewhat demeaned.

2. *dilectionem vestram:* cf. Sermon 4 n. 2.

3. *ortum,* i.e. either a rising or a birth, and hence an untranslatable play on words. The verb form *oriri* is used in the following lines.

4. Cf. Jer. 10.7.

5. Isa. 7.14; Matt. 1.23.

6. *naturae.* Inasmuch as *natura* can mean either nature or birth, the phrase is ambiguous. The author may be saying either that the mystery of the birth bears witness to the divine nature of Christ—which is the meaning indicated by the translation—or that the mystery of the birth bears witness to the birth itself.

7. Luke 1.35.

8. Deut. 19.15; 2 Cor. 13.1.

9. *sacramentum fidei,* i.e. the faith itself. On the term "sacrament" cf. Sermon 3 n. 3.

10. *Maria enim tamquam in sacrario ventris sui portavit cum mysterio sacerdotem.* Hence also: Since Mary bore the priest with the [or: His] mystery in the sanctuary of her womb.

11. *Templum plane est in quo habitat sanctum quidquid in caelo est, nisi quod super caelos aestimandum est, ubi quasi in secretiore tabernaculo mysterium a divinitate disponitur, quemadmodum a pluribus ascendatur ad caelum.*

SERMON 61C

1. Doubtful. On the feast of Christmas cf. Sermon 60 n. 1. The beginning of §2 recalls Sermon 97.1. Toward the end of §2 is reminiscent of Ambrose, *Exp. evang. sec. Luc.* 2.26.

2. Cf. Sermon 101.1.

3. Cf. Luke 2.40.

4. Luke 2.14.

5. On Mary as a type of the soul cf. J. Huhn, "Ein Vergleich der Mariologie des hl. Augustinus mit der des hl. Ambrosius in ihrer

Abhängigkeit, Ähnlichkeit, in ihrem Unterschied," *Augustinus magister* (Paris 1954) 1.237–38.

6. On the Magi in what follows cf. Matt. 2.1–12.

7. More usually the gifts of the Magi symbolize respectively Christ's royalty, divinity, and human nature: cf. Irenaeus, *Adv. haer.* 3.9.2; Iuvencus, *Evang.* 1.249–51 (CSEL 24.16); Hilary, *In Matt.* 1.5; Jerome, *In Matt.* 2.11 (citing Iuvencus). The interpretation here and in the following lines, however, seems ultimately founded on this symbolism.

8. Cf. Ambrose, *Exp. evang. sec. Luc.* 2.48.

9. The reference is to the pagan celebrations of the kalends of January, the first day of the year: cf. Sermons 63 (with n. 1) and 98.

SERMON 87

1. Spurious.

2. Cf. Luke 7.1–4.

3. Luke 7.4–5.

4. *et demonstrat propterea se tabernaculum amplius addidisse, ut multipliciter domini gloriam loquerentur.* The meaning is obscure, but the following sentence suggests that both Jew and Gentile (the latter represented by the centurion) might thus praise God, the Gentile by having built the synagogue and the Jew by having worshiped in it.

5. *vir clarissimus et providentissimus. Vir clarissimus* was a title usually restricted to persons of senatorial rank and members of their family: cf. *Mittellateinisches Wörterbuch* (Munich 1973) s.v. *clarus.*

6. A *comes* was one who accompanied the emperor on his journeys, but the term also came to signify one who had a particular military authority. The designation "count" is anachronistic at this period. Cf. A. H. M. Jones, *The Later Roman Empire: 284–602* (Norman, Okla. 1964) 104–5; *Mittellateinisches Wörterbuch* (1974) s.v. *comes.*

7. The phrase is unknown in Scripture.

8. Matt. 8.8.

9. *Ibid.*

10. *salutem*, meaning either health or salvation.

11. These persons are otherwise unknown. They seem to have been poor men who nonetheless possessed sufficient to build, or help build, the basilica that is being spoken of.

12. *hi tamen sumptu operati sunt +alter assensu+*. The meaning seems to be that Vitalianus and Marianus were responsible for the building and that the comes gave his assent.

13. 2 Cor. 8.2.

14. Cf. 2 Cor. 6.10.

15. Luke 21.3–4.

SERMON 90

1. *Extravagans*. Spurious. The heretics spoken of in this sermon are unknown; the anonymous preacher passes over their doctrinal errors and in §3 singles out for special reprobation the crime of soliciting money for the forgiveness of sins.

2. 1 Cor. 15.19.

3. *non honestas sed potestas*.

4. *Quantos membrorum sanguinitate pollentes, qui non dei misericordia gubernantur, sed pecudum sanguine crassentur!* The sentence is a difficult one, and the translator thanks Edmund Ditton, O.P., for his help. The cattle spoken of here seem to be ordinary people who suffer from those in power over them.

5. This brief theology of temporalities sees honors, wealth, and health only in the most negative light: they are valueless, fortuitous, and seductive. For a similar view cf. the Pelagian work *De divitiis* 8.1–4 (MLSuppl. 1.1388–90). Contrast Augustine, *Enarr. in ps.* 66.3; Cassian, *Conlat.* 6.3.

6. 1 Cor. 11.19.

7. *presbyteros*.

8. *presbyter*.

9. Matt. 10.8.

10. Matt. 26.75. On the theme of contrition expressed by tears cf. Sermon 76.2–3 and n. 1.

11. *presbyter.*
12. *sacerdoti:* cf. Sermon 3 n. 2.

Sermon 97

1. *Extravagans.* Doubtful. The end of §1 recalls the beginning of Sermon 61C.2. On the feast of Christmas cf. Sermon 60 n. 1.
2. Luke 2.14.
3. pay . . . bestow: *repraesentat . . . praesentat.*
4. Cf. Luke 2.8–14.
5. 1 Cor. 2.8.
6. *sacerdotes,* as in the following sentence: cf. Sermon 3 n. 3.
7. On this image cf. Ambrose, *Exp. evang. sec. Luc.* 2.50.
8. Ps. 72.6.
9. *sine inquietudine omnium totum imbrem per multiplices effu-sum partes toto corpore in se trahit unius meatus scissuram nesciens, solida mollitie plures praebens meatus; et quod clausum videtur per densitatem est patulum per tenuitatem.* The image is considerably forced, and the translator thanks William Conlan, O.P., for helping him to make some sense of it.
10. On fleece and rain as an image of the virginal conception and birth of Christ cf. also Paulinus of Nola, *Ep.* 19.3; *Carm.* 25.155–60; Ps.-Jerome, *Brev. in ps.* 71 (ML 26.1028). On Christ as the rain, without a mention of Mary as the fleece, cf. Ambrose, *De vid.* 3.18–19; Augustine, *Enarr. in ps.* 71.9. For numerous references in this latter regard cf. SC 146.78 n. 1. Often Ps. 72.6 is related to Judg. 6.37–40, the narrative of Gideon and the fleece.

Sermon 104

1. *Extravagans.* Doubtful. This is a fragment, perhaps of the end of a sermon; in any event, it is too short to be able to be attributed with any certainty to Maximus. Most of the fragment is reminiscent of Ambrose, *Exp. evang. sec. Luc.* 8.15–16. If it is in fact dependent on

this section of Ambrose's work, then the wounds referred to are probably the sores of Lazarus (Luke 16.20–21), who is there taken as an image of Christ.

2. John 6.41.
3. Matt. 15.26.
4. Matt. 15.27.

SERMON 109

1. *Extravagans*. Spurious. The present sermon is only a fragment.
2. Luke 2.34.

INDEXES

1. OLD AND NEW TESTAMENT

2. AUTHORS AND SOURCES

3. GENERAL INDEX

Abel, 41
Abraham, 51ff, 69, 196f, 210, 287, 351
abstinence, see fasting
Adam, 108f, 113, 121f, 124f, 143, 185,
    240ff, 315, 318; Christ as second, 121f
adultery, 84, 153, 210
Adventus, 31ff, 278
agapetae, 347
Alaric, 336
Alexander, 2, 4, 232ff, 356
almsgiving, 1, 7, 53ff, 66, 88f, 104f,
    109, 127, 145ff, 152, 174f, 177, 195,
    198, 205ff, 218ff, 288, 290, 325, 343,
    351f; compared to baptism, 57, 290
Amalek, 93, 250
Ammaus, 22, 59, 273
Ananiah, 21
Ananias, 44f
Anaunia, 233; see also Val di Non
angel(s), 94, 98, 113, 128, 152f, 200f,
    225f, 249f, 253f, 260, 307, 315, 343f;
    John the Baptist as an angel, 25
Antichrist, 47
Apostle, the, 18f, 28, 30f, 35, 43, 50,
    56, 59, 65, 67f, 70, 73f, 76, 79, 81,
    83f, 95f, 100 111f, 114, 116, 129,
    131, 143f, 146, 155f, 160, 164f, 169,
    172, 175, 178f, 181f, 187, 192, 196,
    202f, 217, 222, 233, 236, 244, 247,
    257; see also Paul
apostle(s), 1, 15ff, 30, 42ff, 62, 70, 76,
    81, 108, 110f, 117, 125, 128, 132,
    136, 153, 167f, 184f, 188, 190, 203,
    230ff, 314, 333, 349
Aquileia, 282
archigalli, 358
Arcosolium of Celerina, 323
Arian(s), Arianism, 3, 7, 10, 244f, 274,
    293, 308, 310, 323f, 360ff
ark of the covenant, 106f, 155, 160, 313

Armenia, 361
ascension of Christ, 97f, 102, 110f, 136,
    309
Athaulf, 336
Augustine, 2
auspices, 223, 353
avarice, avariciousness, 1, 31, 43ff, 66,
    73, 77ff, 105f, 109, 127, 145, 150,
    162, 169f, 174f, 177, 197, 214f, 293,
    349
Azariah, 21

baptism, almsgiving compared to, 57,
    290; of the apostles, 111, 314; of
    Christ, 33ff, 57, 157ff, 225ff, 249,
    279ff; of Christians, 37ff, 56f, 69, 84,
    86, 111, 113, 119, 127,133, 144, 158,
    164f, 212, 227, 240ff, 282, 284, 302f,
    315, 322; deferral of, 160, 330; as
    enlightenment, 119, 127, 317f; John's
    b. of repentance, 154; seal of, 205,
    249f, 345, 363
barbarian(s), 4, 7, 46, 176, 198ff, 207,
    285, 336
Bar-Jesus, 299
bed, 48f, 286
bees, 211, 348
belt, 145, 293
Benjamin, 149
birds, 179f, 337, 364
birth of Christ, 1, 23, 26, 33f, 93f, 122,
    134, 144ff, 222ff, 228, 250, 259,
    279f, 365; see also Christmas
bishop(s), 2, 8, 19, 43, 52f, 65ff, 104,
    112, 118, 140f, 161f, 173f, 189, 191,
    208, 211ff, 243f, 248, 259, 261, 267,
    272, 278, 287f, 335, 341, 348; Christ
    as, 191, 341; see also priest(s)
breast(s), 275, 354
burning bush, 249, 363